Song *of* Songs

BAKER COMMENTARY *on the* OLD TESTAMENT

WISDOM AND PSALMS

Tremper Longman III, EDITOR

Volumes now available

Song of Songs, Richard S. Hess

Song *of* Songs

Richard S. Hess

BakerAcademic

Grand Rapids, Michigan

©2005 by Richard S. Hess

Published by Baker Academic
a division of Baker Publishing Group
P.O. Box 6287, Grand Rapids, MI 49516-6287
www.bakeracademic.com

Printed in the United States of America

Library of Congress Cataloging-in-Publication Data
Hess, Richard S.
    Song of Songs / Richard S. Hess.
        p.   cm. — (Baker commentary on the Old Testament wisdom and Psalms)
    Includes bibliographical references and indexes.
    ISBN 0-8010-2712-8 (cloth)
    1. Bible. O.T. Song of Solomon—Commentaries. I. Title. II. Series.
BS1485.53.H47 2005
223'.9077—dc22
                                                                    2004023799

Contents

Series Preface

AT THE END of the book of Ecclesiastes, a wise father warns his son concerning the multiplication of books: "Furthermore, of these, my son, be warned. There is no end to the making of many books!" (12:12). The Targum to this biblical book characteristically expands the thought and takes it in a different, even contradictory, direction: "My son, take care to make many books of wisdom without end."

When applied to commentaries, both statements are true. The past twenty years have seen a significant increase in the number of commentaries available on each book of the Bible. On the other hand, for those interested in grappling seriously with the meaning of the text, such proliferation should be seen as a blessing rather than a curse. No single commentary can do it all. In the first place, commentaries reflect different theological and methodological perspectives. We can learn from others who have a different understanding of the origin and nature of the Bible, but we also want commentaries that share our fundamental beliefs about the biblical text. Second, commentaries are written with different audiences in mind. Some are addressed primarily to laypeople, others to clergy, and still others to fellow scholars. A third consideration, related to the previous two, is the subdisciplines the commentator chooses to draw from to shed light on the biblical text. The possibilities are numerous, including philology, textual criticism, genre/form criticism, redaction criticism, ancient Near Eastern background, literary conventions, and more. Finally, commentaries differ in how extensively they interact with secondary literature, that is, with what others have said about a given passage.

The Baker Commentary on the Old Testament Wisdom and Psalms has a definite audience in mind. We believe the primary users of commentaries are scholars, ministers, seminary students, and Bible study leaders. Of these groups, we have most in mind clergy and future clergy, namely, seminary students. We have tried to make the commentary accessible to nonscholars by putting most of the technical discussion and interaction with secondary literature in the footnotes. We do not mean to suggest that such information is unimportant. We simply concede that, given the present state of the church, it is the rare layperson who will read such technical material with interest and profit. We hope we are wrong in this assessment and, if we are not, that the future will see a reverse in this trend. A healthy church is a church that nourishes itself with constant attention to God's words in Scripture, in all their glorious detail.

Since not all commentaries are alike, what are the features that characterize this series? The message of the biblical book is the primary focus of each commentary, and the commentators have labored to expose God's message for his people in the book they discuss. This series also distinguishes itself by restricting its coverage to one major portion of the Hebrew Scriptures, namely, the Psalms and Wisdom books (Proverbs, Job, Ecclesiastes, and Song of Songs). These biblical books provide a distinctive contribution to the canon. Although we can no longer claim that they are neglected, their unique content makes them harder to fit into the development of redemptive history and requires more effort to hear their distinctive message.

The book of Psalms is the literary sanctuary. Like the physical sanctuary structures of the Old Testament, it offers a textual holy place where humans share their joys and struggles with brutal honesty in God's presence. The book of Proverbs describes wisdom, which on one level is skill for living, the ability to navigate life's actual and potential pitfalls; but on another level, this wisdom presents a pervasive and deeply theological message: "The fear of the LORD is the beginning of knowledge" (Prov. 1:7). Proverbs also raises a disturbing issue: the sages often motivate wise behavior by linking it to reward, but in reality, bad things happen to good people, the wise are not always rewarded as they expect. This raises the question of the justice of God. Both Job and Ecclesiastes struggle with the apparent disconnect between God's justice and our actual life experience. Finally, the Song of Songs is a passionate, sensuous love poem that reminds us that God is interested in more than just our brains and our spirits; he wants us to enjoy our bodies. It reminds us that we are not merely a soul encased in a body but whole persons made in God's image.

Limiting the series to the Psalms and Wisdom books has allowed us to tailor our work to the distinctive nature of this portion of the canon. With some few exceptions in Job and Ecclesiastes, for instance, the material in these biblical books is poetic and highly literary, and so the commentators have highlighted the significant poetic conventions employed in each book. After an introduction discussing important issues that affect the interpretation of the book (title, authorship, date, language, style, text, ancient Near Eastern background, genre, canonicity, theological message, connection to the New Testament, and structure), each commentary proceeds section-by-section through the biblical text. The authors provide their own translation, with explanatory notes when necessary, followed by a substantial interpretive section (titled "Interpretation") and concluding with a section titled "Theological Implications." In the interpretation section, the emphasis is on the meaning of the text in its original historical setting. In the theological implications section, connections with other parts of the canon, both Old and New Testament, are sketched out along with the continuing relevance of each passage for us today. The latter section is motivated by the recognition that, while it is important to understand the individual contribution and emphasis of each book, these books now find their place in a larger collection of writings, the canon as a whole, and it is within this broader context that the books must ultimately be interpreted.

No two commentators in this series see things in exactly the same way, though we all share similar convictions about the Bible as God's Word and the belief that it must be appreciated not only as ancient literature but as God's Word for today. It is our hope and prayer that these volumes will inform readers and, more importantly, stimulate reflection on and passion for these valuable books.

As one might imagine, to write a commentary in a series like this one requires a rare combination of skills. It calls for the technical expertise of a scholar of ancient language and culture as well as sensitivity as a reader of literature. Most important, however, this series demands scholars who are also passionate about God and his people. I am for this reason overjoyed that Rick Hess has written the commentary on the Song of Songs. Rick combines the skills of a proven scholar of the Bible and the ancient Near East as well as the literary and theological sensitivities necessary to explicate this intriguing and sometimes enigmatic book. This commentary has succeeded in doing what we expect all the contributions to this series to do. Like most commentaries, it can be read piecemeal with profit. But unlike most commentaries, it can also be read cover-to-cover. I turn you over now to Rick Hess. Enjoy and profit!

Tremper Longman III
Robert H. Gundry Professor of Biblical Studies
Westmont College

9

Author's Preface

THE SONG OF Songs is an adult book. This has always been one of its difficulties when it comes to the public teaching and preaching of this text. Unless one moves immediately to allegory or in some other manner basically ignores the text, it seems that little can be interpreted literally for any audience that includes children. Perhaps one can go directly to the single didactic section of 8:5–7 and use it as a means to summarize the whole of the book. As valuable as such an approach may be for those verses, it loses the importance of the remainder of the book.

And yet the message of the Song needs to be heard more clearly and directly in this world than ever before. In a fallen world in which the first couple was expelled from the garden of Eden, this song offers the hope that couples today may find something of that garden again and may see in their love that which is beautiful and good, from the good God. The book avoids both extremes of the cheapening of sex into promiscuity and of the locking away of this gift, never to be mentioned or appreciated for what it is. It does this despite the insistence of proponents from both sides that the Song belongs to them. It joyfully celebrates physical love and a couple's committed relationship. It does this without concern for issues of theology, procreation, propriety, or even the announcement of marriage (although terminology creeps in throughout the Song). Ultimately, love and its enjoyment are what matter. Thus this amazing book has a wonderful place within the Bible, for the love in which it rejoices is a gift of creation.

Following the introduction, the commentary is presented in seven sections that recognize major divisions in the text. Each of the major sections begins with a translation. The interpretation of the text that follows considers each of the subsections. They are divided according to the speaker. The interpretation of each subsection begins with a discussion of the structure. This then unfolds into verse-by-verse comments that seek to integrate the poetic forms with the images presented so as to understand as completely as possible the intent of the text. Where appropriate, I present theological and other practical notes regarding the implications of the poetic expressions. The poetic structure, at the level of the individual verses, is thus the determining factor in shaping the interpretation. Altogether, the themes and images recur and interweave in this structure so as to form a verbal symphony of beauty and joy. Footnotes deal with technical matters, especially Hebrew linguistics. Interested readers will find profit in the main text of the commentary, without the need for special training. Each of the major sections (except for the first one, which considers only the title verse) concludes with a paragraph or two that summarizes and discusses major theological implications for that part of the Song.

The content is my own and no one else's. The delightful task remains for me to express gratitude to the series editor, Tremper Longman, for entrusting me with this project and for reading the manuscript and providing important comments. I also thank Baker for bravely agreeing to publish it. Further, I thank my Hebrew Song of Songs class at Denver Seminary. The students shared their insights with me and enabled me to learn and to balance this commentary with a collective wisdom. I also express appreciation to Sister Timothea Elliott, who joined us early on and assisted in setting a clear and sensitive course in the understanding of this marvelous book.

While I was completing this manuscript, our two sons, Fraser and Greig, announced their engagements to their fiancées, Elizabeth and Jenna. As we look forward to the joy of two family weddings in the coming year, I gratefully dedicate this work to them and the joy of their marriages. I hope that they will know the same happiness of desire and its fulfillment as the lovers of the Song and as Jean and I know in our marriage.

אֲנִי לְדוֹדִי וְדוֹדִי לִי (Song 6:3)

Richard S. Hess
Denver, Colorado
December 1, 2003

Abbreviations

Bibliographic and General

AHw   *Akkadisches Handwörterbuch*, by W. von Soden, 3 vols. (Wiesbaden: Harrassowitz, 1959–81)

BHS   *Biblia Hebraica Stuttgartensia*, ed. K. Elliger and W. Rudolph (Stuttgart: Deutsche Bibelgesellschaft, 1967–77)

CAD   *The Assyrian Dictionary of the Oriental Institute of the University of Chicago*, ed. I. J. Gelb et al. (Chicago: Oriental Institute, University of Chicago Press, 1955–)

CTU   *The Cuneiform Alphabetic Texts from Ugarit, Ras Ibn Hani and Other Places*, ed. M. Dietrich, O. Loretz, and J. Sanmartín (2nd enlarged ed. of *KTU*), Abhandlungen zur Literatur Alt-Syrien-Palästinas und Mesopotamiens 8 (Münster: Ugarit-Verlag, 1995)

DCH   *Dictionary of Classical Hebrew*, ed. D. J. A. Clines (Sheffield: Sheffield Academic Press, 1993–)

Eng.   English

GKC   *Gesenius' Hebrew Grammar*, ed. and enl. E. Kautzsch, trans. A. E. Cowley, 2nd ed. (Oxford: Clarendon, 1910)

HAL   *Hebräisches und aramäisches Lexikon zum Alten Testament*, by L. Koehler, W. Baumgartner, and J. J. Stamm, 3rd ed., 5 vols. + supplement (Leiden: Brill, 1967–96)

HALOT   *The Hebrew and Aramaic Lexicon of the Old Testament*, by L. Koehler, W. Baumgartner, and J. J. Stamm, trans. and ed. M. E. J. Richardson, 5 vols. (Leiden: Brill, 1994–2000)

Heb.   Hebrew

KAR   *Keilschrifttexte aus Assur religiösen Inhalts*, ed. E. Ebeling, 2 vols. (Leipzig: Hinrichs, 1915–23)

KJV   King James Version

KTU	*Die keilaphabetischen Texte aus Ugarit: Einschließlich der keilalphabetischen Texte außerhalb Ugarits*, vol. 1, *Transkription*, ed. M. Dietrich, O. Loretz, and J. Sanmartín, Alter Orient und Altes Testament 24 (Kevelaer: Butzon & Bercker; Neukirchen-Vluyn: Neukirchener Verlag, 1976)
lit.	literally
LXX	Septuagint
MT	Masoretic (Hebrew) Text
NAB	New American Bible
NEB	New English Bible
NIV	New International Version
NJPS	New Jewish Publication Society Translation
NRSV	New Revised Standard Version
NT	New Testament
OT	Old Testament
REB	Revised English Bible
v./vv.	verse/verses

Old Testament

Gen.	Genesis	Song	Song of Songs
Exod.	Exodus	Isa.	Isaiah
Lev.	Leviticus	Jer.	Jeremiah
Num.	Numbers	Lam.	Lamentations
Deut.	Deuteronomy	Ezek.	Ezekiel
Josh.	Joshua	Dan.	Daniel
Judg.	Judges	Hosea	Hosea
Ruth	Ruth	Joel	Joel
1–2 Sam.	1–2 Samuel	Amos	Amos
1–2 Kings	1–2 Kings	Obad.	Obadiah
1–2 Chron.	1–2 Chronicles	Jon.	Jonah
Ezra	Ezra	Mic.	Micah
Neh.	Nehemiah	Nah.	Nahum
Esther	Esther	Hab.	Habakkuk
Job	Job	Zeph.	Zephaniah
Ps.	Psalms	Hag.	Haggai
Prov.	Proverbs	Zech.	Zechariah
Eccles.	Ecclesiastes	Mal.	Malachi

New Testament

Matt.	Matthew		1–2 Thess.	1–2 Thessalonians
Mark	Mark		1–2 Tim.	1–2 Timothy
Luke	Luke		Titus	Titus
John	John		Philem.	Philemon
Acts	Acts		Heb.	Hebrews
Rom.	Romans		James	James
1–2 Cor.	1–2 Corinthians		1–2 Pet.	1–2 Peter
Gal.	Galatians		1–3 John	1–3 John
Eph.	Ephesians		Jude	Jude
Phil.	Philippians		Rev.	Revelation
Col.	Colossians			

Other Jewish and Christian Writings

b.	Babylonian Talmud
B. Bat.	tractate *Baba Batra*
1–2 Esd.	1–2 Esdras
Hist. eccl.	Eusebius, *Ecclesiastical History*
Jdt.	Judith
m.	Mishnah
Sanh.	tractate *Sanhedrin*
Sir.	Sirach
t.	Tosefta

Introduction

Authorship/Date/Setting

Although the first verse of the Song would appear to attribute the work to King Solomon, it is susceptible to alternative interpretations (see commentary). Indeed, the text does mention Solomon several additional times (1:5; 3:7, 9, 11; 8:11, 12). He is spoken of as though he were alive. In addition, the place-names in the Song (Lebanon, Hermon, and Amana) suggest the kingdom at its greatest extent, as under Solomon.[1] However, he is never designated as one of the speakers.[2] Nor do the anonymous speakers address Solomon directly. Further, the place-names suggest prominent towns and landmarks, but they nowhere imply that these form part of the contemporary empire of Israel.

Solomonic authorship for the Song would date it to the tenth century BC. If the problems with such a conclusion are accepted, then the authorship may be suggested from other evidence. Often the language of the Song is used to identify a later date.[3] Nevertheless, early attributions are not unknown. Gerleman observes that the emphasis this book places on beauty and art implies a time of Egyptian influence such as that experienced by the Solomonic court.[4] However, this remains speculative because little is known about Solomon's reign beyond what may be found in the Bible. Such influence may come as easily during the Persian period or some other time in Israel's history. Nor can geo-

---

1. Goitein, "Song," 63.
2. Murphy, *Song*, 3.
3. For attempts to use the aromatics in the Song for dating, see the evaluation in the comments on 4:14.
4. Gerleman, *Hohelied*, 63–77.

graphical references such as Tirzah (6:4) be of assistance. Although this site served as the capital of the northern kingdom of Israel before Omri moved it to Samaria in the early ninth century, such matters do not touch upon the purpose of the name as it occurs in the Song. The natural beauty of Tirzah could describe any period of time.[5] Again, attempts to date the text early according to appearance of Ugaritic cognates rest on the assumption that these terms cannot occur at a later date.[6] Young's arguments that the isoglosses between the Song and the early poem of Judg. 5 demonstrate archaic Hebrew are the most compelling presented on the subject of dating according to language.[7] However, even here the example of the letter *šîn* as a relative pronoun is more common in later Hebrew, and its usage in Judg. 5:7, if indeed it appears there (contrary to the vocalization), is not with a syntactic form parallel to that most common in the Song or later Hebrew. Nor are the possible appearances of the Greek *phoreion* (Song 3:9), the Persian *pardēs* (4:13), and other possibly late terms certain indications that the whole of the text is late.[8] De Paula Pedro and Nakanose ("Debajo") suggest a sociocultural context from the period of Ezra and Nehemiah. Garbini dates the Song to 69 BC.[9] Yet Müller ("Travestien") can find the Song echoing Amarna Egypt of the fourteenth century BC, as well as a Greco-Roman bucolic. A single word is a slight basis for dating a whole text, especially if one allows for the possibility of later editors and for other sources to originate the word.[10] The village life, the awareness of the "king" close by, the context of a fortified Jerusalem, and the active engagement and enjoyment of the luxury products of the trade routes—these all suggest an environment that is not far removed from the Israelite monarchy for much of the poem's content. Aspects of the language may suggest a postexilic date for the final composition, but the themes portray an earlier time.

For example, there is the question of the female's ability to run through the city streets in the middle of the night (3:1–5). Despite the various opinions of commentators, little is cited in the way of substantial evidence. Only Keel refers to the Middle Assyrian laws (12th/11th centuries BC) that require women to appear in public as veiled unless they are slaves or prostitutes.[11] Of course, this has no necessary relevance for Israel in the first millennium BC. In fact, a woman running through the city streets at night would have been unheard of and unaccept-

5. A possible derivation of the name Tirzah may be "lovely, pleasing."
6. Pope, *Song*; cf. Albright, "Archaic."
7. Young, *Diversity*, 161–65.
8. See summary in Murphy, *Song*, 4n10, and this commentary.
9. Garbini, "Significato"; idem, *Cantico*, 293–96.
10. Goitein, "Song," 62.
11. Keel, *Song*, 122.

able during the intertestamental period (Sir. 42:11), even if it is only a dream. However, in the earlier periods women could walk through a populated area alone at night, as Ruth did in her visit to the threshing floor (Ruth 3).[12]

Nevertheless, none of this is compelling, and the environment of the Song can be situated in a variety of possible times and places. This itself may betray the intention of the Song to speak more widely of love than a defined historical circumstance would allow. Even so, the springtime of the year, with an abundance of new life and vegetation, would be most suggestive for the setting of the Song. Perhaps this is one reason the book is traditionally read at Passover.[13]

The social roles presented in the Song deserve comment. Part of the logic behind the allegorization of the text may have been to reduce the implications of the lovers as truly free and independent individuals. The female in particular is the major character. She speaks first and last, and her words contain the most imperatives for her lover and for others. Indeed, it is she who both seeks his kisses (1:2) and commands him to be gone (8:14). Her feelings are freely shared, unlike those of her partner.[14] Given the female's dominant role as speaker and actor (e.g., she goes out in the night to search for her lover, 3:1–5), the full impact of this Song must include an equality and independence of the female as well as the male—what many traditional societies (to the present day) have been reluctant to recognize.

This then raises the question of a female author or composer behind the Song. Brenner, recalling the manner in which Miriam and Deborah may have composed Exod. 15 and Judg. 5, calculates that the female voice in the Song accounts for 53 percent of the text, while the male voice accounts for 34 percent.[15] This dramatic distinction may be coupled with the tradition that Israelite women could write (1 Kings 21:8–9; Esther 9:29) and the references to women's participation in the composition and performance of victory, lament, and harvest songs (Judg. 11:40; 21:21; 1 Sam. 2:1–10; 18:6–7; 2 Sam. 1:20, 24; Jer. 9:17, 20).[16] Various attempts, however, have not been successful to the point where it is possible to

---

12. So Keel, *Song*, 120, who also notes the rape law of Deut. 22:25–29.

13. In addition, later Jewish allegory associated the Song with Israel's exodus and the coming of the Messiah. Cf. Longman, *Song*, 2, although the attribution of the reading of the Song on the eighth day is not universal. The date has varied since its association with this festival, a phenomenon at least as early as the eighth century AD (Brenner, *Song*, 20).

14. Walsh, *Exquisite*, 106, goes further and notes that while the two are essentially equal in their appreciation for one another, "as desire travels through the levels of discourse, from flirtation to physical want to excitement, however, the man cannot keep up with the woman's desire."

15. Brenner, *Israelite*, 46–56.

16. Bekkenkamp and Van Dijk, "Canon"; Exum, "Developing," 226, 231.

be definite about the gender of the unspecified author of the Song.[17] Nevertheless, this composition clearly provides a stronger female voice in the dialogue than does any other biblical book.

This should be affirmed despite the attempts of Clines ("Why?") to identify the Song as a male composition of soft pornography that was designed for men's entertainment and allegorized (see "History of Interpretation" below) in order to preserve it within the canon.[18] Not only does this fail to deal seriously with its context within ancient Near Eastern love poetry; it also lacks acuity to distinguish erotic literature from pornography (with its brutality and oppressive caricature of women) and cannot explain the emphasis on the shared love and total commitment that the couple enjoys.

Canon/Language/Text Criticism

The Song appears as the first of the five Megilloth, or "Scrolls," in the Hebrew Bible. The others are Ecclesiastes, Lamentations, Esther, and Ruth. Its first appearance in this collection may be associated with its reading at Passover.[19] It forms part of the third division of the Hebrew Bible, the Writings. The books that appear in this section are thought to have been added last to the canon of the OT and therefore the last to be accorded canonical status.

No doubt the Song's canonical status was recognized because of its connection with Solomon (1:1) and its emphasis on human love.[20] It is the teaching of love that has preserved it as a book for the synagogue and the church. The question of the position of the Song of Songs seems to have been affirmed in Judaism. Rabbi Aqiba's (died c. AD 135) famous quote from the Mishnah bears repeating, since it was explicitly intended to counter questions about the canonical status of the Song: "God forbid!—no man in Israel ever disputed about the Song of Songs [that he should say] that it does not render the hands unclean, for all the ages are not worth the day on which the Song of Songs was given

17. Bekkenkamp and Van Dijk, "Canon," 107–8, argue that "the metaphorical language of women's songs seems to be (1) more explicit as far as objects or locations from women's life are concerned, (2) more implicit regarding bodily experiences, and (3) more individual." Brenner, *Israelite*, 90, suggests that the dream sequences of 3:1–4 and 5:2–7 contain "conflicts, contents and symbols" that "are 'typically female' in terms of modern psychology." She also finds less humor in the female lyrics. This all suggests that the composition has achieved an authentic female voice. However, that is not the same as demonstrating the presence of a female author.

18. On this subject, see Exum, "Developing," 218–19, and the bibliography there.

19. Brenner, *Song*, 24.

20. Bergant, "Song."

to Israel; for all the Writings are holy, but the Song of Songs is the Holy of Holies."[21]

Judaism thus accepted the canonicity of the book despite its unique form in comparison with the remainder of the Bible. The Song was read aloud during the Passover. In Christianity, the Song was recognized in an explicit manner as early as the list that Eusebius ascribed to Melito, the second-century AD bishop of Sardis.[22]

The female voice dominates this poem to a greater extent than any other book or text of comparable length in the Bible. Hence feminine forms occur frequently. However, there are occasions when the gender (or at times number) of the verb is unexpected. Thus 2:5 contains masculine plural imperatives spoken by the female, apparently to her female friends. The same is true of the masculine plural object in 2:7. Masculine forms where feminine were expected occur in 4:2; 5:8; 6:5, 8; and 8:4.[23] One may ask whether this does not suggest an epicene usage of characteristically masculine forms as either masculine or feminine, especially in contexts where only women are addressed or otherwise serve as referent. Elsewhere, number becomes unclear. For example, 1:17 refers to "our houses" (*bāttênû*), when the singular "house" is intended.

The Masoretic Hebrew text (MT) provides few problems and is used as the basis for the translation proposed here. The need for emendations and corrections is generally recognized in only a handful of places.[24] There are several fragments of the Dead Sea Scrolls that relate passages of the Song. Thus, 6QCant includes parts of the first seven verses. It represents a proto-MT form and confirms the existence of this text at Qumran. The remaining three fragments come from cave 4. The fragments from this cave choose parts of the Song but are not identical with a continuous text.[25] They seem to have served a liturgical purpose or another intent distinct from the preservation of the Song itself. The LXX represents an attempt to translate a text that also resembles the MT. This is followed as well by the Syriac Peshitta, which in the opinion of some represents

---

21. Danby, *Mishnah*, 782; *m. Yadayim* 3.5. The reference to soiling the hands is used to describe those books considered sacred Scripture. Aqiba's further endorsements of the Song are collected by Murphy, *Song*, 6n16. In the midrash *ʾAggādat šîr haššîrîm*, the scholar is reported to have said, "Had not the Torah been given, Canticles would have sufficed to guide the world." See Urbach, "Homiletical," 250. Better known is the statement ascribed to Aqiba in *t. Sanh.* 12.10, where he denies access to the world to come to any who sing the Song at a party or in an otherwise profane manner.

22. *Hist. eccl.* 4.26.12–14.

23. Murphy, *Song*, 132–33.

24. Cf., e.g., 3:11; 5:12; 7:10 (7:9 Eng.).

25. 4QCant[a] contains parts of 3:7–11; 4:1–7; 6:11?–12; 7:1–7; 4QCant[b] contains parts of 2:9–17; 3:1–2, 5, 9–10; 4:1–3, 8–11, 14–16; 5:1; 4QCant[c] contains a fragment of 3:7–8.

a stylistically more fluent rendering. Specific points of disagreement in the versions will be noted in the discussion below.[26]

History of Interpretation

The most detailed and easily available summary of the history of interpretation of the Song may be found in Pope.[27] It is not the purpose of this study to repeat what has already been stated elsewhere. Instead, a few of the major highlights in the development of the Song's study will be noted.

An allegorical interpretation can be found as early as 2 Esdras/4 Ezra (5:24–26; 12:51; c. AD 100). Israel is described as a lily, a stream, a dove, and a bride; all are images found in the Song (2:2; 4:15; 2:14; 4:8). The even earlier *Life of Adam and Eve* 43.4 may contain an allegorical allusion to Song 4:14.[28] This type of interpretation made an equation of God or Christ with the male, and Israel or the church with the female. The Targum to the Song identified 1:2–3:6 with Israel's victory over Egypt and the wilderness wandering, while 3:7–5:1 became associated with Solomon's temple and the temple cult. Song 5:2–6:1 is considered as the Babylonian exile. Song 6:2–7:11 is allegorized to describe Jewish independence, with the Roman rule found in 7:12–13. Song 7:14–8:4 describes the coming Messiah, and the last ten verses describe the resurrection of the end times.[29]

Allegorical interpretation in the Christian church was stimulated by the suggestion of the marriage imagery in NT texts.[30] Hippolytus (c. AD 200) used the Song as an allegorical vehicle to affirm asceticism. Origen developed allegory in his commentary of five volumes in the third century. This was furthered by Ambrose, Gregory of Nyssa,[31] and Bernard of Clairvaux.[32] Nor has the concept of an allegorical interpretation disappeared. Like Origen, Tournay (*Word*) would affirm both

26. See especially Garbini, *Cantico*. He provides the full texts of the MT, LXX, Old Latin, Vulgate, and Syriac Peshitta, along with text-critical apparatus and notes. Although he sometimes rearranges and emends the text without proper justification, his presentation of variants is without equal.

27. Pope, *Song*, 89–229.

28. See Robert, Tournay, and Feuillet, *Cantique*, 43; Audet, "Sens," 200; Elliott, *Literary*, 3.

29. See the summary of Bardski, "Swiatynia."

30. Matt. 9:15; 25:1–13; John 3:29; 2 Cor. 11:2; Eph. 5:22–33; Rev. 19:6–8; 21:9–11; 22:17. See Elliott, *Literary*, 4.

31. Gregory also recognized an erotic level of meaning as well as a marriage drama (in addition to the allegorical interpretation). See Dünzl, *Braut*.

32. See, e.g., Bernard, *On the Song of Songs*, vols. 1 and 2.

the allegorical and the "literal" interpretation, with the latter necessary for proper understanding of the former. This is accomplished through double entendre, in which the poetry works at both levels. Maier (*Hohelied*) speaks of the outer meaning of a profane love poem and the inner meaning of a poem about the Messiah.[33] Both the figures of the male and female became images of the divine.[34] Allegory flourished in the centuries before the Reformation. Lobrichon ("Espaces") notes how the laity, as well as the monastic tradition, gradually applied this book to their own lives by using it typologically and allegorically for the teaching of morals.[35] Phipps ("Plight") reviews the allegorical interpretation of the Song from the patristic period through the nineteenth century, demonstrating the great lengths to which it went for the purpose of suppressing the erotic message lying at the heart of a literal interpretation. Among the major interpreters, only Theodore of Mopsuestia, John Calvin, Edmund Spenser, and J. G. von Herder attempted to appreciate the work as a description of physical love.[36] Elliott has criticized the allegorical approach on two accounts: there is no plot in the Song such as would be necessary for a successful allegory; and there is no explicit reference to an allegorical interpretation anywhere in the Song.[37]

In addition to allegory, the patristic period saw a wide variety of interpretations, including those nonreligious approaches as represented by Theodore of Mopsuestia (Auwers, "Lectures"). The identification of the Song as a drama may have occurred as early as the fourth-century AD. Codex Sinaiticus and the fifth-century Codex Alexandrinus are two of the three earliest complete Bibles (and complete editions of the Song). Both of these contain marginal notes identifying the various speakers and assigning parts to them. Nilus of Ancyra (*Commentaire*, c. AD 400), like other patristic writers, saw a dramatic element among the themes. For him the female was a prostitute who worshiped other deities. The Song describes the love that converted her. Perhaps as much as any other scholar of the last two centuries, Franz Delitzsch developed this interpretation.[38] For him, the drama consisted of Solomon and

33. Cf. also D. Carr, "Falling."

34. D. Carr, *Erotic*, 127, notes how the beaten woman of 5:6–7 became an image of the crucifixion.

35. In addition, the Song was applied to devotion to Mary.

36. On the struggles of Herder to have his interpretation accepted and on its influence on others, especially Goethe, see Baildam, *Paradisal Love*.

37. Elliott, *Literary*, 6–7. Contrast the allegory on old age in Eccles. 12, which clearly identifies old age. Cf. Murphy, *Song*, 94, who refers to an absence of empirical evidence for this position. The allegorical interpretation continues in modern times. Cf. Joüon, *Cantique*; Krinetzki, *Hohe Lied*; Robert, Tournay, and Feuillet, *Cantique*; and Tournay, *Word*. The last relates the male lover to the church.

38. Delitzsch, *Song*.

the Shulammite female (7:1 [6:13 Eng.]), who taught the king the true meaning of love. The young women of Jerusalem function in a manner similar to a Greek chorus. Scholars such as Ginsburg, Renan, Harper, and Provan expand the number of main characters to three.[39] They add a rustic young lad, who competes with Solomon and his wealth, power, and decadence for the love of the female. At one point its acceptance was so widespread that an OT introduction such as that of Driver could present the dramatic interpretation as the only one to be considered.[40] It remains an interpretation adopted by some.[41] However, despite the fact that the name of Solomon occurs some six times in the Song (see comments on 1:1), he stays in the background and never speaks. The theory of the drama of three characters presents Solomon as a lustful abductor, for which there is no evidence elsewhere. In fact, it would be odd for a poem with Solomon in the heading to portray him as a villain.[42] Further, the presentation of drama seems largely omitted from Hebrew literature, remaining abhorrent to Jewish culture until late into the Middle Ages.[43] Finally, there are no ancient Near Eastern parallels for drama such as is envisioned.[44]

A cultic and liturgical interpretation of the Song arose with the publication of Akkadian and, subsequently, Sumerian texts from Mesopotamia. These revealed the story of Dumuzi (later Tammuz), the shepherd and king, who seeks and is sought by his love, Inanna (later Ishtar). Their adventures take them into the underworld and include rituals of mourning associated with the dry season and its absence of vegetation. Meek used the Akkadian texts to associate vocabulary and themes with the Song; Kramer developed the historical person of Dumuzi and in the Sumerian texts found love songs that he compared with the biblical Song.[45] Pope connected the whole Song with the mourning (and celebration?) rites of the West Semitic institution of the *marzēaḥ* ritual.[46] However,

39. Ginsburg, *Song*; Renan, *Cantique*; Harper, *Song*; Provan, *Song*.

40. S. Driver, *Introduction*; Elliott, *Literary*, 280n41.

41. See V. Sasson, "King," who sees the female as pharaoh's daughter in 1 Kings 11:1–2. Cf. also Provan, *Song*.

42. Webb, "Garment," 19.

43. Elliott, *Literary*, 13.

44. Phipps, "Plight," 83.

45. Meek, "Canticles"; idem, "Song of Songs"; idem, "Babylonian"; idem, "Song and Fertility"; Kramer, *Sacred*.

46. Pope, *Song*, 210–29. The discovery of further texts related to the *marzēaḥ* has resulted in an awareness that much less is known about this practice than was recognized when Pope wrote. For the opposite view, which minimizes funerary associations with this banquet, see McLaughlin, *Marzēaḥ*. Nevertheless, Pope's massive collection of evidence remains an essential starting point, and his analysis continues to convince on many points.

beyond the presence of similar vocabulary and themes (for which one may expect to locate even closer similarities with nonreligious Egyptian love poetry), it is difficult to identify a consistent liturgical form in the Song. It also is unlikely that religious texts based so overtly on foreign deities would have been acceptable to the rabbis in their consideration of retaining it in the canon.[47] Finally, the sheer speculative nature of this connection would find parallels with every love story. In his critical evaluation of Pope's theory, J. Sasson ("On Pope's *Song*") observed how the history of interpretation involved more a shift in "location" than one in actual method. It was not so much that the interpretations became less allegorical or more literal, but that the locus of activity and description moved from the synagogue or church to the palace (drama) and then finally to the temple (cultic).

The second half of the twentieth century saw the emergence of a different type of interpretation of the Song.[48] Perhaps more than any other book of the Bible, the Song lacked a satisfying analysis from the perspective of traditional literary criticism of the Bible.[49] The development of literary analysis emphasizing the unity of a literary piece (rather than its dissection into discrete and originally independent parts) has been combined with the emergence of rhetorical criticism and the application of both comparative Egyptian love poetry and techniques from the social sciences to the Song. All this has led to a rejection of earlier categories that themselves came from literatures later than, and foreign to, the Song itself. The recognition that the Song is poetry and that it should be studied first of all as poetry provided the basis for these new directions. In this light, Keel's observation on the Song as poetry is important: "The whole discussion has often overlooked the fact that poetry does not merely reflect reality—whether the reality of dreams or of conscious experience—but uses artistic means to create a reality of its own."[50]

Social science approaches to the interpretation of the Song have led in several directions. There is the psychological approach, championed by Landy,[51] which seeks to use psychological concepts to explore the

47. Elliott, *Literary*, 14–18.
48. The following section is dependent on ibid., 18–32.
49. Meyers, "Gender," 198, expresses it well: "The critical tools honed and sharpened in the analysis of the pentateuchal, prophetic and historiographic literature of the Bible have been inadequate to deal with a biblical book that differs in essential ways from the rest of the scriptural corpus."
50. Keel, *Song*, 120, while discussing 3:1–5. However, the observation could also apply to the Song as a whole.
51. Landy, *Paradoxes*. Cf. Krinetzki, *Hohe Lied*; Boer, "Second"; Black, "Beauty"; and discussion by Longman, *Song*, 46–47.

underlying relationships expressed in the poetry. Not only is the subjective nature of such analysis problematic, but the use of a brief piece of literature distant in time and culture also creates enormous problems for scientific study. Elsewhere, Stadelmann (*Love*) has resurrected allegory but applied it to interpret the Song in terms of postexilic Judean and Persian politics.[52] Such highly speculative approaches remain unclear as to their interpretive value.

The basic decision about the nature of the poetry that the Song represents could be described as one of two alternatives. Does the Song represent poetry from diverse sources and origins, or does it represent a more unified whole, perhaps even the work of a single author? Within this latter category there remains the question: Does the Song describe a progression of thought, or is it rather a thematic whole that does not intend to take any action within it and to move that action forward in time?

Among those in the first category who see in the Song an anthology of love poems, Horst identifies eight different types of poems and divides the text into relatively small units representing these forms.[53] Falk finds thirty-one different poems.[54] Publication of collections of Egyptian love poems furthered the sense that the Song is a similar collection.[55] The poems themselves were relatively short compared with the Song, and so a direct comparison led to the view that the latter consisted of a composition of originally independent poems.[56] However, Egyptian (and other) love poetry does not need to be limited in length. Indeed, the 117 verses of the Song do not make a long poem—not anything like, for example, an epic. If it is love poetry, then what determines length is not convention but the expression of the ardor and passion of the lovers. Lovers are nothing if not creative and independent, and the same is true for their poetry. In the case of the Song, unlike some love poetry, there is dialogue. This interaction heightens the passion. It also allows for a longer poem.

Egyptian and other comparative material can sometimes assist in the interpretation of the Song. However, many parallels that do exist

52. Weems, "Song," argues for a less specific form of a political/sociological interpretation. She suggests that society, for unclear reasons, seeks to separate and keep apart the lovers. Texts such as 1:5–6, the hasty departures and escapes, and the repeated assertion by the female that her lover belongs to her alone (2:16; 6:3; 7:11 [7:10 Eng.]) contribute to a view of a disparity of the couple in terms of class and perhaps race.

53. Horst, "Formen." Cf. Haupt, *Biblische*; Murphy, "Form-Critical"; idem, "Towards."

54. Falk, *Love*.

55. Hermann, *Altägyptische*. More recent adherents of the Song as a collection include Soulen, "Waṣfs," 215; and Brenner, *Song*.

56. White, *Study*, 163.

do not provide much in the way of an exegetical payoff, and therefore the usage of comparative literature will be limited. The reason for this seems to be the universal nature of love poetry. Thus White comments:

> Not only does the Song's rustic imagery betray a close association with the ways of expressing love in Egypt, but the commonality of love-language denotes archetypal vehicles through which human, sexual love was celebrated in the ancient world. Thus, it is not surprising that specific topoi be common to both Hebrew and Egyptian love literature. The fragrances, sight of the love partners, embracing and kissing, friends and enemies of the lovers, and even specific parallels (scent of garments, the mother figure, love under the trees, gazelles, etc.) denote the Song's participation in the world of human love expression.[57]

A promising direction in interpretation emerged with the acceptance of the Song as a unified collection of love poetry, designed to trace and develop themes but not to advance a particular plot. As Webb notes, the title suggests a single song or poem.[58] Landy represents this view in his study of the Song as a mystical love poem.[59] The lovers are both persons and archetypes. Further, love and death represent creative and destructive forces. He compares the whole poem with the Eden story of the opening chapters of Genesis. Trible argues that the poem develops its motifs from Gen. 2–3.[60] As in the garden of Eden, so here all the senses are involved, plants are everywhere, harmony pervades, water is abundant, animals are suggestive of love, and (Trible contends) sexual play and work are tied together in the Song. Certainly, and no more so than at 7:11 (7:10 Eng.), any conflict of the wills and domination of Gen. 3:16 is reversed in the Song.[61] However, this is not sufficient in itself to establish Gen. 2–3 as the key hermeneutical text. What brings the two texts close together is the intentionally similar reference to the judgment in Gen. 3:16, reversing it by the power of love in Song 7:11 (7:10 Eng.). Thus the woman

> unties the bondage of the ancient curse, exactly as Isaiah invalidates the curse of "I [God] shall institute hostility" between man and serpent by letting a suckling play over a viper's son (Isa. 11:8). In truth, in the pages

57. Ibid., 162.
58. Webb, "Garment," 22.
59. Landy, *Paradoxes*; idem, "Beauty," 36.
60. Trible, "Love's"; cf. Landy, "Two"; Lys, *Plus beau*, 52.
61. See the affirming opinion of Pope, "Song."

of the Song we encounter a new relationship between the two sexes, a relationship of equality and amicable mutuality.[62]

Literary and structural analysis of the poem has in some quarters superseded the historical-critical approach as a means to identify the major themes and interpretations.[63] More than anyone else, Elliott (*Literary*) argues for a thorough unity to the Song, structured on the basis of literary, vocabulary, and phrase connections throughout.

Bloom brings the discussion full circle with his comment: "The question of literal versus allegorical reading of the Song of Songs should be set aside forever; the work is so strong, that it demands every mode that can be brought to it."[64]

Phipps is correct when he rejects as anachronistic a view that the Song deals with free love and sexual experimentation.[65] Parallels with extrabiblical love poetry, especially Egyptian, do not in and of themselves demonstrate that the lovers are unmarried.[66] As will be noted, the use of "bride" (*kallâ*) never occurs other than in contexts of legal marriages (unlike terms of kinship, such as "sister," that can be used to describe a close friendship rather than a blood relationship) or as reference to a daughter-in-law.[67] The repeated appearance of "bride" in the Song's heart (six times in 4:8–5:1) demonstrates a relationship that is one of marriage, whether in fantasy or reality. The language of commitment pervades the whole Song and provides one of the most important interpretive keys for understanding the work. Alter (*Art*) goes further and asserts that any attempt to identify an original setting for this poetry is misplaced. Not only is this true because of the mixture of pastoral, urban, and royal allusions, but also because the

---

62. Goitein, "Song," 59; cf. Munro, *Spikenard*, 105–6. Exum, "Ten," 30, represents the opposite view, denying any equality of the sexes in the poem. She argues that the male is elusive in his freedom to leap about on the hills, whereas the female does not have this freedom and has a greater constraint placed on her chastity. However, gender equality is not gender identity, nor is the man "always off bounding over the hills," nor is the female unable to move from her place. Further, the text nowhere advocates promiscuity for the male.

63. Cf. Pelletier, "Cantique," and most of the commentaries since 1990.

64. Bloom, *Song*, 1.

65. Phipps, "Plight," 83–84.

66. White, *Study*, 81–82, 91–92, 163–64. The same uncertainty may be concluded regarding attempts to establish the Song as a wedding poem, using Egyptian parallels.

67. This disputes the assertion of LaCocque, *Romance*, 108, that the term signifies a bride-to-be. The use of "bride" in the Song is not contrary to usage in the OT and to the lexicons. In fact, the two examples that LaCocque cites to prove his point fail to do so. He refers to Gen. 38:24, which describes Tamar, hardly a bride-to-be. He also cites Hosea 4:13–14, where the term is explicitly used twice in parallel with "daughters." Both of these passages clearly use the term in the sense of a daughter-in-law.

life setting is suppressed so as to provide a universal appeal for this love poetry.[68]

Images/Structure/Theology

As Alter (*Art*) asserts, figurative language is used more prominently throughout the Song than anywhere else in the Bible. Furthermore, the lines of semantic distinction blur in the creative play of the imagery. This means that it is not always clear (from a structural standpoint) which image is the illustration and which is the referent.

Significant emphases occur in the repeated images that dominate the poem. The images include auditory and visual as well as taste, smell, and touch. These images serve as vehicles to define the intimacy of the relationship. The female is enclosed as a locked garden (4:12), a vineyard (1:6; 8:12), a palanquin (3:7–10), a locked room (5:5), and a walled city (8:9–10). She brings her lover into such an enclosure, the room of her mother (3:4). Around these images are scenes of protection: tenders of the vineyard (8:12), sixty warriors (3:7), sixty queens (6:8), watchmen and walls (5:7), lattice (2:9), locks (5:5), and towers (4:4; 7:5 [7:4 Eng.]; 8:9–10).

The vineyards and the gardens dominate the Song with emphasis on the sexuality of the female.[69] Walsh observes an important contrast between the male imagery of sexuality elsewhere in the Bible and that of the female as presented here.[70] Using Samson's metaphor for intimacy in Judg. 14:18, "plowed with my heifer," she demonstrates the extent to which male-oriented imagery emphasizes the farmer's working of the field (often the picture of the passive female) to produce a harvest of dry grains. In contrast, the female of the Song expresses sexual metaphors of moist and succulent fruit, which creates a quite different picture, one of fruitfulness and the many sensual pleasures of touch, taste, and aroma.

Falk provides some of the most helpful perspectives on contexts and themes presented in the Song.[71] There are four contexts where the scenes of the Song occur: the wild country with its destructive natural forces; the cultivated countryside portrayed as a return to paradise; indoors within the city, where a private and supportive world is found; outdoors in the city, where there is hostility and violence. Within these contexts occur five themes, three of which concern the beckoning of, banishment

---

68. This may also explain the absence of personal names given to the chief characters. See Exum, "Ten," 26.

69. E.g., Falk, *Love*, 101–4; Meyers, "Gender," 201.

70. Walsh, *Exquisite*, 81–94.

71. Falk, *Love*. See the summary in Webb, "Garment," 20–22.

of, and search for the beloved. The remaining two concern the evaluation of self in a hostile world and the praise of love. Within these major
contexts and themes, the Song imagery may be construed.

For example, when Meyers ("Gender") observes the architectural and
military images applied to the female, these reflect the fourth theme of
self-worth in Falk's list. Thus in 4:1–4 her neck is a tower (cf. 7:5 [7:4 Eng.])
and her ornaments form layers (or a ziggurat). Shields form a protection
for her. Whether or not the pools of Heshbon were designed for military
defense, they certainly could have been used in such a context. The "house
of the mother" (3:4; 8:2) contrasts with the "house of the father." This
traditional expression would describe the extended family, yet it is never
mentioned. Instead, the "house of the mother" affirms the female presence
and her dominance in the domestic sphere. Along with the male (2:9, 17;
4:1; 5:12; 8:14), she is associated with the more gentle and graceful doves
(2:12; 6:9) and gazelles (4:5; 7:4 [7:3 Eng.]). However, only the female is
associated with lions and leopards (4:8), an apparently unusual connection. More revealing is her simile with a mare let loose among pharaoh's
chariots (1:9). Meyers comments, "The female has a power of her own
that can offset the mighty forces of a trained army."[72] The effect of this
imagery is to provide the female with the tools necessary to control her
destiny and thus to choose her lover even as he chooses her.[73]

Alter (*Art*) finds a fusion of image and referent. In 2:8–9 the figure
at the lattice is both a stag and the lover. The double entendre of the
female's body, which is described repeatedly as a garden, becomes a
garden. There is a continuity of geographical landscape and the aesthetic reality of the female's body. The two cannot be separated. Thus
the imagery of the poem achieves more than a powerful description of
the lovers and their love. It participates in that love by attracting all five
senses into a heady acknowledgment of a matching relationship and a
full correspondence between the poem and the world.[74]

As noted above, the Song is best understood as a structured whole.
Elliott (*Literary*) finds the key to the structure in the refrains that are
repeated, especially in 2:7; 3:5; and 8:4.[75] As represented by the ongoing
dialogue throughout the poetry, the emphasis on the alternation between

72. "Gender," 207.
73. Cf. LaCocque, *Romance*, 131, who notes 6:4 and 6:10, where he translates that the
woman's eyes are "terrible as an army with banners."
74. Exum, "Ten," 27–29, notes that the text is a literary construct and thus lacks reality.
However, literature can strive to depict reality, and that is what the imagery appears to
be doing by drawing the scenes and word pictures with such evocative images. Compare
the comment of Ostriker, "Holy," 46: "Nothing in the Song suggests that woman is the
second sex."
75. See Feuillet, "Drama."

genders also becomes a key for understanding the basic structure.[76] This is the clearest distinction on a level that divides the text according to discourse. However, at a larger level one may identify a prologue (1:2–2:7), an epilogue (8:5–14), and four parts: 2:8–3:5; 3:6–5:1; 5:2–6:3; 6:4–8:4. Near the beginning and at almost every division (1:4; 2:4–7; 3:4–6; 5:1–2; 8:2–4) there occurs a series of key terms. Not all appear at each place, but a cluster appears: "come, enter" (bw'); either "house" (byt), "room" (ḥdr), or "garden" (gn); "wine" (yyn); "embrace" (ḥbq at 2:6 and 8:3); and an adjuration to avoid "love" or "sleep." Each new section begins with the lovers apart and concludes with them finding one another and coming together.

Scattered throughout the Song is a distinctive literary form that appears outside the book in modern Arab cultures. The Song contains three descriptions of the female's body (4:1–7 [8]; 6:4–7; 7:2–8 [7:1–7 Eng.]) and one of the male's body (5:10–16). These reflect a form known elsewhere to derive from an Arabic term for "description" (waṣf).[77] A waṣf is an Arabic love song in which the lover praises the physical attributes of his or her partner.[78] The argument that it is anachronistic to refer to these poems by a term known only from later Arabic sources cannot be sustained because (1) Arabic language and customs may predate the extant texts and (2) the appearance of a literary/oral form in a later period does not preclude its earlier existence. For another early example, see the waṣf for Sarah in the Genesis Apocryphon from Qumran.[79] David Carr ("Gender") compares the nonpublic love poetry sung predominantly by women in Mediterranean and Middle Eastern societies to argue that similar love poems were used for channeling emotions regarding love. The Song may therefore use well-known styles of discourses and create a literary artistry that makes these forms public.

The suggestion of a structural analysis recognizes the poem as a whole. Then the question arises: Does it have a central theme or a key theological emphasis? In terms of a theme, many emphasize the erotic nature of the love described here. In these cases the emphasis often lies upon freedom. Thus, the lovers describe and enjoy their bodies as

76. See, e.g., Fokkelman, *Reading*, 189–206, 224. The girl speaks thirty times, whereas the boy speaks eighteen times (200). Cf. Sonnet, "Cantique."

77. The term will be rendered in this manner throughout.

78. In the nineteenth century, J. G. Wetzstein, "Syrische," observed local weddings in Syria and the songs of the bride and groom that described the body of the other. He reported these to Delitzsch, who recorded them in an appendix to his commentary (*Song*, 162–76). See Soulen, "Waṣfs," 214; Longman, *Song*, 140–41. Thus began the study of waṣfs and their relation to the Song of Songs.

79. Murphy, *Song*, 158. For more on this type of song, as well as Arab examples, see Falk, *Love*.

physically sensual parts of nature.[80] Walsh (*Exquisite*) has determined that the emphasis of the Song lies in the expression of desire between two lovers. It is not sexual consummation that is most important, but the desire itself that drives the lovers together. In this she distinguishes erotica from pornography. The latter is concerned only with sex, and in this it is qualitatively different from the Song. Here sex plays a secondary role to desire. Whether there is any sexual activity at all in the poem—and as a fantasy there may be no such reality here—the key to the Song remains with the desire that drives the reader to appreciate the time of waiting. Hebrew experience placed the greatest value on passion. Here, too, the point of the Song is not that desire should be controlled, but the opposite, that "loss of control is a given."[81] Therefore, there can only be the full realization of desire for the other that forms the expression of love (ʾahăbâ, from a root already occurring six times in 1:2–2:7) most powerful to render absolute commitment and loyalty. The passion of the text separates it from the traditional category of wisdom literature, in the eyes of some; however, the emphasis on commitment prevents a capitulation to promiscuity.[82] It is this emphasis that relates the text to Prov. 5:15–19:

> Drink water from your own cistern, running water from your own well.
> Should your springs overflow in the streets, your streams of water in
>   the public squares?
> Let them be yours alone, never to be shared with strangers.
> May your fountain be blessed, and may you rejoice in the wife of your
>   youth.
> A loving doe, a graceful deer—may her breasts satisfy you always, may
>   you ever be captivated by her love. (NIV)

Some six or seven explicit verbal images relate this passage to the Song and render explicit the theme of exclusive commitment that is assumed in the love poetry.[83] Further, this and other examples of parallels to Israelite wisdom literature in the Song suggest that it has a place in wisdom literature. This is supported in a wider context by the presence of scribal and wisdom texts interspersed with Egyptian love poems.[84] The two are supplemental, not antithetical.

80. Viviers, "Rhetoricity," identifies this as the "ecstatic body," referring to Drew Leder's typology of rhetoric used in describing the human body.
81. Walsh, *Exquisite*, 162.
82. See LaCocque, *Romance*, 8, who, however, insists that "free love" is the chord of the text.
83. So Webb, "Garment," 29–30.
84. Specifically, White, *Study*, 81, refers to the Harper Song between the second and third sections of love poems found on Papyrus Harris 500.

Within the biblical context this positive theme of physical love contrasts strongly with the persistent negative statements on adultery, promiscuity, and the images of Israel as an unfaithful wife as found in the prophets. Hunter ("Song of Protest") argues that this book is a form of protest literature in which human nakedness and sexuality are appreciated and praised. This counters the negative associations of these things with sin as developed in the prophets. It also provides a counterpoint to the institutionalized patriarchalism of much of Israelite society by giving the female lover the dominant voice in the dialogue.

These are love poems whose use of language embraces the erotic but also points beyond this to a greater love.[85] Knight and Golka (*Revelation*) find in the Song a focus on God's redemptive plan for the world. Burns ("Human Love") is not troubled by the absence of God's name in the Song (see, however, comments on 8:6 below), but finds here the manner in which human love achieves a sanctity that grows from God's presence and love. On the other hand, Abécassis ("Espaces") suggests that the Song's central message has to do with personal identity that is defined in relation with others, whether God or people. This relational aspect is examined by Linafelt ("Biblical"), who emphasizes distinctiveness and unity, and the manner in which the Song bridges the connection between God and people. In so doing, he reaffirms the impact of some of the allegorical approaches.

Nor is this love far removed from the same *ʾahăbâ* occurring in contexts such as Deuteronomy. The covenantal love clearly embraced commitment. That same commitment may be found in a text such as the Song. Here it is not directly to God but to the lover. The *ʾahăbâ* of Deuteronomy also embraced a person's emotions.[86] This is because the emotions cannot be separated from the mind and will of the individual. Thus the love of the Song is not unlike the love for God that the community experiences as it joins with God in the fulfillment of its mission.

However, physical love remains the focus of the Song, and this must never be lost in any identification of the major theme.[87] It is this unbridled desire, with its exclusive commitment, that forms the basis for the confession of 8:6–7: "Love is as strong as death" (NIV). This connection of passion with death is not accidental. There is a connection of love with death in which both open the door to the unknown and uncontrolled. Passion, like death, cannot be bought or sold; it is beyond the human economy. Instead, it demonstrates the power of those parts of our being

85. Cogently argued by Murphy, "History."
86. Lapsley, "Feeling."
87. Contrast Webb, "Garment," 23, who asserts that the true consummation of love is in the relationship rather than sex. The Song does not recognize a dichotomy between the two. The same criticism must be directed at allegorical and other interpretations that fail to give proper emphasis to the physical side of love in the Song.

that can lie on the very edge of full encounter with God. Love for God here transcends covenantal fidelity alone and achieves an arousal and joy that is never consummated fully in this life. The saints of Christianity sometimes understood this, and so for them there was no discontinuity between the Song and their passion for God. These two expressions of desire welled up from the same center of their being. For them, then, it became the closest experience this side of the grave of the transcendent knowledge of the living God. As passion was a shortcut to knowing God in this life, so death itself became the door to that eternal knowledge.

How (Not) to Read the Song

The Song is not a drama or a sequential narrative.[88] It is not an allegory. It is not an anthology of diverse erotic poetry. The Song represents a poetic unity, expressing in its pages a most sublime love poetry. It closely resembles love poetry among the various genres of ancient Near Eastern literature. In its imagery and subtlety of metaphor, it is most similar to Egyptian love poetry. As is often the case with love poetry, and is certainly true with the published forms of Egyptian love poetry, the Song does not review a historical event but celebrates a loving relationship. The structural divisions outlined by the refrains repeatedly portray the couple apart and then reunited. Beyond this, the Song explores the passion of desire in more and more ways throughout its stanzas. As a result the reader comes to better understand the meaning of love and the loving relationship that exists between the couple.

The metaphor of the Song is the richest of any book in the Bible. It is, however, not intended to provide a simple one-to-one correspondence. In fact, interpreters are most likely to go astray into absurdities when they attempt to match things up where they are not explicit. The parade example is where the woman's breasts are made to represent the OT and NT (1:13). However, one also wonders about the recent attempts in which the common word for "navel" becomes a symbol of the woman's vagina (7:3 [7:2 Eng.]). The best interpretation is to remain sensitive to the language of imagery and attempt to follow its contours without imposing too much demand on specifics of interpretation.[89]

88. Munro, *Spikenard*, 121: "Moreover the ever-shifting perspectives compel the reader to give up the task of distinguishing between the real and the imaginary, the actual and the hoped for, for it becomes apparent that the lovers are capable of experiencing past, present and future with equal intensity."

89. Fox, *Song*, 298: "Sexual desire pervades the songs, and sexual pleasure is happily widespread in them. But their eroticism is not concentrated where commentators most often seek it: in specific allusions to genitalia and coitus." Exum, "In the Eye," 80.

The Song is not a manifesto for free love, nor is it a description of a married relationship. The Song does not entertain its readers with prurient expositions nor educate them as a sex manual.[90] Instead, the Song is a fantasy that explores the commitment of an erotic love affair. For the Israelites who first read it, as for the Bible readers of later periods, it may presume a sexual relationship within marriage. However, this is never made explicit. Instead, the absolute commitment of the two lovers (and the repeated term "bride" in the center of the text) suggests that this was an expectation of the society in which they lived (or at least for the couple themselves). Although anticipated and sometimes almost achieved, it is not possible to find a clear and certain description of coitus having taken place.[91] Whether as a fantasy of desire or a concatenation of images and words expressing the rapture of physical love, the Song pulls its readers along to teach them first and foremost about erotic love and the desire and joy that come with it.

The Song is unique in the Bible, but that does not mean it has no place there. The Bible takes the reader from the consequences of primeval rebellion and the discipline of the Torah to the unconditional delights of love. There is more to life, and by experiencing this we come to understand why love is so important for the covenantal God. The Song contrasts the abuse of sex in the treaty alliances of the kings of Israel and Judah and the terrible descriptions of rape in the narrative sections of the Bible with the beauty and appreciation of sex as a gift from God. It further enables the reader to appreciate that, while the prophets condemned sex in the service of the worship of gods and goddesses and equated such behavior with adultery, this is not the whole story. The Song fills a necessary vacuum in the Scriptures because it endorses sex and celebrates it beyond all expectation. Although abuse is possible and to be avoided, sex is not inherently evil, nor is it limited to a procreative function. Instead, sex enables an experience of love whose intensity has no parallel in this cosmos and serves as a signpost to point to the greater love that lies beyond it.

Outline

I. Title (1:1)
II. Prologue: First coming together and intimacy (1:2–2:7)
A. Female: Longing for her lover (1:2–7)

---

90. Cf. Webb, "Garment," 18.
91. Cf. Exum, "Developing," 247: "The Song is immediate in another sense: the love is always present, and the lovers just about to take their pleasure."

B. Male: Response with invitation and praise (1:8–11)
C. Female: Her lover as fragrance (1:12–14)
D. Male: Praise of beauty (1:15)
E. Female: Love in paradise (1:16–2:1)
F. Male: My love is like a flower (2:2)
G. Female: A pastoral scene (2:3–7)

III. Lovers joined and separated (2:8–3:5)
A. Female: Her lover pursues her (2:8–9)
B. Male: Invitation to come away (2:10–14)
C. Couple: Protect our love (2:15)
D. Female: Love affirmed, gratification delayed (2:16–17)
E. Female: Search and seizure (3:1–5)

IV. Love and marriage at the heart of the Song (3:6–5:1)
A. Male: Marriage scene (3:6–11)
B. Male: First *wasf* and call to come along (4:1–8)
C. Male: A walk in the garden (4:9–15)
D. Female: Invitation to her garden (4:16)
E. Male: Tasting the garden (5:1a)
F. Chorus: Enjoy! (5:1b)

V. Search and reunion (5:2–6:3)
A. Female: A second search at night for her dream lover (5:2–8)
B. Chorus: Challenge to compare the male lover (5:9)
C. Female: *Wasf* for the male (5:10–16)
D. Chorus: Inquiry for the male (6:1)
E. Female: Reunites with her lover (6:2–3)

VI. Desire for the female and love in the country (6:4–8:4)
A. Male: Second *wasf* for the female (6:4–10)
B. Female: Lingering in the groves (6:11–12)
C. Chorus: Call to return (7:1 [6:13 Eng.])
D. Male: Third *wasf* for the female (7:2–10a [7:1–9a Eng.])
E. Female: Springtime and love (7:10b–8:4 [7:9b–8:4 Eng.])

VII. Epilogue: The power of love (8:5–14)
A. Chorus: Search for the couple (8:5a)
B. Female: The power of love (8:5b–7)
C. Brothers (quoted by the female?): Their younger sister (8:8–9)
D. Female: Her defense (8:10)
E. Female: Solomon's vineyard (8:11–12)
F. Male: Listening (8:13)
G. Female: Departure (8:14)

I.
Title
(1:1)

Translation

¹The Song of Songs that concerns^a Solomon.

Interpretation

1:1. The first verse forms the title for the book. It places the expression *šîr haššîrîm* first and thereby gives it emphasis as the key to the text. The construction may be translated "Song of Songs." *Šîr* (song) occurs as a noun some 166 times in the Hebrew Bible, mostly in the book of Psalms. However, it appears only here in the Song of Songs. Although the noun occurs elsewhere alongside the same root used as a verbal form (1 Sam. 18:6; 2 Chron. 29:28; Isa. 26:1), here the form used is unique to this text.[1] This form implies a superlative statement: The Best Song. It may seem surprising that this text should be designated the best song, given the wide variety of poetry in the Bible. Would not one of the great hymns of praise (e.g., Pss. 19; 100) be a better choice as the best song? This text barely mentions God. None of the customary designations for the God of Israel is present (*ʾĕlōhîm, ʾēl, ʾĕlôah, yhwh*), and the focus of the song seems to involve physical love between a man and a woman. Who would define this song as the best? The answer lies in a careful study of the song and an understanding of the physical love praised here as sharing in the greater love of God, which he created for all those in his image

---

a. Goitein ("Song," 65) follows Nahum Halevi in vocalizing the word as *ʾāšîr*, "I shall sing." While possible, this vocalization is not followed by the versions.
1. The nouns are in construct, with a definite article, "the song of songs."

to enjoy.[2] If the physical love praised in this book is merely a detached symbol separate from the greater spiritual love, then either the title is misleading or its author valued the carnal pleasures of sex above anything else (an example of ancient advertising, propaganda, and seduction). It will be argued here that neither of these alternatives is correct (despite the intense eroticism of the poem). Instead, all the words and desires of the lovers point toward an understanding of love in which this song shares. The apostle may have reflected on such a knowledge when he concluded, "The greatest of these is love" (1 Cor. 13:13 NIV).

The LXX renders the Hebrew *šîr* (song) by *asma*, a term that denotes more of a secular lay or ode than a religious hymn. It is clear from the title that the composition was thought by the author of this verse to constitute a single unified whole. Murphy contrasts this with the book of Proverbs, where the use of the plural term "sayings, proverbs" (1:1; 10:1; 24:23; 25:1; 30:1; 31:1) implies a diverse collection of material (cf. also Amos 1:1).[3]

The expression "that concerns" (*ʾăšer lĕ*) occurs some 221 times in the Bible, always to denote the owner of some sort of property (e.g., Ruth 2:21; 4:3, 9). Although an abbreviated construction could communicate this, there are three reasons why this longer form may be preferred.[4] The first is the desire to provide an unequivocal statement that the psalm is inextricably attached to Solomon. This may mean authorship, or it may refer to the commitment of another author to write along the lines and experience of the king.[5] The formation is never used in the titles of the psalms elsewhere

---

2. Gen. 1:26–28. Cf. the Christian doctrine of the Trinity, in which God shares loves among the three persons of the Deity.

3. Murphy, *Song*, 120.

4. The shorter and more common form (cf. the titles to the Psalms) would be the *lāmed* preposition by itself. Note that in the Song the relative *ʾăšer* occurs only here. Elsewhere the relative is designated some 32 times by *še*. Of the 142 times that the relative appears in the Bible, it occurs some 70 times in the book of Ecclesiastes. Because this latter book is dated as a postexilic work, the appearance of this relative is used as an argument that the Song is postexilic. Further, the appearance of the relative *ʾăšer* in 1:1 is used to argue that this verse was added by an author/editor different from the writer of the book. However, such a form would suggest that the one who added the title did so earlier than the book that follows the title! An argument of deliberate archaizing would seem odd: Surely the author of the title with such a motive would have intentionally wished the form there to resemble the rest of the Song. Hence the author would have either altered the relatives in at least some places in the Song or avoided using *ʾăšer* in the title. Further, it is not certain that the usage of *še* must indicate a postexilic (late) text. Judges 5:7 appears to use this particle in a poem widely recognized as one of the earliest preexilic texts in terms of its language (see the comments on dating in the introduction). For these reasons, we look elsewhere for the rationale for this construction in Song 1:1.

5. Murphy, *Song*, 119, notes both biblical (1 Chron. 24:20) and Ugaritic (*CTU* 1.6.i 1) examples where the *lāmed* is used with a proper noun to introduce a topic.

in the Hebrew Bible. It therefore suggests an authorial style different from such titles, perhaps also implying a different purpose.

The second reason for the longer construction may have to do with the repetitive sound of the opening words in the book. The four words of the title (v. 1) as well as the first two words of the poem (v. 2) all contain a *šîn* (ש), creating a *sh* sound.[6] Indeed, the first word of the book (and only that word in the opening two verses) begins with a *šîn*, signaling the importance of this sound. Further, the first three words each contain a *šîn* followed by a *rêš* (ר, an *r* sound), repeating the *šîr/šer* sound.[7] In poetry, the sound repetition is significant. The *šîr/šer* sound would emphasize the word for "song" three times at the beginning of the book, because it sounds like *šîr* (song). The repetition of the letter *šîn* ties the title "Song of Songs" together with Solomon. Thus the value of the song as the best of songs is enhanced by its association with the key figure of wisdom in the Bible as well as someone whose reputation for marriages exceeds any king or commoner (1 Kings 3:4–28; 11:3). Again, the appearance of the *šîn* sound in the first two words of Song 1:2 (*yiššāqēnî minnĕšîqôt*, let him kiss me with the kisses of) ties the theme of physical love, here in the form of passionate kisses, with the title and thus indicates the direction of this best song and of the association with Solomon. This association suggests the attribution in 1 Kings 5:12 (4:32 Eng.): "He spoke three thousand proverbs and his songs numbered a thousand and five" (NIV).

This association with Solomon provides an anchor for the Song in the biblical wisdom tradition and relates to this material in the canon. No longer separated from the Bible as a collection of love songs, the book takes on a unified significance that cannot be reduced to secular humanism. Nor can its imagery within the context of physical love be ignored and give way to purely allegorical interpretation. The connection to Solomon places the book within a historical wisdom tradition of literature recognized by the church as possessing divine inspiration.[8]

A third and final reason may have to do with the nature of the literature that follows: love poetry that is rich in metaphor and imagery. In this context the extended means of referring to Solomon may intentionally separate this notice from those of authorship or reference elsewhere in poems of the Bible. Here Solomon, as the king and symbol of wisdom and love, becomes an image for the male lover in the poem. Thus the female speaker, who dominates the poem, dedicates it to her Solomon, a figure who embodies her greatest desires for the fulfillment of love.

6. This sound is represented here in transliteration as *š*.
7. So also J. Sasson, "On Pope's *Song*," 190–91.
8. See Childs, *Introduction*, 573–79.

II.
Prologue:
First Coming Together and Intimacy
(1:2–2:7)

Translation

Female

1:2 May he kiss me[a] with the kisses of his mouth,
Because[b] your lovemaking[c] is better than wine.
3Your name[d] is cologne poured out,[e]

a. As vocalized by the MT, this is a Qal jussive (third-person masculine singular) from the root *nšq*, plus the first-person pronominal (object) suffix. The suggestion of Karl Budde ("Hohelied"; cited in Kautzsch, *Heilige Schrift*, 2:392) and others (cf. Gordis, *Song*, 78) is to emend the text and analyze the form as a Hiphil stem of the root *šqh*, with the meaning "cause me to drink," "drown me," and "smother me." This commentary will follow the MT where its consonantal text and vocalization are clear in meaning. For this and other suggested emendations, see Pope, *Song*, 125 et passim.

b. Others take this particle (*kî*) as emphatic and translate "truly." See Pope, *Song*, 298; Murphy, *Song*, 125. Their interpretation is based on Albright, "Archaic," 2.

c. The LXX reads Hebrew *dadayik* (your breasts) for *dōdeykā* (your lovemaking) and renders it as *mastoi sou*, apparently reversing the gender roles of the Hebrew. Interestingly, the other occurrence of kissing in the Song (8:1) does mention breasts. This may have influenced the LXX or its *Vorlage* to identify the word in this location. The initial emphasis of the text on the broader topic of lovemaking suits its location at the beginning of the book.

d. Into the consonantal *šmk* (your name), J. Sasson, "On Pope's *Song*," 191, suggests inserting a *nûn* and translating "your oil/cologne."

e. The major textual problem with this verse lies in the verb, translated "poured out" (*tûraq*). This is a Hophal stem derived from the root *ryq* (to be empty). However, it is a feminine form of the verb. The problem is that there is no feminine antecedent. To allow it to remain suggests a gender incongruency, something known in Biblical Hebrew, especially where the speakers are feminine. However, the form may be a noun that is the object of a

40

It is the fragrance of your best colognes.[f]
Therefore, the maidens[g] love you.
[4]Take me with you. We must hurry.
The king brought me to his chambers.
We will indeed rejoice and be happy for you.
We will indeed recall your lovemaking more than wine.
Naturally[h] they love you.[i]
[5]I am black but[j] beautiful,
O daughters of Jerusalem;
Just like the tents of Qedar,[k]
Just like the curtains of Solomon.[l]
[6]Do not[m] look at me so,
Because I am so swarthy,[n]
Because the sun has "stared" at me.

---

construct relationship with *šemen*. In that case it could refer to a place-name, Turaq, or to a type of strongly scented oil whose term is borrowed from an Egyptian cognate. For the former, see Fox, *Song*, 97. The latter was proposed by Görg, "Salbenbezeichnung." However, these options create forms otherwise unattested in Hebrew. The Dead Sea Scroll text 6QCant reads here *mrqht mwrqh* (an ointment that is clean/for the purpose of cleaning). While not likely in itself, this may explain the presence of a passive participle in the LXX, Aquila, and the Vulgate, all of which may retroject to *mûrāq* (having been poured out; *BHS*). This also provides for the suggestion of *BHS* and the conjecture of *HAL* 1618 (= *HALOT* 1758) to read *tamrûq* (pure ointment). Cf. von Soden, "Nominalform," 81–82. However, it is not clear that any of these options provides a likely translation. Certainly, they require shifts in the meaning to accommodate a text where the emphasis of the oil is upon its fragrance rather than its salubrious properties. It remains perhaps the best option to retain the apparent gender confusion. See also Pope, *Song*, 125, for a similar conclusion and doubts about any certain interpretation of this passage in 6QCant.

f. The LXX renders this line as "and the fragrance of your colognes is better than all the aromatics." Qumran and the Vulgate omit the second-person masculine singular suffix in the same line.

g. Rabbinic interpretation analyzes the consonants of "the maidens love you" (*ʿlmwt ʾhbwk*) as "they love you unto death" (*ʿal māwet ʾăhēbûkā*). Thus they connect love and death early in the Song. See Goldin, *Song*, 116; J. Sasson, "On Pope's *Song*," 191.

h. The Hebrew *mêšārîm* may rather refer to the quality of the wine (smooth wine) in the preceding line. See Fox, "Scholia," 199–201.

i. Here 6QCant reads a passive, "they are loved."

j. The *wāw* here is construed as adversative. Otherwise, it is difficult to understand how the picture of the beauty of this condition in this verse would be reversed in the following one. Cf. Fox, *Song*, 101; contra Pope, *Song*, 126. Cf. also Hostetter, "Mistranslation."

k. Although a proper noun from Arabia, the root *qdr* carries the basic sense "to become dark," similar to the concern of the female in vv. 5–6.

l. The suggestion to alter "Solomon" to the place-name "Salmah" is accepted by Pope, *Song*, 319–20. J. Sasson, "On Pope's *Song*," 191, prefers retaining the complementary simile as translated here with Qedar. He observes that *kîrîʿôt* (just like the curtains) suggests "friend, companion" (*raʿyâ*).

m. The suggestion of Exum, "Assertive?" to argue that *ʾal* is asseverative rather than primarily negative is supported by "neither syntax nor context" (Murphy, *Song*, 126).

n. Hostetter, "Mistranslation"; Longman, *Song*, 95.

The sons of my mother burned with anger against me,
They made me look after the vineyards,
Yet my very own vineyard I have not looked after.[a]
[7]Tell me, you whom I love,
Where[b] do you graze [your flocks]?
Where do you rest[c] them at noon?
Lest[d] I become like a cloaked woman,[e]
Beside the flocks of your friends.[f]

Male

[8]If you don't know, most beautiful of women,
Follow the sheep paths,[g]

a. J. Sasson, "On Pope's *Song*," 191, translates this line as a rhetorical question: "Have I not guarded my own vineyard?"

b. For *ʾêk* as "where?" see 2 Kings 6:13; Hyman, "Multiple."

c. *Tarbîṣ*: Garbini, *Cantico*, 32–33, argues that the consonantal MT inserted a *yôd* in order to transform the more erotic Qal, "Where do you lie?" to the innocent "Where do you cause them to crouch?" He compares four Kennicott manuscripts, the LXX (*koitazeis*), and other versions that preserve the Qal form. However, the argument is not conclusive because the parallelism with the preceding line, "graze" (*tirʿeh*), would suggest exactly the MT form. The two verbs occur together in eleven verses. The only other occurrence where both are finite verbs and possess the shepherd as subject is Ezek. 34:15, which the MT points as a Hiphil (with the consonantal *yôd*): "I myself will tend my sheep and have them lie down" (NIV).

d. This hapax legomenon has been related to the Aramaic *dilmah*. The LXX supports this with *mēpote*.

e. This follows the first meaning of *ʿṭh* (to wrap), here used as a Qal feminine participle meaning "she wraps (herself)." Cf. Ps. 104:2 and the LXX *periballomenē*. Emerton, "Lice?" reviews the evidence and concludes that the best option is to understand here a cognate to the Arabic *ʿaṭā* ("taking/picking lice" off a garment). In this he follows von Gall, "Jeremias"; G. Driver, "Lice"; NEB; and REB. However, G. Driver influenced the latter versions (but not the NRSV's "like one who is veiled"). This option was first identified for Jer. 43:12. Whether or not its application is appropriate there, the many occurrences of *ʿṭh* (to wrap) throughout the biblical text (*HALOT* 813 lists fourteen in the Qal stem, as here) indicate that this should be the first option for consideration. The Old Latin (*sicut operta*), Symmachus (*rembomenē*), the Vulgate (*vagari*), and the Peshitta (*ṭʿytʾ*) understand "wander, stray" from *ṭʿh*, a by-form of *tʿh*, and a metathesis of the MT's *ʿṭh*, the root behind the form in Song 1:7 (Keel, *Song*, 51–52). Again, such an emendation appears to be extreme, nor is it supported by the LXX. In fact, Emerton's objections for the traditional translation seem to be based on the assumption that "wrapping, covering, cloaking" must require either covering a moustache, wearing something distinctive of a prostitute (cf. Fox, *Song*, 103), or wearing something that would conceal the female's identity (Emerton, "Lice?" 128–29). However, the biblical text requires none of these, nor is such a cloak different from ordinary female dress (see comments). The most common root thus remains the most likely.

f. Or "shepherds."

g. This expression is *ʿiqbê haṣṣōʾn* (footprints of the sheep). The root of the first noun (*ʿqb*) normally refers to the heel of a living creature. Several times in the Psalms (56:7; 77:20; 89:52 [56:6; 77:19; 89:51 Eng.]) the contexts suggest footprints or feet.

Graze your goats by the shepherds' tents.
⁹To a mare[h] among pharaoh's chariots,
Do I liken you, my darling.
¹⁰Your cheeks are desirable with earrings,
Your neck with strings of jewels.
¹¹We will make you earrings of gold,
Studded with silver.

Female

¹²While[i] the king is on his couch,[j]
My spikenard gives forth[k] its fragrance.
¹³A sachet[l] of myrrh is my lover to me,

h. There is general agreement that this form, *susātî*, consists of *sûsâ* (mare) plus an old (archaizing) suffix form, perhaps reflecting the oblique case ending. J. Sasson, "On Pope's *Song*," 120, suggests that *susātî* may have been so written to resemble the sound of *raʿyātî* (my darling).

i. Although the straightforward meaning "while" may be applied only to mishnaic occurrences of the prepositional construction *ʿad še*, a form of this occurs already in Judg. 5:7, viewed by most as a second-millennium BC early Hebrew poem. Further biblical occurrences are found in Ps. 123:2 and seven additional times in the Song (2:7, 17; 3:4 [2x], 5; 4:6; 8:4). In all other biblical usage, the preposition means "until," describing a sense of anticipation and of change at a critical point. Cf. the LXX *heōs* for Song 1:12. The preposition in this verse may well be translated "until" in the sense of the lover's expectancy at her partner's arrival. While the male lover's presence achieves a climax for the female's anticipation, it does not change the ongoing portrayal of the fragrances that these verses describe. The fragrances continue, and indeed the whole emphasis of the poem, as suggested by the parallelism, is that the king, the lover, and the fragrances are one and the same. Thus the ongoing nature of the scene suits a translation of the preposition as "while." In support is also the fact that here is the only occurrence of this prepositional construction in all its biblical usage where it is followed by a noun instead of a verb. This, more than the date of the poem, may affect the usage of the form.

j. Hebrew *mēsab*, used of an article of furniture only here. The other two occurrences of a word spelled in this manner describe either the preposition "around" (1 Kings 6:29) or a noun describing the "environs" of Jerusalem (2 Kings 23:5). NIV's "table" is possible but does not lend itself to "spends the night" (*yālîn*) in Song 1:13. Nor is this a banquet scene or one that has anything to do with food. The basic sense of the root *sbb* (around, surrounding) could just as easily describe a couch. Cf. Fox, *Song*, 105. Although Keel, *Song*, 63, renders this "with his table guests," he recognizes the purpose of the banquet as erotic (cf. 2:4).

k. The perfect form of this verb (*nātan*) might suggest a natural translation in the past tense that would describe the action as completed. There is only one other verb in these verses, the imperfect (*yālîn*) at the end of v. 13. The alteration of perfect and imperfect in West Semitic poetry does not necessarily indicate changes in tenses but may have to do with meter and other aspects of the poetry, some of which are no longer clear to the modern reader. In any case, the initial preposition governs the poem and describes the activities as ongoing.

l. The *ṣĕrôr* has suggested a bag, a definition supported by other occurrences of the term (Gen. 42:35; 1 Sam. 25:29; Hag. 1:6; Job 14:17). However, the term does not require a cloth bag. Carrot-shaped and spherical perfume containers, made of alabaster or other

Between my breasts he spends the night.[a]
[14]A bouquet of henna[b] is my lover to me,
In the vineyards of En Gedi.

Male

[15]You are so beautiful,
My darling,
You are so beautiful,
Your eyes are doves.

Female

[16]You are so beautiful,
My lover;
You are so pleasant,
And our bed is a spreading <tree>.[c]
[17]The beams of our house[d] are cedars,
Our rafters[e] are junipers.[f]
[2:1]As for me, I am the asphodel[g] of Sharon,

---

stone, from the sixth and fifth centuries BC, have been found in Palestine. Earlier ones were made of ivory and wood. Thus a "juglet" may be a more accurate description than a "sachet" or some other term for a cloth bag. The reason is that most aromatics were mixed with an olive oil base in Palestine (as opposed to today's common use of an alcohol base). This would be difficult to keep in a cloth container; however, a juglet would allow for it to be opened and poured out from time to time so that the aromas could be enjoyed. On the juglet, see King and Stager, *Life,* 280, 282. Nevertheless, a sachet would be more comfortable. Thus Keel, *Song,* 65, describes the Egyptian *demedh* as "a small bag made of one or two cloth strips. The bag is not sewn but is formed when the cloth is wrapped around one or more objects, which it then holds. It is held together by a pin."

a. The verb here should not be translated "rest" (so NIV), because its many biblical occurrences never refer to spending less time than one night (e.g., Gen. 19:2; 24:23; Judg. 19:7; Isa. 65:4; Ps. 55:8 [55:7 Eng.]). Murphy, *Song,* 132, however, understands it as "rest," citing Job 19:4; Prov. 15:31. However, even in these contexts it suggests a dwelling together for a long period of time.

b. Although the LXX and Vulgate render this term "cyprus," "henna" best fits the context and was well known in the Middle East. See Charbel, "Come tradurre."

c. No term for "tree" occurs here. However, in Biblical Hebrew "spreading" (*ra'ănānâ/ ra'ănān*) is always used of trees, and the following verse suggests that context. Cf. Deut. 12:2; 1 Kings 14:23; 2 Kings 16:4; 17:10; Isa. 57:5; etc.

d. The plural *bāttênû* is not "houses" (G. Carr, *Song,* 87) but a syntactical construction known from Mishnaic Hebrew, in which the *nomen rectum* (modifying noun) matches the number of its antecedent (Fox, *Song,* 106). Murphy, *Song,* 132, refers to it as a plural of generalization.

e. Following the Qere (traditional variant reading), which reads *rhytnw* (our rafters).

f. As *HALOT* 155 suggests, the hapax legomenon "junipers" (*běrôt*) is an Aramaic by-form of the more common Hebrew *běrôš.*

g. The dictionaries also suggest a meadow saffron or narcissus. See *HALOT* 287; *DCH* 3:152. The Akkadian cognate *ḫabaṣillatu* refers to the fresh shoot of a reed and can identify

The lotus[h] of the valleys.[i]

Male

[2]Like a lotus[j] among the thorns,
So is my darling among the young women.[k]

Female

[3]Like an apple among the trees of the forest,
So is my lover among the young men.
In its shade I delight[l] to sit,
Its fruit is sweet to my palate.[m]
[4]He brought me to the house of wine,
And his intent[n] for me is love.

---

a (copper/bronze) musical instrument in a lexical text. See *CAD* 6:8, where it is argued that "fresh shoot of reed" is a better translation for the Hebrew term. Pope, *Song*, 368: "Apart from the rose fanciers, the consensus is that the plant is some sort of common bulb, such as the asphodel, crocus, hyacinth, or narcissus. The crocus or daffodil is taken as a fair guess." Munro, *Spikenard*, 83, is correct that the point of the image, the female's similarity to other flowers, renders insignificant the precise flower to which reference is made.

h. Traditionally, the *lilium candidum* that grows in soil. However, it could also refer to the lotus (sea daffodil, water lily, *pancratium maritimum*), which grows in water, as required in 1 Kings 7:26; 2 Chron. 4:5 (*HALOT* 1455), where the brim of the molten sea at the temple was said to have this shape. Further, lotus capitals are known in Egypt and Israel (1 Kings 7:19, 22). For the early borrowing of this term from the Egyptian word for lotus, see Kitchen, "Lotuses." For the appearance of the lotus in the Plain of Sharon, the identification of the Egyptian lotus as a lily (*krinon*) by Herodotus (followed by the LXX), and the lotus as a favorite object for Egyptian and Phoenician art, see Keel, *Song*, 78–80; Pope, *Song*, 368.

i. Fox, *Song*, 107, suggests that this is a term for a type of flower, a "valley-lotus," because a single lotus could exist only in a single valley.

j. In the Song the feminine form of "lotus" occurs only here and in the preceding verse. It also appears in Hosea 14:6 (14:5 Eng.) and 2 Chron. 4:5. Elsewhere the common noun is masculine gender.

k. The term for "the young women" is literally "the daughters" (*habbānôt*).

l. With G. Carr, *Song*, 90, the Piel stem of this verb, used only here in the Bible, describes "the active accomplishment of the state described by the related noun or adjective."

m. *Lěḥikkî*, as the organ of taste; cf. 5:16; 7:10 (7:9 Eng.); Pope, *Song*, 373.

n. This follows Pope, *Song*, 376–77 (cf. Fox, *Song*, 108; G. Carr, *Song*, 91), who compares the Akkadian *diglu* (look, gaze) with Hebrew *diglô* (his intent) here. This certainly makes better sense than the unexpected intrusion of the noun "banner," whose martial context elsewhere in the OT is far removed from this scene of love. See also Murphy, *Song*, 132, 136 (who nevertheless retains "banner" in his translation, pleading the royal dignity that it represents in the male). Zolli ("In margine," 173–75) and Gordis ("Root") earlier had identified and accepted the Akkadian cognate. Keel, *Song*, 85, accepts the traditional "banner, standard" as being implied here. He points to iconography from Egypt and Assyria, where such standards appear. However, all his examples are martial, not domestic or erotic. See also, Longman, *Song*, 113–14, who sees no reason to abandon the traditional translation but does not address this point.

⁵Refresh^a me with raisins,
Revive^b me with apples,
Because I am faint with love.
⁶His left <arm is> under my head,
His right <arm> embraces me.
⁷I want you^c to promise,
O young women of Jerusalem,
By gazelles and does of the field,^d
Do not disturb,
Do not excite love,
Until it desires.^e

Interpretation

Callow ("Units") follows many others in identifying 1:5–2:6 (with 2:7 as the conclusion) as the first major section after the title.[1] He notes that the female alone speaks in his first subsection, 1:5–6. Of course, this is true for all of vv. 2–6. However, the key point is the absence of the male and the implied distance between the two. His second subsection, 1:7–8, is where the couple interact, although they do not use the customary terms of endearment shared later and throughout the Song. In the division proposed here, which follows the speakers, v. 7 is attached to the female's poem of vv. 2–7, and v. 8 is attached to the following subsection, spoken by the male. In this manner the two verses form a bridge, connecting the two subsections, yet each retaining characteristics of the larger speech of which they are a part. Song 1:9–17 creates a rhetorically ascending

a. The Piel of *smk* appears only here in the Bible. The Qal sense, "to support, sustain," seems to be intensified by the Piel. Murphy, *Song*, 132, notes the masculine plural form of the imperative but suggests that the gender is not specific and in context can reference the young women. Fox, *Song*, 109, suggests "a sort of rhetorical imperative," not unlike G. Carr, *Song*, 92, who recognizes "an appeal to anyone who is within hearing."

b. The Piel of *rpd* occurs only here and in Job 17:13 in the Bible. There and in its one Qal usage (Job 41:22), it takes the meaning of "to extend, spread out." This seems to be the more common sense, with the idea of refreshment being secondary and supported only in this context in the Song by the parallel verb.

c. Again, masculine plural forms. Cf. Song 2:5.

d. The LXX *en tais dynamesin kai en tais ischysesin tou agrou* and the Old Latin *in virtutibus et in viribus agri* reflect a different translation than that found in the MT (or Vulgate *per capreas cervosque camporum*), one that deals with strengths and powers rather than gazelles and does. Cf. Garbini, *Cantico*, 42–45.

e. It is true that there is a homonymic root, *ḫpṣ* II, which *HALOT* 340 lists as occurring only once (Job 40:17) to describe the swaying "loose" tail of Behemoth. The Arabic cognate carries the meaning "to lower." Therefore, it is unlikely on the surface that this means "to stiffen" or that it should constitute a double entendre here, as Grossberg, "Sexual," suggests.

1. He further confirms this division with discourse analysis.

unit in which increasing intimacy is achieved. The terms of intimacy (my darling, my beloved) appear. In the last subsection, 2:1–6, the intensity increases until the final three verses, where the female swoons and the two join in physical embrace at the climax, represented structurally by the chiasm of 2:6.[2] Verse 7 provides the refrain that marks off this first section from what follows. The section as a whole introduces all the major themes in the Song.

1:2–7	Female: Longing for her lover
1:8–11	Male: Response with invitation and praise
1:12–14	Female: Her lover as fragrance
1:15	Male: Praise of beauty
1:16–2:1	Female: Love in paradise
2:2	Male: My love is like a flower
2:3–7	Female: A pastoral scene

1:2–7. *Female: Longing for her lover.* The formal structure of this first address of the female is remarkably diverse.[3] The persons of the verbs and nominal sentences shift back and forth in rapid motion, with several changes in each verse.[4] Likewise, the syntax has no consistent form. The subject can appear in any position, and the verbs include a variety of finite and nonfinite forms.[5] While assonance seems to play a role in the beginning verses, it gradually gives way to lengthier descriptions that hold the lines together by common theme and content. Yet vv. 2–4 hold together structurally. They form ten lines, where each of the first nine contains three words and the tenth has two.[6] This is not followed in vv. 5–7. Thus these verses serve as an introductory unit.

The sense created is the (paratactic) piling on of one descriptive phrase after another. Indeed, the one theme that does run through vv. 2–4 is the appeal to every one of the senses in describing the love envisioned by the female and shared by the couple.[7] There are examples of wordplay, moving from sound-centered assonance in the opening

---

2. Callow, "Units," 474–75.

3. For a fascinating study of the structure of vv. 5–6 and 7–8, with its ambiguity and paradox, and the question as to how these devices contribute to the beauty of the poetry, see Landy, "Beauty."

4. Verse 2 begins in the third person and ends in the second. Verse 3 moves from second to the third. Verse 4 shifts from second to first to second to first. Verse 5—second, first, third, first. Verse 6—second, first, third, first. Verse 7—second, first, second, first.

5. That is, imperfects, perfects, imperatives, and participles.

6. Callow, "Units," 477.

7. Cf. des Rochettes et al., "Mots."

verses to repetitions, paronomasia, and connections of content in vv. 5–7. The opening speech of the female lover flashes from one sensuous image to another, thereby expressing a height of emotion and delight that ignores rules of parallelism or other poetic structure. Instead, the perception of the reader is a breathtaking adventure of love that will be difficult to keep up with.

> **1:2**May he kiss me with the kisses of his mouth,
> Because your lovemaking is better than wine.

In v. 2 the female speaks first, and her speech dominates throughout the Song. Whether or not the author was a female, this text is unusual in the OT (though not unique; cf. Ruth and Esther) in the prominence that it gives to the female voice.[8] She begins by referring to her lover in the third person (he). This gives prominence to her prayer and the expression of desire for her lover. However, the second half of the verse switches to the second person (you) to dramatize the direct address to her lover. The intimacy in the address and the declarations of love will continue for several verses and recur throughout the Song.

The verb "to kiss" (*nāšaq*, 1:2) normally refers to kisses of friendship or family (e.g., 1 Sam. 20:41; Gen. 27:26–27), or even of official or formal recognition (1 Sam. 10:1; 2 Sam. 15:5). Clear attestations of kissing in romantic or sexual involvement occur in the OT only here, in Song 8:1, and in Prov. 7:13. The last evokes a picture of the seductress kissing the young man as part of her enticement. Song 8:1 is the single other occurrence of this root in the Song. In all these appearances it is a female lover who kisses the male or, as here, imagines him kissing her. The noun "kisses" (*nĕšîqôt*) occurs elsewhere only in Prov. 27:6, a context that is neither romantic nor positive. It describes the deceitful and pretended kisses of one who hates. Finally, the reference to "his mouth" as part of the picture of kissing also has only one other biblical occurrence. The act of kissing with the mouth appears in 1 Kings 19:18, where reference is made to those whose mouths have not kissed the image of Baal. Thus the biblical use of these terms does not suggest what one may think. To the reader of the Bible, kissing and kisses on the mouth would not evoke positive images of romance. In fact, their use here might seem surprising. However, that these are romantic and erotic images is not to be doubted. Commentaries note that the act of kissing with the nose has also been attested in the Middle East; hence the Song emphasizes the more sensual kisses with the mouth. The fact

---

8. Nevertheless, there is no suggestion of dominance by the female; rather, the couple share love and mutual respect. See Ndoga, "Is the Woman?"

that the rest of the OT does not dwell on such matters suggests that its interests lie elsewhere. Song 8:1 solves the dilemma as it holds the romantic kiss in tension with the familial kiss. There the lover wishes that her beloved were her brother so that she could kiss him in public as well as private. Thus kissing in public was acceptable and even expected in a variety of nonromantic social contexts (especially related to members of one's family). Romantic kissing was assumed but kept away from the public gaze and thus does not occur in the other narratives of the Bible.

The noun *dôd* often refers to an uncle or another close relative (Lev. 10:4; 1 Sam. 10:14–16; Esther 2:7). However, the singular can refer to one who is loved. It occurs in one certain instance in this manner elsewhere in the Bible. In Isa. 5:1 the composer of the song praises the one he loves, who plants a vineyard. All the other occurrences of the common noun with this meaning of "lover" appear in the Song in reference to the male and are spoken by the female or the chorus.[9] Once, in 5:1, the plural is used in reference to the two lovers. However, in the remaining seven occurrences of the plural form of this noun, where it does not refer to uncles or other family relations (Ezek. 16:8; 23:17; Prov. 7:18; Song 1:2, 4; 4:10 [2x]), the reference is always to love or, more specifically, to sexual relations.[10] In Ezek. 16:8, God observes that Israel, pictured as a female, has blossomed into a youth ready for *dôdîm*. In 23:17, Judah again appears in the guise of a woman who lusts after the Babylonians and who shares her bed of *dôdîm* with them. Proverbs 7:18 continues the picture of the seductress referred to above. She invites the young man to join her in "drinking" *dôdîm* until the morning. The four occurrences in the Song include two where the female praises the male lover's *dôdîm*, and two together in 4:10, where the male praises the female lover's *dôdîm*, with similar comparisons to wine. Thus, although the plural form may suggest an abstract notion, it seems that the physical act of sex is in view here, certainly in the texts from Ezekiel and Proverbs, and therefore also in the more positive description in the Song. This term is different from other Hebrew verbs for sex, such as *yādaᶜ* (know), *bôʾ* (enter), *nāgaš* (approach), *gillâ ᶜerwat* (uncover the nakedness of), *šākab ᶜim/ʾet* (lie with), *zānâ* (fornicate), as well as the term that later (if not already) becomes vulgar, *šāgal* (rape). While these emphasize various components of sexual relations, *dôdîm* expresses the passion and desire in the relationship.

The comparison of lovemaking with wine uses the common Hebrew term for the drink (*yayin*). Wine was a common drink in ancient Is-

---

9. 1:13, 14, 16; 2:3, 8, 9, 10, 16, 17; 4:16; 5:1, 2, 4, 5, 6 (2x), 8, 9 (4x), 10, 16; 6:1 (2x), 2, 3 (2x); 7:10, 11, 12, 14 (9, 10, 11, 13 Eng.); 8:5, 14.
10. Cf. Fox, *Song*, 97; G. Carr, *Song*, 73.

rael.[11] The climate encouraged vineyards, and the juice of the grape was not likely to remain unfermented for long in a warm environment without refrigeration. Wine provided a drink that could be stored for longer periods of time. It provided a drink (sometimes perhaps mixed with water) that would not make the drinker ill through the presence of minerals or microorganisms, as could have been the case with water (e.g., 2 Kings 2:19). However, wine did more than slake the thirst. As a picture of love here, its properties of delight and intoxication certainly would have come to mind.

The comparison with wine is a sensual one, as is the entire description of the verse. Touch and taste combine with the sound of the words as they roll off the tongue. The kisses on the mouth, the lovemaking, and the wine join together to provide readers with an introductory verse that plunges them into the heady waters of this poem. Here is no gradual acclimation, a step at a time, but rather a baptism by fire! With the assonance of the sounds, the word pictures of kissing with desire, and lovemaking that can only be compared to the intense pleasure of drinking wine, the poet leaves the reader or listener in no doubt as to the direction she is taking.

> ³Your name is cologne poured out,
> It is the fragrance of your best colognes.
> Therefore, the maidens love you.

Verse 3 hinges on the reference to "your name" (*šĕmekā*), located in its center as the sixth of ten words. A similar *l* sound appears both at the beginning of the last word in v. 1 and in the first word in v. 3.[12] As such it marks v. 2 as the center. In fact, the connection to v. 2 appears intentional as the male lover will later also compare his partner's lovemaking to wine and, in the same breath, refer to the fragrance of her perfumes (4:10). Indeed, these are the only two verses in the Bible where the expression "fragrance of oils" (*rêaḥ šĕmānêkā/šĕmānayik*) occurs. In the ancient world, perfumes or colognes were made using an (olive) oil base. Hence the literal term "oil" should be rendered "perfume" or "cologne" in this context. Another connection between vv. 2 and 3 is the use of the Hebrew *ṭôbîm*. In v. 2 it is translated "better," while in v. 3 it is "best." Also, v. 3 like v. 2 has a repetition of sounds, here initial consonants (alliteration). Here as well, it appears in the first half of the

---

11. This may be contrasted to the other popular fermented drink, beer, which was used more frequently in Mesopotamia. Canaanites and Philistines, as well as Israelites, tended to drink more wine than beer.

12. This is the *lāmed* prefix that begins this verse and provides a counterpoint to the *lāmed* before the last word in v. 1.

verse. The word for oil or cologne occurs twice with the repetition of *sh* (*šîn*) and *m* (*mêm*) sounds. This is followed by "your name," beginning with these same consonants.

The verse focuses on the senses of smell and hearing. The first line emphasizes the fragrance that the male lover wears, a cologne that is memorable in the senses of the speaker.[13] The cologne is made with the best of oils, and this moves attention to the name of the beloved. More than a means of identity or a symbol of him, the name evokes the presence of the male lover despite his absence. And when he is present, the sound of the name makes him all the more vivid. Indeed, both the address of the female to her lover and the evocation of fragrance that can be sensed only when physically close suggest that the saying of the name, like the aroma of the cologne, provides one more sensual bond between the two. Hence the image is that of the name poured out. Note that there is no preposition or other grammatical indication of a simile here. The name itself is not merely stated; it is "poured out." In a manner similar to the fragrance, its pouring overwhelms the lover as she repeats it and hears it again and again.

The term for "maiden" (*ʿalmâ*) occurs only seven times in the Hebrew Bible. The famous text of Isa. 7:14 is controversial and thus begs the question of whether a virgin is intended.[14] Other occurrences include groups of "maidens," as here, as well as queens and concubines, who accompany singers and musicians in processions (Ps. 68:26 [68:25 Eng.]; Song 6:8). These tell nothing certain, but the distinction in Song 6:8 of the maidens from queens and concubines suggests women who are not married. The text where Abraham's servant uses this term in requesting a bride for Isaac (Gen. 24:43) would support the identification of someone who was a virgin and also not married. Exodus 2:8 may suggest a younger girl, perhaps before puberty. Finally, Prov. 30:19 and its comment on "the way of a man with a maiden [*ʿalmâ*]" identifies a woman sexually mature, but the context does not clarify whether she is a virgin. No text denies the possibility of this term meaning virgins, and several suggest it. Certainly, the maidens in

13. Munro, *Spikenard*, 48: "The particular power of fragrance to convey the innermost essence of a person, to convey that which is intangible and invisible, yet particular and unmistakable."

14. In fact, the strongest argument for the translation "virgin" in that passage may be based on a formulaic context for the announcement of virgin births, as known also at Ugarit. Indeed, the epithet of the goddess Anat uses the cognate term *btlt*. In Hebrew, this cognate is sometimes taken to mean "virgin" and counterposed to "maiden" (*ʿalmâ*), which then, it is argued, cannot mean the same thing. However, synonyms exist in every language, and there would be no problem with the same being true here. The key is contextual usage, not etymologies, cognate languages, or the semantic range of similar terms.

the Song are unmarried women who are, or shortly will be, sexually mature.

The verb for "love" (*ʾāhab*) occurs seven times in the Song (1:3, 4, 7; 3:1, 2, 3, 4), always translated in the LXX by the same verb (*agapaō*, which appears in the Song only in these seven verses). Other than here and in the following verse, where it is used of the chorus of maidens who love the male, it occurs elsewhere always with reference to the feelings of the female lover for her partner (1:7; 3:1, 2, 3, 4). His cologne and name excite her. Perhaps her descriptions and songs, or perhaps a direct encounter with the male, lead her friends to express love for him. Although the emphasis of this love now extends beyond the couple, its purpose at this stage is to increase the arousal toward passionate love. However, it suggests that the male is the desired object of many eligible women, not only the female speaker. He is a valued commodity for whom other females will compete. Thus she loves him all the more, as her prize above all others who desire him. This love of dedication and commitment, this same Greek word (in noun form, *agapē*), is picked up by the apostle Paul as the distinctive type of love he wishes to emphasize in all relations with others and as the greatest of all God's gifts (1 Cor. 13). No longer physical or sexual desire, its intensity and solidarity make it an appropriate term for the apostle to apply to Christian love.

> [4]Take me with you. We must hurry.
> The king brought me to his chambers.
> We will indeed rejoice and be happy for you.
> We will indeed recall your lovemaking more than wine.
> Naturally they love you.

In Song 1:4, three of the first four words are verbs. They shift from the second person (you), to the first person (me/we), and finally to the third person (the king/they). Except for the last verb, the remaining six verbs in this verse either are in the first person or have the first person as an object suffix. Therefore, the focus of this verse shifts from the previous emphasis on the female speaking of her lover to her focus on herself. Not since the beginning of v. 2, where kisses were sought, has the female expressed a desire for some action from her partner. Now, however, this concern is couched in the imperative, using a verb that occurs nowhere else in the Song. It conveys the sense of "draw/drag" and thus describes a forceful, though not violent, movement, as when Jeremiah is pulled out of the pit (Jer. 38:13). Here it is close to the usage of Hosea 11:4a, where God speaks of Israel, "I led them with cords of human kindness, with ties of love" (NIV). Thus the female longs for the male to take her. So intense is the longing that she invokes a form of the verb "to run" (*rwṣ*), which adverbially modifies the previous verb: "Take me to you quickly."[15] In a text whose speakers linger over each description, this verb occurs only here. This line provides an interlude in the passionate description of love that has been constructed to this point. The female lover can no longer bear the wait and invokes a command for her partner to come and take her. Yet this is not enough, for she adds at the end of this desire, "Let us run," expressing a need to end the longing at this instant.[16]

At this point the perspective shifts from desire to narrative. The king now responds to the lover and fulfills her request. There is no time interval or delay. The female does not count time between the climax of her desire and its fulfillment in the male lover's action. Thus, while the female speaks to her partner, he is the one who initiates the action. She accompanies him to his private room (*ḥeder*). Although this term can be used for rooms of all types (including ones in the temple, 1 Chron. 28:11), in marital contexts it refers to the bridal chamber (Joel 2:16).[17] Elsewhere it is the location of the bed (Exod. 7:28 [8:3 Eng.]; 2 Sam. 4:7), the site where Samson falls asleep when with Delilah (Judg. 16:9, 12), where Amnon rapes Tamar (2 Sam. 13:10), and where old King David lay with Abishag (1 Kings 1:15). The plural, "chambers," suggests a suite of rooms as befits a king. As with Solomon in Song 1:1, however, it remains plausible that this figure is a king in the eyes of his beloved.[18] He is the one to whom she directs her desires and attention.

The resultant rejoicing and gladness are emphatically promised (1:4). Precisely the same two verbs and forms (cohortatives) occur in Isa. 25:9, where the joy characterizes God's salvation brought upon the people. The first verb may suggest a dance.[19] However, the contexts of the verb can describe singing (Zeph. 3:17), speaking (Ps. 9:15 [9:14 Eng.]), and even trembling (Ps. 2:11). Both verbs, "to rejoice" and "to be happy" (*śmḥ*), occur only here in the Song. Their associations elsewhere with the salvific work of God suggest, not that this scene has suddenly shifted to a predominantly spiritual reality, but that the strongest possible language

15. The Hebrew form is a cohortative.
16. Paul, "Plural," identifies in the "we/us" a plural of ecstasy, which he finds in ancient Near Eastern love poetry. While this is possible, it is better to find here a reference to the couple acting in unison. See 1:11 and 2:15 for further possible examples. Kramer, *Sacred*, 92, 99, provides examples in Mesopotamian poetry in which the female uses the first-person plural common forms of herself.
17. For the role of this image and its relationship to the "gardens" of 8:13–14, as well as other bridal imagery that unifies the whole Song and ties the beginning and end together, see Horine, *Interpretive*, 114–21.
18. Longman, *Song*, 92, understands the references to the king and the shepherd as not literal but as "love language" used in "creating a poetic world."
19. From the root *gyl*, it may suggest a dance because the root (or a homonymic one) refers to a circle (the root for "Galilee") and thus making a circle in physical movement.

of joy occupies the mind of the female lover as she anticipates physical love with her partner. If the king here is understood as the male lover rather than a third member of a love triangle, then in this single phrase the male is both a participant with the female in joy and celebration and also the object of that joy ("for you").[20] As the female speaks concerning the joy, so the male is the natural object of her rejoicing and love.

The next phrase also begins with the same type of verb, using a verbal root (*zkr*) that appears only here in the Song.[21] This particular stem of the verb occurs in the Psalms with the sense of invoking, petitioning, and proclaiming (e.g., Pss. 45:18 [45:17 Eng.]; 38:1 [title Eng.]; 70:1 [title Eng.]; 77:12 [77:11 Eng.]).[22] Together these describe more than bringing to mind. They identify a verbal act by which the thing called to mind is proclaimed with the purpose of achieving some performance on the part of God or the hearer. In the Song this act is a joint announcement of the lovemaking and the joy that it brings so that even the other most sensual pleasure, the drinking of wine, compares unfavorably. So intense is the joy of this love that the female declares just and right others who love her partner. The end of Song 1:4 uses the same verb root, form, and suffix as at the end of the preceding verse, suggesting that she recognizes that the maidens cannot help but love her partner. The desire of him is greater than any sensual pleasure. To suggest that those who love in this way are right (*mêšārîm*) seems to be less an ethical evaluation and more a recognition that this is the normal course of nature. Of its nineteen occurrences in the Bible, only here does it refer to people. Elsewhere it denotes actions of smoothness (Song 7:10 [7:9 Eng.]) or concepts of justice and integrity (1 Chron. 29:17). Thus its meaning may relate to those people such as the maidens who follow their heart. The maidens cannot help but love one who is so desirable.

> [5]I am black but beautiful,
> O daughters of Jerusalem;
> Just like the tents of Qedar,
> Just like the curtains of Solomon.

With v. 5, the female turns her attention to herself and provides a description that will continue into the following verse. She identifies herself as "black but beautiful" (Song 1:5). The word for "black" (*šĕḥôrâ*) elsewhere describes the color of hair (Lev. 13:31, 37; Song 5:11), of a horse (in contrast with the white, red, and dappled ones that were approved; Zech. 6:2, 6), and of skin during an illness (Job 30:30). It identifies a color,

20. It is *bāk* in pause.
21. It occurs as a first-person common plural cohortative.
22. Where it appears in the Hiphil (causative) stem.

not a race, and here it is caused by the sun.[23] The blackness of the skin is explained in Song 1:6, but in v. 5 it is contrasted with the beauty that she claims. Elsewhere in the Song the term "beautiful" (*nā'wâ*) describes the face (2:14), the mouth (4:3), and the city of Jerusalem (6:4). Together these words focus attention on the one remaining sense not yet considered in the song, that of sight. This is the last sense to which the female appeals, and yet it is the most dramatic of them all. The blackness of her skin may contrast with the fairness of the complexion of her maidens, though we are not told this. However, it serves as a mark of the female that selects her in contrast to others.

In v. 5 her address is not toward her lover but turns to the "daughters of Jerusalem." Are these the "maidens" of v. 3? Perhaps, yet here their association with the city not only locates the song in the nation's capital but also, much more importantly, contrasts the most beautiful women of the nation with this female. She is beautiful in comparison to them all. Her claim to this is not only a boast but also a climactic crescendo of sensual pleasure that her presence brings to her lover. The distinctive beauty exhibits an exotic delight that can be compared with the tents of Qedar. The Bible identifies Qedar as a son of Ishmael (Gen. 25:13; 1 Chron. 1:29) and a land in the east (Jer. 49:28), in the region of Arabia (Ezek. 27:21). Its desert could support flocks and warriors (Isa. 21:17; 42:11; 60:7). It lay at the ends of the known world as a distant and exotic land (Jer. 2:10). This picture of the land fits the image of an exotic beauty who, although perhaps not from this land, could have been by her appearance. Further, the tribe, like the woman, stands on the edge of the civilized world.[24] There is a wildness present in her and evident in her appearance, something outside the conventions of polite society.

The "curtains" (*yĕrî'ôt*) describe those coverings used exclusively for tents, whether religious or personal. Some 22 of the 32 verses where this term appears are found in Exod. 26 and 36, describing the curtains that will hide and protect the holy places of the tabernacle. However, the term can also refer to the temporary residence of the ark during David's time (2 Sam. 7:2; 1 Chron. 17:1), the residence of an individual (Isa. 54:2; Jer. 4:20; 10:20; 49:29), and the dwellings of an entire nation (Cush in Hab. 3:7). Most dramatic of all is Ps. 104:2, where God stretches the heavens like a tent in which to live. The use of a tent for the divine as well as the human has an antiquity found as early as the eighteenth century BC, more than half a millennium before the monarchy.[25] The "curtains of

---

23. So V. Sasson, "King," 413–14, though without accepting the tenuous identification of the female with the daughter of pharaoh in 1 Kings 11:1–2.

24. Munro, *Spikenard*, 139.

25. On comparable tent terminology at West Semitic Ugarit and Mari, see Fleming, "Mari's."

Solomon" may refer to a tent that he used for war or a structure built
by him. There is no clear association of Solomon with any tent other
than the one in which David had placed the ark.[26] It is probably best to
understand this reference as depicting the residence of Solomon, which,
in comparison with all the other tents in which other citizens resided,
would have been the finest one.[27]

The female here identifies her form, contrasting her dark skin with
her beauty. This is compared to dark tents that, like her skin and form,
cover the inhabitant. The woman's "tent" is exotic like those of Qedar,
and it is magnificent like that of Solomon. In this manner she lays claim
to breathtaking beauty that, along with the previous verses, consum-
mates a series of sensuous pictures of all that is alluring and captivating
about the physical love she both offers and seeks.

> [6]Do not look at me so,
> Because I am so swarthy,
> Because the sun has "stared" at me.
> The sons of my mother burned with anger against me,
> They made me look after the vineyards,
> Yet my very own vineyard I have not looked after.

As Song 1:5 turns to the "chorus" of the daughters of Jerusalem, so
v. 6 continues this interlude away from a direct dialogue between the two
lovers. This verse begins with a temporary prohibition that warns against
a specific action. The masculine verb form may imply an audience of
men as well as women, but more likely it reflects the general tenor of the
female's plea. No one, not only the daughters of Jerusalem but also anyone else, is to stare at this woman's unusual appearance.[28] The reason for
the negative characteristic of their gaze has to do with the woman's dark
complexion.[29] Although she has just addressed them with an emphasis on

---

26. 1 Kings 1:39; 2:28, 29, 30; 8:4; 2 Chron. 1:3, 4, 6, 13; 5:5. Notwithstanding the
Kethib (consonantal text) of 1 Kings 7:45, the Qere rightly interprets it as a metathesis
for the plural near demonstrative *ʾēlleh*.

27. This and other occurrences of "Solomon" and "king" can be explained as poetic
and hyperbolic (though not from the perspective of those in love). Thus, it forms a natural part of the poetry and is not to be seen as the consistent insertion of a redactor (so
Loretz, *Liebeslied*, 61–62). Fox, "Scholia," 202–4, understands the references as terms of
affection.

28. Murphy, *Song*, 126, suggests that the second-person feminine plural ending is rare
and does not occur before a pronominal suffix. This could explain its absence here and
the use of the characteristic masculine plural form of the second person.

29. Görg, "Travestie," suggests that vv. 5–6 represent the female's attempt to present
herself to the women of the Jerusalem aristocracy. The verses describe her failure. However,
it is best not to push the context of the passage too far beyond the explicit statements of
the text.

the positive appearance of this feature, she quickly becomes self-conscious of it as something that may not be at all desirable. Therefore, instead of using the term for "black" (*šāḥōr*) found in the preceding verse, she coins a reduplicated stem of the same root (*šĕḥarḥōret*), found only here. The effect of such reduplication is to intensify the adjective.[30] In this case, it makes what is black too black. The female worries about her appearance and wants to avert the gaze of her potentially critical friends.

The next line explains a cause for her dark complexion. It uses two words that are held together in sound by the repetition in each of two *šîn* letters, *šeššĕzāpatnî haššāmeš*. The first word, a verb (*šzp*), occurs only here and in Job (20:9; 28:7), where it describes the sharp eye of a bird of prey. It forms a poetic variant on the common verb "to see" (*rʾh*) in the first line. Therefore, it intensifies the process of seeing. If the daughters of Jerusalem stared at the female lover, the sun (the second word mentioned above, *haššāmeš*) had already "stared" that much harder at her, effecting a darkening of the skin's pigments. Yet the word picture of the burning rays of the sun also ties together the following line, where the female's brothers act in hostility toward her. She uses a form of the verb meaning "to burn, be angry" (*ḥrh*) to describe how they became angry.[31] This is the idiom of burning in rage. Thus the wordplay of verbs connects the fire of her brothers with the heat of the sun to produce her dark skin. And the sun's stare couples with the critical gaze of her companions to tie together the whole picture.

However, the wordplay does not end there. The final two lines use the same principal verb meaning "to guard, watch, keep" (*nṭr*). Of its ten occurrences in the Bible, only those that are found in the Song (8:11, 12, in addition to the two here in 1:6) and in Dan. 7:28 carry this sense. All other occurrences convey displeasure or anger (Lev. 19:18; Jer. 3:5, 12; Nah. 1:2; Ps. 103:9), often with God as the source of the anger. This connotation, though secondary in the usage of the verb in the Song, should not be overlooked. It furthers the brothers' hostility in their act of placing their sister in the vineyard, where they know she will lose her fair complexion under the angry sun. In addition, it suggests that a critical evaluation of the female, when the women stare at her, will only continue the hostility that has begun in her family.

Thus the female's own body has not been cared for as would be appropriate for someone seeking love. She has not devoted herself to her physical appearance because her domestic tasks have not permitted it. Worse than that, they have actively contributed to a skin condition other than what she might have wanted.

---

30. Alternatively, some see this as a diminutive form (G. Carr, *Song*, 78).
31. The passive stem (Niphal).

How is it that what begins as a boast in Song 1:5 so quickly turns to a cause for concern and perhaps even shame? In evaluating this transformation, the key lies with the addressees. At the beginning of v. 5 the female continues to speak to her male lover as she continues the poetic rendition of the senses begun in vv. 2–4. Now, however, she turns in the next line and addresses the daughters of Jerusalem. Thus the first line of v. 5 is a hinge that completes the address to her partner and also begins the monologue to her female companions. It takes place at this point because, of all the senses described, only that of sight must move beyond the intimate sharing of the woman and man to the wider group. The daughters of Jerusalem do not participate in the kisses that taste like wine, or the fragrance that the man's cologne holds, or even in expressing the sound of his name. They do not join the female in the chambers of her lover. These are reserved only for the couple. However, the beauty of form and appearance that the woman claims cannot be withheld from the gaze of her friends.

Although in v. 5 she attempts favorable comparisons with the tents of Qedar and Solomon, she then recognizes that the beauty she is claiming may be seen less as exotic and desirable and more as common and lacking in any attraction. The darkness of the skin forms a badge of her social condition in which her past may not measure up to the expectations of class before the maidens of Jerusalem. Therefore, she admonishes her friends not to judge her but to understand her background. That background now becomes part of the introduction to the love poetry that will follow. The term "vineyard(s)" is mentioned seven times elsewhere in the Song in addition to the two in this verse.[32] Here it becomes a metaphor for the physical body of the female.[33] She has not paid attention to her own body because she has been busy taking care of the needs of her family.[34] Thus the darkness of her physical appearance and her claim to a desirable form become a double-edged argument both for exotic beauty and for her devotion to her family.[35]

In this regard, it is interesting to observe the way the woman identifies her brothers as the sons of her mother. Of course, this suggests that

32. Song 1:14; 2:15 (2x); 7:13 (7:12 Eng.); 8:11 (2x), 12.
33. Munro, *Spikenard*, 41.
34. This is the context of the passage. The view that this statement indicates that she lost her virginity and was therefore being punished by her patriarchal oppressors (Provan, *Song*, 268) cannot be proved from this allusion nor is the issue of virginity ever raised. Indeed, this specter of legal definitions and punishments is alien to the spirit of the Song and its content.
35. This builds on the important theme of commitment that is part of the love expressed throughout the Song. It is this, rather than a hint that the woman has lost her virginity (Pope, *Song*, 326), or even a Cinderella motif (Gerleman, *Hohelied*, 99–101), that should be identified as the point of the female's observations about her own vineyard.

antagonism generated by her brothers' hatred has not promoted close relations between them and their sister. However, it is worthwhile probing this observation more deeply. First, the designation "my mother" (*ʾimmî*) rather than "my father" or some other relative suggests a close relationship between the women of this family. This reinforces the impression that the speaker communicates with an authentic female voice and not merely with the imaginations of a male author writing about a female. Second, the form of this designation implies a separation from the males who might be considered closest in her background. As noted, there is no mention of her father. Her language distances her brothers by relating them only through her mother. Thus the woman's words suggest an absence of a male among her close relations as one who would take care of her and protect her. Like Ruth, she has no immediate male relatives to whom she can turn for assistance. In that patriarchal society, the text suggests that she does not have wealth or other resources to take care of herself (that would have prevented her from needing to obey her brothers and work as a shepherdess). Hence this verse portrays her as a vulnerable woman and yet one possessing both beauty and a commitment to care for her family. These themes provide a reason for the insertion of v. 6.

> 7Tell me, you whom I love,
> Where do you graze [your flocks]?
> Where do you rest them at noon?
> Lest I become like a cloaked woman,
> Beside the flocks of your friends.

Verse 7 dramatically shifts the addressee(s) from the female's companions to her lover. The command is not so much a demand for an answer, because the verse ends with an appeal that the couple not remain separate but be joined together in their daily tasks. Rather, the imperative force captures the attention of the male lover, as perhaps it requires redirection after the female's own diversion to address the maidens of Jerusalem. She commands him to speak but addresses him with tenderness: literally, "whom my soul loves." Here for the first time the female describes her love for her beloved. The use of the verb "to love" (*ʾāhab*) earlier occurred only at the ends of vv. 3 and 4, where the maidens express love for the male. Here, however, the female explicitly confesses her love. Of course, this has been the theme of the entire text up to this point. Its expression here balances the same verbs in the first part of the text and draws a climax to the female's address with a summary of her message. In the verse itself, it functions as a means of identifying her addressee.

59

Of the five lines in v. 7, the first three have verbs in first position that address the male.[36] The female seeks knowledge from her lover. He is also a shepherd who grazes his flock. He takes them out to pasture and gives them rest from their traveling during the heat of the midday. This term is emphasized by the two questions. Both have the same interrogative, "Where?" (ʾêkāh), followed by a verb in the same form. This parallelism of syntax and content is then followed by an adverb that functions to indicate the time, "noon" (ṣohŏrāyim).[37] The female desires to join him at that time so that they may be alone together. The sun's heat (v. 6) that caused her physical appearance contrasts with the midday sun of v. 7 that brings the need for rest and an opportunity to enjoy the company of her lover. Thus the negatives are turned into possibilities of something much better. In order to achieve her goal, however, she must know where he takes the flocks. Twice she repeats the key question: "Where?"

The second half of 1:7 describes the woman's condition. The term "cloaked" elsewhere describes an old man wearing a cloak to protect himself (1 Sam. 28:14). On the Lachish reliefs (701 BC), a Judean woman's outer garment appears as a cloak with a mantle that could be pulled over her head like a hood.[38] The description of the woman is one in which she has been following the occupation of shepherdess as described in v. 6, wearing the commonly accepted dress for a woman. Her objection, therefore, has nothing to do with dressing like a prostitute or avoiding the company of the shepherd's friends.[39] It is simply that she would prefer to be alone with her lover. She grazes her flocks alongside those of her lover's friends. However, she would prefer to join her flocks with his so that they could be together in the pastures.

The mood of the female's address has now shifted from one of rapturous description of her relation with her lover to one in which she seeks a practical means to be united with him during the day. Gone from this verse is any sensual description of the physical love that the two might enjoy. In its place there is an immediate concern for a realistic means to facilitate the desire of the female and so to bring the couple together. The command and question bring the female's concerns to a conclusion and invite a response from her lover.

36. In two cases they immediately follow an interrogative, which always takes first position in a clause.
37. The syntactical form appears to be that of an adverbial accusative.
38. King and Stager, *Life*, 272; on customs of the time, they also refer to Gen. 24:65; 38:14–19; Isa. 3:22–23; Ezek. 16:10–13.
39. For the former, see Emerton, "Lice?" 129, who rejects it. For the latter, see Murphy, *Song*, 131, 134.

1:8–11. *Male: Response with invitation and praise.* The syllable count for lines in v. 8 is 11, 6, and 12; that for v. 9 is 7 and 6; that for v. 10 is 8 and 6; and that for v. 11 is 7 and 6. Structurally, v. 8 is out of sequence among the verses providing the male's response. This is also true in terms of content. Whereas vv. 9–11 focus on the beauty of the female, v. 8 provides an answer to her question. The structure of v. 8 duplicates the female lover's charge, question, and plea of v. 7. This threefold expression is not found in vv. 9–11. There each of the two-line stanzas in the first line contains a single verb whose action carries over into the second. All three finite verbs of v. 8 have the female as the subject, whereas vv. 9–11 have either the male or the cheeks and neck of the female as subjects. Thus v. 8 uses the second-person feminine singular address ("you/your"), whereas vv. 9–11 use either first-person ("my/I"; "we") or third-person forms. Thus v. 8 relates to the previous verse and may be better associated with it. Most commentaries place the two together. Verses 9–11 consistently use the image of jewelry.[40]

The subsections of the Song here follow the speakers. For this reason v. 8 begins a new subsection even though there are close connections between vv. 7 and 8. In addition, the following arguments support connecting v. 8 with the following verses: First, vv. 8 and 10 structurally envelop v. 9, with vv. 8 and 10 using the second-person "you" and v. 9 using "I" or "my." Second, from v. 8 onward the concern is to restore the confidence of the woman by praising her attributes, beginning with "most beautiful of women" in v. 8. The emphasis now moves to the man's praise of the woman's appearance.

> [8]If you don't know, most beautiful of women,
> Follow the sheep paths,
> Graze your goats by the shepherds' tents.

In v. 8 the male lover responds to the female, and he does so with an answer to her question that follows her words in v. 7 closely in form and content. Thus the first line of v. 7, "Tell me, you whom I love," corresponds to the first line of v. 8, "If you don't know, most beautiful of women." In both cases, there is a second-person singular verb ("tell," "know"), followed by similar forms[41] referring to the female (lit., "to me," "for yourself"), and concluding with an endearing form of address composed of two Hebrew words ("whom my soul loves," "the most beautiful among women").

Two repetitive questions follow this in v. 7:

40. Callow, "Units," 470.
41. A *lāmed* preposition with a pronominal suffix.

Where do you graze [your flocks]?
Where do you rest them at noon?

These receive a corresponding answer in the same position in v. 8:

Follow the sheep paths.

After the interrogatives, the first two lines in v. 7 each have a second-person ("you") singular verb, and these are followed by a preposition with a noun of time. Verse 8 also has a second-person singular verb followed by a preposition and a phrase (lit., "after the paths of sheep").

Finally, in v. 8 the male answers the concern of the female:

Lest I become like a cloaked woman,
Beside the flocks of your friends. (v. 7)

Graze your goats by the shepherd's tents. (v. 8)

Both have an initial verb that refers to the female, both refer to the flocks, and both use the preposition "upon/by" (ʿal) followed by a reference to other shepherds. The effect of this remarkably close similarity is to unite the concerns of the couple. What the female expresses, the male answers. In Hebrew dialogue and narrative, assent or obedience is often expressed by the response of the individual addressed in language that closely resembles the original request. The same is true here and suggests the perfect harmony of desire and purpose that the couple enjoys.

Even so, v. 8 itself has a cohesive structure. The grammatical forms following the verbs in the first and second lines are parallel: "know for yourself" and "go out for yourself."[42] The same two consonants occur at the beginning ("follow, come out," *ṣěʾî*) and at the end ("the sheep," *haṣṣōʾn*) of the second line.[43] Further, the same three consonants (*rêš, ʿayin, yôd*) appear in sequence at the beginning ("graze," *ûrěʿî*) and at the end ("the shepherds," *hārōʿîm*) of the third line. Thus this verse has a stylistic integrity of its own that complements its connection with the preceding verse.

The means of identification that the male uses, the first descriptive term he applies to the female, is "beautiful" (*yāpāh*). This is the first occurrence of this term in the Song. The woman has identified herself as "desirable" (*nāʾwâ*, v. 5), a word that describes her form in relation to her lover. However, the term "beautiful" suggests a description of the

42. That is, the *lāmed* preposition plus the second-person feminine singular pronominal suffix (*lāk*).
43. The consonants are *ṣādê* and *ʾālep*.

female form that stands on its own. With the definite article and followed by the phrase "among the women," it creates a superlative expression: "the most beautiful of the women." Note that the term "(the) women" also is definite. It suggests that the comparison is not primarily among all women everywhere, which would itself be a fantasy that the male could not know. Instead, it may refer to the daughters of Jerusalem in vv. 3–5. In so commenting on his partner, the male asserts that he has eyes only for her, no matter how much the others may love him (vv. 3–4). Further, he does not see the imperfection that she senses (vv. 5–6), but affirms that she is all he wants in terms of beauty. Here already the male betrays what will become evident in the following verses: whereas the female's expression of love fills all the senses with marvelous descriptions, the male's focus is on the physical form of beauty.

> [9]To a mare among pharaoh's chariots,
> Do I liken you, my darling.

Verse 9 begins a series of descriptions that capture physical attributes of the female lover. The emphasis in this verse is the repeated first-person common singular forms: "I liken you" and "my darling." Add to this the archaizing suffix on "mare," which produces a form that sounds like "to my mare." Again and again the male lover expresses his desire to have his partner as his own possession. The verse begins and ends with terms of endearment that express this possession: "to my mare" and "my darling." These form an envelope that frames the whole verse with admiration and devotion. In contrast to the 140 times that the masculine term "horse" (*sûs*) occurs, this is the only appearance of the common feminine noun "mare" (*sûsâ*) in the Bible.[44] Thus this term is unique in the Bible, though certainly not unknown among ancient Israelites. Still, horses were not a common phenomenon in Israel or in the surrounding countries. Introduced from central Asia in the early second millennium BC, these animals became associated with war and royalty rather than with the more menial tasks of common transport and agriculture. Most likely the state would have owned virtually all the horses and used them primarily for war, at least before the Persian age. The horse and the mare would thus be associated with the most noble of beasts, possessed by the royal house and used primarily for warfare. While the stirrup awaited invention, horses were not ridden into battle, but these animals were used to pull chariots around the battlefield.[45] This

44. The form occurs once elsewhere (Josh. 19:5) but as part of the place-name Hazar Susah.
45. Pope ("Mare"; *Song*, 336–41) and Keel (*Song*, 56–58) note that stallions were normally used to pull chariots. They cite an incident in an Egyptian battle where the release

provided the quickest and surest means to gain a strategic position from which archers on the chariots could fire their weapons. Therefore, the comparison of the female lover with a mare would first and foremost emphasize her nobility and her value.

Furthermore, the qualification "among pharaoh's chariotry" provides a picture of the finest horses. At the time of Solomon and for a century afterward, the most magnificent and valuable horses and mares would have been in the service of the ruler of Egypt. With its natural sources of gold, this nation always held the upper hand in economics in the ancient Near East. Thus, even though the breeding of horses may have taken place elsewhere, the wealth to purchase the best of the breeds would have brought the finest animals to Egypt. Hence the comparison suggests not merely a noble and special animal beyond the reach of most Israelites, but also the very finest of them all, legendary equestrian orders from the best stock in the world. It is important to note that nowhere in the Song is either lover valued in terms of money, nor is that the point here. Instead, as the male lover turns to the realm of nature, he no doubt is spurred on by the female's own metaphors from this world. Hence he naturally considers what is most precious and valuable of all, that representative of nature whose form and power had become legendary in the ancient world.

Occurrences of this form (Piel) of the verb "to like/want" (*dmh*) often convey a plan or desire (Num. 33:56; Judg. 20:5; 2 Sam. 21:5; Isa. 10:7; Ps. 48:10 [48:9 Eng.]; Esther 4:13). However, the emphasis on a comparison ("to be like") also occurs with this verb form (Isa. 40:18, 25; 46:5; Hosea 12:11 [12:10 Eng.]; Lam. 2:13), and it is this emphasis that occurs here, the only place the Piel verb form appears in the Song. Therefore, it is significant that the male lover produces a simile. This is perhaps characteristic of one who strives to poetry. However, it contrasts with the words of his partner. In her rhapsody, she did not pause to insert words of likeness or similarity. Instead, all her focus remained with the sensuous descriptions that formed metaphors, a more direct and immediate means of describing her lover and his lovemaking. The term for "darling" (*r⁽yh*) occurs in 1:9 for the first of nine times in the Song (1:15; 2:2, 10, 13; 4:1, 7; 5:2; 6:4). Elsewhere it appears only with reference to the friends of Jephthah's daughter (Judg. 11:37, an early usage of this expression). It is no surprise that it is always used of the female lover. However, its occurrences also suggest that it forms a special term of endearment between the male lover and his partner. He alone uses it

of a mare at the battle of Qadesh was an attempt to upset the cavalry. Murphy, *Song*, 131, observes that this text does not focus on sexual excitement but on the beauty of the female. But are the two so easily separated in the Song?

of her. This term "darling" also provides a wordplay with the pastoral images of the shepherdess who "tends" her flock in v. 7, since both words derive from verbal roots spelled with identical consonants ($r^{c}h$).

> [10]Your cheeks are desirable with earrings,
> Your neck with strings of jewels.

Verse 10 continues the male lover's admiration of his beloved. The synonymous parallelism of this verse is reinforced by the identical number of full syllables in the word pairs "your cheeks" and "your neck," and "with earrings" and "with strings of jewels." Both lines have a part of the body followed by a preposition (*bêt*) that introduces a plural form of a piece of jewelry. The initial verb does "double duty" for both lines. The lover uses a distinctive stem or form of the verb that provides a delicate and allusive reference to the female lover's appearance.[46]

Of the twenty occurrences of the term for "cheek" (*lḥy*), only the two appearances in the Song (cf. also 5:13) have a positive description devoid of any violence. The term for "earrings" (root *twr*) occurs only here and in v. 11 with this concrete meaning of "earrings."[47] The only other verse in which the word pair "cheek" and "neck" occurs is Isa. 30:28. There it forms part of a theophany of God's wrath against the nations, in which his breath rises like water up to their necks and he puts a bit in the jaws of the peoples to lead them wherever he wants. Thus the picture is completely different than that found in the Song. Further, there is no real parallel in the description of Isaiah to the Song's picture of the female lover. The earrings and jewels provide enhancement of the woman's beauty. Rather than a necessity to create an attraction that is not there naturally, these accoutrements serve to make more beautiful what already is desirable. They also do more. The earrings and jewels form appropriate adornments for one so noble and beautiful. The male lover wishes to further emphasize the incredible desire that he feels for the woman's beauty. Therefore, he describes her physical form. Her cheeks and neck may be the only parts of her body, along with the rest of her head, that are visible to the public. The male lover thus praises his partner's body in an initially modest manner. All the while he focuses on the physical form.

---

46. The passive form of the verb (Niphal of *ʾwh*) occurs only in this verse and in Isa. 52:7, although formations of verbs and nouns with the same root appear thirty-seven times elsewhere in the Bible.

47. Elsewhere it or its cognate carries the meanings of "turn/order" (Esther 2:12, 15), "bands" (Akkadian), or "borders" (Aramaic). See Keel, *Song*, 59, who suggests jewelry that sets off the cheeks, whether dangling earrings, ribbons of a headdress, or the locks of a wig.

> ¹¹We will make you earrings of gold,
> Studded with silver.

Verse 11 continues the two-line synonymous parallelism of v. 10 as it describes the vision of the male lover to further transform his beloved in terms of beauty and to provide her with the most precious of objects that reflect her value. As in the preceding verse, this one forms its parallelism on the basis of two key nouns: "earrings of gold" in the first line and "studded with silver" in the second line. In both cases, there is first a plural form in construct with a precious metal. The reference to "earrings," the first word in the verse, uses the same plural noun as in the preceding verse and thus ties it with what has gone before. Gold (*zāhāb*) is the most valuable of metals and, in parallel with "silver" (*kesep*), forms a common word pair often used to describe these most precious commodities. Compare the bride queen of Ps. 45:10 (45:9 Eng.), who wears gold of Ophir.[48] The picture here, along with the jewels of v. 10, describes gems and metals out of reach of all but the wealthiest. This alone is appropriate for the female lover in the eyes of her partner. Only such wealth can approach her. However legitimate the parallels with modern bedouin women who carry their dowry and life savings in the jewelry they wear, the point in this Song is the value that the male places upon his beloved, a value that reaches and surpasses all earthly value.

Thus the male promises, "We will make you" all these. But who is the "we"? Could it be the other maidens of Jerusalem, who also recognize the beauty of this woman and how precious it is? Alternatively, Paul ("Plural") identifies a plural of ecstasy in ancient Near Eastern love poetry, a phenomenon he applies to female speakers but one that Longman suggests could be applied here.[49] However, the listener is not told who the other members of the first-person common plural are. As with the single other occurrence of this form of the verb (*na'ăśeh*) in the Song (8:8), the emphasis is not upon the subjects but upon the object of the verb.[50] In this verse the male does not focus on himself but on his lover. The object of the verb, "[for] you" (*lāk*), repeats the same structure that has already occurred twice in v. 8.[51] The preposition in this structure (*lāmed*) thus forms an inclusio, occurring at the beginning and end of the male's first speech. The male longs to focus only on his beloved.

48. Munro, *Spikenard*, 57.
49. Longman, *Song*, 103.
50. Even if the subject in 8:8 is the brothers (see comments), it is implied rather than explicitly stated.
51. That is, the *lāmed* preposition plus second-person feminine singular pronominal suffix.

Whatever the cost, he will honor her. The focus of his love has no limits as to the cost or task that he must undertake to bless her.

Thus the emphasis upon the feminine singular "you" of vv. 8 and 10, where the male focuses upon his beloved, envelops v. 9 with its three references to the first-person singular pronouns: "I/my." In v. 9, nevertheless, the male does not focus upon himself so much as he emphasizes his beloved as his own precious possession. Again, as at the beginning of the male's address, it is worth repeating how the imagery of his words differs from those of the female. Her words delight all the senses and culminate in observations about her physical form that then express reservations. In dramatic contrast, the male dwells only on the female's physical appearance, with no reference to the other senses. Further, from the reference to the kisses at the beginning of her address and throughout the whole of it, the female stresses the relationship between her and her partner. It is in such a context that she speaks as she does. However, the male addresses his beloved from the perspective of how he sees her and what he does for her. Rather than the female's reciprocity, there is much more objectivity. Hence the female's focus on the mutual relationship contrasts with the male's emphasis on his lover. Yet these two different perspectives complement one another.

While the female's address is far more holistic in her delights of love, her words to the maidens of Jerusalem demonstrate an insecurity in her beauty. It is this concern to which the male responds. He reassures her of her beauty and his love for her as he dwells entirely on her physical form and its value. In particular, her head and neck—visible to the other women and her focus of concern in vv. 5–6—are described by her lover as most beautiful and most precious. It is important to stress this point. What is portrayed in the first dialogue of the Song is not a stereotyping of the female as fully open to all the senses and the male as focused on objectifying the physical form of his lover. Instead, the male's concern addresses the one element that threatens to mar the female's otherwise perfect praise of their love. He uses it as a means to restore her confidence by reinforcing his love for her in the one area that she has displayed insecurity.

1:12–14. *Female: Her lover as fragrance.* Translated in a word-for-word fashion as suggested here, the dramatic parallelism of 1:12–14 becomes clear. For those who see the king and the shepherd as two suitors for the love of the female, there is a switching back and forth here that destroys the otherwise clear parallelism. The king (*hammelek*) is best seen as an image in the female lover's mind of her partner. In this scene, the image of royalty allows for the possession of valuable spices and perhaps even for the couch. The latter would be an item found only in wealthier or royal households. While vv. 9–11 consider jewelry, vv. 12–14 reflect on fragrance.

In each of these three stanzas of two lines, the first line describes the male lover from the female's perspective. He is introduced as a king on his couch. However, with the strong focus on the fragrances, he becomes the myrrh and henna of vv. 13 and 14. Of course, this is made clear by the equation of the noun clause in the first line of each of those verses: "A sachet of myrrh/bouquet of henna is my lover to me." Further, the second word in each of the three verses is the king, the myrrh, and the henna. These three are the only words in the entire poem (1:12–14) that are preceded by the definite article. They are all related in the poem and identified with one another.

After the first lines describe the male lover, the second lines identify his relationship to the female. Structurally, this is accomplished in v. 12 by the use of the first-person singular pronoun "my" as a suffix to "spikenard." In vv. 13 and 14, the location of the male lover between her breasts and in the vineyards of En Gedi connects the two. This is explicit in v. 13 and metaphorical in v. 14, where the vineyards become a metaphor for their lovemaking. Finally, the temporal note at the end of v. 13, that her partner spends the night with her, provides the most vivid description of a physical relationship between the two.

Further connections between these verses include the first-person common singular suffix, already noted for "my spikenard," which also appears in v. 13: "my breasts." Verses 13 and 14 repeat the refrain "my lover is to me" (*dôdî lî*). All three verses contain a location of the male lover (his couch, my breasts, and vineyards of En Gedi), and they each describe a fragrant aromatic (spikenard, myrrh, and henna). In light of these parallelisms, it is also appropriate to ask whether the structure does not intend the verb "spends the night" in v. 13 also to be applied at the corresponding location in v. 14. Note that the second lines of vv. 12 and 13 contain verbs, the only verbs in this poem. Verse 14 might be expected to have one as well. If "between my breasts" parallels "in the vineyards of En Gedi," then the single Hebrew word *yālîn* ("he spends the night") might be expected to do double duty—a common phenomenon already noted in v. 10. The poem's sudden stop after "in the vineyards of En Gedi" would leave the readers/listeners to complete the line as in the preceding verse: "he spends the night."

> ¹²While the king is on his couch,
> My spikenard gives forth its fragrance.

Verse 12 has the female taking up her address after the interlude of the male's speech (1:8–11). She begins with an unexpected prepositional construction that leaves the main clause for the second part of the verse. Not since v. 4 has she identified her lover as the king. Here the royal connection allows for the picture of spices and furniture that might be available only to a king. The royal couch would evoke thoughts of lovemaking and the joys the female would experience with her lover. The spikenard or pure nard was a fragrance native to the Himalayan region of India (the word "nard" appears in Sanskrit literature).[52] Its scarcity and the difficulty of manufacturing and transporting it a long distance made it both valuable and exotic. Perhaps this is the reason it is mentioned only three times in the OT and only in the Song (4:13–14). As the most expensive of the perfumes mentioned, it also has the closest association with the king. Yet the female lover refers to it as "my nard." Although all the aromatics are applied to herself, they each represent the sensual pleasure that the physical presence of the king/lover brings. This first perfume, so precious and exotic, would evoke a distinctive fragrance for the female lover, one that would separate the male lover from all the mundane realities around him. Thus the spreading forth of the fragrance provides an environment that presents the male as of the greatest worth and separated from everyone else.[53]

> [13]A sachet of myrrh is my lover to me,
> Between my breasts he spends the night.

Verse 13 identifies a sachet of myrrh as a metaphor for the female lover's partner. Myrrh is a reddish gum resin that occurs naturally in both a solid and liquid state. It is found native to South Arabia and was one of the precious substances used in making incense for the temple.[54] Not as exotic as spikenard, it was nevertheless valuable. Mixed with olive oil, a perfume such as this could be applied to the body after bathing. Whether or not it was customary for a woman to go to bed with some sort of container of myrrh, it could easily have been worn in this manner during the daytime. Here, however, the sensual nature of the perfume between the breasts becomes an entrée into a word picture of the male lover spending the night with the female.[55] The picture of lying between her breasts evokes a scene of sexual pleasure. And yet the verse is not

52. See further Munro, *Spikenard*, 49–50.

53. Fox, *Song*, 106, ascribes to Origen the observation that spikenard emits its scent only when rubbed—a comment that increases the eroticism of the allusion.

54. It has been suggested that myrrh (*mōr*) is so named because it has a bitter (*mrr*) taste. See King and Stager, *Life*, 347–48.

55. It is possible, as Hunt ("Subtle") claims, that this emotion was heightened by the reference here to breast (*šad*), its similarity to the word for love(making) (*dôd*), and the paronomasia (wordplay) with another word for "breast" (*dad*).

a description of the event itself but the fantasy of the female as she expresses rhapsodies of the best of fragrances and the most desirable of physical experiences.

Attempts to allegorize this among Christians (and Jewish scholars as well) reached such fantasies as ascribing the two breasts to the OT and NT, with Christ as the perfume between them.[56] Nevertheless, there is no indication in the Song that this is intended as anything more than the deepest yearning of the female lover for her partner. In her musings she opens to him the most precious parts of her body and longs for his lovemaking as a means to express the love they share. Here in v. 13 is the first of more than thirty occurrences of *dôdî* (my lover). No term expresses more clearly her deep erotic desire.

> [14]A bouquet of henna is my lover to me,
> In the vineyards of En Gedi.

Although the word for "bouquet" (*ʾeškōl*, v. 14) is otherwise used of a cluster of grapes (Num. 13:23–24), the term here applies to the henna. This substance is native to Palestine and thus is the most easily obtained of the aromatics mentioned here. It produces yellow flowers (hence, bouquet), although the plant also serves as a reddish dye for hair and fingernails. Henna is applied directly to the body as a perfume or deodorant. The female has moved from the most exotic and valuable of perfumes, and its association with royalty, to the least expensive and most accessible of perfumes. The textual "movement" from the royal couch to the breasts of the lover through the night suggests a greater intimacy, or at least a more explicit one (since all this could take place on the couch).

Why are the vineyards of En Gedi mentioned? On the one hand this could describe a secret romantic retreat, away from the bustling cities of Palestine. En Gedi is an oasis located on the western shore of the Dead Sea. Occupation dates back to the fourth millennium BC, though there is no archaeological evidence of people living there permanently during the Israelite monarchy before the late eighth or seventh century BC. Nevertheless, David stayed there while fleeing Saul (1 Sam. 23:29; 24:1). This is significant because the name of David is constructed of the same consonants (when written in its older form without vowel letters) as the repeated expression in vv. 12 and 13, "lover" (*dwd*). Thus the mention of her "lover" may have led the female to thoughts of David and his secret hideout. However, the association goes farther. The desert climate of En Gedi supports the growth of tropical plants more than

56. Cited in Pope, *Song*, 352.

any other site in the kingdom of Israel. It would be a natural location for the importation and transplanting of aromatic plants, such as those mentioned here. In fact, excavation of the seventh- and sixth-century strata from the archaeological site at En Gedi, Tel Goren, has revealed what may be a royal and commercial center for the production of perfumes.[57] Hence the mention of this site brings together themes of these three verses: exotic sensual aromatics, royal and valuable objects, and intimate physical lovemaking separated from others.[58] The "vineyards of En Gedi" may describe physical plantations, but more likely it is a metaphor for the physical body.[59] In v. 6 this was clear as the female lover used it to refer to her body. Here the plural "vineyards" may suggest the bodies of the couple as they enjoy one another in a setting particularly appropriate for their love.

> [15]You are so beautiful,
> My darling,
> You are so beautiful,
> Your eyes are doves.

1:15. *Male: Praise of beauty.* The male's response comprises seven words, two of which are repeated. Each of the two identical phrases contains four syllables in Hebrew. In the first instance this is followed by the three-syllable word for "my darling." In the second case the three-syllable word that follows means "your eyes." The seventh word, which extends the last line, provides the focal point to which the reader's/hearer's attention is drawn: "doves." The verse contains three "your" suffixes and one "my" suffix.[60] This latter, with its noun, repeats the expression "my darling" (ra'yātî), first found in v. 9. There it formed the center of the male's first address. While the suffix does suggest the male's possession of his lover, the focus of the noun is as a term of endearment to describe the female. In fact, every word in the verse applies directly to the female. Identical expressions for "behold/look" (hinnēh) begin each half of the verse. With their second-person feminine singular suffixes ("your") they arrest attention and focus it on the male's partner. Both this and the following word, "beautiful" (yāpāh), are repeated as though the male cannot stop calling attention to this fact. The attribution of beauty and

57. King and Stager, *Life,* 284–85.
58. Munro, *Spikenard,* 139, identifies two of these: "a place of refuge for the lovers, a refuge which is also a garden of delight."
59. Cf. Murphy, *Song,* 135, for a parallel between the second line of v. 13 and the reference to the female's breasts, and the second line of v. 14 with the vineyards of En Gedi.
60. That is, three second-person feminine singular suffixes and one first-person common singular pronominal suffix.

the address "my darling" identify the object of the speaker's concern as the same in his first address, the female. This general statement of loving admiration is then repeated with the additional specification of the first place the male's attention turns as he admires his lover, her eyes. The attribution of the female's eyes as doves is repeated, literally as here, in 4:1. Their third mention by the male, in 5:12, is in the form of a simile. However, the first two occurrences possess no "like" or "as." The male does not bother to insert a term of comparison. He creates a direct metaphor, describing a word picture that comes immediately to his mind. The source of this in part may be found in the reference to En Gedi at the close of the female's previous address. The word "En" means "spring" (*ʿayin*) and is identical with the word "eye" (*ʿayin*). The male thus proves himself to be a careful listener and builds his own poetry on the images expressed by his lover.

There are thirty-three occurrences of the word for "dove" (*yônāh*) in the Bible, not counting the appearances of the personal name, Jonah. Only in the Song are they used in love language. Keel (*Song*, 69–71) identifies the word picture as having to do with the eyes, which determine whether one is plain (Leah, Gen. 29:17) or beautiful (David, 1 Sam. 16:12 NRSV). The term for "eyes" can refer to the gleam or glance of the eyes (e.g., eye of wine, Prov. 23:31; eye of bronze, Ezek. 1:7), and so the comparison with doves refers to their liveliness and fluttering about (Pope, *Song*, 356). The image of doves as symbols of love is attested on seals as well as in poetry and in the NT (Matt. 3:17; Mark 1:11; Luke 3:22). If so here, then the metaphor of the male lover describes his beloved as someone whose depth of love and desire is betrayed by her eyes. The dramatic image is that of the couple staring deeply and lovingly into one another's eyes.

1:16–2:1. *Female: Love in paradise.* Verses 16–17 consider the subject of trees and the houses that are built with them.[61] The passage begins with the female repeating the twice-spoken phrase by the male (in v. 15). Of course, the suffixes are changed to address a male, but the first two words are otherwise an exact replica that now appears for the third time. Her designation of "my lover" (*dôdî*), already seen in vv. 13 and 14, now replaces the male's "my darling" as a term of endearment. Thus the precise response of the female, in complete harmony with her lover, sets up the remainder of the structure of this passage. The following two lines are introduced by the particle *ʾap*, which serves to continue the sense of what preceded and in each case could therefore be translated "and also." Structurally, however, the whole of the three verses is driven more by a theme of nature's flora than by a single type of parallelism.

61. Callow, "Units," 470.

Hence the picture of the bed as a spreading growth parallels the cedar and juniper wood of v. 17 and the flowers of 2:1. Although the pronouns of 1:16 and 2:1 indicate that the female must be speaking these lines, there is no clear indication for 1:17. As a result, some argue that the male speaks in v. 17. However, such an assumption would interfere with the imagery as developed by a single speaker in these three verses.

> [16]You are so beautiful,
> My lover;
> You are so pleasant,
> And our bed is a spreading <tree>.

With the NIV in v. 16, it might seem more appropriate to translate the term "beautiful" as "handsome" for a male, but such a translation would lose the sense of a repetition of precisely the same term in the Hebrew. This, as well as the verbal parallel with the male's praise of her in v. 15, allows the female both to express her view of her partner and harmonize with him in a corresponding poetic line. The term "pleasant" (*nāʿîm*, v. 16) occurs only here in the Song. Elsewhere it can describe the quality of the relationship Saul and Jonathan enjoyed and the relationship of brothers in unity (2 Sam. 1:23; Ps. 133:1). Here it also describes the joy and delight of the relationship. The description of the bed as "a spreading <tree>" is of interest in terms of what it suggests. The term for "bed" (*ʿrś*) often describes an artificially made structure with ornate decorations or other items of note, whether the iron bed of Og (Deut. 3:11), the ivory beds of the wealthy of Samaria (Amos 6:4), or the linen-decorated bed of the seducer (Prov. 7:16). This last reference is the only other use of "bed" (*ʿrś*) with sexual connotations. However, in the Song the bed has an explicit relationship with nature in the adjectival modifier that joins it. The term *raʿănānâ* normally describes trees that are luxuriant with growth. It does not identify the tree itself but the growth of the tree. Its usage in describing a bed is unparalleled. However, in the context of the trees described in the following verse, the term is best translated in relation to a tree.

What does it mean for a bed to be a spreading tree? Perhaps it refers to the fruitfulness of the love that the couple enjoys. Perhaps it describes a kind of bed associated with trees or foliage. Numerous texts and commentaries refer to the prophetic condemnation of the worship of other deities with sexual activities under spreading trees.[62] However, there is no suggestion in the Song of a religious activity of any sort. Whatever

---

62. Deut. 12:2; 1 Kings 14:23; 2 Kings 16:4; Jer. 2:20; 3:6, 13; Isa. 57:5; Hosea 4:13; etc. Cf. Keel, *Song*, 75.

the metaphor may intend, the picture introduces the place of the lovers' intended union as one associated with the natural world that follows. Their love appears as fruitful in this verse, whether in terms of children or, more likely in the context, in terms of the hope, meaning, and joy that their lives possess as a result of their love.

> [17]The beams of our house are cedars,
> Our rafters are junipers.

The cedar beams and juniper rafters describe the wood that the builders laid across the top of the four walls of ancient Israelite houses (v. 17). Taller trees, such as those described here, were used so that the beams would be of one piece and have strength and endurance. On top of such a lattice of wood, the branches, plaster, mud, and straw of the roof were placed.[63] As noted in v. 16, this continues the picture there of trees. In both verses (16–17) reference is made to what is intimate and personal, whether the bed the lovers would share or the home in which they would reside. At the same time the descriptions drawn from nature point both to the natural world of beauty that the lovers inhabit and to the following verse (2:1), where the female lover applies the picture of natural flora to herself. The natural world that the descriptions evoke continues a theme begun in the first verses of the chapter. However, the natural elements—wine, perfumes, tents, vineyards, or whatever—reach their state of use only through some human interference. The same is true of these final verses of chapter 1.

As the reader continues in these pictures of nature, it becomes apparent that the lovers inhabit this world. From a theological perspective of the remainder of the Bible (including some of its finest poetry, as in Ps. 19), this is a world created by God. Thus it is good, and the Creator blesses its use. The same is true of these lovers, who celebrate physical love as something created by God and of value. It is true that their emphasis is not upon God but upon the creation itself. From a theological perspective this is ultimately incomplete. But the remainder of the Bible addresses this deficiency. This text embraces the created world and its pleasures with the realization that this all is a gift and to be celebrated and appreciated as such. Even the house and the bed do not originate only from human labor, but have their ultimate source in raw materials that come from the natural and created world. Hence the Song never attempts to worship nature but instead looks to it as the good world that God has created. Within this context the natural joys of the world may be appreciated and celebrated. This is nowhere more

---

63. King and Stager, *Life,* 23–27.

true than in the case of the physical love that the couple enjoys. Their love is part of the natural world.

> **2:1**As for me, I am the asphodel of Sharon,
> The lotus of the valleys.

Having likened her environment to a forest, the female continues the imagery from nature by applying it to herself. What do these pictures of flowers, valleys, and plains suggest? The word for asphodel (*ḥăbaṣṣelet*) occurs only here and in Isa. 35:1. There it describes the blossoming of the desert as fertility returns to a wilderness. It is important to note that this thought continues into v. 2 of Isa. 35, and there it describes the glory of Lebanon and the splendor of Carmel and Sharon. The fir trees of the previous verse in the Song remind the reader of Lebanon, just as the Sharon is explicitly mentioned in both. Thus the asphodel of Sharon portrays an image of fruitfulness.[64] The female goes on to describe herself as the lotus of the valleys (2:1). In parallel with the asphodel, it suggests fruitfulness but also beauty and love.[65] As a lotus this term describes the decorations of the temple (1 Kings 7:19, 22, 26; 2 Chron. 4:5). In Hosea 14:6 (14:5 Eng.) Israel's blessing is likened to a blossoming lotus and a cedar of Lebanon. The Song's earlier images of trees compare with those of a flower in this verse; but in Hosea they describe the resurrection of a nation and its blessings of prosperity and well-being. Thus the self-description of the female lover (in Song 2:1) is one of self-confidence in which her beauty becomes a key to fruitfulness and success for the male.[66] Here it seems that God has created the natural world primarily as a paradise in which the couple may find one another and enjoy their love. The nature imagery will continue throughout the book. Its intensity at this point allows the female lover to develop the thought of her partner and to present their love as a part of the natural world, which God created. In a similar vein, Jesus compares the lotus or lily favorably to Solomon with all his splendor (Matt. 6:29).[67]

64. This is preferable to seeing the image as one among many flowers/women, as do Delitzsch, *Song*, 40; Fox, *Song*, 107; Gerleman, *Hohelied*, 116; Murphy, *Song*, 136; Provan, *Song*, 110. The Song does not develop anonymity and self-effacement as characteristics of the couple. Cf. Provan, *Song*, 284.

65. Keel, *Song*, 80, describes Egyptian love songs in which the lovers use the term "lotus" as one of affection.

66. J. Sasson, "On Pope's *Song*," 192, suggests that the female here quotes a brief poem or the first line(s) of a poem.

67. In this one instance Plato and the philosophers who followed him were correct. They understood that humanly constructed wealth and glory is but a shadow of what is created naturally.

> ²Like a lotus among the thorns,
> So is my darling among the young women.

2:2. *Male: My love is like a flower.* Verse 2 links with the first verse as both use the picture of the lotus.[68] The word order, particles ("like," "so"), and corresponding terms of endearment ("my darling," "my lover") parallel v. 2 with v. 3.[69] From every perspective this verse exhibits an excellent use of synonymous parallelism. Each of the two lines begins with a preposition of comparison. This is followed by three words: the first is a singular noun, the second is the preposition "between" (*bên*), and the third is a plural common noun with a definite article. The first line compares plants from the field, and the second line compares women. The close parallelism suggests that, if one can determine the significance of the first simile from nature, it will yield the significance of the second comparison. So the question remains: How is a lotus among thorns? The lotus continues the nature imagery of the preceding text, and it surely forms a tie with the previous verse as a means by which the male affirms the female's boast of her attractions. Hence the lotus may well continue the theme of prosperity and success, as well as the natural form and beauty that this delicate flower possesses. The word for "thorn" (*hôah*) occurs twelve times in the Bible. Thorns can describe desolation (Isa. 34:13; Hosea 9:6; Job 31:40). Thorns were used to pierce jaws and lead prisoners of war (Job 40:26 [41:2 Eng.]; 2 Chron. 33:11). They were dangerous to the touch (Prov. 26:9) but also served as hiding places (1 Sam. 13:6). However, the one example of a symbolic use of thorns occurs in Jehoash's words to the king of Judah: "A thistle [thorn bush, NRSV] in Lebanon sent a message to a cedar in Lebanon, 'Give your daughter to my son in marriage.' Then a wild beast in Lebanon came along and trampled the thistle underfoot" (2 Kings 14:9 NIV). The clear sense is the insignificance of the thorn. Therefore, the point of comparison between the lotus and the thorns may be the general insignificance of the latter in light of the former. For the lover to compare a lotus among thorns to his partner among the young women suggests that he has eyes for her alone, not for anyone else.

> ³Like an apple among the trees of the forest,
> So is my lover among the young men.
> In its shade I delight to sit,
> Its fruit is sweet to my palate.

68. So also J. Sasson, "On Pope's *Song*," 192–93.
69. Callow, "Units," 471.

2:3–7. *Female: A pastoral scene.* The simile and synonymous parallelism of v. 2 continue in v. 3. Now the female takes up the same forms of expression as her lover and uses them to distinguish him from the other males. Exactly the same prepositions introduce the first and second lines. Again there are three words. In the first line the first word after the preposition is a common noun describing a product of the field, here an apple, whereas in v. 2 it is a lotus. The parallel noun in the second line of v. 3 is the term of endearment "my lover," whereas in v. 2 it is "my darling." In the first line of v. 3 the middle preposition is not "between" (*bên*), as twice in v. 2, but a preposition (*bêt*) followed by "trees of." This forms a single idea with the final common noun, "the forest," which is both definite and plural, just like the corresponding "the thorns" of v. 2. Again, the second line's final "the young men" (lit., "the sons") corresponds with "the young women" (lit., "the daughters") in v. 2.

The emphasis, however, is not upon the lotus with its beauty of form and its distinction among the other plants. Instead, the apple (*tappûaḥ*) serves as the basis for comparison with her lover. Fox maintains that except for the wild inedible kind, apples did not grow in ancient Israel, and therefore he translates "apricot."[70] However, the apple appears to have been known in earlier Sumerian literature.[71] The "apple" occurs six times in the Bible, four of which are in the Song. In Joel 1:12 it appears as one among several different types of fruit trees that have dried up and are no longer available for food. In Prov. 25:11 "apples of gold" may better be rendered as "grapes of gold" in order to describe a cluster of fruit.[72] Together the terms portray a fruit that is delicious and enhanced by the flavor of the whole cluster. Otherwise, apples provide refreshment (Song 2:5) and a pleasant natural fragrance (7:9 [7:8 Eng.]). An apple tree in the forest is one that can distinguish itself by its usefulness in providing something that is nourishing. However, "apples" seem to be used less for sustenance and more for refreshment, the pleasure of their taste, and the accompanying odor. Thus, if the lotus enhances the pleasure of visual form and beauty, the apple tree stimulates the taste and olfactory senses.[73]

---

70. Fox, *Song*, 107.

71. Keel, *Song*, 82.

72. See Heim, *Like Grapes*.

73. For erotic associations of the apple, especially in Sumerian and Assyrian sources, see Pope, *Song*, 381; Keel, *Song*, 82, 88. The use of apples and pomegranates as an aphrodisiac is found in an incantation quoted by Pope and Keel:

> [Incan]tation. The beautiful woman has brought forth love.
> Inanna, who loves apples and pomegranates,
> Has brought forth potency.
> Rise! Fall! Love-stone, prove effective for me. Rise!
> . . . Inanna . . .

In order to clarify the point of the simile, the female goes beyond the parallel of the male's statement. She adds both a chiastically constructed stanza and one that is at the same time synonymous. As a chiasm it begins and ends with the same formation:[74] "in its shade/to my palate." The first occurrence, "in its shade," refers to the male lover as providing relief from the hot sun, which the female has already described as damaging to her (1:6). The last expression, "to my palate," describes another sense that the female employs to encompass as much of her partner's love as possible. The stanza is also synonymous, for each of the two lines begins with a description of the apple tree, with which the female interacts as she might with her lover. Its shade is an occasion for her to sit and to find pleasure in remaining close to her lover. He shelters her as she sheltered him in 1:13.[75] Its fruit serves to delight her sense of taste with sweetness. The third line (of 2:3) begins with "its shade" and continues with "I delight," "I sit." The fourth line begins with "its fruit" as something desirable to the female. Together these descriptions portray the female's relation to her lover as one who provides an abiding physical closeness and refreshment and as one whose physical touch and taste is a heady sweetness. As noted earlier, so here again the female expands the sensuality of the descriptions, accommodating more of them with lengthier and more complete explanations. In contrast, the male focuses on the visual aspect and draws from it his praise and appreciation of the female. However, this verse and the following description go beyond the sensual experiences and their excitement to include physical actions that will describe the closeness and support that the lovers provide one another.

> **4**He brought me to the house of wine,
> And his intent for me is love.

In contrast to the quiet repose of v. 3, the next verse begins with a verb of action: "He brought me." As noted in the introduction to the interpretation of this first unit (1:2–2:7), 2:4–6 constitutes a climax. It also forms an envelope with the beginning verse. The female's request to her lover to take her away and to join him (1:4, 7) is here answered as intimacy

---

She has presided over love.
Incantation. If a woman looks upon the penis of a man.
Its ritual: either <to> an apple or to a pomegranate
You recite the incantation three times.
You give (the fruit) to the woman (and) you have her suck the juices.
That woman will come to you; you can make love to her.
(Biggs, *Šà.zi.ga*, 70 [*KAR* 61, lines 1–10]; 74 [*KAR* 69, lines 4–5])
74. An inseparable preposition attached to a noun with a pronominal suffix.
75. Fox, *Song*, 107.

is achieved.[76] The male lover has now taken the initiative and brought his lover to a place, "the house of wine" (*bêt hayyayin*). With no direct parallels elsewhere in the Bible, Longman notes "the house of drinking wine" (*bêt mištēh hayyayin*, Esther 7:8) and "the drinking house" (*bêt mišteh*, Jer. 16:8; Eccles. 7:2).[77] These describe specific places. Clearly the definite article intends a specific place. However, it is not at all certain that even if one were to establish that the phrase refers to a particular establishment, such is its usage here. The metaphors and symbols of this poetry imply that the drinking house may refer to a particular place where the lovers meet, one that is private and embodies the sensual pleasures of lovemaking already suggested by the image of wine (Song 1:2, 4, 6). Such a place has already received allusions in 1:7–8 and 1:16–17. This is the likeliest interpretation in the context of such poetry. The second line of 2:4, "And his intent for me is love," has no structural parallel to the first line. Instead, it is close to the last phrase of v. 3: "Its fruit is sweet to my palate."[78] In v. 4 this second line follows the action of the first line and describes its purpose. The "house of wine" was not a place for drunkenness but a symbol of the erotic love that formed the reason for going there.[79]

> [5]Refresh me with raisins,
> Revive me with apples,
> Because I am faint with love.

Verse 5 has a distinctive structure that, like v. 3, encompasses two couplets. A similar verb and preposition[80] are repeated, using the same ideas: "refresh me"/"revive me," "with raisins"/"with apples." The word "apple(s)" repeats the first word of v. 3, and "love" repeats the last word of v. 4.[81] The verse concludes with an explanation as to why the refreshment is necessary. The female has become faint from her desire for love. This parallels the previous two verses, in which a final line explains or develops the ideas expressed: "Its fruit is sweet to my palate"/"And his intent for me is love"/ "Because I am faint with love." As the intensity of the passion increases, so does the delirium that the arousal of love brings. Elliott observes how

76. Callow, "Units," 480.
77. Longman, *Song*, 112.
78. Both have a common noun with a third-person masculine singular pronominal suffix followed by a predicate without a verb.
79. Fox, "Scholia," 201–2, suggests any structure or booth that might accommodate a private banquet. Fox, *Song*, 285, finds examples in Egyptian love poetry: "The references to garden booths in the Egyptian songs show that the motif of lovemaking and feasting in booths in fields and under trees was traditional in the love song genre."
80. There is a Piel plural imperative verb with a first-person common singular suffix that is followed by the *bêt* preposition and a noun in the plural.
81. J. Sasson, "On Pope's *Song*," 193.

2:1 begins with the first-person common singular "I" (ʾănî) and v. 5 ends with this same pronoun.[82] It thus forms an envelope for the whole first part of chapter 2. The position of the pronoun at the end of the verse does call attention to it and allows it to emphasize this theme in the verse. It is the female and her joy in her lover that are the concern of the verse.

Note the usage of verbs that describe refreshment and revival. Both verbs are rare forms, and their occurrence here suggests a sophisticated poetic usage. The masculine plural forms are far more puzzling. These can be used for an all-male group or for a mixed group; however, they are not appropriate for the maidens of Jerusalem alone. Perhaps they address both the maidens and the male lover, with the possible addition of his male companions. It is also possible that the addressees are not otherwise identified and represent either servants, family members, or neighbors in the area where the couple meets in their love tryst. However, the likeliest explanation is that found with the imperfect forms in 2:7. These are also characteristic masculine plurals, and yet the context indicates that they must be feminine (see below). Because the imperatives in Hebrew are formed from the imperfects, unusual imperfect forms allow for similar imperative forms.

The noun for "raisin (cake)" (ʾăšîšâ) occurs in only three other cases in the Bible. One is Hosea 3:1, which describes the Israelites as those who love the raisin cakes, a symbol of the worship of other deities for whom these cakes were offerings (cf. "cakes" in Hosea 3:1; Jer. 7:18; 44:19).[83] Its other occurrences are in the parallel texts 2 Sam. 6:19 = 1 Chron. 16:3, where David distributes these (along with a loaf of bread and dates) to the Israelites who attend his procession and celebration of the ark as it is brought to Jerusalem. Although these other occurrences have religious contexts, there is no suggestion of that in the Song. Instead, the food appears to be something served in a celebration. It is a rich dainty that may stimulate the mind (especially if the grapes or whatever fruit is used have had time to ferment). As a special food, it serves as a parallel with the apples, which also appear to describe a food for special occasions. Both are pleasure foods, and the command of the female to partake of them straddles the literal and symbolic. On the one hand, her overpowering sense of passion for her lover leads her to call for a substitute or some distracting nourishment that will give her strength. On the other hand, her comparison of her lover with an apple tree (v. 3) surely brings to mind these foods, which are sweet like her lover and

---

82. Elliott, *Literary*, 60.

83. Oddly enough, the noun appears in a masculine plural construct form, suggesting it can occur in both genders. Fox, *Song*, 109, argues that "raisin (cake)" is too specific in all the occurrences. However, his "apricots" is also speculative.

cause her to think of him. Finally, in a symbolic sense that reaches to
the erotic, they represent a call for her lover to come and provide the
refreshment and revival. Above all, she wishes to taste him.[84]

> [6]His left <arm is> under my head,
> His right <arm> embraces me.

Verse 6 is composed of two lines, each with six full syllables.[85] The
direction could refer to the hand, arm, or any part of the male's body.
The translation "arm" suits the context. This has "his" (a third-person
masculine singular possessive suffix) attached. It is followed in the first
line by "under my head."[86] In the second line it is followed by "embraces
me."[87] Keel describes this as "a classic position" for lovers and points to
examples.[88] Thus the words move the reader/listener from the male (his)
to the female (my/me). The absence of a verb in the first line emphasizes
the lack of action. Instead, the female rests in her lover's arms. In the
second line the verbal motion describes the embrace. The female says
all of this, but the picture is one of her passively yielding to the male's
advance as he supports her fainting head and embraces her supine body.
The sense is one of security and trust. The picture provides an answer to
the concern of v. 5, where the female was dizzy and fainting. However,
it resolves it only by intensifying the sensual, physical contact that the
lovers enjoy. Now they are physically close as only lovers may be. They
melt into one another's arms, and the dizziness of love's overpowering
sweetness is enhanced rather than removed.

> [7]I want you to promise,
> O young women of Jerusalem,
> By gazelles and does of the field,
> Do not disturb,
> Do not excite love,
> Until it desires.

Verse 7 like v. 6 is also repeated later in the Song. In this case,
however, the repetition occurs twice, in 3:5 and 8:4. These refrains
constitute the major structural dividers in the Song.[89] Only the 3:5

84. Murphy, *Song*, 137, correctly rejects the opinion of Pope, *Song*, 380, that these
fruits are aphrodisiacs: "It makes little sense for the woman to ask for an aphrodisiac
here." Cf. Fox, *Song*, 109.
85. This verse is virtually duplicated in 8:3.
86. A preposition and then a noun with a first-person singular possessive suffix.
87. A Piel verb in the imperfect with the first-person singular possessive suffix.
88. Keel, *Song*, 89–90.
89. Cf., e.g., Feuillet, "Drama."

parallel includes the gazelles and does, however. The verse begins with a verb, one that is used of taking oaths. Its stem (Hiphil) suggests the act of forcing someone to swear an oath. Here, however, the sense of the poem does not suggest something that is forced, but rather has the female warning her companions to promise to act in a certain way. The term for "gazelle" (*ṣĕbîyâ*) occurs nowhere else in the Bible as a common noun except in the Song. In addition to the duplicate passage (3:5), 4:5 and 7:3 mention the fawns of a gazelle in describing the female's breasts. The term for "doe" (*ʾayyālâ/ʾayyelet*) is used in describing beauty (Gen. 49:21), sure-footedness (2 Sam. 22:34; Hab. 3:19; Ps. 18:34 [18:33 Eng.]), and motherly devotion (Jer. 14:5; Job 39:1). However, in at least one instance, Prov. 5:19, the doe is used to describe the wife of a man's youth. As with the gazelle, the context in Prov. 5:19 compares the doe with the breasts of the woman. Thus the reference to gazelles and does of the field may symbolize the physical attributes of the women addressed and the female's adjuration to apply the oath with reference to the carnal pleasures of love. If so, then the content of the promise and what is to be avoided follow naturally. The use of these animals in an oath, in place of the customary reference to God, may reflect special sensitivities about invoking God in any oath.[90]

Forms of the same verb (Hiphil and Polal) are used to describe a progressive stimulation, excitement, and arousal. Here again, the forms of the verbs are the customary masculine plural. Yet the addressees, (lit.) "daughters of Jerusalem," make clear that these are female companions of the woman. Therefore, the verb forms must be understood as variant feminine plural forms (imperfect second person). It would seem that Hebrew preserved or developed an alternate feminine plural form (imperfect second person), used sometimes in poetry and perhaps other texts as well.[91]

What does the verse mean? How can love, an abstract concept or an emotion, desire anything? Why should the daughters of Jerusalem restrain their impulses until love "desires"? It would seem that love is the controlling factor. The joys of physical love and the arousal to that ecstasy are not to be toyed with. If the text means anything, it refers to this rather than a

---

90. Gordis, *Song*, 26–28; Fox, *Song*, 110. Murphy, *Song*, 133, observes how the sounds of the customary names of God in Hebrew oaths (*bĕʾlōhay ṣĕbāʾōt* or *bĕʾēl šadday*) resemble the sounds of the words in Song 2:7 for "deer" and "doe" (*biṣbāʾôt ʾô bĕʾaylôt haśśādeh*). Keel (*Song*, 92) disagrees, noting that this replacement of expressions for "God" would be unique in the Bible and that elsewhere in later Jewish literature the technique always uses nonsense syllables. He points to Syrian, Israelite, and Egyptian evidence that associates these animals with the goddess of love.

91. See introduction under "Canon/Language/Text Criticism."

request not to disturb the couple in their love.[92] Love is such a powerful emotion and carries such enormous power that it must not be misused.[93] The appreciation of love as a gift from God is the traditional theological understanding of this book. This verse captures the counterbalance. The full appreciation of the joys of physical love can happen only when love comes at the appropriate time with the partner that love chooses. For the Christian, here are the beginnings of a powerful message of physical love as God's gift according to his will and timing. It is not a decision reached by the daughters of Jerusalem (any more than by the sons) but one that must be received when and in the manner that God has decided.

Theological Implications

Situated within the canon of the Jewish and Christian Bible, the Song celebrates physical desire and carnal love between a man and a woman as created and blessed by God. The Song explores this divine blessing. The female begins the exchange with appeal to each of the senses in her praise of their love. She moves from this description to a desire to be with her lover (1:2–7). The male's response serves to reassure and confirm her appeal to him, by extolling her great physical beauty (1:8–11). The female takes up the dialogue with her "king" on his couch and moves quickly to a picture or fantasy of greater intimacy as he spends the night between her breasts (1:12–14). Following the reaffirmation of the female's beauty (1:15), the female (1:16–2:1) and then the male (2:2) use repeated and intensive images of the natural world and especially the most beautiful and sensual flora of ancient Israel. Here, as well, the beauty created by God in nature corresponds to God's creation of the love that the couple enjoys. The section concludes with the lovers united and with the adjuration of the female to her companions that love will come at its proper time (2:3–7). In the Song of Songs, which almost never refers directly to God, this suggests yet another divine blessing, that God's greatest gift of physical love comes according to his own timing and within the natural world that he has also created.

92. So Viviers, "Besweringsrefrein," and others who appear to object more to the presence of a moral element in these words of the Song than to any clear exegetical explanation. In the most important repeated refrain in this greatest example of love poetry in the Bible, what is more likely to be the repeated message: a caution about the evocation of erotic love or a "Do Not Disturb" sign?

93. For Murphy, *Song*, 137, this is a warning against the artificial stimulation of love and desire. Longman, *Song*, 116 (with credits to R. Hubbard), writes: "Love is not a passing fling but rather a demanding and exhausting relationship." See de Villiers and Burden, "Function"; Grossberg, "Sexual."

III.
Lovers Joined and Separated
(2:8–3:5)

Translation

Female
²:⁸The sound of my lover.
See! He comes,
Leaping over the mountains,
Springing over the hills.
⁹My lover is like a gazelle,
Or a young stag.
See! He stands behind our wall,
Staring through the windows,
Peering[a] through the lattice.

Male
¹⁰My lover responds,[b] saying[c] to me:
"Arise,[d]

a. The participle "peering" (*mēṣîṣ*) derives from the root *ṣwṣ*, which elsewhere describes the budding and blossoming of plants (Num. 17:8 [17:23 Eng.]; Isa. 27:6; Ps. 72:16) or people (Pss. 92:8 [92:7 Eng.]; 103:15; 132:18), and in one case judgment (Ezek. 7:10). Only here does the sense of peering or looking occur. Therefore, this single occurrence is best understood as a hapax legomenon, a homonym of a root separate from that represented by the other occurrences. See *HALOT* 1013–14. The LXX, Vulgate, and Talmud (*b. Yoma* 67a; cf. Murphy, *Song,* 139) all understand here the sense of viewing.

b. The absence of the normal *wayyiqtol* Hebrew narrative form at this point suggests that this statement is not to be seen as narrative and therefore not to be translated in the past tense. Instead, the perfect aspect and the poetry suggest a dramatic presentation so that this phrase becomes a sort of stage direction inserted here for reasons indicated below. Thus the present-tense translation.

c. Hebrew *wĕʾāmar*; this *weqatal* form here indicates the result of the responding and should ordinarily be translated "(he responded) by saying." J. Sasson, "On Pope's *Song,*" 194, translates, "kept on telling me."

d. J. Sasson, "On Pope's *Song,*" 194, recognizes the inchoative nature of this verb with "come" and translates "begin to come."

My darling, my beauty,
Come!
[11]Look!
The winter[e] has passed,
The rains are over and done with.[f]
[12]The blossoms[g] have appeared in the land,
The time of song[h] has arrived,
The cooing of the turtledove is heard in our land.
[13]The fig tree ripens[i] its young fruit,[j]
The vines blossom[k] with fragrance.
Arise,
My darling, my beauty,
Come!

e. Whether with the Kethib (*hassĕtāw*) or the Qere (*hassĕtāyw*), this is a hapax legomenon. Its postbiblical Hebrew usage as well as Syriac and Arabic cognates all support the context here, that in parallelism with *haggešem* it refers to winter and the rainy season.

f. *Hālak lô* provides a modal or intensive sense to *hālap* (with no conjunction), confirming that the rains have indeed ceased. J. Sasson, "On Pope's *Song*," 194, renders this as "has spent itself."

g. *Niṣṣānîm* occurs only here in the Bible. Elsewhere the root appears as *nēṣ* and *niṣṣâ* (Gen. 40:10; Isa. 18:5; Job 15:33), used of the blossoms on grapevines and olive trees. In Ezek. 1:7 the Qal participle *nōṣĕṣîm* refers to the gleaming or glistening of the feet of a calf. See Pope, *Song*, 395.

h. The translation of *zāmîr* could refer either to singing or to pruning. The latter option is chosen by the LXX, Vulgate, and other ancient versions. It recalls the two months attributed to "pruning" on the ninth-century BC Gezer Calendar (Lemaire, "*Zāmîr*"). Pope, *Song*, 396, makes much of the occurrence of a reference to implements of pruning together with the mention of a "blossom" in Isa. 18:5. Nevertheless, this distant parallel does not require such an interpretation in the Song. Instead, the voice of the dove in the following line makes an anticipatory reference to song in the preceding line a distinct possibility (cf. G. Carr, *Song*, 97–99). Although this may be translated as a time of "pruning," the balance of probability favors "song" in the first instance with a double entendre that includes "pruning." See also Albrektson, "Sjunga?"; idem, "Singing?" For this as Janus parallelism (looking backward and forward; as proposed by Gordon, "Asymmetric") and other examples, cf. Paul, "Polysensuous"; J. Sasson, "On Pope's *Song*," 194; Noegel, *Janus*, 12 et passim. Rabbe, "Deliberate," 214–15, refers to it as deliberate lexical ambiguity.

i. Not related to the *ḥnṭ* root meaning "to embalm" (Gen. 50:2, 26; contra Syriac, Ethiopic, and Targum), this homonym, used only here, is cognate with Akkadian *ḥunnuṭu* (ripening). The term also occurs inscribed on a wine jug from Hazor. Cf. Snaith, *Song*, 39.

j. *Pag* occurs only here. Syriac and Arabic cognates designate unripe fruit.

k. *Sĕmādar* occurs only here and in Song 2:15 and 7:13 (7:12 Eng.). Its unusual quadriliteral nature suggests a loanword or at least one of foreign etymology. The Akkadian *samādiru* (blossom) may be cognate through Aramaic (*AHw* 1016; see *HALOT* 759). The LXX *kyprizousin* (they give off a fragrance) and the Vulgate *florentes* suggest fragrant flowers, associated here with the vineyard. The relationship of this noun to "the vines" is that of a predicate, "The vines in blossom." This is followed by the perfect aspect of "give" and the accusative *rêaḥ* (fragrance). Literally, it says, "The vines in blossom give a fragrance."

¹⁴My dove in the clefts^a of the rock,
In the crags^b of the cliff,^c
Let me see your form,
Let me hear your voice,
For your voice is sweet,
For your form is desirable."

Couple

¹⁵Catch foxes^d for us,
Little foxes who ruin vineyards,
Our vineyards are in bud.^e

Female

¹⁶My lover is mine,
And I am his,
He feeds^f among the lotuses.
¹⁷Until the day breezes gently along,^g
And the shadows flee,
Turn!
Become like a gazelle, my lover,
Or a young stag upon the mountains of Bether.^h
^{3:1}Nightly on my bed,ⁱ

a. The term, always in the plural construct (*ḥagwê*), occurs elsewhere only in the parallel passage of the indictment against Edom, Jer. 49:16 = Obad. 3. There as well it is in construct with *hassela^c* (the rock), which may itself be a term for the Edomite stronghold of Petra. In all cases it describes abodes high in mountainous terrain.

b. As a noun or adjective, *sēter* refers to secret places.

c. *Madrēgâ* occurs elsewhere only in the plural (Ezek. 38:20), where it is in parallel with walls and mountains. Aramaic and Arabic cognates of the root support the sense of "steps" or "terraces."

d. Alternatively, some suggest "jackals." Either meaning is possible.

e. See the discussion of this word in the third translation note at v. 13.

f. Although this expression (*hārō^ceh*) can refer to one who shepherds a flock or gives someone else something to eat, the context here is best served by the lover feeding himself.

g. The verbal root *pwḥ* refers to a gentle wind. Although it may be used to describe nightfall (Keel, *Song*, 115, whose attempt to compare Jer. 6:4 ignores the usage of a different verb there), it can also refer to the dawn, and that seems to be confirmed by the following line. As noted, at night the shadows gradually stretch out (*nṭh*; Pss. 102:12 [102:11 Eng.]; 109:23), whereas they flee before the morning sun (Fox, *Song*, 115; G. Carr, *Song*, 103).

h. The term *bāter* is much disputed, with several possible interpretations. See comments.

i. For some, the Hebrew plural for night (*lêlôt*) is a plural of composition or generalization, used with nouns of time to describe the sense of duration through the whole night rather than a group of nights (Pope, *Song*, 415; Snaith, *Song*, 46; Longman, *Song*, 128). Fox, *Song*, 118, disagrees, providing strong comparisons with other biblical poetry: Pss.

I have sought the one whom my heart loves,
I have sought him but I have not found him.[j]
[2]I will now arise,
I will search[k] the city,
In the streets and squares,
I will seek the one whom my heart loves,
I have sought him but I have not found him.
[3]The guards found me,
Those who go through the city,
"Have you seen the one whom my heart loves?"
[4]As soon as I left them,
I found the one whom my heart loves,
I caught him,
I would not release him,
Until I brought him to my mother's house,
To the chamber where she conceived me.
[5]I want you to promise,
O young women of Jerusalem,
By gazelles and does of the field,
Do not disturb,
Do not excite love,
Until it desires.

Interpretation

2:8–9   Female: Her lover pursues her

2:10–14   Male: Invitation to come away

2:15   Couple: Protect our love

2:16–17   Female: Love affirmed, gratification delayed

3:1–5   Female: Search and seizure

2:8–9. *Female: Her lover pursues her.* Verses 8–9 develop the structure
of the Hebrew text. On a larger level, 2:8–17 begin with mountains, ga-

---

16:7; 92:3 (92:2 Eng.); 134:1. He suggests that this indicates how the female has spent
many nights yearning for her lover. Now she decides to do something about her desire. A
similar translation may be applied to this plural form in v. 8. Cf. Garrett, *Song*, 397.

    j. The LXX adds *ekalesa auton, kai ouch hypēkousen mou*, "I called him, but he did
not answer me." Cf. 5:6.

    k. The Polel stem of *sbb* is used here in contrast with the Qal of *sbb* in the second line
of v. 3. Whether the difference is one of greater intensity with the Polel (Krinetzki, *Hohe
Lied*, 143–44; Murphy, *Song*, 145) may be disputed. However, it certainly describes greater
intentionality. The same verb and stem are used of dogs who prowl about the city at night
(Ps. 59:7, 15 [59:6, 14 Eng.]).

zelle, and stag, and they end with gazelle, stag, and mountains.[1] Verses 8–9 begin with an introductory note about the sound or voice (*qôl*) of the male. The expectation is that what follows will be something heard. However, the audio portion of the text does not begin until v. 10. Instead, there is a parenthetical introduction in which the lover is seen to approach the female like an animal that moves rapidly across the terrain. Indeed, that is what happens in a series of verbs, actually participles. These forms can extend the action as an ongoing reality while additional verbs describe what is happening. In both verses an initial identification of the female's partner gives way to an introductory participle that describes the basic purpose of the action: "comes"/"stands." This is followed by two lines, each beginning with a participle, which express in a synonymous manner a picture of the male as a gazelle leaping and then remaining motionless: "leaping"/"springing" and "standing"/"peering." This parallelism and the overall structure serve to emphasize the approach of the female's partner and her eager anticipation for his coming. She longs for his voice, but before she can hear it she witnesses his approach.

> ^{2:8}The sound of my lover.
> See! He comes,
> Leaping over the mountains,
> Springing over the hills.

Verse 8 begins with the mention of the sound of the lover. However, this focus almost immediately shifts as the female desires to look and see his coming. Nevertheless, the whole of vv. 8 and 9 are introductory, expressing her anticipation of the male's approach and the joy of the visual contact that is made before speech begins. The expression "he comes" is a simple single-syllable assertion (*bāʾ*) that the figure is coming and not drawing back. He is on his way, and the economy of language in the use of this one word of a single syllable expresses the initial explosion of joy in his first appearance in the distance. This gives way to a two-line description of the male's approach. The descriptions of leaping and bounding suggest one who acts more like the fastest of animals in his approach rather than like an ordinary human. This is in the eye of the female, who sees his approach as one of eagerness, like her own, eagerness for physical love. This form of "leap" (*dlg*, Piel stem) occurs three times elsewhere in the Bible. In the parallel texts 2 Sam. 22:30 and Ps. 18:30 (18:29 Eng.) it is used in the military context of scaling a wall. However, Isa. 35:6 has the closest parallel: "Then the lame will leap like a deer" (NIV). This forms a commentary on its usage in Song

---

1. Tournay, "Abraham," 550n22; Murphy, *Song,* 140.

2:8. It describes the opposite of immobility and the inability to walk. The leaping is more than walking or movement; it is the embodiment of physical skill and beauty in physical movement. This is what the female appreciates.

> [9]My lover is like a gazelle,
> Or a young stag.
> See! He stands behind our wall,
> Staring through the windows,
> Peering through the lattice.

Verse 9 begins with a word that describes a comparison: "is like" (*dômeh*). It resembles the sound of the second word, "my lover" (*dôdî*). This participle also indicates the simile between the female's lover and the gazelle or young stag, whose actions have already been pictured. Hence this forms the center of vv. 8–9. It connects the leaping and bounding of v. 8 with the peering and gazing of v. 9. Both are depicted according to the animals identified here. The law allowed the gazelle (*ṣĕbî*) to be hunted and its meat to be consumed (Deut. 12:15, 22; 14:5; 15:22). It was served at King Solomon's table (1 Kings 5:3 [4:23 Eng.]) and formed the prime example of a hunted animal (Isa. 13:14; Prov. 6:5). Although it is mentioned only about ten times in the Bible, this animal formed a favorite subject in the personal, glyptic art of stamp and cylinder seals of Palestine during the period of the monarchy. In fact, as the depictions of human figures diminished, the use of animals, and above all the gazelle, increased. Found on other Palestinian art as well, the gazelle may have represented grace and beauty of form as well as a freedom of spirit. Along with the other two occurrences of gazelle in the Song (2:17; 8:14), this occurrence pairs the animal with the fawn of deer (*ʿôper hāʾayyālîm*). Only in the Song is this description used. Its masculine gender invites the translation "young stag." These are two types of animals with power, grace, and beauty. They relate to the action of v. 8 and also possess skills and quiet and stealth, enabling them to approach someone without being detected and to stare at them. This portrays the events of v. 9.

Unable to pass over the wall or to enter into the house, the stag remains outside, his attention fixed on the activities and people within. The term for "wall" (*kōtel*) occurs elsewhere to describe the walls of a palace or temple.[2] Here as well, in parallel with the window and lattice, it identifies the wall of an individual house rather than the defenses of a city. Thus the lover pauses outside his partner's house. Presumably this

2. Although it is a hapax legomenon in Hebrew, it occurs in the Aramaic of Dan. 5:5; Ezra 5:8.

is the house of the female's family, certainly her parents, and therefore the "our." While the complete cessation of motion contrasts nicely with the leaping and bounding of v. 8, there is more. This period of rest allows the lover to stare into the house. The unusual term for "look" (*šgḥ*) elsewhere describes the intent stare of the dead, who are amazed at the fate of Babylon's king (Isa. 14:16), and God's watching over the world (Ps. 33:14). The stare is a fixed one. This idea is repeated in the last parallel phrase of Song 3:9 with a participle and noun that are both unique to this verse in Biblical Hebrew. The noun for "lattice" (*haḥărakkîm*) is so used in postbiblical Hebrew.[3] The picture is one of the lover, like a buck, staring with fixed eyes toward the beauty of his beloved. However, one other structural element in these two verses must not be overlooked. In vv. 8 and 9, before the participle describing the male's activity (coming, standing), there is the interjection "Look!" (*hinnēh*). Translated by some as "Now" (Fox, *Song*) or "Lo" (Pope, *Song*), this particle reminds the reader/listener that the admiration is reciprocal. While the female's vision of her lover is the focus in v. 8, it should not be forgotten in v. 9. There the male gazes toward her, but she sees him, and he is aware of her view. Other than the lattice, the window would have no glass or anything else to obscure her gaze. Instead, there is here the possibility for the lovers to gaze upon one another without barrier or distance. The loving admiration adds to the sense of sight, already expressed by both in this chapter, the longing gaze into the eyes and soul of each. However, it is not fully realized because, as v. 14 will suggest, the male cannot fully see the form of his partner.

2:10–14. *Male: Invitation to come away.* This section, in which the male speaks, begins with a comment by the female introducing his words. This is the first such introduction in the book. Although there have been changes of speaker before, these have been signaled by the alteration of the gender of verbs, nouns, and pronouns. Why is the change of speaker explicitly stated here? The reader/listener is not directly told, but the reason may have to do with the first word in the Hebrew, "he responded" (*ʿānāh*). Although the sense of this verb can convey speaking, it also carries the idea of responding to someone. That sense is stronger in this verb than in the other customary expressions of speaking, saying, or telling (e.g., Qal of *ʾmr*, Piel of *dbr*, Hiphil of *ngd*). The lover's remarks are a response to the observations of his partner. Responses have appeared before, as in 2:1–3, where each verse contains an explicit verbal parallel to the preceding one as the two lovers interact. In this case, however, what follows has no such parallels. Instead, the voice of the male bids the female to follow him. Hence the action that has begun

---

3. Pope, *Song*, 392.

in v. 8 may continue, but now with the two of them. The introductory comment of the female makes this connection explicit in a manner that the previous unstated shifts did not.

> [10]My lover responds, saying to me:
> "Arise,
> My darling, my beauty,
> Come!

The single item that ties together the ten words constituting v. 10 is the suffix -*î*. It appears attached to six of the ten words. Four times it forms the first-person common singular pronominal suffix "my," as in "my lover, to me, my darling, my beauty." Twice it refers to the feminine singular imperative, "Arise! Come!" These latter forms occur as the fifth and ninth words, thus forming an equal distribution throughout the verse. By repeating the identical vowel sounds of these two imperatives, the effect of the verse is to tie together the couple. The same is reinforced since this is the first verse where both the female and the male speak in turn. Thus the two are bound together on a level of sound as well as content.

As the translation suggests, the words of the male in this verse form a grammatical chiasm. The two commands begin and end his words. In between are the two words that designate his lover with affection and compassion, "My darling, my beauty." This refrain will recur in v. 13, word for word. It marks the boundaries to the invitation and the pastoral picture occupying the intervening lines. After reflecting upon the many poetic structuring devices, Watson comments that the dominant technique is the overall alternating pattern of tricolon-couplet-tricolon-couplet-tricolon:[4]

> [10]My lover responds, saying to me:

tricolon:	"Arise,
	My darling, my beauty,
	Come!
couplet:	[11]Look! The winter has passed,
	The rains are over and done with.
tricolon:	[12]The blossoms have appeared in the land,
	The time of song has arrived,

4. Watson, *Classical*, 369.

	The cooing of the turtledove is heard in our land.
couplet:	[13]The fig tree ripens its young fruit, The vines blossom with fragrance.
tricolon:	Arise, My darling, my beauty, Come!

Additionally, the same verb, translated "Come!" and "are over,"[5] occurs in the first and last tricola and at the end of the first couplet (v. 11), where it marks the transition from winter to spring. At the center of this poem is the word for "song" (*zāmîr*), which can also mean "harvest."[6]

Called "the most beautiful song to nature in the Old Testament,"[7] vv. 10–13 provide a description of the natural world in which the lovers rejoice. The male's vivid description of this environment serves to entice the female to join him. However, in an unusual section in the whole of the Song, these verses omit any direct reference to the female, the male speaker, or their love. Instead, the "frames" ("arise, come") in vv. 10b and 13b leave no doubt that this is part of a larger picture with this focus. The repeated address of the male lover to his partner calls her to join him by emphasizing the suffix -*î*. As noted above, this alludes both to the male (first-person singular suffix) and to the female (second-person feminine singular imperative). It is their union that the commands to arise and come seek to fulfill.[8] It is their union that the expressions of endearment "my darling, my beauty" seek to affirm. The verbs are ordinary ones found throughout the Bible. The key is their chiastic formation with the repeated suffix -*î*. In between these commands lie the two expressions of endearment. Again, these are not new. The male has identified his lover as "my darling" three times before (1:9, 15; 2:2). It is his most characteristic epithet for her. The adjective "beautiful" (*yāpāh*) has also appeared earlier. It occurs twice in the mutual admiration that the male and female exchange in 1:15 and 1:16 and a third time in an earlier address of the male (1:8). The combination of these two terms

---

5. *Hlk* plus *lāmed* preposition.

6. See the second translation note at 2:12 and the discussion of Gordon's Janus parallelism.

7. Rudolph, *Hohe Lied*, 134; English translation from Murphy, *Song*, 140.

8. Cf. Blutting, "Go," for a comparison of the charge to "come" in vv. 10 and 13 with Abram's command to depart in Gen. 12:1. She views Song 2:10 as a kind of reversal of the experience of Sarah when placed in seclusion by the pharaoh in the same chapter of Genesis. Although the principle of seclusion there and here in the Song may be compared, of greater interest is the connection of these two texts as part of Israel's experience. Cf. also Tournay, "Abraham."

occurring in 1:15 will appear again (4:1, 7; 6:4). The male lover is not creating new expressions but using customary addresses of love to frame his description of the place where he wishes his lover to join him. In calling her, he provides the means by which he wishes it to happen.

> [11]Look!
> The winter has passed,
> The rains are over and done with.

Verse 11 begins the description of the sensual beauty to which the male wishes to entice his partner. The opening lines that constitute 2:11 affirm that the period of remaining indoors has ended. The initial *kî hinnēh* suggests that all that follows provides the reason for the male's call to his lover to come out. It also directs her attention to look, in this case neither at the male nor at their love, but at the beauty that the outdoors provides. The cold and rain of the winter months have now gone. No longer need one remain inside. No longer does one go out only because of necessity. Now the warm sun of the summer has come. The picture here assumes the climate of Palestine, in which there are two primary seasons during the year: the summer with its heat and dryness, and the winter with its showers, storms, and cold. The latter lasts from October to March, and then the summer begins. There is no autumn or spring, because the appearance and disappearance of precipitation provide the main markers for the two seasons. Thus the male lover declares null and void any former reasons that would have kept the lovers from a rendezvous in the fields and forests. He explains that the period of mourning and separation has ended. On a symbolic level, the lover may here suggest that the couple have now fallen in love, and so all that went before was cold and without joy. Now that has ended and their love begins the early summer with all that the following verses will describe. They were dead; now they can become alive.

> [12]The blossoms have appeared in the land,
> The time of song has arrived,
> The cooing of the turtledove is heard in our land.

Verse 12 continues the structure of v. 11. There is a definite noun followed by a perfect form of the verb in all three lines. The first and third lines add a preposition (*bêt*) followed by "the land/our land" (*hāʾāreṣ/ʾarṣēnû*). The first and third lines describe events that occur naturally and are therefore beyond human control: "appear"/"is heard."[9]

9. Both are Niphal verb stems.

Nevertheless, each line appeals to the senses: seeing the blossoms, hearing the song, and listening to the sound of doves. Only in the springtime do these events occur. With the warmer weather, the rains of the winter leave behind carpets of beautiful wild flowers in the desert as well as on the sown land. The songs mentioned may include a variety of human activities: harvesting the barley and later the wheat crops, celebrating the Passover and the Feast of Unleavened Bread, and simply rejoicing in the pleasant weather.[10] However, the following line indicates that the singing must include birds, especially doves (or turtledoves) that pass through the region in the spring. The atmosphere is enticing to the female lover, who may experience release. Outside is a world of color and music. Indeed, with the second line the male implies that this scene is interactive. The lovers can join in the song of nature and rejoice in God's abundant creation. The sensual nature of this description is compounded by the observation that each of the items mentioned is seeking and achieving fruitfulness. The blossoms of the flowers suggest their generation of new life. The cooing of doves in the spring hints at lovers calling to one another and finding a partner.

> [13]The fig tree ripens its young fruit,
> The vines blossom with fragrance.
> Arise,
> My darling, my beauty,
> Come!

The theme of fruitfulness continues into the following verse (2:13). Figs produce several crops each year: the first is in June. Later harvests occur in August and September.[11] The scene here would take place during the month or two before the first harvest. The fig's high sugar content and the unusual sweetness of the June harvest add to the picture of fruitfulness suggested by the lover. The vines in the vineyards also appear with blossoms and give off a sweet aroma. These buds or blossoms appear in April or May, with the ripening of the grape occurring in June and July.[12] The mature grape is harvested in August and September. As with the fig, the picture describes a time during the spring or early

10. Ehrlich, *Randglossen*, and others are too restrictive when they suggest that the song (*zāmîr*) can be found only in cultic contexts. Among the mere seven occurrences of this noun, Isa. 25:5 is certainly not a reference to a cultic song—"the song of the ruthless." Cf. also Job 35:10; Lemaire, "*Zāmîr*"; and the Gezer Calendar (e.g., Shea, "Song").

11. King and Stager, *Life*, 104. See Müller, "Menschen," for a study of Song 2:8–14 within a third-century BC Palestinian context of hellenization and skepticism, all of which seems to reach beyond the clear statements of the text. Cf. also Talmon, "Prophetic."

12. Fox, *Song*, 113.

summer. This agrees with vv. 11 and 12. The winter is over, and the rains have brought fruitfulness to the land as it begins the dry season. The structure of the two lines in the first part of v. 13 follows the pattern of v. 12: a definite subject, describing fauna or flora, is followed by a verb (in the perfect aspect) and then an object. Unlike v. 12, where the verbs were passive (Niphal stem) and the "objects" described the location of the events, v. 13 uses active verbs to describe the production of fruitfulness. The objects further this by identifying what is produced and how it appeals to the senses: sweet fruit for eating or fragrant blossoms to tantalize the sense of smell. Thus the verses betray a movement in the type of descriptions. Whereas v. 12 emphasizes sights and sounds that can be seen and heard at a distance, v. 13 invites a closer inspection of taste and smell that can come only when the lover leaves the indoors and joins her beloved in the fields of nature and fruit.

The second part of v. 13 repeats the second part of v. 10. The refrain forms an inclusion that calls to the female to join her lover in the fields and forests, which are the mountains and hills of v. 8. The male has thus made his appeal, this time addressing all of his lover's senses and gently repeating words of endearment as he invites her to come away. The whole of these verses ends as it has begun, with the male's invitation, "Arise! Come!" This is the invitation of love that the male makes. It has a powerful significance that calls beyond that of young lovers.[13]

> 14My dove in the clefts of the rock,
> In the crags of the cliff,
> Let me see your form,
> Let me hear your voice,
> For your voice is sweet,
> For your form is desirable."

The first five words of Song 2:14 constitute two lines. The initial "my dove" (*yônātî*) forms the subject for both of them. This is followed in each case by a preposition and a phrase describing the location of the male's "dove."[14] This is the customary term for doves that inhabit Palestine.[15] Pope notes two places in Palestine that go by the term "Valley of the Doves."[16] One is northwest of the Dead Sea in the area of Jericho, and the other is northwest of the Sea of Galilee. Each may be described as a valley with steep sides filled with caves in which the doves live. Many

---

13. See further below under "Theological Implications."

14. In both cases, the preposition is *bêt*, and the phrase consists of two words in a construct relationship.

15. G. Carr, *Song*, 100, identifies the common rock dove (*Columba livia*).

16. Pope, *Song*, 400.

thousands of doves have been seen in one or the other of these sites in the premodern era. That such rocky clefts and crags formed the natural home for doves seems apparent from these illustrations. Of special interest is the connection of doves with mountain strongholds in Jer. 48:28: "Abandon your towns and dwell among the rocks, you who live in Moab. Be like a dove that makes its nest at the mouth of a cave" (NIV).

The use of the term "dove," a feminine noun, here symbolizes both the female and the concept of love. This resembles the symbolism of the dove in the Mediterranean world, in Mesopotamia, and elsewhere in ancient Palestine itself.[17] More even than form, beauty, and love, the context of parallel lines implies the inaccessible nature of the dove and therefore of the female lover. Although the female sees her male partner as coming close, for the male there remains an inaccessible wall and stronghold into which he cannot go to find his princess. This is clear in the second half of v. 14.

Verses 10–13 formed the plea of the male lover for his partner to come away with him. Here, however, he moves away from that request to one in which he desires to hear her voice, to see her visage. The location of this request at the end of his address suggests that he has not abandoned hope that his partner will leave her home and join him. Instead, it suggests that, having made his plea and being unable to reach her, he now wishes her to show herself and make her response known. Phrased in poetic language, the male lover speaks in terms of desire and love for his partner. This is nevertheless a call for her to respond to him. The structure is one of two lines of synonymous parallelism followed by the same again. In order the lines describe form, voice, voice, form. Thus they demonstrate a chiastic construction already noted in the refrains of vv. 10 and 13, as well as elsewhere. The first two lines begin with "show me/tell me."[18] A following noun identifies what is to be shown: "your form/your voice."[19] "Because" (kî, a causal particle) introduces the last two lines, each comprised of two words: "your voice [is] sweet"/"your form [is] desirable."[20] The word for "sweet" (ʿārēb) also occurs in Prov. 20:17: "Food gained by fraud tastes sweet to a man, but he ends up with a mouth full of gravel" (NIV). The term "desirable" (nāʾweh) appeared in 1:5 as the female's description of herself. Here it is the last word in the male's address. He hears his lover and he affirms

17. Ibid., 399–400.

18. Feminine singular imperatives (both in the Hiphil stem) and first-person common singular pronominal suffixes.

19. This is introduced with a direct object marker and has attached to it a second-person feminine singular suffix.

20. "Your voice" and "your form" are each a single word in Hebrew.

her. The emphasis here, as in v. 13, involves both auditory and visual imagery. The lover longs for the voice and form of his beloved.

> [15]Catch foxes for us,
> Little foxes who ruin vineyards,
> Our vineyards are in bud.

2:15. *Couple: Protect our love.* Verse 15 provides no hint as to whether it belongs to the male's previous address or should be part of the female's response. The former option seems out of character with either the descriptions of nature in the heart of the male's speech or the exhortations to his lover, which are filled with encouragement interspersed with terms of endearment ("my darling, my beauty").[21] Neither appears here. On the other hand, there is not a lot of similarity with what follows.[22] Although the female does exhort her lover to do something (v. 17), she does not address him in the plural as in the initial command in v. 15. In fact, the whole meaning of the verse is difficult. Nevertheless, the preferred option is to understand here metaphors for those who would threaten the couple and their love. Therefore, it seems best to attach this to the words of the couple, an intermezzo that both sing.[23]

The structure of this verse is of interest. There are three lines. Each line has a different subject and seems to carry the thought in a new direction. The structural tie is the manner in which the last word of each line forms the first word of the next line. Thus "foxes" (*šûʿālîm*) appears as the last word of the first line and the first word of the second.[24] The same is true with respect to "(our) vineyards" (*kĕrāmîm/kĕrāmênû*) for the second and third lines. The LXX ignores this structure, with only one occurrence of "foxes" (*alōpekas*). Fox cites examples from Egyptian love poems in which lustful lovers are designated as wolf cubs or jackals (Egyptian *wnš*), other possible meanings for the word here translated "foxes" (cf. Ezek. 13:4; Lam. 5:18).[25] It would fit the context here. In this picture, the couple pleads with those around them to restrain the young men and women from taking advantage of them and undermining their love. The vineyards represent the couple's love, a metaphor common enough in the Song (1:6; 7:13 [7:12 Eng.]; 8:12). The budding

---

21. Contra Snaith, *Song,* 41.

22. Contra Bergant, *Song,* 31; Murphy, *Song,* 139.

23. Fokkelman, *Reading,* 196.

24. For this first example, cf. Sivan and Yona, "Pivot Words," 399. This phenomenon is also known as anadiplosis.

25. Fox, *Song,* 114. Cf. the images in Keel (*Song,* 109–10) and Fox (*Song,* 10), where the female describes her lover in this manner: "My heart is not yet done with your lovemaking, my (little) wolf cub!"

and blossoming of the vineyard portrays fruitfulness in the spring or early summer, as noted in 2:13. The symbolic meaning of the relationship between the lovers suggests a preparedness for sexual relations. The vineyard is a metaphor for the female's body as well as a picture of their union of love. Their mutual desire to share their love with one another is expressed by the use of "our." This is a powerful statement about the need to protect the love that the lovers possess.[26] Those in romantic relationships know all too well how quickly a relationship can be upset, especially by interlopers. There is no certain solution, but it makes a great deal of difference if the couple together pledge to come against any attempt to interfere with that relationship, and then make this a public declaration.

> [16]My lover is mine,
> And I am his,
> He feeds among the lotuses.

2:16–17. *Female: Love affirmed, gratification delayed.* The expression "my lover is mine and I am his" occurs only here, although related expressions using "I am my lover's" (*ʾănî lĕdôdî*) occur in 5:6; 6:3; and 7:11 (7:10 Eng.). Song 6:3 preserves the inverse of this statement: "I am my lover's and my lover is mine." These first four words of 2:16 divide into two lines of three full syllables each (not counting the *wāw* connective). The female expresses her love in a simple but elegant statement that defines the relationship as one of commitment and possession of each other. Each of the first three words ends with the same long vowel (*-î*). This vowel sound expresses the first-person singular possessive suffix ("my"), as it does in the first two words. The third word is the first-person singular pronoun, "(and) I." To this point the emphasis of the female's declaration focuses upon her possession of

---

26. Murphy, *Song*, 141, describes the verse as a "tease" in which the female sings a popular poem both to answer the male's request to hear her voice and to seek mock protection against the "threat" of aggressive males, especially her own lover (cf. Fox, *Song*, 114). The teasing nature of this is established by the "provocative" (so Keel, *Song*, 110) last line that invites him to know she is ready for his love. The first-person common plural "us" is difficult here and without an obvious connection to the larger context. This is not a "strategy of last resort" (Longman, *Song*, 124), nor does it seem that the foxes represent general obstacles rather than aggressive males (Budde, *Hohelied*). However, there is no marking or other indication in the Song that a quoted poem has been inserted, and the first-person common plural pronouns are retained without indication as to whom they might refer. Instead, the couple can use the imagery to express a common concern, as suggested here. Rather than a "tease," the final line asserts both the reality of the threat from outside the love that the couple enjoys as well as the implicit temptation to which the couple is physically (if not psychologically) capable of succumbing.

her partner.[27] Only with the last word does it become clear that the intent is to balance the relationship with the affirmation of mutual possession of one another in love. The picture of feeding among the lotuses is that of a deer or other caprid munching on these beautiful flowers. Yet the direct connection that the verse makes between the female's lover and the one who feeds among the lotuses prepares the reader/listener to associate the lover with the act of feeding.[28] The image of a lotus has already been used of the female, in the self-identification of 2:1 and the simile of 2:2. The plural is applied to the female in 4:5, where her breasts feed among the lotuses; and in 6:2, where the male goes to gather lotuses among the spice beds. The association is not yet clear, but the image of the male feeding among the lotuses is one of his physical relationship to the female.[29]

> [17]Until the day breezes gently along,
> And the shadows flee,
> Turn!
> Become like a gazelle, my lover,
> Or a young stag upon the mountains of Bether.

As used in 2:17, "until" carries a sense of time.[30] The picture of a gently blowing breeze could signal the beginning or the end of the day. The fleeing of the shadows, however, describes the morning. The sudden appearance of the sun brings to an end all the shadows; light replaces darkness. The image of lovemaking remains just an image as the female now addresses her partner. She utters one request in contrast to the many requests that he has given her in vv. 10–14: "arise," "come out," "show me," "let me hear." Her response is "turn" (sōb). This term uses a root that by itself cannot mean "turn toward me" but must mean "turn away."[31] The four other occurrences of this same form all imply turning away from a previous course of action (cf. 1 Sam. 22:18; 2 Sam. 18:30).[32] Most revealing is the double usage in 2 Kings 9:18–19. Twice riders from the enemy approach Jehu as he rides to battle. In both cases he uses this command to persuade them to change sides and join him. Now in the Song the male has just finished addressing the female (2:14). His

27. See also Bergant, "My Beloved," for a reversal of customary categories of honor and shame at this point.
28. Contra Gerleman, *Hohelied*, 127–28, who sees here verbal decoration to create atmosphere.
29. Bergant, *Song*, 23; Longman, *Song*, 115.
30. Rudolph, *Hohe Lied*, 136: "When."
31. Although he opts for the opposite interpretation, Murphy, *Song*, 139, compares the parallel 8:14, where bĕraḥ (flee) replaces sōb.
32. Qal masculine singular imperative.

last position is that portrayed by a gazelle or a young buck who stares directly at the female (v. 9). Hence his turning requires that he leave the presence of the young woman (a presence where he may not yet be able to see her clearly, as v. 14 suggests) and go away. This seems contradictory to the remainder of the text. How will the young lovers enjoy one another? How will they consummate their physical love? Indeed, how will they protect it (v. 15)? The answer lies in the female's address to her lover at this point. In the midst of the passionate poetry, at the height of desire and longing, the female completes the poem of chapter 2 with the admonition to her lover to depart. She is not ready for his love, and he must await her own decision as to when she will appear.

The picture here is then completed by her repetition of the description of her lover in v. 8. There she spied him approaching her and described his coming as that of a gazelle or a young stag bounding over the mountains and hills. Here the same animals are mentioned. As a stag the male is to return to the mountains. Is he leaving for the present, or is this a metaphor that actually invites him to the female's sexual pleasures? The key lies with the final word: "Bether" (*bāter*). Pope's review of the possible interpretations, ancient and modern, tends to favor one of two options.[33] There is the suggestive "mountains of spices," in which the word is a kind of abbreviation for longer forms of Sanskrit and other derivations meaning "spices" (cf. Peshitta; Keel, *Song*, 115, 117). This also recognizes a parallel with 8:14. The second option identifies a physical description of the mountains as rugged, pocketed with openings (cf. LXX), or as a "cleft" in the mountains. This last term is Pope's translation and provides him with an opportunity to discuss in detail the female pudenda and the way in which this image is appropriate. However, this is not the likeliest meaning for the word. The ancient versions of Aquila, Symmachus, and the Vulgate (as well as the KJV) all understood this as a proper noun used to describe a mountainous area to the southwest of Jerusalem. Bar Kochba identified a village, Beitar, eleven kilometers from the capital city, and it is mentioned in the LXX addition to Josh. 15:59. Fox summarizes this evidence, noting that gazelles are visible in this area even in the present day.[34] The proximity to Jerusalem and the natural images that this term provides contribute to the suggestion

33. Pope, *Song*, 409–11.

34. Fox, *Song*, 116. Because the Hebrew text was not originally vocalized, it is impossible to know for certain the vowels used to read this term when it was written. Therefore, attempts to deny any possible relationship between *btr* and the place-name suggested by the versions seem puzzling (cf. Murphy, *Song*, 139; Longman, *Song*, 126). Morfino, "Cantico," seeks to identify this and other terms in the Song with Abraham (Gen. 15:10; as the mountain where God met him and made a covenant with the patriarch), Isaac, David, Solomon, and other aspects of earlier biblical narratives.

that this is a place-name rather than an adjective. Thus, as the female beheld her lover coming from this direction, so she admonishes him to return and to await the coming of a new day for their love.

How can it be that in the midst of passion and pictures of erotic love, the female should send her lover away? The full explanation must await the completion of the Song. However, she is not ready to participate with her partner in a time of amorous pleasure, despite her strong feelings for him. One therefore suspects that lovemaking is anticipated but not yet consummated. Instead, the poetry, with all its suggestive imagery, awaits fulfillment at a future time. This picture of delayed gratification challenges all who would see this book either as a biblical license for free sex or as a manual for a successful marriage. It is neither, although it may have insight for marriage. It is erotic love poetry that makes no apology for appealing to all of the senses that God has created. Yet it also affirms that there is an order to this wonderful gift of sex. Its potency and wildness does not mean that there is no restraint.

3:1–5. *Female: Search and seizure.* The first line of 3:1–5 sets the initial place and time. Structurally, the first four verses are linked by an action on the part of the female that is then identified as seeking "the one whom my heart loves." This is followed in the first two verses by a failure to find him, stated explicitly. The third verse brings her no closer to her goal, and the beginning of v. 4 indicates that her mission was not yet successful. In v. 4 she finds him. The second half of that verse completes the action in which she takes her lover to her mother's bedroom. The first four verses are linked by the repetition of "the one whom my heart loves." As the key object of each of these verses, its frequent appearance acts as a refrain, drawing the reader/listener back again and again to the object of the female's search. The verb introducing this phrase in vv. 1 and 2 is "I sought/seek" (*biqqaštî/ʾăbaqšâ*). It identifies the pursuit. The failure to find is reported in these verses with the same verb (*māṣāʾ*) that recurs in vv. 3–4. Although its usage in v. 3 appears to be irrelevant to the purpose (the guards find the female instead of the male), it announces by its first position in the verse that a change has taken place. Indeed, it is directly from this encounter that the female goes on to find her lover. Thus the front or first position of the verb "to seek" in vv. 1–2 introduces the reader/listener to the chief purpose of the narrative: the quest. Its double appearance, twice in v. 1 and twice in v. 2, further gives it prominence.[35] The final position and negative marker on the verb "to find" in vv. 1–2 may lead one to discount the significance of this action. Yet it emerges as key in vv. 3 and 4 and ultimately serves

35. Elliott, *Literary*, 79, notes that the repetition of the initial *bêt* in the midst of v. 2 emphasizes the intensity of the search.

as the only other verb, in addition to "love," to occur in all four verses. Thus the fourfold occurrence of each of the verbs—seek, love, find—and their sequence cooperate to mark the themes and general movement of the narrative. The seeking without finding gives way to finding, and all has as its source and goal "the one whom my heart loves," a phrase that remains constant and unchanged throughout the story.[36]

> [3:1]Nightly on my bed,
> I have sought the one whom my heart loves,
> I have sought him but I have not found him.

If there is a chronological sequence to be followed from the preceding chapter, then one may assume that the male lover's previous appearance on one spring evening leads to the exchange and his departure. That night the female longs for his presence beside her upon her bed. What is expected here? The nouns "bed" (*miškāb*) and "night" (*laylâ*) occur together elsewhere only in 2 Sam. 4:7, where the treacherous murder of Ish-Bosheth is described, and in Job 33:15, where a nightmare is described. In neither case is there any sexual intent. Thus, although the Song is a work of an erotic nature, by themselves these nouns do not require that the female is seeking sexual relations with her lover in bed at night. Indeed, the expectation that she should find her lover in bed with her contradicts the previous verse (2:17) where she sends him away. Instead, the opening line of 3:1 suggests that she cannot sleep because of the feverish excitement of longing for her lover, wherever he might be. Nevertheless, the direct connection with the rest of the verse suggests a search for her lover on her bed and around her. It may be that she expects him to return or wishes for it. Or it may even be that, as she would doze occasionally and then awake, her dreams of desire mingle with her hope to see her lover in reality.[37] It is this desire that sends her out into the night in a search for him. The repeated statement that "I sought (him)," like the plural form of "night" in the first line, defines an extraordinary intensity to her yearning and desire.[38] It is only because she is driven in such a way that she would venture out into the dangerous

36. Contrast this with the seeking and finding that yields no satisfaction; Fox and Porten, "Unsought."

37. Murphy, *Song*, 145, concurs: "One cannot be sure if this is a dream." Many see the whole passage as a dream: Krinetzki, *Hohe Lied*, 141; Würthwein, "Hohelied," 48; Rudolph, *Hohe Lied*, 155–56; Lys, *Plus beau*, 139. I do not. However, the focus of desire, rather than success in the search, forms a theme that links the whole of the Song. Desire presents itself both awake and asleep, and this is suggested by the time (night) and the arousal to search beyond the place of sleep.

38. Keel, *Song*, 122, compares the use of this verb in Ps. 27:4; Jer. 2:33; 5:1. Cf. Bergant, *Song*, 34.

world of night in a city (v. 2). Thus the "search" upon her bed does not lead to finding her lover. He is not present, and neither anxious dreams nor fervent desire can bring him to her.

The periphrastic designation of the male partner as (lit.) "whom my soul loves" (*šeʾāhăbāh napšî*) occurs four times in this section, once in each of the first four verses. It thus serves as a key statement for understanding the female's motivation. The use of "soul" here is of interest. It can carry a variety of meanings, as discussed in detail by Wolff.[39] It can, of course, function as a pronoun (1 Kings 20:32) or refer to the more abstract life situation of a person (Exod. 23:9). However, it also conveys the sense of the life of a person, as in Lev. 17:11, where it is the "soul" (*nepeš*) of the person that is in the blood. This is fundamentally the desire for life. In Prov. 16:26 a worker's *nepeš*, like his (hungry) mouth, encourages him to work so that he will live. The term as used here seems to convey this sense of desire. The female's desire for her lover, equal in intensity to her desire to live, will cause her to go forth and seek him.

> ²I will now arise,
> I will search the city,
> In the streets and squares,
> I will seek the one whom my heart loves,
> I have sought him but I have not found him.

In v. 2 the female ventures into the city. Although the term for "city" (*ʿîr*) may refer to little more than a village, such is not the case here. The references to the daughters/young women of Jerusalem (1:5; 2:7; 3:5; 8:4) and to the mountains of Bether (2:17) suggest the capital as the scene for the events of this poem. In any case, the population center is large enough to possess streets and squares for people to gather, as well as a contingent on patrol through the night. The first three verbs—arise, search, seek—all have the same tense/aspect, that of a cohortative. This form indicates an intentional search, one that looks eagerly, holding nothing back: I *will* arise, I *will* search, I *will* seek. She intends to search through the streets and squares. The word for "streets" (plural of *šûq*) seems to occur only three other times with this meaning, in Prov. 7:8 and Eccles. 12:4, 5. It is a place where one might meet others, onto which one's house opens, and where mourners may be found. However, similar ideas may be covered by the noun "squares," a word that occurs some forty-three times in the Bible. Not only does the addition of "streets"

39. *Anthropology*, 10–25. The observations summarized here remain cogent despite the recognition of greater complexity to the overall issue of the "soul" and personal identity. See Di Vito, "Old Testament Anthropology."

balance the line; along with the *bêt* inseparable preposition it also is similar in sound to "seek," since both contain the consonants *b*, *q*, and *š*. Hence this preposition and noun combination link the female's search with the places where she searches.

The second half of Song 3:2, with the minor exception of the tense/aspect of the first verb, "seek," is a duplicate of the second half of v. 1. Although this may be a refrain, repeating the problem after the initial search of v. 1 and following the further search of v. 2, there is another possibility. It could be that these are envelope constructions, similar to "I" in 2:1 and 2:5, to 2:9a and 2:17b, and to 2:10b and 2:13b. If so, then the center, 3:2a, forms a description of the female lover's specific intention to search for her lover, while the surrounding statement of searching and not finding states in a general way the plan and its failure up to this point. In that case, v. 1a would be separated in thought from v. 1b. This would provide support to the bedroom scene as one of more generally seeking the lover rather than expecting him to be in her bed.

> ³The guards found me,
> Those who go through the city,
> "Have you seen the one whom my heart loves?"

In v. 3 the subject of the verbs suddenly changes from the female to the guards. These patrol the city at night and keep watch for any threat to its security (cf. Jer. 6:17). The use of these figures here is without prejudice. They will appear again in 5:7, where they beat the female. Their purpose here seems to be one of reinforcing the search that the female makes and to provide for the third appearance of the verb "find." In v. 3 is also a repetition of the verb "search/go (through)" (*sbb*), which the female declared she would do in v. 2. Thus the female need not search at length, for she relies upon the watchers to inform her of her lover. She asks them for information, but they appear to be silent. In fact, the absence of a response in this verse is intended as a response. The watchers have nothing to say because they have not seen the lover. They who should know all the news in the city have nothing to say that would assist the female in her quest. At this point the drama appears to have no resolution. There seems to be no way that the male can still be in the city. No one has seen him. Perhaps the female's pursuit is in vain. Yet the verbal structure, as noted above, hints that a resolution is coming. In v. 3, for the first time, there is no statement that the female does not find him. Instead, the verb "find" is used in a positive sense. As v. 4 shows, this anticipates a positive resolution to the female's search. In fact, it is literally just around the corner!

<blockquote>

[4]As soon as I left them,
I found the one whom my heart loves,
I caught him,
I would not release him,
Until I brought him to my mother's house,
To the chamber where she conceived me.

</blockquote>

Verse 4 carries forward the female's adventure. She has departed from the patrol. As soon as she leaves them, she comes upon the object of her search. Note the courage and daring implicit in the opening phrase of this verse. The expression (lit.) "I had passed over from/behind them" (*ʿābartî mēhem*) suggests that she does not at this point return to her home. The female has met the guardians of the city, and they have nothing to tell her. The reasonable thing to do would be to give up her search and return home, perhaps with their escort. However, her love and dedication will not allow this. She will go further, down the street, around the corner. Whatever the risk, she will not be deterred from the object of her desire. With this additional leap, brought about solely by her devotion to her lover, she finds her lover. How this speaks of love at every level: the devotion of the lover to the object of her desire.

It is this devotion that characterizes the female's search for her lover, a devotion that expresses itself through love at many levels. The love that the woman feels for her lover is expressed through seizing him and not releasing him (Song 3:4). The verb for seizing (*ʾḥz*) has already appeared at the beginning of 2:15 in describing the capture of the foxes. Here it is not an enemy who is captured, but the lover's determination is no less intense. The parallel expression conveys the intent in the opposite way: "I will not release him," using the root *rph*. This root is used by God in his promise to Israel and to Joshua never to forsake them or to let them go (Deut. 31:6, 8; Josh. 1:5). It has overtones of loyalty and faithfulness. This is what the female has sought and is prepared to give to the male. She seizes him in order to bring him to "the house of my mother." This expression appears only twice outside the Song. In Gen. 24:28 it describes the place to which Rebekah runs after first encountering Abraham's servant. It may indicate a special relationship between Rebekah and her mother or, more likely, the household of one of several wives of a single husband. Then in 24:67, Isaac takes Rebekah into the tent of his mother to marry her. When Naomi addresses her two daughters-in-law, she exhorts each to return to her mother's home. This occurrence in Ruth 1:8 suggests that the primary association of a young woman is with the house of her mother rather than her father. It may imply something similar to the

105

house of the father, in the sense of an extended family that includes all relatives. However, its exclusive use with reference to daughters, never sons, suggests a place where the daughter could go to find security and acceptance. As in Sumerian love poetry, the groom may normally enter the house of the bride's parents.[40] One additional item that the mother provides occurs in Song 8:2. There the female lover again speaks of leading her partner to her mother's house, describing it as either where "she taught me" or where "you [her lover] will teach me." Either is possible. In parallel with "house" (*bêt*) is the "room, chamber" (*ḥeder*, 3:4). However, it is not merely a simple parallelism. As has been the case throughout this section, there is a movement forward. Here the female seeks to move her lover from the house in general to the inner chamber of conception, the place of lovemaking.[41]

> [5]I want you to promise,
> O young women of Jerusalem,
> By gazelles and does of the field,
> Do not disturb,
> Do not excite love,
> Until it desires.

The fifth verse of this chapter repeats Song 2:7. The female again cautions her companions that they should not attempt to seek out and arouse love before the appropriate time. However, here it is surprising that this comes immediately after a picture of the female pulling her lover into her home and bed. Is this a complete disjunctive? Is there any relation between vv. 4 and 5? The answer lies in the understanding of the Song as a whole and in the structure of the Song in relation to 2:7 and 3:5. In fact, these verses appear as markers at the end of some of the longest, most active, and most intimate descriptions by the female. These markers guide the reader/listener through some of the major ideas and passions of the Song. Here the female's search culminates in a dramatic meeting and journey to her home. Her address to the daughters of Jerusalem follows immediately upon this sexually charged scene. Like 1:1–2:7, so 2:8–3:5 begins with the lovers apart and culminates with them united in an intimate relationship. As in 2:7 (cf. also 8:4) the poetry reaches a high point of erotic celebration and union

40. Longman, *Song*, 129, 131, referring to Sefati, *Love Songs*, 3–5, 104. Cf. Gen. 2:24.
41. Lundbom, "Song of Songs 3:1–4," compares this passage with Mary Magdalene's search for the body of Jesus and his subsequent promise to take her to his house (rather than she taking him to her house; suggested but not clear in John 20:18). The themes are similar, although it is difficult to remove the erotic element that is so obviously present in the Song and absent from John 20:11–18.

and then suddenly interrupts with a message of caution. The caution betrays not only the awareness of an element of control in this poem; it also suggests that the Song portrays a picture that itself is a fantasy, a poetic celebration of carnal love as a gift.

Theological Implications

Characteristically, the female introduces this section. Here she praises the male for his movement, a movement toward her that expresses his desire for her (2:8–9). The male's appeal looks forward to their love as to the blossoming of spring after the coldness of winter (2:10–14). With the new life comes a rush of desire, which the male expresses with an appeal to all the senses. In this manner, it resembles the opening statement of the female in 1:2–7. His request to his lover to arise and come forms an expression of this release and the central theme of the section. The desire creates the invitation of love, a desire to come close and unite. On each level of love in the Christian life, that invitation remains. The Christian family hears it as parents invite their children to follow them in their faith. His disciples hear it as Jesus calls them to greater commitment and dedication. The church hears it while following the Bridegroom. Christ heard the invitation of love and followed his Father, passing through death to the glorious resurrection of life. Did the poet have such symbolism in mind when he voiced these words? Certainly not in the fullness suggested here. However, the all-encompassing nature of love, love that is accessible to all humanity at the physical level, is not intended for this couple alone. Their physical and sexual love partakes of the greater reality of the One who is love. To affirm that love of partners in the poetry and images of this text is also to affirm love on all human and divine levels. In the words of the apostle, "Dear friends, let us love one another" (1 John 4:7, 11).

At this central climax of the section, the couple speaks together of the need to protect their love from any compromise (Song 2:15). In the midst of such affirmation of love, the female sends her lover away (2:16–17). She remains in love but unprepared to consummate that love. The fulfillment is yet to come. On one level, Christian ethics may see here a couple's love that, despite erotic elements, will remain unconsummated until marriage. On another level, delayed gratification describes an important principle of the disciple's life (Rom. 12:1–2; James 4:7).

Despite the female's statements to drive away her lover, her desire has not abated (Song 3:1–5). Unfulfilled passion drives her from her bed to seek her lover and find him. Yet the nocturnal context and the musings or dreams of the female upon her bed suggest a fantasy. The section concludes with the same refrain as that of its predecessor (2:7). This expression of restraint parallels the female's own delay in consummation of their love. As with sexual love, the consummation of God's love for his people follows a similar principle—it achieves its final goal of true union with God in a life beyond this world.

The search that represents the female's devotion to her lover brings to mind the command to love God with all one's heart in Deut. 6:5, one of two commands that summarize the law according to the words of Jesus (Matt. 22:37; Mark 12:30, 33; Luke 10:27). Similarly, the apostle Paul encouraged Christians to work with all their hearts as to the Lord (Col. 3:23). However, it is in the promises of God to his people that this search finds its closest match. Thus Jer. 29:13: "You will seek me and find me when you seek me with all your heart" (NIV). This itself recalls the wonderful promise of God at the beginning of the giving of the Deuteronomic law: "But if from there you seek the LORD your God, you will find him if you look for him with all your heart and with all your soul" (4:29 NIV).

IV.
Love and Marriage
at the Heart of the Song
(3:6–5:1)

Translation

Male

³:⁶Who is this[a] ascending from the desert,
Like columns[b] of smoke,
Perfumed[c] with myrrh and frankincense,
The best of all the powders of the merchants?
⁷Look! It is Solomon's palanquin,[d]

a. Zō'ṭ is a feminine singular demonstrative. Thus this would seem to indicate a female, despite the objection that this form could be translated as a neutral "what?" (Longman, *Song*, 133). See Murphy, *Song*, 149. However, as Murphy notes, 8:5 asks the same two-word question, and there the female is clearly intended as the answer. Cf. Fox, *Song*, 119; Keel, *Song*, 126. Dirksen, "Song of Songs iii 6–7," examines the usage of *mî* as "what?" and observes that it is rare. The question asked is, "Who is coming?" The implied response is, "The bride cannot be seen, but look at the entourage."

b. Keel, *Song*, 126–27, likens this noun (*tîmārâ*) to the date palm tree (*tāmār*) as a symbol of royal splendor. This would provide a common root that could signify something vertical and tall. Dahood, "Hebrew," proposes a derivation from Akkadian *amāru* (to see), but that is unnecessary.

c. *Měquṭṭeret* is the only Pual stem form of the verbal root *qṭr*. Its use as a feminine singular construct participle suggests that its subject must be the only previous feminine singular noun, or in this case, a demonstrative, "this" (zō'ṭ).

d. *Miṭṭâ* refers only to a bed or a place of lying down. Thus NIV's "carriage" is not adequate. Although as here it could be portable, the contexts show that this noun must be translated as something where one lies down, not where one sits to ride. Compare the other occurrences of this noun in the poetic books: Ps. 6:7 (6:6 Eng.); Prov. 26:14. The word has a third-person masculine singular suffix that is anticipatory: "his palanquin, that is, Solomon's."

Sixty warriors surround it,
From the warriors of Israel.
[8]All of them skilled with a sword,[a]
Experienced in battle,
Each with his sword at his side,
Because of the nightly terrors.[b]
[9]A[c] litter[d] did King[e] Solomon make for himself,
From the wood of Lebanon.
[10]Its posts he made of silver,
Its underpart[f] of gold,
Its seat of purple,
Its interior lovingly[g] inlaid[h]

a. Lit., "seized by a sword." See comments.

b. A plural noun as in 3:1. See the discussion there.

c. Keel, *Song*, 130, insists that vv. 9–10 are not spoken by anyone but are an objective account, the only one in the Song. This itself should give pause to such a theory. Given the previous verses, both their context as well as that of the whole Song, this probably forms part of the male's delivery. Nevertheless, it may be from a different period than the remainder of the text, as some of the vocabulary may imply.

d. *ʾAppiryôn* possibly derives from the Greek *phoreion* (Rundgren, "*ʾprywn*"), as the LXX translates. Putative Sanskrit and other derivations are possible but involve the presence of additional consonants. The derivation may have come indirectly through Aramaic or Phoenician. However, the earliest attestation of *phoreion* coming from a third-century BC Greek author does not guarantee a terminus a quo for the Song. Gerleman, *Hohelied*, 139, derives it from Egyptian *pr* (house) and translates "throne room." See also Fox, *Song*, 125–26, who translates "canopied bed." Görg, "Sänfte Salomos," hypothesizes a Hamito-Semitic root *pry* (to appear), which would also fit the context.

e. Longman (*Song*, 134, 137) and G. Carr (*Song*, 111) break the line between "King" and "Solomon" to allow for a greater balance between the two.

f. *Repîdâ*, a hapax legomenon, could refer to the back (LXX and Vulgate; G. Carr, *Song*, 112), the top (Gerleman, *Hohelied*, 139; Murphy, *Song*, 149; Munro, *Spikenard*, 58), or the bottom (cf. Fox, *Song*; Falk, *Love*) of the palanquin. In light of the root *rpd* (to support), this may be best understood as the underpart of the litter that supports the rest. Görg, "Sänfte Salomos," suggests the Egyptian *rpw.t*, which refers to the sacred palanquin or canopy that housed the image of a goddess when carried in procession. As Görg admits, however, this normally referred to the image of the statue itself rather than the covering.

g. The unusual usage of *ʾahăbâ* (love) as an adverbial accusative (cf. Elliott, *Literary*, 88) in a context where it adds little to the interpretation of the text has led to the emendation *hobnîm* (ebony; Graetz, *Shir*, followed by others, including Gerleman, *Hohelied*, 139, 142; Pope, *Song*, 445). However, none of the versions supports this emendation. While difficult, in the context of love songs the use of a term for "love" is not unexpected. G. Driver's theory ("Supposed"; Grossberg, "Canticles 3:10," interprets a double entendre, "leather" and "love") that the noun *ʾahăbâ* should be rendered "leather" here lacks contextual support and seems unnecessary. Less likely is Barbiero, "Liebe," who combines the last two lines for the interior as "decorated with the love of the daughters of Jerusalem." Gerleman (*Hohelied*, 140) and Fox (*Song*, 126–27) unnecessarily emend the text to *ʾăbānîm* (stones). Cf. LXX *lithostrōton*, "(stone) pavement" or "mosaic."

h. *Rāṣûp* occurs only here. The root is known from Akkadian, where *raṣāpu* means "to layer, to erect structures." Less persuasive is Provan, "Terrors," 153–54, who cites three

By[i] the daughters of Jerusalem.
[11]Come out and see,
Daughters of Zion,
King Solomon,
With the crown,
That his mother crowned him,
On the day of his wedding,[j]
On[k] the day his heart rejoiced.
[4:1]Look at you, so beautiful, my darling!
Look at you, so beautiful,
Your eyes are doves
From behind your veil,[l]
Your hair is like the flock of goats
That descend in waves[m] from Mount Gilead.

---

occurrences of a possibly related noun, *rispâ*, as referring to the paved floor of a temple or palace (2 Chron. 7:3; Esther 1:6; nor does its contextual meaning refer to a room at all [Isa. 6:6]). He also notes that the common word for "posts" in the preceding line refers only to a fixed structure, even though he admits that it can describe columns of smoke. On the basis of these two terms he argues that v. 10 depicts a room inside Solomon's palace. But three occurrences of one word (and not one that is identical to the form used here) and a common noun that has some variety in its usage do not seem to demonstrate the case Provan attempts to make.

i. This accepts the MT, where the *mêm* of *min* is attached to the "daughters of Jerusalem." Cf. LXX, *apo thygaterōn Ierousalēm*. Pope (*Song*, 446) and Murphy (*Song*, 150) suggest an enclitic *mêm* attached to the preceding word. They translate the "daughters of Jerusalem" as a vocative. This has no versional support. Murphy's resultant chiastic construction with "daughters of Zion" in v. 11 seems forced and unnecessary. Keel, *Song*, 134, opts for the same emendation but claims the *mêm* as the plural marker to allow a translation "inlaid with [scenes] of love." Setting aside the question of where the *yôd* went (in a text not known for defective writing), there remains the observation that this translation of the plural form of "love" has no parallel. Proverbs 7:18, the only text cited by Keel in support, requires no such translation ("joys of love") for the plural because the "joy" is in the verb of that proverb: "Let's enjoy ourselves with love!" (NIV).

j. Although the root *ḥtn* (to marry, intermarry) is known throughout the Bible, this particular noun form for marriage (*ḥătunnâ*) occurs only here. It is found in later Hebrew, but it also occurs in a Late Bronze Age letter from Taanach as *ḥatnūtu*. The fact that its one early association is with a second-millennium BC form no more proves an early date for the Song than does the late appearance of the Greek cognate of "bed" (*ʾappiryôn*).

k. The initial *wāw* is pleonastic, so Gordis, *Song*, 86; Murphy, *Song*, 150.

l. Based on a diverse reading of the versions, Garbini, *Cantico*, 69–72, 152–53, reads this line as *mbʿd lšytk* (from upon your hips). The whole reconstruction of 4:1–7, involving the interpolation of parts of 6:4–5, remains speculative.

m. Tuell, "Riddle," argues for this translation by demonstrating a Ugaritic cognate, *glt*. Longman, *Song*, 142, translates, "Like a flock of goats streaming down." He rejects Tuell, arguing that the emphasis is on goats and their movement and that goats "stream" but do not produce waves. However, hair does wave and does not stream, and it is not clear that the goats might not be thought of in the same manner. The image is in the eye of the beholder.

111

²Your teeth are like a shorn[a] flock
That ascend from the washing,
Every one of them with its twin,[b]
There is no "miscarriage" among them.[c]
³Like a scarlet thread are your lips,
Your mouth[d] is lovely,
Like pieces of pomegranate are your temples,[e]
Behind your veil.[f]
⁴Like the tower of David is your neck,
Built in layers,[g]
A thousand shields hang on it,
All the armor[h] of warriors.
⁵Your two breasts are like two fawns,
A gazelle's twins who feed among the lotuses.[i]
⁶Until the day breezes gently along,[j]

a. This Qal feminine plural passive participle from the root *qsb* occurs elsewhere in the Bible only in 2 Kings 6:6, where it is used of cutting a piece of wood. Compare the Akkadian *kasābu* (to lessen, be stunted [of the feet]) and the Hebrew noun of occupation *qaṣṣāb* (butcher). Murphy, *Song*, 154, prefers the sense of a flock about to be shorn.

b. This is the Hiphil feminine plural participle of the root *tʾm*. It occurs only here and in the parallel verse, 6:6. A plural noun form ("twins," *tĕʾômîm*) occurs in Gen. 25:24; 38:27; Song 4:5; 7:4 (7:3 Eng.). The first two occurrences refer to twin boys born to Rebekah, while the appearances in the Song describe twin fawns of a gazelle that are likened to the female's breasts.

c. Murphy, *Song*, 155, observes more examples of the lack of gender agreement between the masculine plural suffixes "every one of them" (*šekkullām*) and "among them" (*bāhem*) and their presumed antecedent, the feminine "shorn flock." However, if the reference is to "teeth," there would be no lack of agreement.

d. This accepts the Qere, "your mouth," rather than the Kethib, "your mouths." The LXX has *hē lalia sou* (your speech; cf. Vulgate *eloquium*). For the translation of this unusual word, see the comments.

e. *Raqqātēk* from *raqqāh*. This term appears in Judg. 4:21–22; 5:26 as the part of Sisera's face into which Jael drove the peg in order to kill the Canaanite general. There it is the temple above the eyes, where the skull would easily give way to the blows of her hammer. It remains possible, however, that it describes a larger part of the face, as the LXX "cheeks" (*mēlon*) suggests here and in Song 6:7. Nevertheless, the Ugaritic cognate *rq[t]* and the likely derivation from or relation to Hebrew *rqq* (to be thin) with the significance as described above suggest that "temples/brow" should be retained. So also Gerleman, *Hohelied*, 147–48; Murphy, *Song*, 159, who nevertheless translates "cheek."

f. This phrase, identical in the MT to the one in v. 1, has numerous variants attested in the versions. See Garbini, *Cantico*, 69–72. Nevertheless, the MT remains an acceptable original reading.

g. Honeyman, "Two Contributions," identifies *talpîyôt* as a *taqtîlah* form of the root *lph* (to layer; Aramaic *lpy*). See Pope, *Song*, 467.

h. A term that may be a synonym for "shields," as used in 2 Sam. 8:7; 2 Kings 11:10; Ezek. 27:11. The LXX renders its seven OT occurrences variously, as quiver, bracelets, ornaments, and arms. See Fox, *Song*, 131. Here the LXX translates the term as *bolides* (darts/javelins).

i. See comments on 2:16.

j. See comments on 2:17.

And the shadows flee,
I will go to the mountain of myrrh,
To the hill of frankincense.
[7]All of you is beautiful, my darling,
There is not a blemish in you.
[8]Come[k] with me[l] from Lebanon, my bride,
Come with me from Lebanon,
Travel from Amana's peak,
From Senir's peak,
From Hermon,
From the dens of lions,
From the mountain lairs of leopards.
[9]You have beguiled me,[m]
My sister <and> bride,
You have beguiled me,
With a single <glance>[n] of your eyes,
With a single strand[o] of your necklace.

k. The single verb "come" (*tābô'î*) appears at the end of the second line and serves both the first and second lines. This is a backward ellipsis construction, which can occur only with the verb in final position on the second line (see Miller, "Linguistic"). This renders unnecessary the apparent reading of the LXX, which takes the first "with me" (*'ittî*) as "come" (*'ĕtî*) and renders it *deuro*. Cf. Keel, *Song*, 154; Murphy, *Song*, 155–56.

l. So the MT against the LXX and other versions that read *'ĕtî* (come) here and in the second line. To follow the versions, as many modern translations do, results in three verbs "come" in the first two lines, or in placing the final verb with "travel" in the following line. In either case, it creates an awkward syntax that is problematic for poetry. It also vitiates the parallel with v. 1, where none of the first five words is a verb.

m. The question of how to translate the first word in v. 9, repeated as the fourth word, has occasioned much discussion. *Libbabtînî* (written defectively?) seems to form a Piel perfect verbal form from the root *lbb* (heart). The question of its meaning is tied up with whether it is based on a positive meaning such as "you have aroused me sexually), you have given me virility" (where the heart conveys the idea of arousing the emotions), or whether it may carry a privative meaning such as "you have stolen my heart." Elsewhere this verb occurs only as a Niphal, in Job 11:12, with the meaning "to acquire wisdom." The privative sense, followed by Fox, *Song*, 136, seems preferable. If so, it nevertheless serves to increase interest and desire and therefore may be rendered as "beguile." See Waldman, "Note," and for parallel uses of this expression in Mesopotamian love poetry used by females to seduce men, see Biggs, *Šà.zi.ga*.

n. This is added for style. It does not occur in any of the versions, despite the gender problem between "one" and "eyes."

o. *'Ănāq* with the numeral "one" before it carries the sense of a single strand of jewelry (Fox, *Song*, 136, following the LXX and the related Mishnaic Hebrew meaning, "chain"), or it may refer to a single gem or jewel (Pope, *Song*, 482). Either meaning is possible. Pope notes the plural in Prov. 1:9 with reference to women's neck jewelry and to that on the necks of camels in Judg. 8:26. His citations of an "eye" type of jewel from Mesopotamia seems somewhat removed from the context, especially since the function has not been determined. Nor is Pope correct in identifying the parallel "eyes" in Song 4:9 as necessarily a singular. The older understanding of a strand of jewelry seems more likely.

[10]How delightful[a] is your lovemaking,
My sister <and> bride,
How much better[b] is your lovemaking
Than wine,
And the fragrance of your perfumes
Than all the spices.
[11]Your lips drip virgin honey,[c]
O bride,
Honey and milk are beneath your tongue,
And the fragrance of your garments
Is like the fragrance of Lebanon.
[12]<You are>
A locked[d] garden,
My sister and bride,
A locked pool,[e]
A sealed fountain.
[13]Your plants,[f]

a. *Yāpû*, a Qal denominative verb from *yph* (to be beautiful), here used as an adjective.

b. *Tōbû*, a Qal denominative verb from *twb* (to be good), here used as an adjective.

c. *Nōpet* refers to the best honey, directly from the honeycomb. Murphy, *Song*, 156, compares Ps. 19:11 (19:10 Eng.).

d. Used twice in this verse, *nāʿûl* is a masculine singular Qal passive participle of the root *nʿl*. This root appears to have two primary meanings, depending on the period in which it occurs. Later texts, such as Ezek. 16:10 and 2 Chron. 28:15, apply the term to shodding someone in sandals. Earlier texts, such as Judg. 3:23–24 and 2 Sam. 13:17–18, apply it exclusively to locking the doors of a building or room. Comparative Semitics also supports this distinction. Thus Ugaritic and Arslan Tash texts use the root with the meaning "tie/close; bar"; later Hebrew and Aramaic dialects take the sense "to bind on a sandal." Cf. also the Arabic cognate with the meaning "to shoe a horse or camel" (see *HALOT* 705). The context of the Song clearly favors the locking of the garden rather than shodding one in sandals.

e. *Gal* can refer to a wave of water. However, it is not clear that such is the intent here. One can imagine a karstic spring such as the Gihon in Jerusalem, a "gusher" that shoots out water periodically, and this may suggest an origin to the sense of "wave" as it appears here. Pope, *Song*, 488–89, gathers evidence for this term as related to Hebrew *gullâ*, Ugaritic *gl*, Akkadian *gullatu*, and Greek *gaulos* (bowl). All of this suggests a pool of water in the shape of a rounded bowl or cup.

f. *Šĕlāḥayik* comes from a root *šlḥ*. If the basic sense of this is "to send," then the noun form here may refer to the "shoots" of the plants, the plants themselves on which the fruits grow. Alternatively, a homonymic root seems to carry the sense of a gift, a wedding gift, as it is used in 1 Kings 9:16, where the pharaoh gives Gezer to Solomon on the occasion of his marriage to pharaoh's daughter. This may also be the sense of the Ugaritic *tlh* (see *HALOT* 1517). Less likely is Görg, "Kanäle?" who translates "branches" and relates it metaphorically to the pubic area via the Egyptian *sr/lh* (branches), used to represent that part of the body in female deities of the Middle Bronze Age. So also Keel, *Song*, 176, who cites Sumerian and Egyptian love poems that associate garden and canal with womb and vagina. He also refers to Lev. 12:7 and 20:18, where the Hebrew word for "fountain" or "spring" refers to female genitalia. Of course, in these OT legal texts the association is clear. That is not the case with poetry. See the comments for allusions to these terms and the argument that they refer in a general way to the female's body and its fruitfulness.

A garden[g] of pomegranates,
With the best of fruits,
With henna and spikenard.
[14]Spikenard and tumeric,
Spice cane and cinnamon,
With all the trees of frankincense,
Myrrh and aloes,
With all the best spices.
[15]A garden fountain,
A well of living water,
Flowing from Lebanon.

Female

[16]Awake, O north wind,
Come, O south wind,
Blow upon my garden,
Let its spices spread,
Let my lover come to his garden,
Let him eat its best fruit.

Male

[5:1a]I have come to my garden, my sister and bride,
I have plucked my myrrh with my spices,
I have eaten my nectar[h] with my honey,
I have drunk my wine with my milk.

Chorus

[1b]Eat, friends,
Drink, and become intoxicated with lovemaking.[i]

g. The word for "garden" here is not the customary *gan* but *pardēs*. This word occurs elsewhere only in Eccles. 2:5 and Neh. 2:8, with the meaning of "forest" in the last reference. It is widely recognized as a loanword from the Old Persian (Avestan) *pairidaēza* (*HALOT* 963) and the source, through Greek, of the English word *paradise*. If so, then it appears to guarantee that this word signifies a late text. However, one may be excused for asking if so great a conclusion should rest on a single word. If so, then other evidence that would argue for an earlier date must be ignored. Perhaps this word, line, or verse is itself a later addition or adjustment to the text.

h. The term *yaʿar* often refers to a "forest" or "thicket." Here, however, as in 1 Sam. 14:27, it denotes the honey found in a honeycomb.

i. As in Song 1:2, 4; 4:10, the plural of *dwd* occurs with the meaning of "lovemaking." Contra Pope, *Song*, 508, who takes this word as referring to the abstract idea of love, following NEB, NAB, and NJPS. Certainly, other texts (such as Ezek. 16:8; 23:17; Prov. 7:18) define this as sex. For example, see the words of the adulteress in the Proverbs text:

Interpretation

    3:6–11 Male: Marriage scene
    4:1–8   Male: First *waṣf* and call to come along
    4:9–15 Male: A walk in the garden
    4:16   Female: Invitation to her garden
    5:1a   Male: Tasting the garden
    5:1b   Chorus: Enjoy!

3:6–11. *Male: Marriage scene.* These six verses describe a scene that appears to have been witnessed by the male, as suggested by the feminine "this (one)" in the first line.[1] More so than anywhere else in the Song, the emphasis is on things that are seen.[2] If so, it is one in which the royal lady appears on a palanquin. At first this is perceived only dimly, as from a distance the procession approaches. Then the nature of the procession comes into focus and is identified by the male (v. 7). His eyes begin with the male guards who surround it. He describes their military attire and fierce appearance (vv. 7–8). His eyes then move to the litter itself. Here he observes each part of the glistening and majestic object, culminating in the inner part where the king would recline. In the final verse his attention turns to the female's companions, last mentioned in 3:5, and he calls them to witness the king and to see his crown (v. 11). The crown, however, is not described in terms of its form or accoutrements, as with the previous objects. Instead, the crown serves as a means to introduce the wedding that the king experiences. The focus of this section is King Solomon, who is mentioned three times, in vv. 7, 9, and 11. The suffix "his" (-ô) refers to the king once in v. 7, again in v. 9, and four times in the second half of v. 11. Indeed, the final word in the section is "his heart" (*libbô*), a direct reference to the essential part of King Solomon's person, and the aspect of a person that has the most relevance in the love poem of the Song. Furthermore, the king is

---

"Come, let us drink deeply of sex till morning; let's enjoy one another with lovemaking." Others, including ancient versions such as the LXX's *adelphoi,* the Vulgate, and the Syriac, as well as the NIV and other modern translations, read here a parallel to "friends" in the first line of Song 5:1. The plural of this root is not used in the Bible as a noun meaning "lovers." Therefore, it is best to see the plural as the singular form, an adverbial accusative that conveys the idea of lovemaking.

1. Fox, *Song,* 119, prefers the daughters of Jerusalem as the speakers because it would not seem appropriate for the male to "express surprise." However, it seems no more likely that the daughters of Jerusalem should be surprised than the male. Further, the male does not clearly express such great surprise in the text. The initial observation could be better seen as an exclamation motivated by his love and desire for the female.

2. Gerleman, *Hohelied,* 135.

the subject of every verb and participle in vv. 9 and 10a. His royal body-guards and the daughters of Jerusalem/Zion serve as subjects of verbs in vv. 7, 8, 10b, and 11a. The king's mother is the subject of the single verb in v. 11b. However, in every case these other figures relate directly to the king, serving him and his interests in one way or another. Thus the king remains the key figure and theme of this portion.

> **3:6**Who is this ascending from the desert,
> Like columns of smoke,
> Perfumed with myrrh and frankincense,
> The best of all the powders of the merchants?

The male begins his description with a question: Who? This hints that the key emphasis of the verses will be a person. Although the initial verse (3:6) does not answer this question, it provides the background for an important figure with a dramatic entrance and an abundance of wealth. The first line describes an ascent (*ʿlh*). While this may appear to the male speaker as a physical ascent as the caravan comes into view, it may also imply the "ascent" to Jerusalem, for so the approach to the Holy City has always been described (see, e.g., Isa. 2:1–2 [= Mic. 4:1–2]). The term for "desert" or "wilderness" (*midbār*) can describe a variety of places throughout ancient Israel. For example, it can include the hill country to the east and south of Jerusalem (Josh. 8:20, 24; 2 Sam. 15:23). It is possible that this is the area from which the procession is pictured as approaching. The term for "columns of smoke" (*tîmărôt ʿāšān*) occurs only here and in Joel 3:3 (2:30 Eng.), also the only other use of the first noun, "columns." The Joel passage lists this among various wonders (*môpětîm*) that God will display in the heavens and earth. The others are blood and fire. This context suggests that columns of smoke would identify and single out a phenomenon such as the traveling caravan. Thus, as the male surveys the landscape of the desert, perhaps to the east and south of Jerusalem, he observes columns of smoke rising. His attention is drawn to the source of this smoke, which forms the subject of the second half of v. 6.[3]

The word "perfumed" (*mĕquṭṭeret*) describes something completely filled with fragrance or incense. This feminine singular participle cannot refer directly to the columns, in plural, although the columns of smoke may be the result of the burning of the incense. Indeed, the root of the term means "to go up in smoke" and is often used of sacrifices and of-ferings. However, the expression must refer to "this one" in the initial

---

3. Ibn Ezra appears to have interpreted this statement as a vision of a mirage in which the woman appears by herself. The male's mention of Solomon then demonstrates how inferior is all that Solomon has compared to their love. See LaCocque, *Romance,* 97.

question. The use of the feminine singular suggests that the female is here identified.[4] Myrrh is a spice that has been mentioned in 1:13 to depict the male lying between the breasts of the female. The picture there suggested both the great value and pleasure that the female has in her lover and the sexual intimacy that they enjoy. The myrrh and the frankincense, called "whiteness" (*lĕbônâ*) from its color, were imported spices used in incense for sacrifices, in medicines, and in cosmetics.[5] Only kings and other wealthy classes would use these valuable commodities for their own deodorants and perfumes. Their burning produced a pleasant aroma that could be detected at a distance. The need to import them from traders and merchants who exchanged goods with distant Sheba (Saba) in southern Arabia would explain the final line. The male understands that what approaches is no ordinary group of people, but one whose opulence is signaled in advance by columns of smoke burning fine aromatics. Already in this first verse the male has addressed the senses of sight and smell. Whenever the senses go beyond what is seen and heard, the male directs his attention toward his lover or something wonderful that reminds him of her physical presence and lovemaking.

> [7]Look! It is Solomon's palanquin,
> Sixty warriors surround it,
> From the warriors of Israel.

The next verse (3:7) begins with an interjection to draw attention: Look! (*hinnēh*). This signals the most important piece of information in this section, the identification of the key figure, the one for which v. 6 built its description. It is the king and the greatest of kings, Solomon. However, his name appears as a note of ownership. Solomon himself is not on the bed. The bed belongs to Solomon, but he is not the occupant. Instead, the male sees his lover. This scene portrays the most luxuriant method of travel, one that only the wealthy could afford. Yet, although the wealthy are indicted for their leisure and lack of social concern ("beds of ivory" in Amos 6:4), the term is almost never used in sexual contexts. Only in Esther 7:8, where the king mistakenly assumes that

4. Such an identification renders unlikely the observation of Holman ("Fresh Attempt") that the litter is a metaphor for the bride. Of course, there is no direct reference to the female, and the litter does point to her as the other objects are described. However, it is not likely a metaphor (despite Sumerian analogues), given both the lack of metaphor in this section and the absence elsewhere in the Bible of imagery of a litter being used in this manner.

5. Both spices were native to southern Arabia, Djibouti, Somalia, and southeastern Ethiopia. See King and Stager, *Life*, 81–82, 347.

Haman is molesting Esther as he falls on her bed (or couch) to beg for mercy, is there any sexual connotation. This is true even though it is one of the most common nouns for a place of rest. The male's thoughts are not of sexual matters simply because he mentions the bed. Rather, he revels in the opulence and indulgence that the appearance of this object brings. The number sixty may anticipate the sixty queens of 6:8 and describe a complete and royal entourage. Twice the number of David's men (2 Sam. 23:18–19, 23), sixty is associated elsewhere with Solomon's temple (1 Kings 6:2; 2 Chron. 3:3), provisions (1 Kings 4:22), and, in the form of six hundred sixty-six, tribute (1 Kings 10:14; 2 Chron. 9:13).[6] Later, sixty conscripted men are taken from Jerusalem as part of the Babylonian captivity (2 Kings 25:19). Hence sixty is associated with Solomon and his wealth and power. It also remains a number that can describe a contingent of men used for a particular purpose. Generally overlooked is the parallel noted by J. Sasson that describes the seventh-century Assyrian king Esarhaddon being protected by sixty great gods.[7] The number emphasizes the royal security that the female enjoys. The "warriors of Israel" (*gibbōrê yiśrāʾēl*) first appear in Exod. 17:11, where they form the army that defeats the Amalekites. These battle-ready warriors form the honor guard for the passenger. For her to control a contingent of this size suggests great power and prestige.

> [8]All of them skilled with a sword,
> Experienced in battle,
> Each with his sword at his side,
> Because of the nightly terrors.

Song 3:8 provides a further detailed description of the warriors at the king's side. The term for wearing a sword is a passive form of *ʾḥz* with the general meaning "seize, grab."[8] The phrase thus literally means, "All of them are held fast by a sword." This expression is unique in the Bible.[9] Yet the verbal root occurs three other times in the Song: 2:15; 3:4; and 7:9 (7:8 Eng.). Of special interest is 3:4, where it is used to describe how the female, having gone through a dangerous search, holds on to her lover and refuses to yield him to anyone. The sword is a weapon of war.

6. However, it is his son Rehoboam who possesses sixty concubines (2 Chron. 11:21).

7. J. Sasson, "On Pope's *Song*," 195.

8. A Qal passive participle.

9. Delitzsch, *Song*, 63. Pope, *Song*, 435 (and Fox, *Song*, 124), interprets this as "skilled," citing Akkadian and Ugaritic parallels. G. Carr, *Song*, 110, rejects the translation "skilled" because "the idea is better expressed in the next colon." However, the repetition of a similar or identical idea is basic to parallelism.

Of its nearly five hundred occurrences, it appears only here in the Song, and twice in this verse. Hence this is not a special image or symbol. Rather, it further outfits the warriors and demonstrates that they are indeed ready, able, and skilled to defend their passenger. The same is true of the second phrase, "experienced in battle." The passive form of the verb *lmd* describes one who is skilled.[10] Elsewhere it is used as an adjective to describe people skilled in rules of religion (Isa. 29:13) and a heifer trained to thresh (Hosea 10:11). In only one other context does it occur as a participle in construct with a noun, as here. In 1 Chron. 25:7 it describes individuals who are skilled in music. Thus the same idea appears in this verse in the Song. These are warriors trained for war and experienced in war. They are the best of Israel's military. Again, there is nothing erotic in this description. However, the emphasis of the strength, power, and danger that these warriors personify could easily lead the male to a sense of security and well-being when they protect his lover. Indeed, that is exactly the direction of his thoughts, as the last line of Song 3:8 demonstrates. The "terror of the night" also appears in Ps. 91:5, where it describes how one who trusts in God will not know fear, either of this night terror or of the arrow of the day. Arrows would be shot in the daytime, when the archer could see the target. However, what is the terror of the night?[11] The term in Ps. 91:6–7 appears to head a list of dangers to which one who trusts in God will not be subject:

> nor the pestilence that stalks in the darkness,
> nor the plague that destroys at midday.
> A thousand may fall at your side,
> ten thousand at your right hand,
> but it will not come near you. (NIV)

Although the king's warriors could not shield the passenger from plague or pestilence, they could protect her from attack in battle or a covert plot against her, most dangerous at night. Hence the picture becomes one of security in addition to wealth and prestige. This would make the figure a desirable partner and lover. However, it is of greatest interest that the woman herself is not described in this section. Instead, only the outward signs of power and position receive attention.

10. A Pual participle.

11. The inevitable association with demons derives from ancient Near Eastern comparisons (Pope, *Song*, 435–37). The Ps. 91 context suggests it, insofar as "pestilence" (*deber*) in 91:6 may be personified as a force of evil. Note, however, that the most often cited usage of *deber* in this manner (Hab. 3:5) implies that its power remains completely in God's control. Thus "demons" seems an unlikely implication in the canonical context of the Hebrew Bible (G. Carr, *Song*, 111).

> ⁹A litter did King Solomon make for himself,
> From the wood of Lebanon.

If, as the text states, Solomon has made this bed for himself, then how does it happen that the female rides in it? This question is not asked or answered. It is not that the king made the litter only for his own personal use, but that he made it for the use of whomever he wished to be carried on it. Of course, Solomon would use the finest of materials in constructing such a royal device. Cedarwood from Lebanon was most prized in construction. Cedar was already mentioned in 1:17.[12] Its recurrence here suggests a bed made of the finest wood, imported from the north as the aromatics were from the south.

> ¹⁰Its posts he made of silver,
> Its underpart of gold,
> Its seat of purple,
> Its interior lovingly inlaid
> By the daughters of Jerusalem.

The wood formed the frame and the basic construction. To this would be added the materials described in v. 10. The posts of the bed were made of silver. This may suggest that they were covered with the precious metal. Of the thirty-seven verses in which "columns/posts" (ʿammûdîm) appears with "silver" (kesep), thirty-five describe the construction of the tabernacle (e.g., Exod. 26:32; 27:10, 11, 17; 36:36; 38:10, 11, 12, 17, 19). The remaining occurrence is Esther 1:6, where the Persian king's garden is described in terms similar to those here: "The garden had hangings of white and blue linen, fastened with cords of white linen and purple material to silver rings on marble pillars. There were couches of gold and silver on a mosaic pavement of porphyry, marble, mother-of-pearl and other costly stones" (NIV).

As in the Song, gold and silver were used to make couches. In addition, gold was used to construct the base in the Song. In Esther gold is merely listed as one of the metals used in the preparation of the couches. It is the most prized of all metals. In the ancient Near East the country renowned for its gold was Egypt. African mines produced gold that was valued throughout the known world. The most precious of all colors was purple. The dye was made from murex shells found along the coast of the eastern Mediterranean Sea. Refineries for the production of murex purple were discovered at Dor and were known to have existed at

---

12. For its earlier usage with the construction of Jerusalem's temple and palace, see 1 Kings 5:13, 20, 22–23, 28 (4:33; 5:6, 8–9, 14 Eng.); 7:2; 10:17, 21.

Sidon and above all at Tyre. During the Roman period, laws restricted who could wear clothes so dyed. Earlier it was used in the curtains of the tabernacle and the garments of the priest.[13] Purple therefore was a sign of royalty and of highly prized cloth. The interior of a special object could be inlaid with precious stones and metals as well as ivory. Here the details are not given, but the figures responsible are named, the daughters of Jerusalem. As a female contingent corresponding to the male warriors of Jerusalem, this reference is unusual because they are for the first time not merely passive recipients of advice from the female. Instead, they participate in making ready the royal couch for conveying the female to the wedding.

> [11]Come out and see,
> Daughters of Zion,
> King Solomon,
> With the crown,
> That his mother crowned him,
> On the day of his wedding,
> On the day his heart rejoiced.

The term "daughters of Jerusalem" in Song 3:10 is likely a poetic variant of "daughters of Zion" in v. 11. These figures are commanded by the male to appear and bear witness to the king. Their role in producing the bed and its beauty now changes. Like the virgin attendants of Ps. 45:15 (45:14 Eng.), they will serve a function in the royal wedding. They are called to view the king. He has a crown, a symbol of royalty (Ps. 21:4 [21:3 Eng.]). This crown seals his kingship. It is one that Solomon's mother made for him on the day of his wedding. Although royal mothers are sometimes associated with crowns (Jer. 13:18), their role in the manufacture of the royal crown is not otherwise attested. Whether this is a formal recognition of the discharge of the son from the care of his mother,[14] the text does not say. The mention here of the mother brings to mind "my mother's house," to which the female led the male in 3:4. Here, however, it is not the female's but the male's mother that is mentioned. The solution to this unusual reference lies in the following line. Here and only here in this section, and indeed in the whole of the Song, is a wedding (*ḥătunnâ*, 3:11) explicitly mentioned.

---

13. Exod. 25:4; 26:1, 31, 36; 27:16; 28:5, 6, 8, 15, 33; 35:6, 23, 25, 35; 36:8, 35, 37; 38:18, 23; 39:1, 3, 5, 8, 24, 29; Num. 4:13; cf. 2 Chron. 2:14; 3:14 for Solomon's temple.

14. Keel, *Song*, 136–37, argues that the adornment of crowns at a wedding is a late custom from the intertestamental period. His observation that there is no evidence for this practice earlier must, of course, cut both ways. This feature thus says nothing about the date of the custom.

The entire section has been building to this climax, the announcement of a wedding. This is what brings joy to the heart of the king, rather than wealth or power or anything else. So significant is this happiness that the term *śimḥâ* occurs only here in the whole of the Song, despite its frequency elsewhere in the Bible (some 95 appearances) and the joyous tone of the Song. Contrary to some commentators, the Song does not portray sex as the great and final goal in order to experience true joy. Nor does it suggest that mutual admiration of the lovers, their physical bodies and sensuality, is the source of joy. Rather, the Song directly associates the joy of the heart with the final commitment of marriage.[15] It is only within this commitment that all the joys of the male and female lovers come together, for it is only here that they realize the freedom to express those joys without restraint, knowing that the marriage bond seals their love in a lifetime commitment to each other.

How then is "Solomon" to be understood? Is this a literal picture in which the bride of Solomon (one of his hundreds of brides? cf. 1 Kings 11:3), perhaps Abishag (1 Kings 2:17, 21–22), appears as the king looks on and refers to himself in the third person ("his")?[16] Is it some sort of rivalry between a lowly shepherd boy and the great King Solomon, as they vie for the hand of the female? Neither of these scenarios is likely, because it is not certain that the primary focus of the Song is King Solomon. That is not necessarily true of this section, which may have had an earlier origin outside the Song itself.[17] However, if this section

15. Even Fox, *Song,* 121, finds here a wedding, but not the couple's wedding day.

16. After reviewing the options of Phoenician and Egyptian queens, Fox, *Song,* 120, concludes that none of these is likely to approach Jerusalem from the desert. However, he does not consider a wedding procession from the eastern nations of Moab or Ammon or one that comes from an Arabian origin. Nevertheless, like Fox, it is best to conclude that this whole scene, in its present context, is fiction or fantasy. He suggests that the phrase "ascending from the desert" is itself an idiom for coming from a long distance and has no bearing on the actual direction of approach. For the three-person drama, see Provan, *Song,* 298–305, for whom the story of Song 3:6–11 is one of Solomon on an adventure of forced sexual conquests among the women of his kingdom. The column of smoke rising represents these women as sacrifices, and the guards keep the women on the bed as much as they protect the king from any advances. This modern-day allegory allows for much preaching application but has little value as a serious exegesis of the poetry. It further emphasizes the negative evaluation of Solomon, for which see Andiñach, "Crítica," who places Solomon over against the couple in his analysis.

17. Thus Gordis, *Song,* 56: "This song is the oldest datable unit in the collection. It was written to mark the ceremonies connected with King Solomon's marriage to a foreign princess, perhaps from Egypt, across the desert. Another example of a royal wedding hymn, not connected with Solomon, is to be found in Psalm 45." Murphy, *Song,* 151, declares that "it is impossible to reconstruct this with any certainty" and that the purpose of the ceremonies in the present context is different from that of a wedding. However, his comments at the end of 152 seem to allow for a wedding interpretation.

is to be integrated with the rest of the Song, then it is necessary to understand how these verses function as an expression of romantic love that extends beyond the experience of one particular couple. The references to King Solomon, like the crowns worn up to the present day by Jewish brides and grooms on their weddings, represent the images that the male and female possess in the eyes of one another. The female here appears perfumed with the finest of aromatics, guarded by a retinue of the strongest of warriors, and housed in the most gorgeous and exotic of chambers. She presents an altogether magnificent spectacle of one who might well have come from the ends of the earth to her lover. The male is the greatest of all kings of Israel, whose crown and glory are unsurpassed. Previous sections have considered their passion and pure sensual desire for one another. Later chapters will turn to describe in detail their physical bodies. Here the erotic poetry pauses as it considers only the manner in which the lovers appear in the eyes of one another. They are queen and king. Is this hyperbole? Of course it is, from the perspective of those of us who read this poetry. Of course it is not, from the perspective of those of us who find here our own beloved and recall how beautiful or handsome they seemed to us on our wedding day. For the lover, the object of his or her love is one who exceeds everyone and everything else. We gaze upon the object of our love in desire, admiration, and ultimately joy because we want to do so, because we see there the fulfillment of all that we long for. In the Song it is the male and female lovers, the bridegroom and bride. For interpreters throughout history, it has been God and his people, and for Christians, Christ and the church.

4:1–8. *Male: First* waṣf *and call to come along.* This is the first of several waṣf forms that occur throughout the remainder of the Song.[18] In most cases the male addresses the female, but at least once the female turns to the male. Murphy sees the song as one in which the word pictures are appropriate to, and representative of, various parts of the body.[19] The actual waṣf is limited to vv. 1–7, although v. 8 is closely related and by the same speaker. In the view of some, it continues through the remainder of the chapter as the male continues to speak in vv. 9–15. The waṣf provides an opportunity for the male to affirm his lover in her beauty.[20] His words of praise and adoration set aside feelings of insecurity and uncertainty and provide a direct means of access between the inner feelings of the couple. For the male, riches, power, and strength

18. The introduction (under "Images/Structure/Theology") discusses the waṣf: a love song in which the lover praises the physical attributes of the partner.
19. Murphy, *Song*, 158–59, also finds symbolic and evocative aspects to these comparisons, something already emphasized by Soulen, "Waṣfs."
20. Cf. Provan, *Song*, 325–26.

are found in the beauty of the one he adores. This one he adores is not the generic beauty who fulfills the requirements of lust, but rather an individual, a person who is like no other. She is special and significant, unique among women. And he will know her (and no other) in every way possible. Thus the *waṣf* is a prelude to sexual intimacy, not primarily because it arouses the passions, but because its honesty of expression and detail of observation place the desire within a loving respect for the woman.

The structure of this poem begins and ends with verses that exhibit staircase parallelism.[21] Verses 1a and 8a also contain repeated lines that frame an address of endearment: "my darling/[my] bride." In between, the verses move from the lover's eyes to her hair, teeth, lips, mouth, temples, neck, and breasts. Each one is compared to something either from nature or from military imagery. Verses 2 and 5 begin and end this description with comparisons with animals, including sheep and fawns. The initial metaphor and simile of v. 1 are brief, at most possessing two lines. However, the teeth and neck have longer similes, lasting the entire four lines of the verse. The breasts also receive a full verse (5); though with only two lines, it has eight words. Verses 6–8 depart from this physical description and focus on the desire of the male to visit "the mountain of myrrh" and to be joined there by his partner. This itself may form a metaphor. Beginning with the head and moving his eyes downward, the male does not complete his description but stops with the bust of his partner. At this point, as though overcome with passion, he expresses his desire in terms of a sensual pursuit. Now his lover's body becomes a mountain upon which he finds perfumes. Hence the summary statement in v. 7 concludes the description with a general statement of perfection. His invitation to his bride then turns into a call to come away from the impregnable heights and to join him. At both the beginning and the end of this section, specific geographical locations are mentioned to imbue the Song with a sense of reality. Yet these descriptions also portray phenomena unique to their respective concerns, whether the precipitous heights of Gilead or the even greater distances of Hermon.

In vv. 2 and 5, there is common structure to the bodily descriptions. The part of the body to be described is named along with the second-person feminine singular suffix, "your *x*." This is followed by the prefixed *kāp* preposition, except in the first description, that of the eyes. The preposition is prefixed to the object of the simile. This is normally followed by a relative pronoun that introduces a verb of action to describe how the compared

21. Watson, "Note," who also finds examples of this in vv. 9 and 10, comments that it may be a characteristic of direct speech.

object functions in order to make the comparison vivid. Thus one flock of goats descends from Mount Gilead, another flock ascends from washing, and fawns feed among the lotuses (though this last omits the relative). In vv. 3 and 4 there are no such action verbs, and the comparison, beginning with the *kāp* preposition, begins the line. Verses 5b and 6a repeat lines from 2:16 and 17. And v. 6b continues the theme of chapter 2 as the lover desires to go mountaineering. All of these similes tend to flow forward in their descriptions, adding to the images. The summary of v. 7 frames its comments with two second-person feminine pronominal suffixes on the first and last words, "All of you/in you." There is no verb in this verse, unlike all the others. Instead, there are two designations that surround the term of endearment. The whole produces a chiasm:

> All of you
>> is beautiful,
>>> my darling,
>> There is not a blemish
> in you.

The structure of v. 8a has already been noted. Verse 8b contains two parallel expressions that frame the central expression "from Hermon":

> Travel
>> from the peak of Amana,
>> from the peak of Senir,
>>> from Hermon,
>> from the dens of lions
>> from the mountain lairs of leopards.[22]

In this manner Mount Hermon becomes the focus of the end of the verse and the concern of the male lover as a metaphor for the distance he feels from his lover when he is not in her arms. In connection with a similar structure in v. 7, the twin centers of "my darling" and "from Mount Hermon" beautifully summarize the concern of the male lover for access to his partner.

The whole of the text may be an address without the female being present, although the Song seems to suggest that words are spoken while

22. The structure of this verse is discussed at length by Jakobson, "Grammatical"; Zevit, "Roman"; and Landy, "In Defense." Jakobson, followed by Landy, tends to see here a great many interconnecting repetitions of sound that rise to the level of meaning in interpretation. Zevit downplays the significance of some of these, noting (among other things) the absence of many techniques in Hebrew poetry that call for a sequence of more than three items.

both are present.[23] Theologically, this and the succeeding *wasf*s (5:10–16; 6:4–10; 7:2–10a [7:1–9a Eng.]) demonstrate a value to the human body that lies at the heart of the Song. The body is not evil but good and worthy of praise. The *wasf*s respect the body with a focus that is appreciative rather than lurid. Nevertheless, they reflect the fundamental value of God's creation as good and the human body as a key part of that creation, whether at the beginning (Gen. 1:26–28) or redeemed in the resurrection (1 Cor. 15:42–44; cf. Araújo, "O corpo").

> 4:1Look at you, so beautiful, my darling!
> Look at you, so beautiful,
> Your eyes are doves
> From behind your veil,
> Your hair is like the flock of goats
> That descend in waves from Mount Gilead.

Song 4:1 begins with a twofold repetition of "behold/look" (*hinnēh*) with the feminine singular suffix "you" (-*āk*) followed by "beautiful" (*yāpāh*). This repeats 1:15. These two occurrences are the seventh and eighth times the word "beautiful" has appeared in the Song and the second time *hinnēh* and *yāpāh* have occurred together twice in the same verse (cf. 1:15).[24] Verse 7 will repeat *yāpāh* and thus form an envelope construction with 4:1. Indeed, the whole of vv. 1–7 deals with the beauty of the female and the male's response. "My darling," the male's characteristic term of endearment and address to his lover, occurs in 4:1 for the sixth time and in v. 7 for the seventh time.[25] Although the random nature of such occurrences is a distinct possibility, it is perhaps more than coincidence that the sixth occurrence and the key seventh occurrence of the male's central words of address to his lover are in this section. The repetition emphasizes his point, and the six words (eleven syllables) of 4:7 altogether demonstrate the elegant simplicity and power of this introductory address to his lover.

Some commentators suggest that the male begins at the top of the female in his description. This is not precisely true. Later he describes her hair and temples. He begins with her eyes. This was true in 1:15 as well, where the verse is identical with the first seven words of 4:1. In the first chapter the male may have been cut short by the passionate outburst of his lover as she responded and addressed him in a similar manner. Here he is allowed to undertake his description of his beloved in as full a manner as his own passion will allow. The focus on the eyes,

23. For the former, see Schweizer, "Erkennen."
24. Previously *yāpāh* has appeared in 1:8, 15 (2x), 16; 2:10, 13.
25. Previously "my darling" has appeared in 1:9, 15; 2:2, 10, 13.

which perhaps evoked due wordplay in 1:15, here relies on no such connection. Instead, 4:1 pictures the loving gaze of the lovers into one another's eyes. Where better for the lover to begin his *wasf* than with the eyes into which he loves to stare? For the dove metaphor, see comments on 1:15. Here the eyes are hidden, at least in part, behind a veil (*ṣammâ*). Other than its occurrence in v. 3 and the parallel in 6:7, this noun appears in Isa. 47:2, portraying the humiliation and defeat of the city and kingdom of Babylon as a woman. She must grind flour and lift her skirts to bare her legs while crossing streams. In the midst of these acts of humiliation, she is commanded to remove her veil. Thus for the biblical writers the veil serves as a symbol of modesty and reflects the same sense for the woman of the Song. Does the male merely fantasize about her eyes, or has he actually seen them? The reader/listener is not told; however, his boldness in describing them and the other parts of her body suggests an acquaintance. Hence veiling may have been an act of modesty, but it was not performed so rigidly or so completely that any revelation of the eyes would be inappropriate. Indeed, neither Egyptian reliefs nor Palestinian drawings of women portray them with veils over their eyes.[26] Van der Toorn describes it as "a piece of cloth covering the head and partially concealing the face; the eyes and the cheeks were usually left exposed."[27] Here it serves to intensify the impression of the grace and beauty of her face.[28]

The region of Gilead in Transjordan included the Jabbok River (Josh. 12:2). The presence of sites such as Ramoth (Josh. 20:8; 21:38; 1 Kings 4:13), which means "heights," would suggest a hilly and perhaps mountainous area. Although this as well as the deep gorge formed by the Jabbok suggest steep precipices, the area was better known for its pastoral land and products (1 Chron. 5:9; Jer. 22:6; 50:19; Mic. 7:14; for the balm of Gilead see Jer. 8:22; 46:11). There was a Mount Gilead (*har haggil'ād*) west of the Jordan River, where Gideon assembled his army at the spring of Harod (Judg. 7:3). This would be located on the south

26. The latter is not limited to the Lachish reliefs of Judean prisoners, who may have been humiliated. There are also pictures of females at Kuntillet ʿAjrud in the Sinai and at Samaria that date from the time of the monarchy and do not include veils over the eyes.

27. Van der Toorn, "Significance," 328.

28. Ibid., 339. As he and others observe, the Middle Assyrian laws, dating from the latter half of the second millennium BC, are a major source of information for understanding the practice of women wearing a veil. In those laws, it was required for most free adult females to wear it, except for prostitutes and slave women, who were forbidden to wear a veil. Hence it is not true that nothing is known about the practice of wearing a veil in the ancient world, although how much this practice corresponded to ancient Israelite custom is not clear. However, Gen. 29:23–25 and 38:13–15 suggest that in that particular culture both prostitutes and brides did wear veils.

side of the Jezreel Valley. Either would be a possible location for goats to descend. However, the parallel passage in Song 6:5 mentions only Gilead (*haggil'ād*), with no reference to a mountain. Further, Mount Gilead of Song 4:1 has no definite article as in Judg. 7:3. Finally, the context of flocks of sheep fits well with the Transjordanian region of Gilead, as does the later mention of Mount Hermon. Therefore, the weight of evidence tips the scales in favor of the Gilead east of the Jordan. The picture of goats descending a steep terrain en masse conjures the appearance of a dark waterfall of waves in which the light plays off the innumerable reflections of each animal and creates a shimmering and enchanting spectacle.[29]

> ²Your teeth are like a shorn flock
> That ascend from the washing,
> Every one of them with its twin,
> There is no "miscarriage" among them.

The second verse continues the structure already noted. Here the teeth become the focus of attention. Having gazed at his lover's eyes, he observes her smile, and this evokes a verse of praise for this beautiful aspect. The image of the goats in the preceding verse naturally leads to this picture of another flock. In this case it is sheep, as the adjectival participle "shorn" suggests. Although this adjective does not appear in the otherwise parallel 6:6, it remains an important additional piece of information. It is not true to argue, as Pope does, that this must be a synonym for "ewes" (*hārĕḥēlîm*) that occurs in this position in 6:6.[30] In fact, in the preceding verse that also had a duplicate (6:5), there likewise was additional information not found in the repeating section—that Gilead is Mount Gilead. The same occurs in v. 2, where the word "shorn" should be treated seriously. As the backs of dark-colored goats create the effect of the lover's hair in v. 1, so the backs of shorn sheep create the effect of whiteness and cleanliness here. The image of teeth that have no spot or decay, or food particles, remains an attraction to this day. These sheep ascend from a watering hole,[31] though perhaps the sense here directly relates to the root "to wash" (*rḥṣ*). It is thus a place of washing, perhaps a watering hole or a similar spot in a topographical depression where water collects. The picture is further enhanced in that the ewes have just been washed, and therefore their shortened hair is as

---

29. Munro, *Spikenard*, 96: "her head of tumultuous curls."

30. See Pope, *Song*, 461. His description tends to focus on the teeth of the ewes in this verse. Thus the wash becomes a means by which the teeth of these sheep are cleaned, improving their appearance. However, this is certainly not the point of the verse.

31. So *HALOT* 1221.

clean as possible. Again, the cleanliness and whiteness of the teeth are in view. Of course, teeth yellow as one grows older. Therefore, there is also a sense in which this praise describes the youthfulness of the lover. The image of youthfulness and especially fecundity will continue into the second half of the verse.

Verse 2b is chiastically structured. Each line consists of six full syllables. The five words, in which the two last words form a single group, form an A-B-B'-A' pattern. Further, the first and third words sound almost identical: *šekkullām* and *šakkulâ*.[32] The first and last words also end in the characteristic *mêm* suffix (*-ām/-hem*) of the third-person masculine plural. The Hebrew pattern looks and sounds like this:

šekkullām
 matʾîmôt
 wĕšakkulâ
ʾên bāhem

This translates as:

Every one of them
 with its twin,
  Miscarriage
is not among them.

If the simile of ewes continues into this part of the poetry, then the feminine plural participle "twins" and the feminine adjective "miscarriage" describe the ewes as fertile. Indeed, it would appear that the birth of twins among sheep in the ancient Near East was both rare and desirable. In the Gilgamesh Epic, one of the blessings that the goddess Ishtar promises the hero is that "your nanny-goats will bear triplets, your ewes twins."[33] Hence the verse may suggest fecund ewes, and this would apply to the nubile female as well. However, the continuing theme of the lover's teeth is the primary purpose of this description. These lines portray teeth that are whole and straight, where each of the upper teeth has a matching correspondent among the lower teeth.[34] They are identical twins; there is no "miscarriage," where one of the teeth is not present. Given the amount of money spent for cosmetic dentistry in the modern age, nothing has changed regarding the beauty that "a perfect smile" evokes.

32. Fox, *Song*, 129.
33. Gilgamesh Epic 6.18, as quoted in Pope, *Song*, 462. Ishtar was associated with fertility, and her purpose in this promise was to seduce Gilgamesh.
34. Longman, *Song*, 144, notes that the point for the sheep is that each one's image is reflected in the washing pool.

> ³Like a scarlet thread are your lips,
> Your mouth is lovely,
> Like pieces of pomegranate are your temples,
> Behind your veil.

The third verse is carefully composed of four lines, with eight full syllables in the first and third lines and six in the second and fourth. Its content turns to consider the lips, an appropriate adjunct to the description of the teeth and a sensual one that reminds the lover of kisses. In sequence unlike the previous metaphor and two similes of vv. 1–2, this one begins with the comparison ("like a scarlet thread") and then identifies the part of the body compared ("your lips"). This reversal heightens the vivid picture of a scarlet thread. The thread (*ḥûṭ*) describes a cord that is not as thick or strong as a rope. Samson breaks the ropes as easily as if they were threads (Judg. 16:12). Although the picture of Rahab hanging a scarlet *ḥûṭ* outside her window as a sign to the Israelites (Josh. 2:18) may signify something broader and easier to see, such as a ribbon or cord, Eccles. 4:12 describes a rope of three *ḥûṭ* that is not easily broken. Nevertheless, the ideal of reddening lips to make them appear thick and desirable was common to the ancient world. In fact, the phrase "scarlet thread" (*ḥûṭ haššānî*) as it occurs in the Rahab story is identical to the one in the first line of this verse. The comparison goes on to summarize the mouth as "lovely" (*nāʾweh*). This term also carries the idea of "fitting" as praises that are fitting for God (Pss. 33:1; 147:1). The closest sense occurs in Prov. 17:7, where arrogant or lying lips are not fitting for a fool or ruler. This is the opposite of the picture here, in which the female's teeth and lips describe a perfectly formed mouth, one whose proportions are fitting and whose shape is beautiful. For the third time now the female has been described as *nāʾweh*. In Song 1:5 she identified herself in general with this adjective. In 2:14 the male spoke of her face as *nāʾweh*. Here the object of beauty becomes even more focused: the mouth. This word for "mouth" (*midbār*, 4:3) occurs only here. From the root *dbr* (to speak), it refers to the place of speech. This unique term is unexpected, given the fact that much more common terms for mouth (*peh*, above all) exist in Hebrew. The longer term may help achieve balance in the number of syllables. Fox suggests a better explanation, however.[35] The homonym *midbār* is a common noun referring to a wilderness. It has already appeared in 3:6. The adjective "lovely" (*nāʾweh*)[36] resembles a common word that describes grazing

35. Fox, *Song*, 130.
36. The *ʾālep* is quiescent.

land for animals (*nāweh*). Fox suggests that this refers to an oasis, and he finds a double meaning with this second phrase: "You are so lovely, so flawless, that whatever part of you might in comparison with the other parts be reckoned a wilderness, as somehow defective—even that 'wilderness' is an oasis, fresh and refreshing."[37]

Is this justified? A close examination reveals that the structure of this phrase is unique, and its position among the other metaphors and similes is central. The grammatical structure of the description provides two words with no preposition. In this manner it resembles only the first description, that of the eyes. Although in 4:1 that is followed by a second line elaborating their beauty, here with the mouth there is no second line. Further, in v. 1 the eyes are metaphorically identified as doves, a predicate nominative in the clause. Here in 4:3 the mouth is described as lovely, a predicate adjective. Thus the structure of this comparison, in its brevity and use of an otherwise unattested noun (*midbār*, mouth), arrests the reader/listener. Further, the poet places this remarkable comment in the middle of the comparisons. It follows four comparisons (eyes, hair, teeth, lips) and precedes three (temples, neck, breasts). Along with the lips, whose simile provides the other line of the first two lines of this verse, this description is centrally located in the *waṣf*. Hence the location and structure focus attention on a double entendre: the male lover delights in the form of his partner's mouth and uses the same words to praise her as his source of refreshment in the wilderness.

The second half of 4:3, duplicated in 6:7, turns to consider another part of the face, the temples. That the location of this part of the body is associated with the face becomes clear from the reference to its position "behind your veil," a repetition of the fourth line of v. 1. There it described the eyes and introduced the male's praise of his lover's face and head. Here it concludes complimenting her for those attributes. After this line the male's attention will leave the face and move to the neck. Since the temples are the part of the face closest to the eyes, this shows that the male has come full circle in his description of his lover's face and hair. The pieces of a pomegranate can take on two hues, yellow and red, or red and darker red.[38] These colors may well reflect the dual appearance of the female's skin on her forehead. There is the lighter part that is exposed and the darker part that is covered by her veil. This portrayal thus pictures both mystery and beauty. The juicy fruit of the

37. Fox, *Song*, 130. One could simplify this metaphor by understanding the implication of the text as "you are an oasis in the wilderness." However, this would not do justice to the pronominal suffix as possessive (your wilderness).

38. See Pope, *Song*, 464, and his discussion of the portrayal of pomegranates in Egyptian art.

pomegranate is filled with small seeds, a factor that contributed to it as a symbol of fertility and life.[39] As with the double message of the line concerning the lover's mouth, this image also describes what is fertile and full of life-giving potential.[40] The same was true of the ewes in v. 2. Hence the poem contains another theme that underlies many of these images, that of fertility.

> [4]Like the tower of David is your neck,
> Built in layers,
> A thousand shields hang on it,
> All the armor of warriors.

As with v. 3, Song 4:4 begins with the *kāp* preposition and the object of comparison followed by the body part. The tower of David is unknown other than here and in a parallel expression in 7:5 (7:4 Eng.). Lovers in Egypt appreciated the ideal of a long and graceful neck. In at least one poem a male describes his female partner as "long of neck."[41] However, the comparison with a tower suggests not someone who has a long neck as much as a woman whose neck is made strong and secure by what guards and protects it. In this case it is the shields and armor that appear in the following lines. The structure of this verse changes after the first line. Participles mark the boundaries of the two descriptions that occupy the center of the verse and create an A-B-B'-A' pattern:[42]

Built [*bānûy*]
   in layers,
   A thousand shields
hang [*tālûy*]

This provides a clue to the meaning of the word picture. The layers that are built, one upon another, create a strong fortress. They provide a parallel to the "shields." These are not literal shields but what appear to be shields in the fortification of the tower.[43] Small round leather shields

39. King and Stager, *Life*, 104, also observe its role in the temple decorations.

40. For the life-giving imagery of the pomegranate from the time of Thutmose III (1450 BC) onward, see Keel, *Song*, 143–47. Keel understands that the cutting of the pomegranate must refer to a single slit and that this is understood as the female's mouth. However, such a long veil covering the mouth does not seem likely. Bergant, *Song*, 46, follows Keel and argues for an opened, seductive mouth from the previous observation regarding the female's teeth. However, this element is nowhere explicit in these verses.

41. Fox, *Song*, 52, 130.

42. The participles are both third-*hê* verb Qal passive forms.

43. Contra Pope, *Song*, 468, who compares the five hundred gold shields (two hundred larger shields and three hundred smaller) that Solomon possessed in 1 Kings 10:16–17 with (attestations of) the hanging of shields on the wall of a tower (cf. this description

would resemble the outcroppings of various stones in the layers. For example, in the header-stretcher construction of the ancient Near East, those blocks of stone with their heads projecting outward could take on the appearance of shields added to the wall. How does this resemble the female's neck? Her neck would hold much of the jewelry that a woman might wear. Such jewelry was often layered, where strands of jewelry were placed one on top of the other. This formed a layered appearance that could ascend from the shoulder and reach as far as the top of the neck.[44] The martial imagery connotes defense and security.[45] If this interpretation of strands of jewelry is correct in reference to the image of the shields and armor, then the picture also conveys a scene of wealth and prosperity. The male lover may praise the female for the beauty and gracefulness of her neck, but the metaphor's focus on adornment suggests her own security and perhaps wealth. The point would then be that the female does not require the male to provide her with financial security or to guarantee her safety. Instead, she remains secure in who she is and what she has. His admiration recognizes that and seeks to approach her from a position of equality rather than subordinating her in class or status. Further, her security guarantees that her choice of his love will be voluntary and not pressed upon her by economic or other needs. The freedom of choice in the love that the couple shares remains an essential and important part of any couple's relationship. They must recognize their mutual need for one another in love but not such a dependency of one upon the other that provides opportunity for the "smothering" of one lover by the insecurity of the other or the abuse by one assuming a superior posture in the relationship.

> [5]Your two breasts are like two fawns,
> A gazelle's twins who feed among the lotuses.

The fifth verse considers the two breasts of the female. Here the structure returns to the opening comparisons in which the bodily part of the female is mentioned first and then the comparison follows (4:1–2). Given the emphasis upon the two breasts, it is significant that the eight

---

of the defenses of Tyre in Ezek. 27:11; LaCocque, *Romance*, 105). He seems to suggest hyperbole with the doubling of the number from five hundred to one thousand.

44. Fox, *Song*, 131, whose interpretation of the appearance of shields with strands of necklaces has its closest parallel in pictures of Egyptian females. These, however, do not have necklaces reaching all the way up their neck. In most cases, the strands lie on their shoulders and reach no higher than the base of their necks. Nevertheless, the imagery remains similar.

45. Garrett, *Song*, 105, suggests that the text conveys the sense of something impervious.

words of v. 5 are divided into four groups of two words each. The first three each contain a plural noun followed by a second noun.[46] They are each four full syllables in length. The final phrase, "who feed among the lotuses," contains a special form distinct from the preceding lines.[47] In addition, definite articles mark both words, a verb appears, and there are seven syllables in this phrase. The first three phrases of 4:5 form a word-for-word parallel with 7:4, and the last phrase coincides with the final words of 2:16. Thus this verse continues a theme previously expressed and anticipates descriptions to come.

This is the first appearance of "two" (*šĕnê*, here in masculine construct, 4:5) in the Song.[48] More significant structurally is the common *šîn-nûn-yôd* consonantal formation and sound that appears four times, as the first word in 4:2 (your teeth, *šinnayik*), the second word in v. 3 ([the] scarlet, *haššānî*), and the first and third words in v. 5 (two [of], *šĕnê*). This distinctive sound joins together three key comparisons: the female's teeth, which receive the longest description of any part of her body; the lips, which (with the mouth) form the center of the *waṣf*; and the breasts, the last part of the woman's body to be mentioned. Their position as last, along with this repeated sound that is doubled in v. 5, suggests a climax is reached at this point. Another structural observation also emphasizes this comparison as special. Verse 1 began with repetition of the phrase "look at you, so beautiful," with "my darling" standing between the two occurrences. A similar phenomenon occurs here. Literally, the first three words may be translated, "The two of your breasts, like the two of. . . ." As at the beginning of the first verse, so here as well, a central idea, "your breasts," lies between two repeated expressions (*šĕnê*) and demonstrates the key importance of this part of the female's body in the male's description. Finally, except for the inseparable prepositions, the first three words of v. 5 and the last word all begin with the same letter, *šîn: šĕnê šādayik kišnê . . . baššôšannîm*. This seems more than coincidence. All these structures highlight this simile.

The section of 4:1–7 thus focuses on this verse, which emphasizes the female's breasts. It highlights their duality as though to express the manner in which they complement one another. Previously the term fawn (*'ōper*) was used in the singular and followed by "the fal-

---

46. The nouns are in construct relation.

47. It is a definite plural participle followed by an inseparable preposition prefixed to a definite plural noun that forms the object of the participle.

48. The eyes of 4:1 were not explicitly numbered, but the use of the dual form would have indicated that fact if it were not for its similarity with the plural when the plural formation second-person feminine singular pronominal suffix is added. In 4:5 the same is true of the word for "breasts."

low deer [plural]" (*hāʾayyālîm*; 2:9, 17), with the two words translated "young stag."[49] In 4:5 *ʿōper* appears as a plural noun by itself and can be understood as "does." The following phrase begins with the expression for "twins" (*tĕʾômê*), whose root already appeared as a verb in the discussion of teeth in v. 2. This plural construct noun refers to the does as twins and connects them with the (female) gazelle or ibex (*ṣĕbîyâ*). The gazelle's does are pictured as identical twins. They symbolize the beauty and grace of the female's breasts. These animals also provide a picture of those who bring life.[50] (For the same phrase, see 2:16, where the female declares that her lover feeds among these lotuses.) The image of a lotus in the Bible is one of a fruitfully blossoming plant (Hosea 14:6 [14:5 Eng.]) whose shape was so beautiful as to be included in the decorations of the temple of Solomon.[51] When used of the female in the Song, it may refer to her special beauty (a lotus among thorns, 2:2) and her waist (7:3 [7:2 Eng.]). In 4:5 the lotuses could describe the physical body of the female lover as they seem to do in 2:16.[52] Thus the breasts appear as nourished by the body of the female. The emphasis again is upon life and fertility. Pope observes how the biblical texts can identify the breasts as givers of milk and life (Isa. 28:9; Joel 2:16; Ps. 22:10 [22:9 Eng.]; Job 3:12), as well as objects that sexually attract (Ezek. 16:7; 23:3, 21; Hosea 2:4 [2:2 Eng.]).[53] They represent the part of the female that, in the eyes of her lover, combine beauty and grace with fertility and youth. The twin fawns enhance this image with a picture of perfect balance between the two as well as a doubling of all these characteristics.[54] This brings the description full circle, as one is reminded of the two-word structure that forms most of the verse.

49. The nouns are in construct relation.

50. Keel, *Song*, 150–51, observes that gazelles and ibex inhabit the steppe, a land that has no properties of life. They thus represent life and the ability to triumph over the powers of death. He finds the idea of regeneration and a lust for life present in the portrayal of these animals on Egyptian amulets and scarabs, including more than a hundred found at Palestinian sites. Further, the iconography show gazelles and lotuses together in a manner to suggest that as the gazelle triumphs over the deadliness of the arid wasteland, so the lotus triumphs over the watery chaos.

51. See 1 Kings 7:19, 22, 26; 2 Chron. 4:5.

52. Cf. 7:3 (7:2 Eng.), where lotuses encircle the waist of the female.

53. Pope, *Song*, 470.

54. Budde, "Hohelied," 21; Longman, *Song*, 147; Rudolph, *Hohe Lied*, 147; Würthwein, "Hohelied," 52, all prefer the view that the point of the image is the two rumps of the does wiggling back and forth as they munch away on the plants. The ancient Near Eastern iconographic context, where does and other caprids are either portrayed in side views or from the front, as well as the absence of a specific visual indicator in the text, seems to favor the interpretation suggested above rather than this otherwise unattested perspective.

> ⁶Until the day breezes gently along,
> And the shadows flee,
> I will go to the mountain of myrrh,
> To the hill of frankincense.

The first half of 4:6 repeats the first half of 2:17. (See comments there for the view that the poet here describes the coming of the morning.) In 2:17 this was quoted by the female, who then urged her partner to turn away and bound like a gazelle into the hills and mountains. In 4:6 the male responds with a different impression. He will not leave his beloved but will come to her. The gazelles are not images of the male and his companions roaming in the distance, as in 2:16–17. Instead, in 4:5 they have become the breasts of his lover, where he will find love. The mountain is not distant as in chapter 2, but close by.[55] It is the mountain of myrrh, a theme already connected with his lover's breasts in 1:13, where she imagined him as a sachet of myrrh between her breasts.[56] The mountain has myrrh and frankincense, two spices previously attributed to the female as aromatics that signaled her "royal" approach in 3:6. It is as though the male, having joyfully praised one part of his lover's body after another, reaches the breasts and can go no farther. A torrent of sensual images and passions come cascading down upon him as he determines in his mind to spend the night with her and to realize the love that he has imagined. Altogether overcome, he expresses a collection of images selected from earlier expressions of love by his partner and himself. The overpowering aromas of the spices betray a fever pitch of excitement in his own heart as he thinks only of his lover.

> ⁷All of you is beautiful, my darling,
> There is not a blemish in you.

It is to her that he now turns his word directly in 4:7. The chiastic structure of this verse has already been outlined above. The lover begins with his summary and total expression, "All of you" (kullāk). This completes the description of the female, so that rather than delay with more praise of individual features, the male includes everything together in "all of you" and thus rushes to complete his address. It also prepares

---

55. As already noted, these spices are not indigenous to Palestine, so it is not possible for these to be geographical locations within reach of the lover, making a figurative meaning for "mountain" more likely.

56. Keel, *Song,* 152, cites a line from the Hellenistic (first-century BC–first-century AD) romance *Joseph and Aseneth*: "And her breasts (were) like the mountains of the Most High God" (18.9; cf. 8.5, "like handsome apples").

to emphasize that his statement of beauty leaves no part of his lover's body untouched. Each and every part has been identified and honored in this single Hebrew word. "All of you" at the beginning corresponds to "in you" at the end of v. 7, meaning "in any part of your body." In a similar manner, the word "beautiful" (*yāpāh*) refers to every part of the lover's body as described and to parts left unmentioned. Its twofold use at the beginning of the address in v. 1 and its recapitulation at the end of this section frame the *waṣf* with a declaration of its main purpose. Here in v. 7, however, the term "beautiful" is not repeated. Instead, the second, parallel position is occupied by "there is not a blemish." Within the context of the passage, this refers to a physical blemish just as the description of beauty applies to the lover's physical body.[57] Central to this verse is "my darling," just as it was central to the first part of v. 1. Like the word "beautiful" it frames the description and asserts that the male has not drifted off into another world or to a dream lover, but continues to address the one with whom he began. The chiastic structure of three levels—asserting the lover's body, her beauty without blemish, and the male's pet name for her—provides a threefold outline of the address: her body in its whole and in each part is praiseworthy, the blemish-free beauty is affirmed, and this is the male's special and only lover.

> [8]Come with me from Lebanon, my bride,
> Come with me from Lebanon,
> Travel from Amana's peak,
> From Senir's peak,
> From Hermon,
> From the dens of lions,
> From the mountain lairs of leopards.

Verse 8 forms a "hinge" between what has preceded and what follows.[58] As already noted at the beginning of this section, there are structural links between vv. 1 and 8. There are also vocabulary links between v. 8 and the remainder of the chapter. The themes of movement and of mountains have already appeared in vv. 1 and 6 and again are expressed here. The suggestion that the female depart from her home and join her partner has also received some comment in v. 4, where the tower imagery suggests distance and removal from the embrace of her male lover. The connections of v. 8 guarantee that the *waṣf* of the first half of this chapter will not be separated from the garden imagery of the second half. Only here in the entire Song does the preposition "with" (*ʾēt*) appear, and it does so twice. Further, the homonymic and omnipresent direct object marker *ʾēt*,

57. Cf. Eph. 5:27.
58. The term Janus parallelism may be appropriate here.

which occurs many times in the Song, remains absent from this chapter. The repeated use of this preposition and pronominal suffix as "with me" provides a significant marker by which the lover emphasizes his desire to partner with his beloved, to be physically present with her.

He calls her to come from Lebanon. This is the second of six occurrences of the noun. It appeared earlier in 3:9, which described the litter as constructed of wood from Lebanon. Perhaps the male calls to his lover to leave her room and home, a palace constructed of the finest of wood (cf. 1:17). However, that would not make sense of the other place-names in the verse, all of which describe mountains in either the Lebanon or Anti-Lebanon range. These ranges, reaching above 10,000 feet in height at the northern end, represent areas visible yet far out of reach. The male sees his lover as unattainable at this point.[59] She is somehow removed from him and he cannot reach her (compare a similar situation in 2:14). Hence he calls her to come away with him and to leave the far regions of Lebanon, where he has no access to his lover. Lebanon, like the place-names that follow, becomes a metaphor for what is inaccessible, lending weight to his demand that the female make her move toward him.[60]

The word "bride" (kallâ) appears here for the first time in the Song. It will occur another five times, four in this section (4:9, 10, 11, 12; 5:1). Coming as it does after the wedding procession at the end of chapter 3, this represents a continuation of the sense of a marriage relationship.[61] In this case, the image is one of a committed love relationship in which the full experience of passion and sensuality, as described in the preceding verses, can be realized. Amana appears as a river in 2 Kings 5:12.[62] There it identifies a clean river that flows through Damascus, thus coming from a source in the mountains. The Targum equates it with Mount Taurus. Pope identifies it with Baradam, whose source is Jebel Zebedamni, in the Anti-Lebanon range.[63] This may be the mountain envisioned. Senir

---

59. Loretz, "Cant 4,8," cites Ugaritic and Assyrian parallels for the Lebanon and Anti-Lebanon ranges as symbols of inaccessibility. So also Murphy, *Song*, 160.

60. Here there may be an additional image of paradise and its restoration (Munro, *Spikenard*, 141).

61. Fox, *Song*, 135, for whom the unmarried status of the lovers of the Song is a matter of doctrine, argues that the term "bride" is one of affection and close relationship, not one of a legal marriage. He compares this with "sister" in the following verse (cf. Murphy, *Song*, 156, 160). However, nowhere in the Bible or in the comparable Egyptian love songs that he cites does any evidence exist for "bride" used merely as a term of endearment (unlike "sister," for which see comments on 4:9 below). In Israel and other societies, *kallâ* defined a legal relationship, with certain obligations and rights. It would be misleading in the extreme to use such a term in a love song where that relationship was not intended.

62. It appears in the Qere. The Kethib has "Abana," but other Hebrew manuscripts as well as the Syriac and the Targums support "Amana."

63. Pope, *Song*, 475, who refers as well to Akkadian records. See also Cogan, "From"; Murphy, *Song*, 156.

is identified with Mount Hermon in Deut. 3:9 and 1 Chron. 5:23.[64] In the former it is identified as the Amorite name of the mountain area. Hermon is the tallest mountain in the southern Lebanon region, rising above 10,000 feet. It represents the most inaccessible of places on land. Like Senir and Amana it lies to the north of ancient Israelite territory and in the region of the Lebanon. For this Israelite poet it is an image of his lover's distance from him. If she is not with him and in his arms, it is as though she is on the far corners of the earth.

There is, however, another connection with these mountains and in particular with Lebanon. The name Lebanon (*lĕbānôn*) closely resembles the word for frankincense (*lĕbônâ*), which already appeared in 3:6 and 4:6 and will recur in 4:14. However, it is the connection with 4:6 that is most interesting. There the male intends to ascend the mountain of myrrh and the hill of frankincense. Surely the connection of these nearly identical words should not go unnoticed. The male seeks to ascend the hill of frankincense/Lebanon and longs for his lover to come from there and to join him. On the one hand this is the female's body that the lover longs to hold in his arms and to enjoy in sexual pleasure. On the other hand it is the most distant of places from which he longs for his bride to come.[65] The fantasy of proximity and the reality of distance meet in the presence of his lover, and he longs for her to yield to him so that his enjoyment of her love might be complete.

The phrase "dens of lions," in parallel with the "mountain lairs of leopards," completes v. 8 and parallels the peaks of Amana and Senir. With Hermon in the center of this structure, these final two lines describe further the difficulty of achieving access to the female. She alone must come out from these places and join her lover. The association of "den" (*mĕʿōnâ*) with "lion" (*ʾaryēh*) occurs in Amos 3:4; Nah. 2:12–13 (2:11–12 Eng.); and with synonyms in Ps. 104:21–22; Job 38:40; and Dan. 6:8–25 (6:7–24 Eng.). The last line literally describes the "mountains of leopards."[66] Some suggest "hole, den" (*ḥōr*) rather than "mountain" (*har*), but there is no textual support for this emendation. Instead, the

---

64. For this reason it is not clear why Keel, *Song*, 158, suggests that Senir, Amana, and Hermon represent the northern, middle, and southern parts of the Anti-Lebanon range.

65. G. Carr, *Song*, 119, suggests that the preposition *min*, usually translated "*from* [Lebanon]," should be translated "*in* [Lebanon]." It remains unclear whether this is a legitimate translation for the Hebrew preposition.

66. Although not apparent in modern times, in earlier periods these animals inhabited the regions named here. Albright, "Archaic," 3, finds here the remnant of an Adonis myth in which he invited his lover to go hunting in the Lebanon. However, nothing significant remains of any possible myth in its present context (Murphy, *Song*, 156). Further, the associations that Keel, *Song*, 155–60, draws between mountains, these animals, and goddesses demonstrate a frame of reference for their connection with females. It does not prove a portrayal of the female as a goddess, as Keel suggests. Cf. Murphy, *Song*, 95–97.

emphasis on the mountains continues the primary theme of the verse, the inaccessibility and difficulty/danger of reaching the female. Her lover thus calls her to leave her "fortress" and to open to him the joys of her companionship and love. As he does this, he addresses her as "bride" and thereby lays claim to her presence with him.

4:9–15. *Male: A walk in the garden.* These verses continue the male's address begun in v. 1 and carried through the chapter. As noted in the preceding section, v. 8 forms the center of this address, with the male's call to his lover to come with him and join him in lovemaking. Verses 9–15 revert to a theme similar to the *wasf* that begins the chapter. Verses 9 and 10 exhibit staircase parallelism (see also 3:1, 8). Verse 9 begins with a direct address to the female, describing twice how she has stolen his heart. Verbs with the female as subject then give way to nominal clauses where aspects of her are described. As in the first part of the chapter, the male begins with his lover's eyes and then proceeds to her neck. However, characteristics of these are not detailed, only their attraction to the male. Verse 10 also begins with two repeated clauses that in this case are not identical but do resemble one another. No verbs appear, but again two groups of lines occupy the second half of the verse, where they compare the female's lovemaking and fragrance. Verse 11 considers her lips and mouth. Here the two lines of parallel expression at the beginning of the verse disappear, as does the dual address, "sister and bride." In their place the two lines describe different parts of the lover's mouth, and the term of endearment is "bride" alone. Throughout these three verses the imagery used in comparison of different aspects of the female has gradually grown in quantity and become more sensual. In v. 9 only jewels are mentioned. In v. 10 wine, perfume, and spices occur. In v. 11 honeycomb, honey, milk, and the fragrance of Lebanon appear. As the images increase in number, the senses to which the poet appeals also grow. In v. 9 sight alone is mentioned. In v. 10 taste and smell are used. In v. 11 taste and smell reappear, and touch may also be added with the comparison of the lover's lips to a honeycomb.

After 4:11 the structure changes. There are no verbs other than participles used as parts of the description. The only time the female is identified occurs in the familiar "sister and bride" in v. 12 and in the feminine singular pronominal suffix at the beginning of v. 13. Otherwise, the verses provide a list of what one might find in the enclosed garden that begins v. 12: wells, fountains, fruits, spices. Verses 12 and 15 provide the envelope that describes the overall garden as enclosed and full of water sources.[67] Verses 13 and 14, between 12 and 15, also go

67. See Elliott, *Literary*, 113; Müller, "Hld 4,12–5,1," for further descriptions of asyndetic and unusual lines and descriptions in the structure of this section (which he terms a paradigm of poetic speech).

inside the garden and inspect the plants that grow there. As noted, both of these two parts begin with a recognition that the descriptions apply to the female.[68] However, the reader/listener is left without the direct relationships that the earlier verses have established by mentioning specific parts of the female's body or active aspects such as lovemaking. The structure betrays a sense in which the male's passion and ardent desire for the female blur individual traits and push his poetry into near total metaphor. No longer is an individual aspect of the female represented by this or that aspect of nature. Now the whole of his lover has become a garden rich in sensual delights.

> [9]You have beguiled me,
> My sister <and> bride,
> You have beguiled me,
> With a single <glance> of your eyes,
> With a single strand of your necklace.

The ninth verse begins with a comment on the part of the male lover. His female partner has led him into greater desire. She has beguiled him. As noted in its appearance in v. 8, "bride" (*kallâ*) is best understood literally. The term never carries a symbolic connotation when used in love poems. It indicates a married state, or at least a condition in which the lovers are about to marry. The same is not true with "sister." This term derives from a different category of relationship. It is not one legally created nor one that could be dissolved as in a divorce. Instead, a sister, like a brother, represents the closest of peer relationships, wherein one is prepared to share intimacies and every part of life. It is often used in Egyptian love songs to describe the lovers without any prejudice toward incest.[69] It also appears with this usage in the Bible: Job 17:14; Prov. 7:4; and elsewhere in the Song. Here the expression will recur in vv. 9, 10, and 12, establishing its thematic significance. The reference to the female's role as sister and bride is intended to convey both the closeness of the brother/sister relationship and the commitment of the marriage. The threefold repetition establishes this as of the highest importance for understanding the relationship. It is a marriage relationship, for that is the only explanation for the use of the term "bride." Yet it also remains a personal bond on the order of siblings. What the last verses of chapter 3 have hinted at in their description of the king's intention to hold a wedding, these verses now confirm.

68. Whether "my sister and bride" (v. 12) or "your plants" (v. 13).
69. Fox, *Song*, 136.

The line following this introductory section remarks how the female stole her lover's heart with one glance from her eyes (4:9). The word "glance" is missing, but this is the most reasonable explanation of the text. As already noted, the focus of the male on the eyes of his lover has begun in the first part of his address, in 4:1. Their appearance at the beginning of this second half of the lover's description may suggest one of two things. Perhaps the eyes summarize the whole of the adorable traits of the female, and as the lover gazes longingly into them, he therefore mentions them again at the beginning as a summation of everything else that he longs for in her. Alternatively, perhaps the lover finds in his partner's eyes the most magnificent and beautiful representation of all parts of her body. More than anything else, the eyes transfix and attract. There may be elements of both aspects in the first position of the eyes here. The reference to strands from the female's necklace may recall the discussion of her neck and the layers of "shields" (strands) that surround it (v. 4). Here, however, a strand is singled out. This is the strand of greatest value and prize. Its unique position of radiance makes it the most attractive of all the strands displayed. Perhaps, as in Egyptian neckwear that appears to rest on the shoulders, it is the lower strand that has the most color and area for radiance. This line regarding the necklace parallels the one regarding the lover's eyes. The synonymous parallelism suggests that the poet identifies the necklace with his beloved's eyes.[70] It is not one eye but both eyes together, luminous and glittering as the finest of neckwear. The strand represents the "glance," which first catches the attention of the admirer. The necklace is then understood as summing up all the charms of the female, all the characteristics that have been and will be described. The second line thus answers the question raised by the previous line. The eyes represent to the male the most alluring part of the female's body. They are what one looks at first, and they increase the value and beauty of the whole of the female.

> [10]How delightful is your lovemaking,
> My sister <and> bride,
> How much better is your lovemaking
> Than wine,
> And the fragrance of your perfumes
> Than all the spices.

The tenth verse provides an enthusiastic assessment of the lover's lovemaking. This central expression of physical love is assessed and

---

70. For this connection as an example of Janus parallelism (cf. 2:12) expressed in the actual word "eye(s)" (*ʿayin*), see Malul, "Janus."

pronounced both "delightful" and "better" than wine. The denominative verbal form of "delightful" (*yāpû*) occurs for the first time here.[71] Its form in v. 10, like that of its parallel "better" (*ṭōbû*), functions as an adjective to describe the lovemaking (also in the plural). The latter comparison is a direct reference back to the second verse of the Song, where kisses were described as better than wine. This comparison is itself enlightening, for it demonstrates that the sense of lovemaking embodied in *dōd* is not solely or necessarily a reference to sex, but may describe physical expressions of love such as kissing. The next line mentions the fragrance of the female's perfumes and continues to track with the opening verses of the Song. This expression is used of the male's name in 1:3. In fact, that is the only other occurrence of the phrase in the Bible. Hence the poet recalls these initial themes, placed on the female's lips in 1:2–3, but here spoken by the male. The reciprocity of description suggests a mutual love characterized by similar passions evoked by describing similar aspects of the partner's form, name, and lovemaking. Of course, it is not the name of the female that evokes desire in 4:10, but rather the actual scent of her perfumes. Nevertheless, the similar forms and expressions suggest that the couple continues probing the depths of their desires and discover that their love is characterized by what they share and express with similar sentiments. The final phrase establishes the fragrance of the female as best of all by using the superlative expression "more than all/any" (*mikkol*). The word for "spices" (*bĕśāmîm*) appears in 4:10 for the first time in the Song.[72] This is surprising because it is not an unusual term, occurring thirty times in the Bible, and yet it has remained absent despite frequent reference to aromatics. It is used here to introduce the garden of spices that will appear in the following verses. Indeed, the term recurs in vv. 14 and 16.

> [11]Your lips drip virgin honey,
> O bride,
> Honey and milk are beneath your tongue,
> And the fragrance of your garments
> Is like the fragrance of Lebanon.

71. Cf. also Song 7:2, 7 (7:1, 6 Eng.). Elsewhere it appears in Jer. 4:30; 10:4; Ezek. 16:13; 31:7; and cf. Ps. 45:3 (45:2 Eng.).

72. It may refer to spices in general or, in the view of some, to balsam oil, a valuable commodity later attributed especially to Judah. Josephus (*Jewish War* 4.8.3 §469) regarded it as the most valuable of Judea's exports in his time. Pliny (*Natural History* 12.111) likewise identified the balsam fragrance, a favorite among Romans, as original to the balsam of Judea. See Keel, *Song*, 165.

The eleventh verse begins with a powerful image of the female's lips dripping the best honey. The object of the line, the honey, appears first in the Hebrew. This unusual order increases the emphasis of the line. It is the honey and particularly its sweetness that portray the lips of the female. This image plays upon the senses of touch and taste. In 1:2 wine was the heady intoxicant that the female used to compare with her partner's lips. Here the male uses honey, an image of sweetness in which the male can become lost. Honey, especially in the form of the sweetness from dates, but also including bee honey, was the major source of sugar for the ancient Israelite diet. Therefore, the allusion emphasizes the sweetest-tasting food of which the male was aware. An active verb also appears in this line and forms a structure distinct from most lines, where either a preposition such as "like" occurs or a metaphor is used without a linking verb. The identical phrase "drip honey" (*nōpet tiṭṭōpĕnâ*) appears in Prov. 5:3, where it describes the adulteress whose mouth is smoother than oil. The enticement of the words of her mouth forms the source of the image in Proverbs and perhaps also here. There are some 48 occurrences of the words for honey (*dĕbaš*) and milk (*ḥālāb*) appearing together in the OT, including Song 5:1, another poem of praise to his lover's joys. However, most of the occurrences appear in the descriptions of the promised land of Canaan as flowing with milk and honey.[73] Again, the honey in those contexts is likely date honey, or dibs, and the milk is more often that of goats than of larger cattle. Such milk is richer in fat and protein, providing an important source of these nutrients.[74] Hence the lover describes a source of sweetness and richness below his partner's tongue. On the one hand the lines portray kissing that becomes more and more intimate as it moves from the lips into the mouth. On the other hand the union of the two lovers becomes a source of sustenance and energy for the male. She is all he needs.

Complementing the senses of taste and touch in the first half of the verse, the sense of smell appears in the second half. Here the sense of touch is carried by the lips and tongue, and taste and smell are all related to the mouth and nose area. Their connection is demonstrated as the loss of smell leads to a loss of taste. Thus perhaps in this verse the greater stimulation of taste heightens the sense of smell. The result is a powerful aphrodisiac in the form of the fragrance of the bride's garments.[75] Of course, the bride might wear special garments, as suggested

73. Exod. 3:8, 17; 13:5; 33:3; Lev. 20:24; Num. 13:27; 14:8; 16:13, 14; Deut. 6:3; 11:9; 26:9, 15; 27:3; 31:20; Josh. 5:6 et passim.

74. King and Stager, *Life*, 103–4, 106.

75. G. Carr, *Song*, 123, objects with the observation that the term used here for "garments" (*śalmâ*) is never used in Ps. 45, the one wedding psalm in the Bible other than the Song. This term refers to the outer garment of Ruth 3:3 and the cloak used for sleeping in

in Ps. 45:14–15 (45:13–14 Eng.). As in the case of the groom, these garments might possess special fragrances that exemplify the pleasant and desirable nature of the couple's love and their wedding: "Myrrh, aloes, and cassia are all your garments" (Ps. 45:9a [45:8a Eng.]).

Thus the closest allusion to this description in Song 4 is Ps. 45 and its portrayal of a wedding. The "fragrance of Lebanon" may describe the fresh scents of pine and other woods. However, the word "Lebanon" (*lĕbānôn*, Song 4:11) resembles frankincense (*lĕbônâ*). In this richly aromatic song it is more than coincidence that these two words occur several times: Lebanon, six times (3:9; 4:8, 11, 15; 5:15; 7:5 [7:4 Eng.]); and frankincense, three times (3:6; 4:6, 14).[76] The one passage where the two terms interweave is this section, 4:6–15. The majority of their occurrences are here, five out of nine. There thus may be an intention to express both terms within this single passage. Although Lebanon appears in topographical contexts in vv. 8 and 15, here in v. 11 it defines an aromatic. This context suggests an intentional mixing of frankincense (or the more general idea of incense that this term can convey) with the location of Lebanon itself as a source of pleasant scents. Whatever the case, the fragrances combine with the senses of touch and taste in a captivating verse of praise to the female's beauty and as a source of desire.

The address of the female as "bride" (*kallâ*, 4:11) is not new. It has been seen in the previous verses. However, in vv. 9 and 10 it is "my sister and bride." Not since v. 8 has "bride" appeared by itself. The structure suggests that this form of address signals a change, one that will come with vv. 12 and 13, in which the imagery shifts from praise of the female for her desirable traits to a simile comparing the female to a garden.

> [12]<You are>
> A locked garden,
> My sister and bride,
> A locked pool,
> A sealed fountain.

Verse 12 turns to the theme of the female lover as a garden. More than any other metaphor, this one serves the purpose of the poet. This image is common in the ancient Near East and evokes senses of leisure,

---

Exod. 22:25–26 (22:26–27 Eng.); Deut. 22:17. However, the context leads him to modify the usage elsewhere and to suggest here a form of sleepwear, perhaps a negligee. Yet the point of the garments is their fragrance. Therefore, whether outerwear or underwear, the comparison with Ps. 45 stands. It alone considers the fragrance of garments.

76. Elliott, *Literary*, 107, regards the use of Lebanon here as an inclusion with 4:8.

happiness, and intimacy.[77] Here it provides opportunity for an extended discussion of a garden. Without making specific connections, it allows the reader/listener the opportunity to visualize multiple metaphors and images in constructing the picture of this garden. The term for "garden" (*gan*) occurs here for the first time in the Song. However, it will recur another seven times, four of which are in this context (4:15, 16 [2x]; 5:1; 6:2 [2x]; 8:13). The identification of the female with the garden is assumed but never explicitly stated. However, the juxtaposition of "a locked garden" in the first line of v. 12 with "my sister and bride" in the second line is performed in such a manner that it implies an association of the two. The locked garden provides an image of the female, whose physical love is not open to anyone. It thus continues the image of inaccessibility exemplified by the mountains of v. 8. However, as the verses continue, it becomes clear that the male does visit the garden and knows of the fruits and beauties found in it. The appearance of the address form "my sister and bride" occurs here for the last time. Its final appearance links it with vv. 9–10 and the previous section. However, it serves as well to introduce vv. 12–15 and to associate this verbal picture with the previous section.

The three images that precede and follow the address are each constructed of two words in which the common noun appears first: garden/pool/fountain. This is followed by a participle used as an adjective to modify the masculine singular noun: locked/locked/sealed.[78] The first two expressions are almost identical: *gan nāʿûl* and *gal nāʿûl*. Only the second consonant of the first word distinguishes the two, *gan* versus *gal*.[79] This near identity of sound associates two images that are otherwise distinct: the closed garden and the closed pool (for this meaning of *gal*, see the second translation note at 4:12 above). The second and

---

77. Keel, *Song*, 169–74, commenting on 169: "The inner court of every house had some kind of garden. A few herbs for the kitchen, a grapevine, or a fig tree usually had to suffice. To sit under these trees in peace and to enjoy their fruits without disturbance was the highest form of happiness (1 Kings 4:25 [5:5]; Mic. 4:4)." Of interest is the association with trees and shrubs, rather than vegetables and flowers, which formed the flora to be found in an ancient garden. Lebanon was thus considered an ideal garden in ancient Mesopotamia and in the Bible, where it is called the garden of God (Ezek. 31:8). The garden of Eden is also identified with trees and becomes the model of a place of intimacy between God and the man and woman (Gen. 2–3).

78. In each case, it is a Qal passive participle. Munro, *Spikenard*, 74, observes: "The effect of the epithets on each occasion is to slow down the description, and to communicate the delicate process by means of which the garden opens to welcome her lover."

79. The LXX translates both by "garden" (*kēpos*), reading both words as the same. This raises a text-critical issue regarding the more likely original reading. However, as "wave" (*gal*) also forms a connection with the following line, and "garden" would not, it seems best to retain the MT. For more on the paronomasia, see Gordis, *Song*, 87–88; Schoville, "Impact," 80–81.

third descriptions, while continuing the same structure, do not need to sound so much alike because their identity is a semantic one: "a locked pool" and "a sealed fountain." A garden that contains its own water source can be securely locked. The sealed fountain, like the locked pool, suggests a close identity with the female's body and with her physical love. Is this a description of the vagina? Perhaps, although the delicate allusion is so carefully disguised that it becomes virtually impossible to achieve certainty that a particular physical part of the genitalia is envisioned here. Rather, as with the remainder of vv. 12–15, the allusions evoke sensations that correspond to those obtained in the acts of lovemaking. Indeed, the erotic image of the garden can refer to female sexuality in general as well as the pudenda in particular.[80] In this case, the pool and fountain are sealed, like the garden, and thus not available to anyone. However, the male lover enjoys them. A fountain or pool would provide him with refreshment and all the more so in the spring and early summer of Jerusalem's desert climate. Hence the love is one that refreshes, as in v. 11, where scents, honey, and milk revitalize the partner. Of course, these waters also serve the necessary purpose of watering the garden so that the exotic plants may grow there. These plants are described in vv. 13 and 14.

> [13]Your plants,
> A garden of pomegranates,
> With the best of fruits,
> With henna and spikenard.

The structure of v. 13 appears to be an A-B-A'-B' order. The reference to "your plants" corresponds to "with the best of fruits." Both describe the garden in general terms. However, the B lines define specific fruits. The garden of pomegranates is an ideal picture of the garden as a whole. Pomegranates are a fruit mentioned some fifty-five times in the OT and are already seen in 4:3. Due to their many seeds, they embody fruitfulness. And this is the symbol of the female's garden. It is a place of great fecundity.

The combination of henna and spikenard (pure nard) recalls their only previous appearance, in 1:12 and 14.[81] There the two represented the most expensive and exotic perfume (spikenard) and what was most easily available (henna). Here as well it is a combination of spices. Again, it may be a merism that introduces the list of spices in v. 14 by includ-

---

80. See Paul, "Lover's," who provides the context for this observation from a wide variety of ancient Near Eastern examples.

81. Keel, *Song*, 178, suggests that the plurals of henna and nard refer to the individual henna bushes and the nard plants.

ing them all. Perhaps it merely indicates that these two aromatics were often associated in their use or for some other reason.

> 14Spikenard and tumeric,
> Spice cane and cinnamon,
> With all the trees of frankincense,
> Myrrh and aloes,
> With all the best spices.

The list that began at the end of v. 13 continues in v. 14. Three lines of v. 14 each contain two aromatics joined by a *wāw* conjunction. The first spice named in v. 14 is nard (*nērd*), written in the singular but otherwise identical to the plural form (*něrādîm*) at the end of v. 13. If spikenard has its origins in the Himalayas, tumeric or curcuma (*karkōm*) was native to Southeast Asia.[82] Spice cane (*qāneh*) and cinnamon (*qinnāmôn*) appear along with myrrh in Exod. 30:23 as the ingredients for the production of the sacred anointing oil. Spice cane was an exotic fragrance with its origins in South Arabia.[83] Like spikenard, cinnamon also came from the east: East India, Sri Lanka, and China. These were both therefore associated with exotic fragrances and were most likely brought from the east in the same caravans. Frankincense, *lĕbônâ*, has already appeared in Song 3:6 and 4:6, where its origin in southern Arabia and eastern Africa was noted. The name refers to its white resin. Only here does it follow the form "trees of" (*ʿăṣê*).[84] The envisioned garden has trees that contain these spices. Alternatively, perhaps these are general plants that produce incense. In fact, this line

82. Keel observes that tumeric or curuma is "a slender, herbaceous plant native to Southeast Asia; its roots contain a yellow substance used as a spice and a dye" (ibid.). He also recognizes the translation of "crocus" or "saffron" for *karkōm*, coming from regions immediately south of the Black and Caspian Seas. However, noting a later association of the Hebrew term among products from India and points east, and relying on the more exotic nature of distant Southeast Asia, Keel prefers "tumeric." However, many commentators prefer "saffron," though they provide no justification for this. Brenner, "Aromatics," argues that nard and *karkōm* demonstrate a Persian period (or later) date for the Song because these terms do not appear elsewhere in early biblical sources, and they most closely resemble the Persian (period) cognates. This argument remains unconvincing because spices from India would have been transported most easily overseas around South Arabia, not through Persia. Contacts between Palestine and India are known as early as the Late Bronze Age, when some of the personal names of rulers and leaders from Palestine are Sanskrit (Hess, *Amarna*).

83. See Ezek. 27:19, 22; Pliny, *Natural History* 12.48; Pope, *Song*, 493–94. Keel, *Song*, 180, however, prefers to identify it with palmarosa, "a tall reedlike grass cultivated in India for the sake of its aromatic oil." Other than the more exotic location, however, he does not explain his preference.

84. The nouns are in construct relation.

and the final line of v. 14 display a similar construction. In both, "with all" (*ʿim kol*) is followed by a masculine plural noun, "trees of/best of" (lit., heads of, *rāʾšê*),[85] and then a masculine plural noun that generally describes spices. These lines form a refrain that brings to an end the list of spices and provides a twofold emphasis on the variety and the quality of the spices. The myrrh has already appeared, usually with frankincense (1:13; 3:6; 4:6). The aloes (*ʾăhālôt*) appear here in the Song for the first time. The term identifies aromatic woods, especially the aloe tree of northern India and eastern Africa.[86] This exotic aromatic was a spice used along with myrrh for royal wedding robes (Ps. 45:9 [45:8 Eng.]) and for perfuming the bed of the adulteress (Prov. 7:17). The spices enumerated in this verse all originated in distant lands. A garden could contain all of them only in fantasy or by transplanting, so only the wealthiest could afford it. Even so, such a transplanted garden would thrive only in a climate such as that of En Gedi. Both the variety and quality of the spices would provide a wonderful collection of fragrances that could overload the sense of smell with delight. This is the impression that the male wishes to convey to the female regarding the effect of her love on him. The fragrances themselves may have erotic associations, although there is no evidence other than the myrrh, aloes, and cinnamon mentioned in Prov. 7:17.

> [15]A garden fountain,
> A well of living water,
> Flowing from Lebanon.

The metaphor continues in v. 15. Although translations begin with the male saying "You are," this is not found in the text. As in v. 12, the image is everything, and the person embodying this picture is assumed. The poet waxes rapturous in his phrases and does not bother with the explicit identifications. As noted above, vv. 12 and 15 form an envelope that encloses the description of the garden. Each verse has eight words. Both are structured so that each line begins with the key description as the first word. The first line of v. 15 uses the last noun of v. 12 in construct with the first noun of v. 12: (lit.) "fountain of gardens" (*maʿyan gannîm*). The resulting description portrays the fountain in the garden, rather than the garden itself. The second line, "A well of living water," contains three Hebrew words. The "well" (*bĕʾēr*) corresponds to the "pool" (*gal*) in v. 12. There, however, the emphasis

---

85. The nouns are in construct relation.

86. Keel, *Song*, 180. G. Carr, *Song*, 126, suggests the *Aloë succotrina*, "a spicy drug extracted from the pulp of the leaves of a large shrub native to the island of Socotra at the southern end of the Red Sea."

was on the inaccessibility of the water. In v. 15 the opposite is true. The fountain is the best one for producing water. The well provides fresh or living waters that can create life and give water to the spice garden.[87] This is not merely a cistern collecting water, but a pool with a spring bubbling up a fresh supply of water.[88] Such waters grant the maximum potential for growth and fertility. Their property to "flow" (*nzl*) adds to their portrayal as fresh. Lebanon appears as the top of the world, the highest source from which the waters may flow. This is another envelope construction, bringing the whole of the second half of the male's song to a conclusion. In 4:8 the image of coming from Lebanon was that of the woman in an inaccessible place. There it was parallel to Hermon, the tallest mountain in the region. Now Lebanon again appears. However, the altered purpose of the mountain range in v. 15 is that of a source of water. The streams from Lebanon water the area around Dan and form the upper courses of the Jordan River, which flows into the Huleh basin and south to the Sea of Galilee (Tiberias). From there the river continues to the Dead Sea, picking up all the watershed on the eastern side of the hill country. That would include the area around Jerusalem. From high points even in this city, Mount Hermon, at the southern end of the Lebanon, is visible on a clear day. Further, the streams from Lebanon contrast with the well of water. Not only the lower water sources but also the highest sources of water provide nourishment for this garden. Thus, the picture ends with the portrayal of an Eden, a well-watered garden in which the male may stroll and find many delights.[89]

An ancient Sumerian poem provides a significant parallel in the third "sign" of Lu-dingir-ra's description of his mother:

> My mother is rain from heaven, water for the finest seed.
> A harvest of plenty. . . ,
> A garden of delight, full of joy,
> A watered pine, adorned with pine cones,
> A spring flower, a first fruit,

87. For other occurrences of the phrase "living waters," see Lev. 14:5, 50; 15:13; Num. 19:17; Jer. 2:13; 17:13; Zech. 14:8. See also the same line, "well of living waters," in Gen. 26:19. There it is used to describe the type of water that Isaac's servants drew from a well they dug.

88. Keel, *Song*, 180–81. Note that this would be true of the Gihon Spring in Jerusalem.

89. Hess, "Eden"; Brenner, *Song*, 84. Cf. Landy, "Song"; idem, *Paradoxes*, 189–265; Keel, *Song*, 158–64; Murphy, *Song*, 161. Landy suggests the poem as a whole is a picture of the garden of Eden. He quotes Lys, *Plus beau*, 52: "Le Cantique n'est rien d'autre qu'un commentaire de Gen. 2" (The Song is nothing but a commentary on Gen. 2). See also Barth, *Church Dogmatics*, 3/2:293–300; 3/1:309–21.

An irrigation ditch carrying luxuriant waters to the garden plots,
A sweet date from Dilmun, a date chosen for the best.[90]

Imagery in this earlier Mesopotamian poem is similar to that in Song 4:11–15. Both describe a woman who is close to the poet, and both portray her as a source of life-giving water. Both emphasize her fecundity in terms of a garden as well as plants and trees found in the garden. Finally, both make an initial identification with the woman and then move on to avoid repeated reference to her.

> [16]Awake, O north wind,
> Come, O south wind,
> Blow upon my garden,
> Let its spices spread,
> Let my lover come to his garden,
> Let him eat its best fruit.

4:16. *Female: Invitation to her garden.* Every line of v. 16 begins with a verb. The first three verbs are feminine imperatives, the last three are jussives (commands). The purpose of the first three lines is realized in the fourth line: the winds are to blow so that the garden's spices will become more intense to the male. This logically leads to the final two lines, in which the male is attracted to the female's garden and partakes of it. For this reason the final two jussive verbal forms have the same subject, the male. This corresponds to the address to the north and south winds in the first two lines. Both of the line pairs refer to the same concern. The two lines in between provide a transition from the winds to the male's visit to the garden. Thus there is a connected movement through this verse. For this reason it seems unlikely that more than one speaker is involved. The fifth line indicates that the female is speaking. There has been a change from the male to the female, likely at the beginning of this verse, which forms a response to the male's call to her and to the metaphor of the garden.

The initial imperative, "Awake" (*ʿûrî*), uses a root that occurs nine times in the Song. Six of these are double occurrences in the three verses where the female charges the maidens of Jerusalem not to arouse or awaken love (2:7; 3:5; 8:4). In 8:5 the female also mentions how she aroused her lover. Finally, in 5:2 the female's heart remains awake while she sleeps. Hence every other occurrence of this verb in the Song refers to the sexual arousal and excitement of lovers for one another. The female alone uses the verb and most often addresses others with a warning not to arouse love. However, she herself appears aroused in her heart only two verses

90. See Cooper, "New"; cited also in Pope, *Song,* 496.

after 4:16. In v. 16, therefore, the command of the female to awaken the north wind may have overtones of sexual desire. If so, the unique reference to the north (ṣāpôn) as the north wind—only here in the Bible is it so used—suggests a call to those elements of the north already mentioned in chapter 4.[91] Most of all, this describes the male's call to the female to come from her mountain stronghold in the Lebanon (v. 8) and the presence of the woman as a source of flowing waters from the Lebanon (v. 15). The second imperative, "Come" (bôʾî), is a common verb that appears some ten times in the Song, twice here in this verse. Except for the occurrences in 4:8 and 5:1, the Hebrew root otherwise appears on the lips of the female (1:4; 2:4, 8; 3:4; 8:2, 11). It normally appears in the causative (Hiphil) stem (meaning "take/bring"), but here and in 4:8 (as well as 2:8 and 5:1) it is in the Qal, with the meaning "come." The male has called for the female a few verses earlier (4:8) and will shortly use the verb to refer to his own entry into his garden (5:1). Here the female commands the south wind to come and perhaps bring its warmth to the garden and their love. The south wind (têmān) occurs in Ps. 78:26, where God cares for his people in the desert, and Zech. 9:14, where it forms part of God's retinue when he appears as a warrior to defeat his enemies. This suggests more than warmth; it implies a powerful wind that effects change. The female calls for this as she commands the winds to blow upon her garden. The root of "blow" (hāpîḥî) occurs two other times in the Song. In 2:17 and 4:6 it describes the blowing of the wind at the breaking of the day. The winds in 4:16 also blow, perhaps in the early morning; but with equal probability the time of day is irrelevant. It is the desire of the female for her lover and his appearance. And so she calls the winds to stir up passions through the circulation of her fragrance. In this way the young man will be reminded of the desirability of her garden and enter it. The female is prepared to yield her body to him in this love, and so she describes her body as "his garden." Although earlier in the verse it was "my garden," her alteration of the person of the possessive indicates a desire to fully share herself with her lover. The noun for "spices" last appeared at the end of v. 14 and designated the aromatics of the female's garden and their fragrances as described by the male. Now the fragrances will "flow" to him; here v. 16 uses the same verb as in the final line of v. 15. The result will be his presence and his partaking of the joys of lovemaking, described as eating of the garden's best or luscious fruit.[92] Even this adjective is a

91. For the life-giving symbolism of this wind in Egypt and its occurrences in West Semitic, see Grave, "Northwest."
92. For Pilch, "Window," this, along with Prov. 5:15 and 30:20, forms the basis for eating and drinking as a biblical picture laden with sexual significance. Keel, Song, 181, concurs and adds Sir. 23:17 and the Qur'an, Sura 2.183.

response to the male's praise of his partner's garden and occurs in v. 13 (and later in 7:14 [7:13 Eng.]). Thus the female expresses her longing for her lover's presence.

> **5:1a**I have come to my garden, my sister and bride,
> I have plucked my myrrh with my spices,
> I have eaten my nectar with my honey,
> I have drunk my wine with my milk.

5:1a. *Male: Tasting the garden.* The structure of this address is simple. There are four lines, each introduced by a perfect verb form. The first line is different after this because it serves as an introductory comment in which the new speaker is introduced and the action of the speaker summarized. In the remaining lines each verb is followed by a noun describing the object of the verb, and the preposition ʿim joins a second, related noun to the first. Except for this preposition and the noun "bride" (kallâ), every word in these four lines ends with the long vowel -î. With nouns, this forms the suffix "my." With perfect verb forms it indicates the subject "I." The repeated emphasis of the sounds of these lines lets the male stress what he does and what belongs to him. This self-emphasis on the male is unusual up to this point, although the female's switch from "my garden" to "his garden" in the previous verse may have anticipated it. The emphasis on the role of the male in this verse looks forward to the *wasf* describing the male in 5:10–16. Here, however, it has nothing to do with the physical attributes of the male. Instead, he lays claim to what the female has offered him—her body personified in the form of a garden.

The perfect form of the verb "I have come" (bāʾtî) in v. 1 introduces a verbal aspect that has not been seen since 4:10. Of the 108 occurrences of the perfect in the Song, only seven occur in chapter 4, in vv. 1, 2, 6, 9, and 10. Both vv. 9 and 10 have this form appearing twice, as though to emphasize it. The extremely common nature of the perfect aspect makes its omission in 4:11–16 surprising. Nevertheless, the previous occurrences (vv. 9–10) form part of the male's address to his partner. This address continues here with the male now describing his approach to the female. The perfect aspect suggests that this took place in the past. However, that is not the only tense it can describe. In poetry, especially, there are a variety of possibilities. Further, the absence of the male in the following verses, as the female hears him knock and then seeks him, suggests that the joining of the two has not taken place. The male has not yet visited the female, but here he speaks with anticipation and a sense of certainty that he will come. His assertion that this is indeed his garden affirms that offer of the female in the previous verse. His designation of his lover as "my sister and bride" recalls this phrase in 4:9, 10, and 12 and affirms the continuation of the garden theme there. It concludes the use of this double term of endearment, and appropriately so. Now the male enjoys the anticipated garden, described with so much detail.

The verb "I plucked" (ʾārîtî) in 5:1 is much disputed as to its possible meanings.[93] In later Hebrew the root ʾrh is used of gathering figs. Its other appearance in the Bible, in Ps. 80:13 (80:12 Eng.), seems to support this. Hence the reference to collecting the spices seems appropriate. Nevertheless, some refer to Arabic cognates that suggest a root related to eating. In both the Psalm passage and here the verb appears in parallel with expressions referring to the eating of fruit. Much has also been made of an Arabic cognate root that refers to honey. Thus it is thought that the poet wishes to convey a triple meaning here: the plucking of the fruit, the eating of it, and the sweetness of it. Thrown into the mix of possible allusions is the word for "lion" (ʾărî), which also resembles the root used here. The suggestion that these allusions lie behind Samson's riddle in Judg. 14:14 and 14:18 ("honey" and "lion" occur) presumes a scribal error in which an older word for "honey," related to this root, was replaced with the word that now appears there. The whole set of allusions remains speculative and would be better demonstrated if some of the words (especially the one for "honey") actually occurred in Hebrew and if the association with a lion could be shown to have some reasonable significance at this point. The connection with a verb of eating is indeed possible and may be the original meaning of this term. However, that is not proved, and the versions support the traditional interpretation. Further, myrrh is not eaten, though it may be mixed with wine for drinking.

The male's enjoyment of the spices and their fragrance uses terms that recall the garden just described. There myrrh (4:6) and the general term for spices or balsam oil (bōśem, 4:10) both appear. In 4:14 they occur together as here. In addition to this appealing odor, the consumption of honey addresses the taste. The two terms "nectar" and "honey" suggest poetic variation of a synonymous expression.[94] As with the myrrh and spices, the honey is a particularly sensual image denoting something that would have special appeal to the tongue. In 4:11 honey is associated with milk as a sensation of sweetness found in kissing. In 5:1, however, the milk is associated with wine, again an image that has had connections with kissing, as in 1:2. Also, this repeats the picture of something whose sweetness is emphasized and whose sensuality is the reason for its choice

93. Pope, *Song,* 504–5; Fox, *Song,* 139.
94. The second term, *dĕbaš,* appeared in 4:11.

as a word picture. In 4:10 it was compared with the general lovemaking that the couple enjoys. The images go beyond what was described as part of the garden in 4:11–15, reaching back to pictures in 4:10. Because this was also true of the perfect verbal aspects, which last appeared there, it suggests that this verse forms an envelope with 4:10 and brings to an end the pictures of various forms of sensuality. The garden, the chief image, is not the only one. As always, however, all the expressions draw upon images from nature. The honey, wine, and milk describe abundance in food and drink: the best and most desirable produce of the land. The verbs "I have eaten" and "I have drunk" depict the activities of joy in receiving nourishment. The male has visited the garden and exposed himself to its heady fragrances. Now the senses of taste and touch are overloaded with the produce described here. Sweetness, intoxication, and the rich taste of creamy goat's milk all describe a full indulgence. This most closely resembles the lover's experience with his partner.

The use of six gifts, paired and each carrying the suffix "my," has a close parallel with Hosea 2:7b (2:5b Eng.): "She said, 'I will go after my lovers, who give me my food and my water, my wool and my linen, my oil and my drink'" (NIV).[95] However, in Hosea the gifts are cheaper and reflect the necessities of life. The woman there receives them as pay from her paramours; here in the Song she gives gifts of love to her lover.[96]

> [1b]Eat, friends,
> Drink, and become intoxicated with lovemaking.

5:1b. *Chorus: Enjoy!* The imperative verbal forms that occur three times in this passage demonstrate that more than one person is addressed.[97] Previously in this text similar imperative verbal forms have been used of the couple addressing whoever will listen (2:15) and in an anomalous context where the addressees are not at all certain (2:5).[98] These are the only occurrences of this verbal form in the Song other than here. Again, it is not clear who is being addressed or even who is doing the talking. It may be that the male and female address young men and women who are their companions. The couple exhorts them to join in the joy of their love with food and drink. On the other hand it is possible that a group such as the daughters of Jerusalem forms a chorus here and addresses the couple. They encourage the pair in their expressions of love and in finding love. This is even more likely if the final word is translated "lov-

95. Van Selms, "Hosea and Canticles," 88.
96. Cf. LaCocque, *Romance*, 115.
97. The imperatives are masculine plurals.
98. The feminine imperative plural is used when addressing the daughters of Jerusalem in 3:11.

ers" rather than "with lovemaking." However, it is true even in the latter case. In the five Hebrew words that constitute this part of the text, three are the same type of imperative.[99] The first part of 5:1 was dominated by the suffix that indicates the first-person common singular form, "I/my"; this latter part of the verse is dominated by the plural suffix -*û*. The result is a dramatic change of sound that signals a different speaker. The first two imperatives, "eat, . . . drink," repeat the roots that the male used in the first part of the verse. It is the only place in the Song where these two verbs appear together, and here they are repeated. The final verb (*šikrû*) contains a root used in Semitic languages to refer to intoxication. It occurs only here in the Song but some eighteen additional times in the Bible. Elsewhere it refers to intoxication,[100] though it can be used simply to refer to drinking without restraint (Gen. 43:34; Deut. 32:42; Hag. 1:6). Since the context of Song 5:1 does not otherwise clarify the scene, it is best to interpret the reference in the Song to a state of inebriation.

The command to eat is made up of one verb. The command to drink continues with the additional exhortation to become intoxicated. The third imperative in a text where there are elsewhere no more than two commands places special emphasis upon the third action. The reason for the additional verb is that it allows the speakers a transition from the image of feasting to that of lovemaking. The lovemaking has already been likened to wine and intoxication, so it is appropriate for the chorus to introduce this final reference to their relationship with a picture of drinking. The wine of love has reached its full potency, and the couple is ready to share in its giddy pleasures. The chorus encourages the lovers to partake of their feast. The image here of lovemaking suggests that the eating and drinking involve more than a marriage feast or other special event with foods and drinks. The picture of lovemaking in the context of the preceding use of verbs of consumption implies feasting upon one another's bodies in the satisfaction of sexual desire. As the male lover declares (5:1a), so the chorus also recognizes no limit to the joys that the lovers may find in one another (5:1b). To the contrary, they command indulgence in the fullness of these pleasures.

Theological Implications

Since the female has previously relished the delights of her experience with the male, it is now the male's turn. His fantasy, however, is not

---

99. They are masculine plurals.

100. Gen. 9:21; 1 Sam. 1:14; 2 Sam. 11:13; Isa. 29:9; 49:26; 51:21; 63:6; Jer. 25:27; 48:26; 51:7, 39, 57; Nah. 3:11; Hab. 2:15; Lam. 4:21.

one of searching and seizing his lover, as was the case with the female (3:1–5). Instead, the male pictures the value of his lover as a princess safe in his protection and consummating their commitment in a marriage ceremony (3:6–11). Is it not this ideal of love and protection that the apostle envisioned when he wrote of the bride, the church, coming toward Christ (Rev. 21:2)?

The first *wasf*, praising the female's body, opens with a stress upon her physical form and ends with the desired intimacy inhibited by physical distance (4:1–8). This and the remaining *wasf*s may stress the value of the physical form and its desire by the admirer, a form so beautiful that it transcends and excludes all others. Theologians such as Hans Urs von Balthasar rightly lament the loss of the aesthetic element in Western Christian theology.[101] Its proper recovery lies in an appreciation of the incarnation and the ultimate exhibition of Christ on the cross—at once a terrible and horrifying spectacle and yet also the sacrifice of love that transcends all other forms as the most beautiful and desirable subject the world has ever known. This portion of the Song and the later *wasf*s begin that journey because they recover the original value of the human body as created by God and significant in its own right, despite sin (Gen. 1:26–28). This is the focus for the remainder of this section (Song 4:9–5:1).

The male's rhapsody continues, with a new focus (4:9–15). Here commitment emerges as a key theme that will remain throughout the Song. The male expresses his commitment with his designation of the female as his bride. Whether reality or a hoped-for fantasy, this designation can refer only to a permanent commitment. The male recognizes this commitment in the female, with his description of her as a locked garden and a locked pool. Her love is reserved for him. Love begins with commitment, and no true love is possible without it.

The whole of chapter 4 and the first verse in chapter 5 bring together an epicurean delight that exults in the senses and pleasures of the physical world. More than any text in the Bible, these verses reject the suppression of physical pleasures as though in themselves somehow evil or unworthy of God. The poet masters all of the physical senses and their indulgence in magnifying the experiences of physical lovemaking. In so doing, the male lover recognizes the fullness of divine blessing in the gifts of this world and the joy that they bring. Self-denial and asceticism have their place in the Christian faith. Jesus fasted in the wilderness (Matt. 4:2). He assumed that his disciples would fast (6:16–18) and deny themselves (16:24; Mark 8:34; Luke 9:23). Further, the early Christians shared sacrificially with others in need (Acts 2:45; Rom. 12:13; 2 Cor.

101. Von Balthasar, *Seeing*.

8:2; 9:5, 11, 13; Eph. 4:28; 1 Tim. 6:18) as they also shared in the sufferings of Christ and the apostles.[102] Yet Jesus and his disciples practiced a ministry of relieving suffering and caring for others. They never denied the goodness of this world. On one occasion, when the Pharisees asked Jesus why he and his disciples were not fasting, he responded, "How can the guests of the bridegroom mourn while he is with them? The time will come when the bridegroom will be taken from them; then they will fast" (Matt. 9:15 NIV).

Above all, Christians looked forward to the time of reunion with their Messiah and the full enjoyment of salvation, which they portrayed as a wedding feast of eating and drinking (Matt. 8:11; Rev. 19:7, 9; 21:6). This picture is not only consistent with that of God's first creation for humankind in the garden of Eden (Gen. 2–3); humanity also approaches it from time to time in the present life, despite the fallen condition of the world. It is found first and foremost in the joys of marriage. The erotic pleasures of sexual love are not a capitulation to sin. They instead are the most excellent sign in this world pointing to the joys that God has in store for those who love him (1 Cor. 2:9). Here as much as anywhere, the Song affirms that the physical world, though fallen, remains capable of redemption by God and that it still contains something of the value and love he put into it. Humanity, created in the image of God, preserves that goodness in the physical body as in our spiritual capacity. The world was created as something good to be enjoyed. Despite the absence of this experience for many in a fallen world and our call to sacrifice for the sake of the gospel, that joy has not departed from the world. Sexual love in its proper context of committed love remains a sign of God's good world and those elements of it that remain forever (1 Cor. 13:13). In this context denial and sacrifice become an expression of love and commitment toward God, not by counting the world that God has created as bad, but by appreciating it as good. The surrender of what is good becomes acceptable only because it embraces a greater good and a greater beauty, the eternal Bridegroom.

---

102. Rom. 5:3; 6:5; 2 Cor. 1:7; Phil. 4:14; 1 Thess. 1:6; 2 Thess. 1:5; 2 Tim. 1:8, 12; 2:9; Heb. 10:32; James 5:10; 1 Pet. 4:12.

V.
Search and Reunion
(5:2–6:3)

Translation

Female
5:2I slept,[a] but my heart remained awake,[b]
The sound of my lover knocking,[c]
"Open to me, my sister, my darling,
My dove, my perfect one,
My head[d] is drenched with dew,
My locks[e] with the night's damp."[f]

a. *Yĕšēnâ* is a feminine singular form from the root *yšn*. It is used as an adjective, although its form appears to be that of a Qal participle of the root.

b. *ʿĒr*, a masculine singular Qal participle form of *ʿwr*, occurring in 2:7 and 3:5 as "arouse, excite" and in 4:16 as "awake."

c. *Dôpēq*, a masculine singular Qal active participle of the root *dpq*, occurs three times in the Bible. Elsewhere it describes the hard driving of flocks of sheep, so hard that it would cause them to die (Gen. 33:13). In Judg. 19:22 (in the Hithpael, "they themselves knocked") it describes the pounding on the door by a hostile crowd demanding to rape the stranger who has entered the house. This one other related occurrence, involving knocking on a door, also involves sexual intentions, but in a violent manner, unlike the picture here in the Song.

d. The expression begins with the relative *še*, prefixed to the following word. It is used causally. However, the absence of the customary particle *kî* suggests that this is a weaker causal construction implicit in the juxtaposition of the clauses rather than the particular word chosen.

e. The form *qĕwwuṣṣôtay*, from the root *qṣṣ* (to cut), appears elsewhere in the Bible only in 5:11. In light of postbiblical usage (later Hebrew describes one who is bushy haired; *HALOT* 1090), "locks" is appropriate. See Pope, *Song*, 512–13.

f. The word for "damp" is the plural construct form of *rāsîs*. It occurs elsewhere only in Amos 6:11 in the sense of "fragments." A cognate appears in Jewish Aramaic and

3"I have taken off my robe,[g]
Must I put it on?
I have washed my feet,
Must I dirty them?"
4My lover stretched his hand through[h] the keyhole,[i]
My inmost being was overcome[j] <with desire> for him.
5I arose[k] to open to my lover,
My hands dripped with myrrh,
My fingers with myrrh,
Flowing over the guides[l] of the bolt.
6I opened to my lover,

Syriac with the meaning of drops of dew; in Mishnaic Hebrew it occurs as something chopped, such as lentils. Thus the basic idea seems to be fragments of a larger mass, whether liquid or solid.

g. Murphy, *Song*, 165, notes that *kuttōnet* refers to an undergarment removed before sleeping.

h. The preposition *min* normally conveys the sense of "from." However, in many languages prepositions are dependent on the context for their meaning. The sense here may be that the lover reached his hand "from" outside the keyhole and in through it. Pope, *Song*, 518, compares Prov. 17:23 and 21:14, where the same expression uses two different Hebrew prepositions: "a bribe from [*min*] the bosom" and "a bribe in [*ba*] the bosom."

i. *Ḥōr*, lit., "hole." The six remaining occurrences of this common noun in the Bible refer not to a keyhole but to a variety of holes—whether caves for people (1 Sam. 14:11; Job 30:6), lairs for lions (Nah. 2:13 [2:12 Eng.]), money chests (2 Kings 12:9), a hole in a wall (Ezek. 8:7), or eye sockets (Zech. 14:12). The limited number of occurrences of this noun, its wide variety of usages, and the absence of a reference to a keyhole elsewhere in Biblical Hebrew—all argue that the term as used here is not extraordinary, nor does its usage automatically suggest a sexual overtone (contra Longman, *Song*, 167).

j. The combination of "my loins/inmost being" (*mēʿay*) and "heave/pound/yearn" (*hmh*) occurs elsewhere in Isa. 16:11; Jer. 4:19; 31:20. The first occurrence describes a lamentation. The two appearances in Jeremiah suggest a pounding heart full of fear (heart attack?) and the overwhelming compassion that God feels for his child Ephraim. Thus the term expresses the emergence of very strong emotion brought on by another. The last example, Jer. 31:20, is in parallel with an intensive infinitive absolute plus finite verb construction: "I do indeed have compassion for him!" There is no sexual connotation elsewhere but the strongest of emotional reaction. Hence the context of Song 5:4 lets a sense of clear sexual arousal emerge.

k. Dobbs-Allsopp, "Ingressive," 43–44, suggests that this is an ingressive use of *qwm*. Thus it does not describe the female as arising but as beginning to open the door. According to this theory, at the beginning of v. 5 she is already at the door. This would be more persuasive if the verb were followed immediately by the narrative tense (*wāw* consecutive plus imperfect/preterite). It is not. The pronoun "I" follows it and then the verb "to open" as an infinitive construct with a *lāmed* prefix.

l. *Kappōt* is from *kap*, a term for the hollow of the hand. This feminine plural form is a metaphor for objects resembling this hollow, as in a hip socket (Gen. 32:26 [32:25 Eng.]) or a sling (1 Sam. 25:29). Here it refers to the guides (or sockets) through (or into) which the bolt is slid. This holds the bolt secure so that the door cannot be opened. See King and Stager, *Life*, 32–33, and the illustration of an "Egyptian" lock.

161

But my lover had turned,[a]
He had departed,[b]
I fainted at his flight,[c]
I sought him but I did not find him,
I called for him but he did not answer me.
[7]The guards found me,
Those who go through the city,
They beat me, they wounded me,
They removed my shawl[d] from me,
Those guards on the walls.
[8]I want you to promise,
O young women of Jerusalem,
If you find my lover,
What will you tell him?
That I am faint[e] with love.

a. So Pope, *Song*, 525, who compares the passive participle in 7:2 (7:1 Eng.), where it describes the curves of the dancer's hips or thighs; the reflexive stem of Jer. 31:22, where it is applied to a perverse girl; and the Arabic cognate, having the sense of one who is stupid. Cf. Murphy, *Song*, 165. Garbini, *Cantico*, 80–86, 156–57, notes that Aquila, Symmachus, the Vulgate, and the Syriac translate a form different from the combined witnesses of the MT, LXX, and Old Latin. He suggests the root *ḥbq* (embrace) and translates it in a manner suggesting that the male embraced the female before turning (but not for Garbini; see next note, below). This is textually possible, but I prefer the MT and LXX, both as an equally strong witness and also for the powerful effect of the verbal sequence as suggested in the commentary.

b. *ʿĀbār* is omitted in the LXX and Old Latin, but preserved in the Syriac, Vulgate, Aquila, and Symmachus. See Garbini, *Cantico*, 80–86, 156–57, who reconstructs here *rbʿ* (to lean/copulate). However, this is without warrant because the same root and consonantal form occurs in v. 5 as "flowing" (*ʿōbēr*). One may well ask whether this is an insertion in the MT caused by a scribe's eye moving up to v. 5 (perhaps a line above the present line) and reading this verb. However, there is no other evidence of dittography, and since *ʿābār* fits with the repeated sense of the female's loss, it is best preserved.

c. Literally, "my soul went forth when he went away." The use of "my soul" (*napšî*) is a common substitute for the first-person common singular "I/me" (see 1 Kings 1:29). The "going out" (root *yṣʾ*) of one's soul occurs in Gen. 35:18, where it describes the death of Rachel. A similar expression, replacing "soul" with "spirit" (*rûaḥ*), appears in Ps. 146:4, where it also refers to death. Thus the idea may be one of fainting to the point of death (Fox, *Song*, 146). The final verb in line 4 of Song 5:6, *bĕdabbĕrô*, is a Piel infinitive construct with a third-person masculine singular suffix and a *bêt* inseparable prepositional prefix. Related to the Akkadian D-stem *duppuru*, it conveys a similar sense of "go away." Longman, *Song*, 163, 168, prefers to interpret the verb as from the root "to speak" and translates the line idiosyncratically as "My spirit had gone out at his speaking."

d. *Rĕdîd* occurs elsewhere only in Isa. 3:23, where it is part of the finery worn by the women of Jerusalem. Perhaps "headband" would be a better translation in Song 5:7, although later Hebrew would use this term to describe a thin outer garment. The context of beating and wounding suggests that what was removed from the female caused her suffering or humiliation. A shawl better serves this understanding, whether or not it also held the hair in place.

e. The form is a Qal feminine singular construct participle from *ḥlh*.

Chorus

[9]How does your lover compare with other lovers,
Most beautiful among women,
How does your lover compare with other lovers,
That you wish us to promise like this?

Female

[10]My lover is dazzling[f] and ruddy,[g]
Better looking[h] than ten thousand.
[11]His head is refined gold.[i]
His locks[j] are date panicles,[k]
Black like a raven.
[12]His eyes like doves,
By streams of water,
Washed[l] in milk,
Sitting by a brimming water basin.[m]

f. Elsewhere *ṣaḥ* appears in contexts that describe the heat of the sun (Isa. 18:4), the force and clarity of the healed stammerer (Isa. 32:4), and wind from the desert (Jer. 4:11). The verbal root *ṣḥḥ* conveys the sense of shining or glimmering and of heat, as do Syriac and Arabic cognates of this root.

g. *ʾĀdôm* describes the color of blood (2 Kings 3:22) and grape juice (Isa. 63:2). Brenner, "*Dôdî*," argues that *ʾādôm* and *ṣaḥ* should be taken together with the meaning of "bright pink," but the redness of the male's skin seems to be the emphasis here. See comments.

h. *Dāgûl* from the root *dgl* appears only here in the Bible. It is related to the Akkadian *dagālu* (to see; Pope, *Song*, 532). Murphy, *Song*, 166, notes the LXX *eklelochismenos* and translates as a similar "outstanding."

i. The expression *ketem pāz* consists of two words to describe special gold (*ketem*) of Ophir (Isa. 13:12; Ps. 45:10 [45:9 Eng.]; Job 28:16) of a highly refined quality (Arabic cognate *fadda*, to be alone, separated). See the expression *zāhāb mûpāz* in 1 Kings 10:18, rendered as *zāhāb ṭāhôr* (pure gold) in 2 Chron. 9:17. In Isa. 13:12 the two terms occur in parallelism, and in Dan. 10:5 *ketem ʾûpāz* describes how the waist of a man was girded in a vision. However, only here do the terms stand side by side, whether in a construct relationship (Fox, *Song*, 147) or not (Pope, *Song*, 535). The description suggests the best of highly refined gold. See also Görg, "Lexikalisches zu HL 5,11," who traces the term from Akkadian through Egyptian and thence to Hebrew.

j. Cf. this same term in 5:2.

k. The *taltallîm* occurs only here in Biblical Hebrew. It may relate to the Akkadian *taltallū*, pollen most likely related to the date panicle (*AHw* 1312a). The rabbinic usage of "curls" derives from an interpretation of this passage. Pope, *Song*, 536, observes how elsewhere the pattern of this noun denotes plant shoots or branches: *zalzallîm* (Isa. 18:5), *salsillôt* (Jer. 6:9), and *sansinnîm* (Song 7:9 [7:8 Eng.]). For this rendering, see Fox, *Song*, 147; Keel, *Song*, 196. Less likely is the proposal of Görg, "Lexikalisches zu HL 5,11," to associate the term with the Demotic *tltl.t* (drops).

l. Vaccari, "Note," followed by Rudolph, *Hohe Lied*, 158–59, and Murphy, *Song*, 166, inserts "his teeth" at the beginning of the line. There is no versional support for this. The lines can be understood as descriptions of the eyes. See comments.

m. Both the LXX and the Vulgate render *millēʾt* as a fullness of waters (*plērōmata hydatōn*). Keel, *Song*, 199–201, records examples of a basin with doves portrayed around

¹³His cheeks like beds^a of spice,
Abundant^b with perfumes.^c
His lips are lotuses,
Dripping with myrrh.
¹⁴His arms are gold rods,^d
Set with gems.^e
His body^f a bar^g of ivory,
Overlaid with lapis lazuli.^h
¹⁵His legsⁱ are pillars of alabaster,
Set on sockets of fine gold.

---

its rim, ca. 2000 BC from Cyprus, as well as a second-century AD Roman painting of a similar scene.

a. ʿĂrûgâ occurs elsewhere only in Ezek. 17:7, 10, where it refers to a place for planting, a plot or bed. It is best to follow the LXX and read the plural. Dahood, "Philological," 393–94, suggests a connection with Eblaite *a-ru ga-tu*^{ki}, a sweet-smelling place, perhaps a garden. Murphy, *Song,* 166, and Provan, *Song,* 336, speculate that a perfumed beard is intended.

b. With Murphy, *Song,* 166, reading here the Piel participle, *mĕgaddĕlôt.* Cf. the LXX's *phyousai* and the Vulgate's *consitae a.*

c. *Merqāḥ* occurs only here as a masculine noun (with a plural suffix). It appears in Job 41:23 (41:31 Eng.) and Ezek. 24:10 as a feminine form with the meaning "container of ointment."

d. The root *gll* refers to rounded or circular objects. The name Galilee is derived from this root.

e. *HALOT* 1798 renders *taršîš* as "topaz." However, Pope, *Song,* 543, noting the variety of types of stones translated here in the history of the Song's interpretation, remains unconvinced that the precious stone can be identified and translates "gems."

f. Hebrew *mēʿîm* uses the same noun as the female's "innermost being" in 5:4. Provan, *Song,* 337, observes the sense of a belly or loins in the Aramaic of Dan. 2:32–33. Longman, *Song,* 167, 173, identifies this with the sexual organs of both the male and female. This would be distinct from its usage elsewhere, where it customarily means "intestines," "body," or "inner being." Certainly, this is not the customary word for "penis" (*yad*) that occurs elsewhere. Nevertheless, Goulder, *Song,* 6, also accepts this interpretation and borrows the proposal of Lys (*Plus beau*) that the first word of the following line (*mĕʿullepet,* here "overlaid") should be translated "veined." Goulder concludes that this suggests "a part of the male body, between the hands and the legs, which is heavily veined, and which . . . resembles a column of ivory," which must be "a tusk." Thus, building conjecture upon conjecture, he returns to the elephant's tusk and a putative symbol of a penis.

g. *HALOT* 898 renders "panels," comparing the usage of this term in "bars of gold" in 3Q15 1.5 and 2.4. However, it would then seem better to follow the Dead Sea Scroll example and translate "bar" here. See Fox, *Song,* 149, who finds here a description of the "youth's flat and muscular stomach."

h. Although *sappîrîm* appears here, *HALOT* 764 suggests lapis lazuli, which is easier to cut than sapphires. Cf. Murphy, *Song,* 166.

i. Despite the *normal* reference of *šôq* to thighs, Pope, *Song,* 546, prefers "legs" because no other part of the young man's legs are named. He also cites the description of a woman in Sir. 26:18, where her legs and feet resemble gold pillars set on silver sockets. See also Keel, *Song,* 205, who, however, prefers "calves," a translation also found in the LXX (*knēmai*).

His looks are like Lebanon,
Choice as the cedars.
[16]His mouth[j] is nectar.[k]
He is totally desirable.
This is my lover,
This is my partner,[l]
Daughters of Jerusalem.

Chorus
[6:1]Where has your lover gone,
Most beautiful of women,
Where has your lover ventured,
So that we can seek him with you?

Female
[2]My lover descended to his garden,
To the spice beds,
To graze in the gardens,
And to gather lotuses.
[3]I am my lover's
And my lover is mine;
He gathers among the lotuses.

Interpretation

5:2–8   Female: A second search at night for her dream lover
5:9   Chorus: Challenge to compare the male lover
5:10–16   Female: *Waṣf* for the male
6:1   Chorus: Inquiry for the male
6:2–3   Female: Reunites with her lover

5:2–8. *Female: A second search at night for her dream lover.* Although chapter 4 has presented the lovers in terms of the male's description of the female and the metaphor of her body as a garden, chapter 5 presents primarily the words of the female with respect to her partner. In vv. 10–16

j. *Ḥēk* describes the interior of the mouth, particularly the palate.

k. *Mamtaqqîm* occurs elsewhere in the Bible in Neh. 8:10, where it is something that is drunk along with rich foods (*mašmannîm*) that are eaten on a special day dedicated to God. The *mtq* root describes what is sweet. In Ugaritic, *mtqtm* describes the sweetness of the lips when kissed (Pope, *Song*, 549).

l. So Pope, *Song*, 549–50, who observes the use of *rēaʿ*, often translated "friend," also for a sexual partner in Jer. 3:1, 20; and Hosea 3:1.

she describes his body just as the male did hers in the previous chapter. However, in the first part of this chapter the female does not relate anything comparable to what the male has expressed in chapter 4. She neither looks at her lover's body nor does she create a metaphor such as a garden and use it to praise her lover's physique. Instead, she narrates a scene of passion and frustrated desire, of terror and commitment. This theme is that of the *exclusus amator,* "the excluded lover." Lucretius identified the theme, and commentators have applied it to this text. However, this only works as a general theme: there is a great deal of variation.[1]

The connecting forms of the whole narrative are found in key words that recur.[2] There is the reference to opening, the root *ptḥ* that appears three times in vv. 2, 5, and 6. There is the expression "my lover" (*dôdî*) that appears in vv. 2, 4, 5, 6 (2x), and 8. Finally, the lover identifies herself as "I" (*ʾǎnî*) four times at the beginning, middle, and end of the address, vv. 2, 5, 6, and 8. This constitutes one-third of the total number of occurrences of this pronoun in the entire Song. It represents a leitmotif that ties together the entire address and provides a focus. It is both the female ("I") and the male ("my lover") who together provide the basis for the relationship that is here desired.[3] Although both the male and the female seek lovemaking, it is not here realized. Thus, although the most frequently used verb, "to open," appears along with the pronoun "I" and the endearment "my lover," in vv. 2, 5, and 6, it does not occur in the final section (5:7–8) where these other terms appear. The "opening" of the earlier part of the narrative is frustrated and does not achieve its objective, the consummation of the lovers' passion. Instead, it leads only to the harming of the female and the absence of the male. A further aspect of this narrative is the complete absence of the common narrative tense.[4] This form, which occurs regularly in virtually every biblical narrative, is not found in this poetic recitation. Instead, the use of the perfect aspect consistently appears throughout this narrative and carries the action forward. It is perhaps the choice of the poet and may be due to the general absence of the characteristic "narrative tense" form in poetry. However, there are few examples of a first-person narrative

1. Thus *De rerum natura* 4.1177–79. Cf. Murphy, *Song,* 168–69, who notes that the "lament at the door" (*paraklausithyron*) is missing. Nevertheless, Pope (*Song,* 522–24), Gerleman (*Hohelied,* 165), and Bergant (*Song,* 62–63) pursue the matter. It is preferable to that of Walsh ("Startling Voice"; idem, *Exquisite,* 105–14), who argues that this is the female's "wet dream," in which her fantasy arouses her. In her analysis, everything (hand, feet, keyhole, etc.) becomes a symbol of the female genitals.

2. Elliott, *Literary,* 122–24.

3. Bergant, *Song,* 59, notes that of the thirty-two occurrences of "lover" (*dôd*) in the Song, sixteen appear in 5:2–6:3.

4. The *wāw* consecutive plus the imperfect.

related in poetry. This may instead suggest that the female uses the perfect as her partner did in 5:1, to correspond to his form of expression and thereby affirm their complete harmony.

> 5:2 I slept, but my heart remained awake,
> The sound of my lover knocking,
> "Open to me, my sister, my darling,
> My dove, my perfect one,
> My head is drenched with dew,
> My locks with the night's damp."

The initial "I" (*ănî*) indicates both the key word of the section as well as an emphasis on the subject. The female relates her own story. She is asleep, as the descriptor, the second word, indicates. The feminine form of the term expressly indicates that the speaker is the female, not the male. Thus the reader/listener understands a change of person from the preceding verse. Within seven words, the speaker has changed twice, from the male to the chorus of maidens to the female. The use of three participles in the opening statement by the female contrasts with the imperatives that precede (5:1b) and follow, both spoken by others. For the female, the first line consists of two cola, each comprising three full syllables. The first, "I slept," describes the apparent peacefulness that she enjoys. The second, "but my heart remained awake," contrasts this with an unyielding desire that disturbs the quiet of the night. The third participle remains unclear: Does it describe a literal knocking, or is this the knocking on the door of the heart, a metaphor that suggests a desire for deep communion and is the cause of the heart's disquiet? A similar picture occurs in Rev. 3:20, where John apparently drew upon Song 5:2 for his image of Jesus knocking at the door of his beloved.[5] If so, vv. 2–8 form a word picture of a dream sequence, rather than a "real" action.[6] Such an explanation might find support from the last verb, also a participle, at the end of the narrative (v. 8): "I am faint" (*ḥôlat*). The lover is in a state in which her consciousness is overwhelmed and she has lost the full use of her faculties. This is not unlike the image of sleep with which this section begins. Thus the impression is given that vv. 2–8 take place in a dream state.[7] The lover dreams of this event, and the dream suggests how her heart is awake and filled with romantic

5. Cf. Feuillet, "Double," 18. Because of his highly eroticized interpretation of this chapter in the Song, Longman, *Song*, 161–62, denies any relationship.
6. Murphy, *Song*, 165, observes that "sleeping" and "awake" are intentional contrasts demonstrating that the composition is "a dream or fantasy."
7. Garrett, *Song*, 409, asserts without qualification that the dream interpretation is "meaningless." Other than a brief note of Pope's argument that the customary word for

and erotic thoughts about her lover. It is the heart—the source of the emotions, will, and decision-making processes in Hebrew thought—that forms the source for the lover's own desires in the following verses, as well as her unyielding pursuit of his presence and embrace.

The second line begins with the phrase "the sound of my lover." As often the case, the sense of hearing serves as the first level of contact with another person. Their voice or the sound of their approach signals their presence. Here, however, it provides both good and bad news. On the one hand, her lover is close and the sound of his movement signals the desire to approach and to come into her presence. On the other hand, however, the sound of his knocking provides the only evidence of his presence. He is on the other side of the door and otherwise inaccessible to the female. So the sound of his coming stimulates the female's desires and hopes but ultimately frustrates her realization of them. The knocking or pounding on the door itself is an expression of the male's own desire and need to be close to his lover. It is followed by his voice, a voice with which the female would be familiar and that would intensify her longing for his presence. The male's words have a dramatic dimension to them that, along with the unexpected assonance, arrests the reader/listener's attention. The drama appears with the first of the twelve words that the male uses. It is a command to her: "Open" (*pitḥî*). This common word appears here for the first time in the Song.[8] As a command, it occurs elsewhere in the Bible to describe the opening of a cave (Josh. 10:22), a window (2 Kings 13:17), gates (Isa. 26:2), granaries (Jer. 50:26), and one's mouth (Prov. 31:8–9). Twice in poetry it is used symbolically, as an entrance to Lebanon (Zech. 11:1) and in opening "the gates of righteousness" (Ps. 118:19). Thus it may be used as a metaphor and should so be understood here, but as a secondary meaning. The primary meaning is that of opening the physical door that separates the lovers. The secondary meaning has erotic overtones as the lover appeals to his partner to open her will, her body, and her being to him. He calls to her with four terms of endearment, more in sequence than in any other address of the Song. In doing so, however, he creates a repeated sound that begins with his first two Hebrew words, "Open for me" (*pitḥî lî*). The long -*î* sound occurs in Hebrew on the first seven words of the male. And on the four terms of endearment the final sound is always -*tî*. In occurrences two through seven of the -*î* sound, it is used as the possessive pronoun "my." The whole first part of the male's speech uses this sound to tie together his

---

"dream" (*ḥălôm*) does not occur here, he provides no evidence to justify his assertion. Yet this may not be an ordinary dream, and therefore the traditional vocabulary would be inappropriate.

8. It will occur again in 5:6 and also in 7:13 (7:12 Eng.) but never in the imperative.

appeal and at the same time to express his close relationship with his lover. The first two expressions, "my sister, my darling," are commonly found on the lover's lips as descriptions of his partner.[9] However, they occur together only here. They summarize all the titles of endearment that have been used to this point to describe the female. The address "my dove" occurs as a term of endearment also in 2:14 and 6:9. Otherwise, the lovers compare one another's eyes to doves (1:15; 4:1; 5:12). The eyes as the organs of sight represent the desire of the lovers to see one another, a desire that is denied to them. The whole line "my dove, my perfect one" is repeated in 6:9. Although the root *tmm* (complete, perfect) may refer to upright ethical character and obedience to the law (Job 9:22; Prov. 19:1; 20:7; 28:6), it may also carry the meaning of a perfect physical form (Exod. 26:24). The obvious emphasis here is on the flawless physical beauty of the female, whose description in chapter 4 is summarized in this single word.

The second part of the male's statement is a dependent clause explaining why the female should open the door for him. The initial word, "my head" ([*še*]*rrō'šî*), is the seventh one in the sequence to have the final *-î*. This connects the subsequent causal clause with what preceded it. The clause consists of two lines in synonymous parallelism, literally translated as follows:

> My head is filled with dew,
> My locks with the drops of the night.

The subjects that begin each line, "my head/my locks," both refer to the wetness of the lover's head, and each contains the pronominal suffix, "my." The verb appears only in the first line and does double duty for both lines.[10] Perhaps surprisingly, three of the six words occur only here in the Song: the verb "is filled," and the nouns "dew" and "drops."[11] Nevertheless, the primary position of "head" and "locks" in each line suggests that the emphasis lies here. In any case, the male longs for entry into the female's dwelling and gives the reason as the dampness of the night. In Palestine, such dampness can soak a fleece such as Gideon's (Judg. 6:38). Hence the complaint could well be valid for someone out in the night, especially if they were attempting to sleep in the open.[12]

---

9. For "my sister," see 4:9, 10, 12; 5:1, 2. For "my darling," see 1:9, 15; 2:2, 10, 13; 4:1, 7; 5:2; 6:4.

10. Cf. a similar pattern in 1:10 and 1:13–14.

11. The root of "to fill" (*ml'*) does appear again in 5:14, but in a different stem and with the meaning "to be set."

12. In ancient times, the areas of the desert fringe developed techniques to take advantage of the dew and use it for farming when it provided the only source of irrigation.

It is possible that the male also had trouble sleeping and his heart's desire drove him to this nocturnal visit. This would further explain the complement of the last two lines of this verse to the first two lines. At the beginning of the verse, the female struggles in her sleep and is aroused (if only in a dream) by the arrival of the male. In the final line of the verse, the male cannot sleep and seeks admittance to his lover's room. The loving correspondence or complement of the lovers for one another at this point extends beyond the verbal—shown repeatedly by the responses of each for the other—to the active. Apart and away from one another, their love nevertheless draws them together as the male seeks his lover in the night.

> [3]"I have taken off my robe,
> Must I put it on?
> I have washed my feet,
> Must I dirty them?"

The third verse constitutes the female's response. Exactly complementing the last two lines of the male's request, this verse is also composed of synonymous A-B-A′-B′ parallelism. In fact, each word in the first two lines matches the corresponding word in the last two. Thus, literally:

I have taken off	I have washed
my robe	my feet
How	How
shall I clothe it?	shall I dirty them?

As the male provided two parallel reasons for seeking admittance (wet head/wet locks), so the female gives two reasons for refusing admittance. Why? If she desires him so much, as she has often indicated, why should she refuse admission now? The reasons do not address matters of ethics and morality, but the bother of putting on clothes and dirtying feet. She has already observed how her desires have been aroused. Is this then a coyness, an objection designed to further arouse her partner? If so, it seems to have failed. There are eight content words in v. 3.[13] Of these, seven occur only here in the Song, while one, "wash" (root *rḥṣ*), appears only one other time, in 5:12. Yet this also parallels the male's previous two lines, where many of the words occurred only in that verse in the Song. There is one more sign of complementarity in the female's response to her lover: her objection is intended to counter the request of the male. His request is couched in the words of complaint about the

---

13. Not counting the two markers of a definite direct object (ʾēt) before "my robe" and "my feet."

weather and the dampness of his head. Her response is therefore also a complaint that she has gone to bed and does not wish to be disturbed again. Would she prefer the presence of her lover to her remaining alone? Certainly, as the following verses indicate, she desires him. However, the playful subterfuge of shifting attention is fully in accord with the tenor of dialogue initiated by the male lover.[14] His concern about the wetness of his head is no more the true reason for desiring admittance to her bedchamber than her objections betray her true feelings about opening her door to him.

However, as is so often the case in this world of image and metaphor, a second level of meaning lies beneath the surface, one that plays upon the words as much as it lays bare the intentions behind what is explicitly stated. The dampness of the head and locks may suggest a natural means of emphasizing the physical attributes of the male that would be most desirable, that would provide the greatest sexual interest. Indeed, in her description of his body, the female begins with his head and hair (5:11). The female in a similar manner focuses on her robe and her feet. The foreground verb that describes how she has removed the robe is one that normally would be translated "I have stripped (myself)" (*pāšaṭṭî*). This particular verb coupled with a reference to "my robe" could have been intended to arouse erotic interest in her partner. Further, the notice of "my feet" (*raglay*) also plays upon the symbolic interpretation of the feet as a reference to the male sexual organs.[15] Thus, while nothing explicit is stated, both statements carry erotic overtones that could stimulate the sexual feelings in the one addressed.

> [4]My lover stretched his hand through the keyhole,
> My inmost being was overcome <with desire> for him.

---

14. Murphy, *Song*, 170, describes it as a tease. Pope, *Song*, 515, uses the term "coy." Longman, *Song*, 166–67, however, suggests that the woman objects to physical intimacy at this point. He argues that her reference to "feet" is a metaphor for genitalia (although some of his examples are not explicit) and that the "door" in the previous verse "clearly" symbolizes the vagina. Nevertheless, as Longman admits, all this lies in the realm of double entendre, possible but notoriously difficult to pin down. G. Carr, *Song*, 130, 133 (cf. also Glickman, *Song*, 60–65, 182–85), argues that the woman has no interest at that instant and suggests that the "must I . . . ?" question should not be regarded as coy because it has negative implications. However, he never attempts to prove this observation with examples. Further, a teasing response is more likely than a lack of interest, something that the couple never appears to suffer anywhere else in the Song. This also remains only a possibility.

15. See, e.g., Longman, *Song*, 166–67; Exod. 4:25; Judg. 3:24; 1 Sam. 24:4 (24:3 Eng.); Isa. 7:20; Ruth 3:4, 7.

All this leads to the fourth verse, in which a further attempt at physical contact is made. As in v. 2, the subject of the first clause appears in the first and therefore emphatic position in the verse. In v. 2 it was "I"; in v. 4 it is "my lover." With this emphasis, the focus of the narrative shifts from the female and her concerns to her partner and the evocative nature of his actions. The two lines of the verse have a grammatical parallelism, but the content seems to move forward as the second line functions as a consequence to the first line. Both begin by expressing the subject with the suffix "my": "my lover/my inmost being." There follows a verb: "stretched/was overcome."[16] Finally, both lines have something following the verb, whether a noun or a preposition, with an attached third-person suffix, "his hand/for him." The one remaining element, the prepositional phrase "through the keyhole," appears at the end of the first line but functions as the key element that ties together both lines (cf. 1:6). The keyhole marks the turning point from a pursuing male and a passive or resistant female, to a retreating male and a pursuing female. The keyhole is the logical opening to which the phrase "through the hole" refers. An ancient keyhole would form a large enough opening to place an adult's hand through because the key would be large.[17] Although someone with a key would need to put the object through the keyhole in order to open the door, it is not clear that there would be any pragmatic purpose to thrusting one's hand through the keyhole if the door were locked. Without the key, the lover cannot open his partner's door. Nevertheless, the action would signify the one remaining means by which the male might come closer. Perhaps he hopes that the door is unlocked and he needs only to lift or slide the bolt to enter. More likely he wishes to provide a sign to his lover that he desires to be with her and that only the lock on the door separates them.

His desire is communicated to good effect. The female reacts with a torrent of emotion that wells up from within. Some have seen in the reference to the "hand" (*yad*) an allusion to the male genital organ, as it seems to be used in Isa. 57:8 and clearly occurs in Ugaritic.[18] This text would then describe a sexual act in metaphorical terms, using the door, the lock, and the hand. However, the whole point of the passage is the failure of the couple to reach and touch one another. It is not sex but lack of sex that is the focus. Therefore, the imagery of sexual participation seems out of place.[19] Nevertheless, it has already appeared in the preceding verses.

16. Both are in the perfect tense/aspect.
17. King and Stager, *Life*, 31–33.
18. See especially the Birth of the Gracious Gods and references to El's *yd* as he impregnates two females.
19. See especially the persuasive arguments of Fox, *Song*, 144–45. Cf. also Bergant, *Song*, 64.

Perhaps the subconscious power of the desire the female has for the male, and vice versa, directs the mind of the poet toward expressions that allow for a suggestive meaning, even where it does not make obvious sense within the brief narrative form here. Thus such images and metaphors as may be found in this verse were not explicit and exist at all only as the result of the fervent passion that grants poetic inspiration.

> [5]I arose to open to my lover,
> My hands dripped with myrrh,
> My fingers with myrrh,
> Flowing over the guides of the bolt.

The female arises in v. 5. The opening words of this and the following verse are emphatic.[20] This verse evokes as much in what it describes as in what it does not. There is mention of her hand and fingers, as well as the bolt and its guides. There is no mention of the robe that she complains of needing to don in v. 3. This absence does not require her to have answered the door undressed. Yet it does suggest that the concerns of v. 3 play no significant part in keeping her from the object of her passion. Verse 5 begins with the verb "I arose" (*qamtî*) followed by the first-person common singular pronoun "I" (*ʾǎnî*). This combination (although in reverse order) last occurred at the beginning of the section as the first words in 5:2. The combination introduces a new movement for the female: first lying in her bed, then a scene of arising and going for the door. The third word that describes her intention "to open" (*liptōaḥ*) the door responds to the male's command of v. 2. The expression "my lover" (*dôdî*, v. 5) also occurs in v. 2 as an address of endearment from the female for the male. The entire first line, except for the verb root, repeats words found in v. 2. Thus the line summarizes and responds to v. 2, forming a new introduction to the subsequent action of the female.

However, there is a delay in the poem as the female observes how myrrh flows off her body onto the bolt and its guides, which she touches. Myrrh had previously appeared as what the male found in the female's "garden" (4:14; 5:1) or her "mountain" (4:6). The female used it to describe her love as a sachet of myrrh between her breasts (1:13). Hence it is a description of the exquisite sensual delight that the female enjoys in respect to the male and vice versa. As myrrh might cover their bodies with an intoxicating fragrance, so it describes the pleasure that each finds in the other's body. The central theme of this passage is this pleasure, or more precisely its expectation, that the female lover yearns for. The myrrh, in an olive oil compound, might well represent a physical

20. Murphy, *Song*, 165.

oil that exudes from the flesh of her hands. However, it also expresses fervent love and desire. The two parallel lines each begin with the part of the female's body that will open the door (plus a suffix): "my hands/ my fingers." In the first line this is followed by the verb, "dripped." No similar verb occupies this place in the second line. Instead the first verb does double duty for both lines. The spice, myrrh, forms the last word in both lines. Its act of "flowing" (participle, unlike "dripped") down onto the bolt guides forms the concluding line in a verse that moves from synonymous parallelism describing the dripping myrrh on the lover's hands to the myrrh flowing onto the lock itself and specifically onto the bolt guides. Syntactically, this structure moves the reader's/listener's attention toward the bolt/lock where the male was. Semantically, the picture is one of increasing desire that reaches a climax as the female grasps the door to open it. Poetically, the hand of the lover reaches out for the hand of her partner. The intent is to join one another fully and completely, with their hands meeting at the keyhole as the first step.

The term for "bolt" (*manʿûl*) occurs only here and in Nehemiah.[21] However, its root (*nʿl*) has appeared as a verb in Song 4:12. There it twice describes the female as a "locked" garden. Thus the lock here is a bolt that slides through the guides and into the socket, thereby securing the door. It alludes to the earlier description by the male. His attempt to enter the "garden" of the female has been thwarted. The myrrh that the male has sought in 4:14 now exudes from the female as a promise of the full sensual delights of the garden of her body. Hence the imagery and allusions continue to draw upon chapter 4 and provide this section with a strong connection to the preceding address of the male.

> [6]I opened to my lover,
> But my lover had turned,
> He had departed,
> I fainted at his flight,
> I sought him but I did not find him,
> I called for him but he did not answer me.

The opening of v. 6 answers the command of v. 2, although time to recite more than forty words has passed. The structure of this verse uses a variety of forms to convey its role as the turning point in the narrative.[22] The first line of three words and the first word of the second line

---

21. Neh. 3:3, 6, 13, 14, 15: "bolts," paired with "bars."

22. Murphy, *Song*, 165, observes that the first verb, followed by an independent personal pronoun as its subject, is emphatic, exactly as at the beginning of v. 5. He considers the following two verbs emphatic as well, due to their asyndetic relationship.

all end with the familiar -*î* suffix, signifying "I/my" and referring to the female. The last word of the first line is identical to the first word of the second line, "my lover" (*dôdî*). These techniques move the attention from the female to the male and bind the two together in the repetition of this by-now familiar form of endearment. However, the next two words after the twofold "my lover" are verbs in which the male is the subject. They describe his departure. Since each line of this first half of the verse consists of one verb, an unusual structure results in which the first line has three words, the second has two, and the third has one. The first line has six full syllables, the second has four, and the third has two. This reduction focuses on the verb "he had departed" (*ʿābār*). The final three lines return to an expected form of parallelism. Each contains three words, with 6, 8, and 6 syllables respectively. The subject is the same in all three. The fourth line, however, is distinct. It records the reaction of the female and uses the expression "my soul went out." Used elsewhere of death, here this expression may identify the near-death experience caused by disappointment at the absence of her lover. The final two lines each begin with the same grammatical form of the verb followed by the same object suffix. There is then the "but . . . not" (*wĕlōʾ*) and another verb.[23] The effect of this structure is to portray a kind of disintegration in the first half of the verse. The first full line continues the action of the preceding verses with the optimism that this will bring the female into the arms of her lover. The second line, however, announces that something is wrong. Using an unusual verb, it suggests a turning. The third line, with its single word, conveys the full impact of the loss. The male is gone. There is a poetic pause at this point as the female attempts to take in the devastation of the scene. Her desolation is conveyed in the fourth line as she approaches death. At the same time this line reestablishes a poetic pattern that continues through the remainder of the verse.

> [7]The guards found me,
> Those who go through the city,
> They beat me, they wounded me,
> They removed my shawl from me,
> Those guards on the walls.

The narrative moves on as the female regains her role as subject. In v. 7, the final lines summarize the remaining action. She seeks without finding. She calls without a response. The sequence of seeking and call-

---

23. All the verbs are in the perfect tense/aspect. The first verbs in each line are first-person common singular forms with a third-person masculine singular object suffix.

ing forms a chiastic construction with vv. 2–4. There it is the sound of her lover and his voice that she first encounters (v. 2). Only afterward does he actively demonstrate how he seeks her by thrusting his hand through the keyhole (v. 4). Thus he has called and sought her without result; and now she experiences the same.

The question remains as to why the male departed. No answer is given in the text. In 3:1–4 he was also absent, and she found him only after a search. Elsewhere he appears as a chimerical figure who leaps about on the hills and mountains, who comes and goes as he pleases (2:9, 17). However, the texts also suggest that his desire for his partner remains as passionate as hers for him (2:10–14; 4:1–8). Nevertheless, the sense of this departure may reflect the unpredictability of the lovers and their actions. For reasons known only to the male, he departs.[24] His love is no less for his lover nor his passion diminished (as further reading will demonstrate). So it is often true with love, and no less the love of the Christian church for its lover, Christ. The unexpected elements interfere with the expectation of love consummated. The sense of the presence of the lover is gone when we most seek to have it present. Yet the lover is always true and ultimately present.

The first two lines of v. 7 duplicate the first lines of 3:3.[25] In both cases the female goes in search of her lover and is found by the guards on their rounds.[26] This time, however, she does not find her lover. Instead, the guards beat and bruise her. Following the duplicate lines, a series of three verbs appears, with the guards as the subject and the female or her garment as the object. Is this the picture of a young girl who wanders wantonly and half-dressed through the streets of the city in the middle of the night? Is she then seized by the guards, who punish her for her brazenness or for the shame her act might bring to her family? Perhaps; however, such punishments would be customary for the family itself to decide, not for guards. This may be the rough treatment she receives while being pushed along, back to her home, by guards who feel they have more important things to do.[27] Nevertheless, there is a sense that the first wandering in chapter 3 was tolerated, perhaps

24. LaCocque, *Romance*, 53, understands here a parallel between the male lover and the wildness of his state in nature. He cannot tolerate the bed and the images of civilized society. However, LaCocque does not address the question as to why he would try to enter a ("civilized") room in the first place.

25. The first verb of 5:7, *mĕṣāʾunî*, is written defectively.

26. Müller, "Hohelied," 56; idem, "Mond," 208–9, proposes a connection between the rounds of the guards and the moon and Pleiades, on the basis of the poem of Sappho. However, there is not a clear allusion to astronomy in the Song itself.

27. Garrett, *Song*, 412, is unique to my knowledge in asserting that the guards rape her. The term is not used here, nor is any term for sexual relations.

with a warning, whereas the second one here receives a greater punishment. The verbs for beating and bruising occur only here in the Song, as does the description of lifting the shawl. Indeed, the appearance of the three verbs in sequence one after the other crowds this action into a sudden and swift activity, a denouement that brings the whole scene to a sudden, frustrated, and unpleasant conclusion. Again, the meaning is not clear. If it is all she is wearing, it would serve to shame her and form a greater punishment than the beating. However, her reference to her robe in v. 3 suggests that she would not have left home so scantily clad. Perhaps it was some signifier of her identity that would serve to aid in locating her home (especially if she was uncooperative in telling the guards where she lived). It might be held until claimed by the head of her household, who could then be informed of her escapades. In any case, these are not pleasant experiences, and the female surely suffers humiliation as a result of her impulsive actions. The final line repeats the first line's identification of the guards. It forms an inclusio that brings the scene with the guards to an end. This is her last dash into the night in search of her lover. The text moves on to other matters after this. However, it never judges the female for her brave adventure. Instead, she describes it in terms of desire that becomes action as she seeks her lover at any price.

> [8]I want you to promise,
> O young women of Jerusalem,
> If you find my lover,
> What will you tell him?
> That I am faint with love.

The final verse of this section has the female addressing the young women of Jerusalem (5:8). As in 2:7 and 3:5 (cf. also 8:4), she elicits a promise from them. However, unlike the other texts, she does not advise her friends about the character of love. Instead, she seeks from the other females a means to reach her lover. If she cannot go in search of him, perhaps they will encounter him. If she is barred from public appearances, perhaps they will have access to him. Following the initial charge, the third and fourth lines have synonymous grammatical parallelism. A particle ("if/what") is followed by a verb addressed in the second-person plural to the young women of Jerusalem ("you find/you tell").[28] Finally, each line concludes with a reference to the object of the female's affection ("my lover/him"). This is the seventh of nine occurrences in the Song of

28. For the unexpected masculine gender of this address, see the comments on 2:7, where (like 3:5 and 8:4) this apparent incongruence occurs.

the verb "find."[29] Three appear grouped together in this section, and this is the third. In v. 6 the female does not find her lover. In v. 7 the guards find her and prevent her continued search for him. Here in v. 8 she asks her friends to find him, because she has no other recourse. The verb "tell" (*ngd*) occurs only one other time in the Song, in 1:7. There the female wishes to join her lover and seeks knowledge as to where he is. In that case she asks him directly to tell her where he pastures his flock. In 5:8 she seeks from her friends a means of passing along to her lover a communication of her desire for him, so that he will join her.

The final line of 5:8 repeats 2:5 but under different circumstances. In the earlier section the female was with her lover, in his house and in his arms (2:4, 6). Here she has lost her lover. His presence is no longer there to thrill her. She seeks him, and as she seeks she remembers their time together. As a result, her longing increases and she cannot contain it. As with his presence, so with his absence, her longing desire drives from her all sense of well-being. She nearly loses consciousness. The passion for love in this section becomes an ideal: the intensity of love does not change when the object of that love has left. His absence may alter the way in which the love is expressed, but it does not affect its power.

The first part of this scene has an interesting parallel in Anglo-Saxon and European tradition, as observed by J. Sasson:

> C. R. Baskerville has written a very interesting article on "English Songs on the Night Visit" (*Publications of the Modern Language Association* 36 [1921]: 565–614) describing a practice that was deeply rooted in Europe as far back as the medieval period, if not earlier. One night before marriage, a highly conventionalized custom was reenacted in which (a) the groom stealthily arrives at the future bride's window; (b) raps on it and asks to be admitted; (c) the girl refuses, citing her parents as her reason for her failing nerves; (d) the groom threatens to leave; (e) the girl capitulates. It is assumed that in some areas the future couple did take their own pleasure at that point. In New England, however, the sweethearts, fully clothed, "bundled" together.[30]

The Sumerian sacred marriage parallel that Pope (*Song*, 515–16) cites suggests an ancient tradition to this practice. Perhaps this passage in the Song reflects a similar custom in ancient Israel. If so, the erotically charged poetry looks forward to the joys of the marriage.

> [9]How does your lover compare with other lovers,
> Most beautiful among women,

29. The root *ms²* appears in 3:1, 2, 3, 4; 5:6, 7, 8; 8:1, 10.
30. J. Sasson, "On Pope's *Song*," 195.

How does your lover compare with other lovers,
That you wish us to promise like this?

5:9. *Chorus: Challenge to compare the male lover.* The function of v. 9 as a response to the preceding one is obvious in terms of the content. The two verses also share similar vocabulary. The initial verb of v. 8 is the same form as the last word of v. 9, "I want you to promise/you wish us to promise."[31] This serves as an envelope construction that wraps together the beginning and end of this exchange. In addition, most of the words in v. 9 are found in v. 8. Only the comparative marker (*min*), the expression "most beautiful of women," and the marker of result at the beginning of the final line (*kākāh*) do not appear in v. 8. The two verses thus contain vocabulary connections that culminate in the inclusio. However, the overall structure of the verses differs. Whereas v. 8 adds new information with each line, v. 9 parallels its lines and repeats the same idea. In v. 8 each line moves the story forward; in v. 9 the whole idea is summarized in the first line. Lines 1 and 3 are identical in v. 9. Lines 2 and 4 add the information identifying to whom the question is addressed and the reason for their question. In fact, except for the final verb, all the other language in lines 2 and 4 is new for vv. 8–9.

If v. 9 forms a response to v. 8, exactly how is the question related to the charge? The women speakers of v. 9 wish to understand what is so special about the female's lover that he arouses the feelings of illness or fainting with which the female's words of v. 8 conclude. By their own confession the female is the most beautiful of all. So why should she be so concerned about finding this male? Surely she could attract the love of the best man of the kingdom. What is so special about her intended partner that she holds out for him alone and risks all? The chorus also wishes to understand why they have been made to promise that they will pass this message along to the male if they find him. Such a message places the female at a disadvantage in the game of love, because it makes her feelings vulnerable to manipulation by her lover. On the other hand, the female's message in the final line of v. 8 also opens that dimension of her life to the male and thereby enables her to further attest to her absolute and undying love for him. Of course, this question also functions to introduce 6:10–16 and the female's description of the lover. Her description answers the question as to what is so special about this partner. However, the open vulnerability of the female, especially in light of the suffering she has experienced for her love (5:7) and his own unexplained departure (5:6), demonstrates a fundamental prerequisite

31. Both are Hiphil perfect forms of the root *šbᶜ*. Both also have either an object suffix or an object pronoun.

for any enduring love. Love must be open and freely express its commitment and need, whether directly to the one loved or to those around the lover. The lover cannot remain silent but must express the intense emotion and yearning.

5:10–16. *Female:* Waṣf *for the male.* Although *waṣf* forms in which males describe females are relatively common in ancient Near Eastern literature, those where females describe males are rare. Nevertheless, all of them tend to begin with a general all-encompassing observation and then move from the head downward.[32]

With the exception of a few participles used as adjectives in the descriptive phrases, there are no verbs in this section. It is composed entirely of nominal clauses, so that the translation must add the necessary "is/are" in order to render it into readable English. Each verse and sometimes each colon begins with some aspect of the male by using a possessive pronoun: "my lover," "his head," "his locks," "his eyes," "his cheeks," "his lips," "his arms," "his waist," "his legs," "his looks," "his mouth." The initial "my lover" secures the whole person and being of her partner to the speaker. Following this, individual areas of the lover's body are described, beginning at the head and moving downward. Then the two lines introduced by "his looks" return to the general description with which the poem begins. Like a camera that begins with a view of the whole figure and then focuses on each specific part, the final shot pulls back and again looks at the whole figure that has been described. However, an additional verse returns to the top and more importantly to the most sensuous part of the male's body that is described. Here the lovemaking would begin.

The full syllables of each line average between five and six, with fewer in the lines of the first verses and more in the lines of the later verses (except v. 16). In most cases, the identified part of the male is followed by two lines that describe it. This two-line rule is violated by the head, which has only one line in v. 11, and by the eyes, which receive four lines (v. 12). Most often visual imagery is employed. However, the cheeks and lips (v. 13) and the mouth (v. 16) appeal to other senses, those of smell and taste. If words connected by the Hebrew *maqqēp*[33]

---

32. Bergant, *Song,* 68–69. It is difficult to accept the contention of Whedbee, "Paradox," 273–74, that this is a satire "of the male who appears as bigger-than-life, standing somewhat awkwardly as a gargantuan, immobile, distant figure." While his citation of Landy's *Paradoxes,* 90—who says that the description is cold and disjointed (except for the face, which has feminine features)—may have merit, this does not justify labeling the *waṣf* a comic description. Instead, the context suggests words of praise by the female for her lover.

33. The hyphen that connects closely related terms, such as a preposition with its object or two words in a construct relationship.

count as a single unit, then the first lines of each description contain two or three word-units, and the second lines virtually always contain two word-units.[34] The overall effect is a poem of remarkable regularity, with descriptions that create an intense impression by adding one phrase to another. Such a paratactic style works well in poetry and is characteristic of Hebrew syntax.

> [10]My lover is dazzling and ruddy,
> Better looking than ten thousand.

The general description of v. 10 begins with the endearment term most frequently used by the female for the male: "My lover."[35] Four terms of description follow, all of which are unique to the Song and used only here of a person. The sense of one who is shining or dazzling and ruddy is a description of the lover as he appears in the mind of the beloved. "Shiny" or "dazzling" can describe heat (Isa. 18:4; Jer. 4:11) and may suggest one who appears fresh from the rigors of hard labor, glistening with perspiration. The ruddy condition is reminiscent of the description of Esau at birth.[36] His skill in hunting and his other name, Edom, associate redness with an outdoor life.[37] Compare the Egyptian use of red in their portrayal of males in art and the act of a king applying rouge after washing (*CTU* 1.14.ii 9) as part of appropriate preparation to offer an acceptable sacrifice. These examples suggest that redness was a color admired in males. If the derivation of "better looking" is correct, it is the only use of the root *dgl* (to see) in the Bible.[38] The sense of the lover's appearance as unique among ten thousand surely attests to the female's admiration of him and her certainty that these words of praise will persuade her friends of his value.

34. The single exception is the last line of v. 13, where there are three word-units. Contrast the use of the *maqqēp* here with its use in 8:8–9. In 5:10–16 all such connections are with prepositions and construct forms that are closely related semantically. In 8:8–9 all the connections are with interrogatives or conditional words. These latter represent independent semantic units and are counted separately in the commentary.

35. This is the seventeenth occurrence. Earlier expressions appeared in 1:13, 14, 16; 2:3, 8, 9, 10, 16, 17; 4:16; 5:2, 4, 5, 6 (2x), 8.

36. Genesis 25:25 uses a similar expression, *ʾadmônî*. Several commentators point out that David is also described as "ruddy" (*ʾadmônî*) in 1 Sam. 16:12; 17:42. In particular, Pope, *Song*, 531–32, observes how men (Keret) and women (Pugat) in the Ugaritic mythological epics redden themselves as part of their grooming. So this may be a cosmetic application, though that is not necessary.

37. Genesis 25:30; 27:27, 30; 36:1, 8, 19. Edom (*ʾĕdôm*) is derived from the same root for redness, *ʾdm*.

38. For a verbal form spelled in the same manner, see Ps. 20:6 (20:5 Eng.). Cf. also the comments on Song 6:4, 10. The psalm text has to do with raising banners, and the verbal root behind it is best understood as a homonym of the root used here.

> [11]His head is refined gold.
> His locks are date panicles,
> Black like a raven.

As the poetic description moves from the general persona to the specific features, the first area of focus is the head. More than any other part of the body, the head represents the person. It is the place that receives marks of identity (Ezek. 9:4–6). The head of the statue that appears in the visions of Daniel is always the starting point for the description of the statues and their interpretations (Dan. 2:32, 38; cf. 7:9). There as well as here it is composed of the choicest of metals, gold. The sense appealed to in this verse is sight. The text produces the strongest contrast possible between gold, the color of the sun, and blackness, the image of darkness. Together they provide an image of dazzling brightness set in the absence of light. Indeed, the picture of the hair as black provides a dramatic contrast for the light of the reflected gold, much as the sun is set in a context of the blackness of space. The image of the locks of the male as date panicles proposes a picture of the naturally curved and fluted plants that suggest perfect and attractive forms. These frame the head of the lover in a beautiful setting of perfect harmony. The curves of the face and its pleasant appearance are accentuated and enhanced by the flowing and perfectly formed locks of hair.[39] The word associations decline in terms of general value, from refined gold to date panicles to a raven. This decline is considerable since the raven is an unclean bird that has few admirers (Lev. 11:15; Deut. 14:14; Job 38:41). Nevertheless, the darkness of its coat allows for its easy observation when sent on missions (Gen. 8:7). Thus it is this one strikingly visible feature, rather than the raven's general worth, that allows its inclusion in the image of praise regarding the lover's head and hair.

> [12]His eyes like doves,
> By streams of water,
> Washed in milk,
> Sitting by a brimming water basin.

The picture of the eyes as doves in the twelfth verse continues the emphasis on color. The doves imagined here may be white, an image reinforced by their association with a milk bath. However, they may also be another color and thus describe the pupils. The pupils of her lover's eyes are then set in a field of white within the eye. Although the

---

39. See 2 Sam. 14:25–26 for an association of a handsome figure with the length and weight of his hair.

analogy may not provide a one-to-one correspondence, it does suggest the whiteness of the eyes in lines 1 and 3. In lines 2 and 4 the imagery shifts to water, a possible allusion to the tears that the eyes may produce. In this poem, however, there is no emphasis on actual tears, only on the potential of tears streaming forth from the male's eyes. Because the Hebrew word for "eye" (ʿayin) is also the term for a spring of water, it is not surprising that the poet should evoke this image, even where no crying is suggested.

The four phrases used to describe the eyes in v. 12 suggest a special focus upon this feature. The male lover began with the eyes in his first *wasf* of the female (4:1). He finished with a reference to their power to render him a slave of her love (4:9). That was neither the first nor the last time he spoke of her eyes.[40] Thus the eyes have a special and powerful effect upon the lover. Only here does the female describe the male's eyes as objects of beauty. In accordance with the male's focus on her eyes, however, she also devotes more time to his eyes than to any other part of his body.

> [13]His cheeks like beds of spice,
> Abundant with perfumes.
> His lips are lotuses,
> Dripping with myrrh.

The "cheek" can refer to various parts of the side of the face: the jawbone (Judg. 15:15–17), the area beneath the eyes where tears flow (Lam. 1:2), and the part struck to inflict pain (Lam. 3:30).[41] In Song 1:10, in its one other occurrence in the book, it describes a place decorated by earrings. Here in 5:13 the cheeks become the area fragrant with aromas of exotic spices. Whole farms of perfume-producing plants are described, evoking the most powerful of appeals to the olfactory senses. Nor is the image complete with the description of the cheeks. The lips also exude (or flow with dripping) myrrh. Along with the spices, myrrh again appears when the wish is to describe the finest and most fragrant of aromatics. As in 1:13, where the female refers to her partner as a container of myrrh lying between her breasts, here as well the myrrh provides an image of erotic sensuality. The term for "perfumes" in the second line of 5:13 occurs elsewhere (see the third translation note at 5:13) with the meaning of containers of ointment, providing a further

---

40. See Song 1:14, 15; 6:5; 7:5 (7:4 Eng.).

41. Longman, *Song*, 172, argues that the beard is intended. Although this is possible, it seems doubtful because the common Hebrew word for "beard" (zāqān) is not used (see also the first translation note at 5:13 above). This does not suggest that the male was beardless but means only that the part of the face described here had no beard.

connection with the holder of myrrh in 1:13. The kisses of the lips bring the lovers into a fantasy of desire not unlike that intoxication of strong sweet aroma such as myrrh and oil. The sense of smell, however, is interrupted by the picture of lotus blossoms. Their graceful curves and form evoke the contours of full lips, which invite the female to happily think upon the joys that they hold for her. Myrrh is among the most vivid of aromas. Its origin in lotuses or blossoms is poetic imagery, and yet the intoxicating effects of lotuses were known in the ancient world.[42] The entire description suggests that the face, with its cheeks and lips, forms as sensual an image for fragrant smells as the eyes do for visual impressions. The lips associate most powerfully of all, not only with the sense of smell, but also with that of touch. The myrrh, mixed with olive oil, would form a smooth and inviting perfume. Applied after a bath, it invigorated the skin in a dry climate. Thus the sense of touch is reflected in this word picture as well. With the lips and their suggestion of kissing, the picture of the lover's head reaches its climax.

> [14]His arms are gold rods,
> Set with gems.
> His body a bar of ivory,
> Overlaid with lapis lazuli.

The poet's attention turns to the arms of her lover. Their description as rods or cylinders of gold implies value, beauty, and strength. Like the use of gold to describe the head (*ketem paz*), the same metal as applied to the arms (though with the more general and less refined *zāhāb;* cf. 1:11; 3:10) suggests how precious the female regards them. In ancient Israel no metal was more costly than gold. Its appearance on the arms as well as the head goes beyond even the statue of Daniel, where the arms are of the less costly silver (2:32). The glistening character of the gold implies the beauty of the gold rods. The metal, formed into perfectly round arms, would describe an ideal of appearance that might contrast with the muscular physique of the modern age. Alternatively, the term for "rods" may suggest something more than smooth cylinders. It is used twice elsewhere as a common noun. In Esther 1:6 is it used for rings of metal, while in 1 Kings 6:34 it describes how the doorjambs turned on their sockets. Hence the possibility of sinews in the female's use of this term cannot be discounted. The precious stones that decorate the gold rods may also serve to further strengthen the gold, a softer metal by itself. In any case, they add even more to the value of the arms. The female draws upon the substances of greatest value, beauty, and

---

42. Cf. Odysseus and the land of the lotus-eaters in Homer's *Odyssey*, 9.82–104.

strength to describe her lover's arms. Commentators observe that the term for arms here (*yād*) is more often translated "hand(s)," although the sense of "(fore)arm(s)" is widely recognized.[43] In the Song the term has appeared in 5:4 and 5:5, where the hands of the lovers seek to touch through the hole at the door, but do not. The term thereby recollects this image of frustrated intimacy. The female's attention upon her lover's arms expresses this intimacy, no doubt with the sense of resting in his embrace. The value and strength of the image can therefore suggest a security that the presence of her lover brings.

The second half of the fourteenth verse describes the central part of the male's body, above the thighs and below the chest. Often translated "loins," it (*mēʿîm*) includes the area of the belly and below, as well as the lower back. The picture of a bar of ivory is one that evokes strength in its smooth and solid form. Such is the male's stomach. As strong and powerful, the stomach takes on the characteristics of the arms. It possesses the might necessary to carry the rest of his muscular frame and to protect the female from harm, such as the beatings the guards inflicted upon her (5:7). The use of ivory also suggests a substance highly prized for its value, beauty, and ability to be carved into artistic forms. King Solomon's throne was thus formed of ivory and overlaid with gold (1 Kings 10:18; 2 Chron. 9:17). An ivory engraving from Megiddo (c. 1300 BC) displays a king on his throne receiving food, and the many ivory engravings from Israelite Samaria demonstrate the wealth of their owners.[44] The decorations of lapis lazuli suggest a style common in the ancient Near East. This blue stone was a popular royal adornment in artistic creations. In Egypt the throne of King Tutankhamen, as preserved in his tomb, possessed decorations primarily composed of gold and lapis lazuli. It thus provided an ideal color to contrast with the gold so that each would set off and complement the other in their beauty.

> [15]His legs are pillars of alabaster,
> Set on sockets of fine gold.
> His looks are like Lebanon,
> Choice as the cedars.

Verse 15 continues the lover's view of her partner as she moves farther down his frame. The term for "his legs" (*šôqāyw*) sometimes describes only the thighs.[45] However, the term *šôq* can also refer to the leg, especially

---

43. *HALOT* 386; cf. Exod. 17:11; Isa. 49:2; Jer. 38:12.

44. These beds of ivory also provide evidence of their decadence according to Amos 3:15; 6:4.

45. This is especially true of sacrificial animals and the priestly portion: Exod. 29:22, 27; Lev. 7:32, 33, 34; 8:25; 9:21; 10:14; Num. 6:20; 18:18.

in descriptions of people rather than animals (Ps. 147:10; Prov. 7:8; 26:7; Isa. 47:2). That is clearly the sense here. Like the term for "hands" used to describe the arms in v. 14,[46] a smaller component of the intended body part refers to the whole. This principle may be used to emphasize the specific part of the arm or leg that provides special significance for the female. For example, the hands of her lover would hold her and touch her. So also the thighs of the male could be the most muscular part of the leg, revealing his strength and endurance. However, the translation "legs" is not only appropriate semantically but also poetically serves as an inclusive reference to the remainder of the male's physique. The image to describe the legs is that of white alabaster, a hard substance that could be used to carve human and other forms. For example, the canopic jars holding the viscera of King Tutankhamen of Egypt were decorated with full-relief carvings of figures in alabaster. Like ivory, alabaster was thus a beautiful and strong stone, susceptible to sculptors who might carve and shape it into fine forms. The description therefore admires the male for his handsome form, for his great worth, and for the security that his strength can provide. Sirach 26:18 describes an ideal woman with the following picture: "Like golden pillars on secure bases, so are shapely legs and steadfast feet" (NRSV). In that text both the legs and the feet are identified with gold. Here the refined gold is *paz*, mentioned previously only in v. 11 as a description of the male's head. The merism of this metaphor should not be lost. The female delights in describing her lover with images of multiple precious substances. However, pure gold tops them all for its value. Here she portrays him as composed from head to foot of the most valuable metal known.

With the second half of v. 15, the "camera" looking at this figure pulls back to the whole of his appearance. It thus concludes where it began in v. 10. There his form was compared favorably with ten thousand other men. Here it is likened to the cedars of Lebanon, the strongest and tallest of living things. They too would number in the thousands. However, the point here is their special value. All the best parts of the tabernacle, temple, and other buildings of the kingdom used cedarwood. It was renowned for its strength and ability to support great weight. Further, the pleasant aroma of cedarwood, and indeed the verdant forests of Lebanon, would add the sense of smell to the overall picture. Like the myrrh of v. 13, the aroma of the cedar forest would further demonstrate the beauty and precious value of the lover.

> [16]His mouth is nectar.
> He is totally desirable.

---

46. Cf. also, perhaps, the "cheeks" of v. 13.

> This is my lover,
> This is my partner,
> Daughters of Jerusalem.

The picture of the lover has come full circle with a return to a perspective of his whole form, and yet the female does not cease with her praise. She finds her thoughts of desire for her lover turning once more to that most sensuous part of his body, the mouth. Although she had already dwelt upon his lips as the climax of her description of his head (v. 13b), the female turns again to consider this area. Now, however, she moves for the first time beyond what can be seen to the interior of the mouth (*ḥēk*). Here she describes his palate, not in terms of what is visible but according to what can be tasted. This additional sense, suggested previously only with the lips (though there the lotuses and myrrh described primarily the senses of sight and smell), provides a more complete experiential (though imaginary) encounter with the female's lover. Not only is he beautiful to behold; he is also pleasant to kiss. Here the female's desire reaches its peak: she exclaims about both the sweetness of his mouth and his all-encompassing desirability. Although the particular term for nectar occurs only here, a different word conveying a similar idea appeared previously in 5:1. There the male described how he had tasted this sweetness in the garden that is identified with the female. Here the nectar is in his mouth, perhaps as a result of that taste or, with the use of a different term here, as a reference by the female to her experience with his love. From the giddiness of such pleasures, it is a simple matter to move to praise of her lover's whole being. The transition is further eased by the similarity of the terms for "nectar" (*mamtaqqîm*) and "hot, desirable" (*maḥămaddîm*). With this expression the female concludes her paean of praise to her lover's body, his sensuality, and his desirability.

In the second half of v. 16 she returns to the question of the young women (daughters) of Jerusalem in 5:9. There they requested proof that her lover was special and the best of all. She has now provided that with her *waṣf*. She concludes by identifying him with herself. The two phrases "this is my lover" and "this is my partner" comprise two Hebrew words, each with three syllables: *zeh dôdî* and *zeh rēʿî*. The repetitive rhyming effect of this synonymous parallelism emphasizes the type of relationship the female has with her lover. "My lover" of the first phrase both recalls her favorite term of endearment for him and also addresses the term that the young women used to describe him in v. 9. Thus she says to them that this person she has described is one and the same person about whom they have inquired. Of course, her affirmation that he is her lover hints at their relationship, one that should not be minimized by potential rivals such as these other young women. The second term can describe a friend or close acquaintance. Indeed, it can be used for a variety of positive associations between two or more people.[47] However, its significance here is that it forms the masculine counterpart to the feminine "darling" (*ra⁽yâ*). The latter is the male's favorite expression of endearment for the female. Thus her use of the masculine form of the same word acknowledges his love by reciprocating the form of address he uses for her. In this manner, the term suggests much more than an acquaintance. It demonstrates the partnership of the two. The female thereby identifies her lover as the one about whom she has been speaking. At the same time and with as much importance, she asserts their partnership as an exclusive relationship rather than a casual association that can be challenged by other interested parties, such as the daughters of Jerusalem.

The fifth chapter of the Song begins with the female's desire for her lover and ends the same way. Throughout, she is the primary actor, although her interaction with both her partner and the young women provides opportunities for her to seek and to praise her lover and their relationship. A key point of emphasis that accompanies the yearning passion for her partner is the female's willingness to risk all in her pursuit of his presence. She runs out into the night in a manner that invites danger and provokes her own harm. However, this drama does more than provide a context for the young women to invite her to praise him physically. Her suffering forms a backdrop for the description of the male's strength by which she establishes his ability to provide her protection against assaults such as those she has endured. She will find security in the arms of her lover, more than she has found in her own house or with the guards of the city. Hence the strength to which the various pictures of the male allude also underscores the protection that the male gives to his female lover. He is her knight in shining armor. His protection and safety form a key part of their love and allow that love to develop between them even as it allows them to grow in their own respect for themselves and for one another.

> [6:1]Where has your lover gone,
> Most beautiful of women,
> Where has your lover ventured,
> So that we can seek him with you?

6:1. *Chorus: Inquiry for the male.* The speech of the chorus stands on each side of the *waṣf*, with questions structured in a similar manner in

47. See Hess, "*Rēa⁽*."

both (Brenner, *Song,* 38). The question "where?" (*ʾānāh*) occurs only here in the Song, and here it appears twice in parallel.[48] Further, the use of the word pair "gone/ventured" (*hālak/pānāh*) appears only here in the whole of poetry. The two verbs do not often occur with the same subject, and when they do they normally appear in the reverse order, to convey the sense of turning away and departing (Gen. 18:22; Deut. 16:7; Josh. 22:4; Judg. 18:21; 1 Sam. 10:9; 1 Kings 10:13; 2 Kings 5:12). An exception is 1 Kings 17:3, where Joshua is commanded to leave (*lēk*) and turn (*ûpānîtā*) eastward. The expression "most beautiful of women" occurs in Song 1:8; 5:9; and here for the third and final time—always from the chorus. The verb "to seek, look for" occurs here for the fifth and last time in the Song. Previously it appeared in 3:1 (2x), 2; and 5:6, always used by the woman about seeking her lover. Only here does the chorus express a desire to search out the male with her. In fact, this usage recalls 5:6, a verse that certainly connects to the narrative suggested by 6:1. It was the last time the lover was mentioned. He had appeared at the door, but by the time the female arrived to open it, he was gone. Her quest for him began there but was interrupted by the *wasf* of his characteristics. This verse now renews the concern and also draws the whole chorus in as participants. Their question, directed at the female, seems odd. In 5:6 she sought her lover but did not find him. Why would they ask a meaningless question? However, as the subsequent verses of this chapter reveal, she does know his location and soon enough is conversing with him. Thus the connections with 5:6, while useful as thematic indicators, are overtaken by a whole new scene and perspective. The female is no longer searching but has found the object of her desire. Rhetorically, the skepticism of the female chorus in 5:9 has been transformed into positive desire by the intervening response of the woman. The point may be to sweep along the readers as well. The descriptive power of the man's beauty, as related by the woman, brings us all into a common mission, the pursuit of the lover.

²My lover descended to his garden,
To the spice beds,
To graze in the gardens,
And to gather lotuses.

6:2–3. *Female: Reunites with her lover.* This dramatic change, in which the female's previous search for her lover now seems to have ended, leads some commentators to identify a new section at this point. In fact, it

48. The Ugaritic myth in which El has Anat request the whereabouts of her lover Baal from Shapshu, who then promises to seek for him (cf. *CTU* 1.6 III), may provide an interesting parallel (Pope, *Song,* 553). However, the search of a woman for her lover is a universal theme, as is the role of others in assisting in the search.

continues the theme stated by the male in 5:1, so that the intervening text takes on the sense of a dream or vision of separation enhancing the desire and joy of the union. At this point there is a realization of the female that her lover has always been found and is ever present with her. He has "descended" (used here for the first time in the Song), and this is followed by four phrases, each introduced by the preposition "to" (lĕ). The first and second such phrases describe the lover's destination as the "garden," "spice beds." Throughout the Song these terms have been used to describe the body of the female in which her lover takes delight.[49] The two thus are together, their bodies joined in love. The second set of phrases in this verse describes the purpose of the lover's presence in the "gardens."[50] He is there "to graze" and "to gather." In other words, he partakes of the love of her body. The two are joined, and the lover is fully engaged with his beloved. Hence there is no need for the other women to seek out the male. The female knows where he is. Further, he has no interest in any of the other women, only in her. The verse concludes with the metaphor of gathering lotuses, suggesting the beautiful, delicate, and intoxicating effects of physical love.

> [3]I am my lover's
> And my lover is mine;
> He gathers among the lotuses.

Verse 3 continues the use of the preposition "to" (lĕ), which has already occurred four times in the previous verse. Here it appears twice more in the four-word statement of unity with which the verse continues. A similar expression, conveying the same idea and followed by "he gathers among the lotuses," has occurred in 2:16. Similar to that case, each of the first three words ends with the same long vowel -î. In addition, however, the fourth word also ends in this manner in 6:3. Thus the binding together of the lovers with the phrase and the repeated ending that conveys the sense of the first person suffix "me/mine" completes the picture of their unity.

The term "my lover" (dôdî) introduces v. 2 and occurs three times in 6:2–3. The word "lotuses" (šôšannîm) appears twice, as the last word in each verse. In both cases it describes where he may "gather" (lqṭ) and where he "gathers among" (rᶜh). The resulting sense is that the act of gathering among lotuses embodies the relationship between the female and her lover. These two verses represent the sixth and seventh occur-

49. For the garden, see 4:12, 15, 16; 5:1. For the spice beds associated with the garden, see 4:16; 5:1; 8:14.
50. With Fox, Song, 149, this plural describes the various places in the garden as different parts of the body.

rences of the term "lotuses" in the Song. Seven times it is applied to the female's body and once to the male's lips.[51] Other than the parallel (2:16), the only occurrence that describes gathering among lotuses is 4:5. There the female's breasts are described as twin fawns that gather among lotuses. In all cases, lotuses form images of the bodies of the two lovers or some aspect of them. Thus the act of gathering among the lotuses carries the sense of physical love and, with it, the joyous union of the two lovers. In the light of chapter 5, this becomes a reunion of the female with her lover and an affirmation of the unity they share.

Theological Implications

The first part of this section (5:2–6:3) describes a scene of passion that is frustrated. Despite this, the female launches a pursuit that ends in her suffering and the loss of her lover (5:2–8). As in 3:1–5 she goes forth into the night. But this time her search for her lover leads to her suffering a beating. The whole picture suggests an intensification of desire as well as the difficulty of its fulfillment. This ratcheting up of emotions suggests that love does not limit itself to a certain degree of passion or of suffering. Instead, those who are in love willingly pay both desire and its price. The high price of love pushes the scene forward as the reader approaches chapter 8 and the ultimate sacrifice for love.

In contrast to 3:5, the female's statement to the daughters of Jerusalem in 5:8 no longer instructs them but requests the location of the male lover. The reason for her public quest becomes clear with the only *wasf* in the Song that celebrates the physical features of the male lover (5:10–16). The male attributes focus on protection and security, the sort that would resolve the insecurity and suffering of the female in the first part of the chapter. Love in the forms of risk, suffering, and protection also characterize the love of Christ for his church (Rom. 5:6–8). This mutual respect is a key ingredient of love and the loving commitment between a man and a woman. The family nurtured by this kind of relationship is one in which the children, like their parents, have a strong sense of self-confidence, which allows them to love unconditionally, without guilt or suspicion. It is also a key ingredient of all loving relationships, not least that between the believer and the Lord. For the Christian, the knowledge of God's presence in the struggles of the world provides a security in which the disciples are able to risk all and venture through-

51. For the female, see 2:1, 2, 16; 4:5; 6:2, 3; 7:3 (7:2 Eng.). For the male, see 5:13.

out the world in their proclamation of his kingdom (Matt. 28:18–20; Mark 16:15; Acts 1:8).

Once more a section concludes with the lovers reunited in a committed relationship (6:2–3). However difficult the search, however hopeless the cause, the lovers' desire for each other assures that they will find one another. Love between couples, and between God and his people, never surrenders hope (1 Cor. 13:7).

The union of the male and female may form an image of many aspects of unity in the life of the people of God. In this world, any claims of unity ring hollow unless there is physical evidence for such oneness. Those who share faith in Christ are called to a unity that the world will see and that will convince them of the truthfulness of the faith (John 17). However, the more direct and clear application of this passage has to do with unity in the loving relationship of marriage. One of the reasons the lovers are not clearly described as married may be the concern to emphasize the unity of their physical relationship as more substantial and fundamental than that of the words of a marriage ceremony. This is not to deny the importance of marriage in the context of physical love. Rather, it affirms the opposite: the most profound basis for a life of commitment in marriage arises out of the loving relationship that the man and woman have for one another. This relationship can be confessed by the four Hebrew words of 6:3, "I am my lover's and my lover is mine."

VI.
Desire for the Female and Love
in the Country
(6:4–8:4)

Translation

Male
6:4 Beautiful[a] as Tirzah[b]
Are you, my darling,
Lovely as Jerusalem,
Terrible[c] as the banners <of war>.[d]
5Turn your eyes from me,[e]
Because they overwhelm me.
Your hair is like the flock of goats
That descend from the Gilead.
6Your teeth are like the flock of ewes

a. Although the translated syntax is somewhat awkward, this rendering preserves the initial position of *yāpāh*.

b. Rejecting emendations that would remove the place-name, J. Sasson, "On Pope's *Song*," 196, cites the parallelism with Jerusalem. The versions translated a form of the root *rṣh*, "pleasing" (*eudokia* LXX; *ṣbynʾ* Syriac; *suavis* Vulgate).

c. *ʾĂyummāh* occurs only here and in 6:10 in the Song.

d. Landy, "Beauty," 38–39, suggests "constellations," in parallel with the celestial imagery of v. 10. However, the implication of war needs to be expressed. This Niphal participle occurs only here and in 6:10. Murphy, *Song*, 175, translates by using the *dgl* root, as in 2:4: "awe-inspiring as visions!" See also Long, "Lover." While possible, it seems less likely than the more common and here appropriate use of war banners. Indeed, Murphy notes that the early versions have a martial sense: LXX: *tetagmenai* (drawn up); Vulgate: *castrorum acies ordinata* (camps in battle array). For further on the military imagery, see Longman, *Song*, 180, who also cites Schroeder, "Love Song," for the use of military imagery in Ps. 45, a marriage psalm.

e. For vv. 5–7, cf. identical expressions in 4:1–3 and the discussion there of various translations.

That ascend from the washing,
Every one of them with its twin,
There is no "miscarriage" among them.
[7]Like pieces of pomegranate are your temples,
Behind your veil.
[8]There are sixty queens,
Eighty concubines,
And maidens without number.
[9]She is unique, my dove,
My perfect one, she is unique.
She is special[a] to her mother,
To the one who bore her.
Daughters saw her,
Queens and concubines blessed her,
And they praised her.
[10]Who is this who gazes down[b] as the dawn,
Beautiful as the full moon,
Special[c] like the sun,
Terrible as the display <of the stars>?[d]

a. The LXX, Syriac, and Vulgate all render *bārâ* as "select" or "chosen." Fox, *Song*, 153, contends that such a meaning, derived from *bwr*, would have to be active ("she chooses") rather than passive. Nevertheless, most translations prefer a sense of "special" or "chosen" to that of "pure," as found in the geminate root *brr*. Such a translation apparently assumes that the word is an adjective rather than the verb form that Fox had in mind. Longman, *Song*, 182, combines both senses to translate "favored," and this allows him to argue the same for the word in v. 10. The context, however, requires a term describing one who is special and distinct from those around her. "Special" preserves the emphasis on one who stands out among so many (vv. 8–9a) and who receives the accolades of her peers (v. 9b). Garbini, "Note," 163–65, hypothesizes that the word is an Aramaism for "girl." However, this does not follow the parallelism of the preceding line and adds no new information to the line in which it appears.

b. The Niphal form of *šqp* always conveys the sense of looking down or peering from above (Num. 21:20; 23:28; Judg. 5:28; 1 Sam. 13:18; 2 Sam. 6:16; Jer. 6:1; Ps. 85:12 [85:11 Eng.]; Prov. 7:6; 1 Chron. 15:29).

c. This retains the same translation as that in v. 9. Others prefer "pure" (Keel, *Song*) or "bright" (NIV; Fox, *Song*), emphasizing the alternative root. While this is possible, purity is not the focus regarding the female, nor is her brightness under discussion. Nor do the two other occurrences of these poetic expressions of "moon" and "sun" together in Isa. 24:23 and 30:26 prove brightness as the main concern. Only Isa. 30:26 describes the brightness of the sun, and there it does so by considering the "light of the sun" rather than the sun itself. Thus it is not the word for "sun" that conveys something special about brightness but the "light of the sun" that does so. Here in Song 6:10, the sun is unique in the heavens, without parallel. As with the preceding verse, the emphasis falls on the female's unique beauty.

d. See 6:4, where this same line is used but with the contextual meaning of war. Here the context requires the starry host of heaven instead of the banners of earthly conflict. See also Goitein, "*Ayumma*," who places the emphasis upon "terrific, awesome."

194

Female

11To the grove of nut trees I went down,
To see the plants[e] in the valley,
To see if the vine has blossomed,
If the pomegranates are in bloom.
12I did not realize,
My desire set me,
In chariotry,
With a prince.[f]

Chorus

7:1 (6:13 Eng.) Return! Return! O Shulammite!
Return! Return! That we may gaze on you.
How would you gaze on the Shulammite?
Like the dance of Mahanayim.[g]

e. *ʾĒb* (plants) occurs elsewhere only in Job 8:12. There it describes plants that are still growing by sending out shoots.

f. The last two words in the MT are *ʿammî nādîb*, literally, "my people, noble." This translation alters *ʿammî* (my people) to *ʿim* (with). The translation of this verse is much disputed. Cf. LXX: *ouk egnō hē psyche mou; etheto me harmata Aminadab* (my soul did not know; it placed me as chariots of Amminadab); Vulgate: *nescivi; anima mea conturbavit me propter quadrigas Aminadab* (I was ignorant; my soul disturbed me because of Amminadab's chariots). A sample of commentators includes Murphy, *Song*, 174: "Before I knew it, my heart made me <the blessed one> of the prince's people"; Longman, *Song*, 184: "I did not realize that my desire had placed me in a chariot with a noble man"; Pope, *Song*, 552: "Unawares I was set in the chariot with the prince"; Keel, *Song*, 225: "Before I was aware, my [desire] set me in [the chariots of Amminadab]"; Snaith, *Song*, 95–96: "I did not know . . . my soul set me . . . chariots . . . my willing people"; Deckers, "Structure," 194: "I don't know, my being determines me, vehicle of my noble people." For the last phrase as "Die Wagen meines edlen Volkes," see Barbeiro, "Wagen," who connects the passage with 6:4–10. For earlier attempts, see the survey of Tournay, "Chariots." Mulder, "Does?" introduces the highly speculative topic of *merkabah* (chariot) mysticism (cf. Ezek. 1). Holman, "Pleidooi," examines cultural anthropology.

g. *Hammaḥănāyim* (the two camps) is understood by some as a reference to a "dance of the two camps" rather than as a place-name. See Delitzsch, *Song*, 120–21; Loretz, *Liebeslied*, 42; Murphy, *Song*, 181; Gruber, "Ten"; Longman, *Song*, 189; Keel, *Song*, 225. Fox (*Song*, 158) is creative in translating "a camp-dancer," and Orel ("Textological") compares 1 Sam. 18:7 and suggests two circles of dancers. Provan, *Song*, 352n3, tries to relate the two camps to the female's two breasts—a usage without parallel. However, he must change the vocalization of the Hebrew text to do so. The major reason for translating the term as a common noun seems to be based on negative evidence: the otherwise lack of an attested dance associated with this place-name. The same is true of the "dance of the two camps." See also the usage of place-names in the previous context and the further discussion in the comments.

Male

[2 (1 Eng.)]How beautiful are your feet in sandals,

O daughter of a prince,

The curves[a] of your hips[b] are like ornaments,[c]

The work of an artist's[d] hands.

[3 (2 Eng.)]Your navel,[e]

A round bowl,[f]

a. *Ḥammûq* (here as plural construct) is a hapax legomenon. In Mishnaic Hebrew, it can refer to a round piece of wood. In Biblical Hebrew, the *ḥmq* root describes the act of turning. It appears in the Qal only in Song 5:6, where the male lover turns and is gone. The sense in this verse is one of curves or a rounded area.

b. This term may refer to the upper thigh and the region of the genitals (Gen. 24:2, 9; 47:29; Exod. 1:5; Judg. 8:30). Yet it can also refer to the outer area of the hips as the place where the sword is worn (Exod. 32:27; Judg. 3:16, 21; Ps. 45:4 [45:3 Eng.]; Song 3:8), a region easily struck by someone engaged in repentance or mourning (Jer. 31:19; Ezek. 21:17 [21:12 Eng.]).

c. *Ḥălāʾîm*, from *ḥălî*, found elsewhere only in Prov. 25:12 and Hosea 2:15 (2:13 Eng.). In the latter it appears in parallel with a word for a nose ring or an earring (*nezem*). In Mishnaic Hebrew the singular comes to mean a link in a chain. LXX has *hormiskos* (necklace).

d. For *ʾāmmān* as a loanword from the Akkadian *ummānu* (specialist, expert in crafts), cf. *HALOT* 64. Hurvitz, "Toward," comes to a similar conclusion on the basis of a parallel usage in Prov. 8:27–30 and because of similar nominal forms. He renders the term "skilled worker."

e. *Šōr* occurs in Ezek. 16:4 with the sense of an umbilical cord. The other occurrence in Prov. 3:8 must either be a homonym or metaphor for "strength" or (*pars pro toto*) "body" (*HALOT* 1650–51), but this is not the intent in the Song. The latter is proposed by Pope (*Song*, 617), who understands a scribal error for *šĕʾēr* (flesh) and translates the occurrence in the Song as "vulva." Ratzhabi, "Biblical," agrees with this translation and regards it as a euphemism. Cf. also Goulder, *Song*, 56; Brenner, "Come Back," 263–64. However, this is without warrant from the Ezekiel context (Keel, *Song*, 234), nor is an appeal to a possible Arabic cognate preferable to the straightforward understanding of its usage as similar to that in Ezekiel. The prominent depiction of the navel on female figurines from Egypt and especially from Palestine and Syria is noted by Keel, who also observes the confusion between the navel and the vulva in some depictions. He thus arrives at a similar conclusion to that of Pope (and Haupt, *Biblische*, earlier), that the image portrayed is that of the moist vulva that, in Sumerian sacred marriage texts, provides an intoxicating drink for the male lover. Murphy, *Song*, 183, comes to a similar conclusion by suggesting that the Hebrew *šōr* is cognate to Arabic *surr* (umbilical cord, navel, valley). He argues that it cannot be the navel because it occurs between the thighs and the belly. However, I translate "hips" and "waist," the latter of which, of course, is close to the navel (as is the belly). It is the navel that is described in the Song, not the vulva. The usage in Ezekiel and the Arabic cognate support this. Further, the wine is related to the bowl, not the navel (Fox, *Song*, 159; Bergant, *Song*, 82, 84). It is the function of such a bowl to contain wine; it is the perceived beauty of the navel to be large and deep like such a bowl. The appearance of figurines with prominent navels suggests that they were considered objects of significance and perhaps of beauty in their own right (contra Provan, *Song*, 353n6).

f. *ʾAggān*, a mixing crater for wine (with water, spices, or stronger narcotic substances), with cognates in all ancient Near Eastern languages and with many examples in archaeo-

It does not lack spiced wine.[g]
Your waist,[h]
A heap of wheat,
Encircled by lotuses.
[4 (3 Eng.)]Your two breasts,
Like two fawns,
Twins of a gazelle.
[5 (4 Eng.)]Your neck,
Like an ivory tower;
Your eyes,
Pools in Heshbon,
By the gate of Bat-Rabbim;
Your nose,
Like the tower of Lebanon,
Espying Damascus.
[6 (5 Eng.)]Your head above you,
Like Carmel;
The loose hair[i] of your head,
Like purple,
A king is bound with locks.[j]
[7 (6 Eng.)]How beautiful you are,
How desirable,
O love,
O daughter of pleasures.[k]
[8 (7 Eng.)]Your stature resembles[l] a palm tree,
Your breasts <resemble> clusters of fruit.
[9 (8 Eng.)]I said,
"I shall climb the palm tree,
I shall seize its branches."[m]

---

logical sites of the ancient periods. Normally, this can be identified with a relatively larger, two-handled, ring-based, round bowl. See also Exod. 24:6 and Isa. 22:24.

g. *Māzeg*, a hapax legomenon. For the connection with Semitic cognates and similar sounding Indo-European terms for "mixed," see Pope, *Song*, 620.

h. *Beṭen* (lit., belly). For a female, it is the area of the womb (Eccles. 11:5; Judg. 16:17; Pss. 22:11 [22:10 Eng.]; 139:13).

i. The root *dll* conveys the sense of that which dangles or hangs and is descriptive of female hair, presumably unbound.

j. *Rĕhāṭîm*. Other suggestions include "leather strips" and "a weaver's beam" or some other aspect of weaving. See Pope, *Song*, 630, for a discussion of etymology and the versional support. He translates "tresses" (cf. Longman, *Song*, 190), but the basic sense seems to be that of a runner or something along which water can flow.

k. The MT preserves this as a single term: *battaʿănûgîm*.

l. Longman, *Song*, 190, translates: "This—your stature—is like . . . ," citing Snaith (*Song*, 106–7), who declares that *qômātēk* ("your stature") is Janus parallelism, used with both what precedes ("this is your stature") and what follows ("your stature is like . . .").

m. *Sansinnâ*, a hapax legomenon that Murphy, *Song*, 183, relates to the Akkadian *sissinnu* (the upper branches of the date palm).

May your breasts become as clusters of the vine,
May the fragrance of your breath[a] become like apples.
10a (9a Eng.)Your palate,
Like the best wine[b]. . .

Female

10b (9b Eng.). . . flowing[c] smoothly[d] to my lover,
Gliding over sleepers'[e] lips.
11 (10 Eng.)I am my lover's,
And his desire is for me.
12 (11 Eng.)Come, my lover,
Let's go out[f] to the countryside.
Let's spend the night in the villages.
13 (12 Eng.)Let's go early to the vineyards,
So we can see if the vine has blossomed,
If their blossoms have opened,
If the pomegranates are in bloom,
There I will make love to you.
14 (13 Eng.)The love fruits give off their fragrance,
At our doors are all the best fruits,

a. *'Ap* is used here, as elsewhere in Hebrew, of the nose. Its reference to the breath is neither surprising nor impossible in the context of metaphorical poetry (cf. Gen. 2:7). Pope, *Song*, 636–37, must reach beyond Hebrew to cognate languages to find a more general sense of "opening/aperture," and reach even further beyond any sense in the context to translate "vulva." It was Dahood, "Canticle 7,9," who compared the term with the text from the Ugaritic myth the Birth of the Gracious Gods (*CTU* 1.23.61), where the newly born gods suck *b'ap dd* (on the nipple of the breast). Dahood thus suggests "nipple." While this is possible, the most common Hebrew meaning of *'ap* fits well within this context of a fragrant odor.

b. *Yên haṭṭôb*. For this form of the superlative, see GKC §133h.

c. *Dôbēb*; Murphy, *Song*, 183–84 (noting versions and Rudolph, *Hohe Lied*, 174), suggests that this is a hapax legomenon related to *dwb* (flow) rather than *dbb* (murmur). Because *dwb* does not occur as a transitive verb, the final *bêt* may be attached to the next word as a preposition.

d. *Mêšārîm* describes what is smooth or level. Here it suggests a fine wine that slips into the mouth with no bitterness or acidity. The term is used adverbially with the *lāmed* preposition.

e. *Yěšēnîm* in the MT carries the sense of "sleep(ing)," a masculine plural adjective. Aquila and Syriac read the word for "(my) teeth" (from *šēn*), as in 4:2; 6:6; and as "ivory" in 5:14; 7:5 (7:4 Eng.), omitting the initial *yôd* (dittography) and dropping the final *mêm* (Murphy, *Song*, 184). However, Fox, *Song*, 163, translates "scarlet" (*šānîm*), which requires only the omission of the initial *yôd*. We remain with the MT in this translation, as do the majority of commentators.

f. *Nēṣē'*, though having the form of a first-person common plural imperfect, functions as a cohortative along with the marked cohortatives that form the two subsequent verbs. In fact, this first verb in the sequence may have been so marked originally. The *hê* that begins the following word may have caused the scribe's eye to skip over a *hê* at the end of the verb (haplography).

Both new and old,
That I have stored up for you, my lover.
⁸:¹If only you were like my brother,
Nursed at the breasts of my mother,
I would find you in public,
I would kiss you,
And no one would despise me.
²I would lead you,
I would bring you to my mother's house,
Youᵍ would teach me;
I would give you spiced wine to drink,
From the crushed juiceʰ of my pomegranate.
³His left <arm is> under my head,
His right <arm> embraces me.
⁴I want you to promise,
O young women of Jerusalem,
Do not disturb,
Do not excite love,
Until it desires.

Interpretation

6:4–10	Male: Second *wasf* for the female
6:11–12	Female: Lingering in the groves
7:1 (6:13 Eng.)	Chorus: Call to return
7:2–10a (7:1–9a Eng.)	Male: Third *wasf* for the female
7:10b–8:4 (7:9b–8:4 Eng.)	Female: Springtime and love

6:4–10. *Male: Second* wasf *for the female.* The male responds to the woman's song of praise with a second one of his own regarding her. Rather than developing from her imagery, he returns to his first *wasf* (4:1–8) and develops from there the words of 4:1–3, repeating many of the phrases in 6:5–7 and then expanding upon them. As might be expected, the imagery overall is less sensual and more focused on martial and architectural themes. The latter in particular begins the song. However, the theme of beauty is by no means absent (6:5b–7), although it tends to be expressed in terms of a favorable comparison to everyone

g. The verb here can be either the second-person masculine singular, "you would teach me," or the third-person feminine singular, "she would teach me."

h. ʿĀsîs most often describes the juice of grapes that have been freshly crushed (Isa. 49:26; Joel 1:5; 4:18 [3:18 Eng.]; Amos 9:13). Here, however, it is the juice of a pomegranate that has been squeezed out.

else (vv. 8–9). The text begins and ends with similes, which seem to enjoy a status as the favorite literary form in these verses. Added one upon the next, they present an impression of incomparability, such as may be found explicitly declared in v. 9.

> **6:4**Beautiful as Tirzah
> Are you, my darling,
> Lovely as Jerusalem,
> Terrible as the banners <of war>.

In 6:4 the male begins and uses his first word as his theme for the whole of the *waṣf:* "beautiful" (*yāpāh*). The initial comparison with cities is perhaps not surprising. Cities were often likened to women.[1] It may be surprising for biblical literature to reverse this simile. Yet the nature of its subject—more often dealing with cities than with individual females—may imply that in love poetry and other popular art forms where females play a greater role than cities, such reversed comparisons were not at all unusual. The comparison to Tirzah has surprised commentators, so much so that Pope followed the versions and attempted to find here a common, rather than proper, noun with the sense of "pleasing."[2] The city of Tirzah, identified with Tell el-Farah North, lies six miles north and east of the city of Shechem. It was an early capital city of the northern kingdom. It was also the name of one of the daughters of Zelophehad (Num. 26:33; 27:1; 36:11; Josh. 17:3). The city later served as the residence of Omri and some of his royal predecessors (1 Kings 15:21; 16:6–23; 2 Kings 15:14–16). Excavations of the Israelite site have revealed unusually well-built houses, which, along with the natural beauty of the area situated above the Wadi Farah and bedecked with natural flowers (not unlike the lotuses of the previous verse), suggest a city renowned for its beauty and strength.

The further comparison with Jerusalem allows for a merism between two cities that would encompass all of Israel and Judah. While Jerusalem might be mentioned alone in a prose text, the parallelism of poetry allows for and expects a second city. By choosing a northern as well as southern center, the writer can include all the Israelites of both kingdoms as sympathetic readers or listeners. The contrast of the loveliness of these cities with the awe-inspiring fear of their power is manifest in the final

---

1. Above all, compare Babylon and Jerusalem as they are described in Isa. 47 and 54, respectively. See also Jerusalem in the book of Lamentations.
2. Pope, *Song,* 559–60. He understands the *kāp* preposition as an asseverative, as in Ugaritic. However, this would break its parallel with the same structure for Jerusalem in the following line. Nevertheless, the root *rṣh* does follow the LXX's *eudokia* (well pleasing) as well as related forms in the other versions.

line. Other than vv. 4 and 10, the term "fearful, terrible" (*'ym*) occurs in this form only in Hab. 1:7, where it describes the Chaldean army. Thus the scene in Song 6:4 includes battlements that defend a city and standards that are raised over them as proud symbols of the identity and power of a nation and city. It is this theme that inspires both desire and fear, that radiates both beauty and power. Such is the expectation of the lover as he proceeds with this theme in the following verse.

> ⁵Turn your eyes from me,
> Because they overwhelm me.
> Your hair is like the flock of goats
> That descend from the Gilead.

Verse 5 explains the source of the fear suggested in the previous line: the eyes of the female. It is not that they are dreadful to behold. Rather, they possess a power of attraction that the male cannot resist. They overwhelm him; their beauty enchants him. Unlike 4:1, where her eyes were likened to doves, here they possess a much greater power. The theme of the strength of their attractiveness, and its association with the image of martial power in the preceding verse, introduces a new aspect of the love that the male describes. From the desire emerges a strength in which the female holds him fast. Such is her power that he cannot avert his own gaze; he must seek from her the means to break the eye contact. Is the new focus of attention in the second half of the verse the result of a quick swing of the head, in which the female's acquiescence to his request now leads to a new fascination, her hair? The male's statement of admiration for his partner's hair is identical to his observation in 4:1, yet with the single difference that instead of Mount Gilead (*har gil'ād*) this is "the Gilead" (*haggil'ād*). Whereas "Mount Gilead" occurs only in 4:1, "the Gilead" appears some 43 of the 136 times that the name Gilead appears in the OT. It describes the entire region, though here the effect of the image is the same. The glistening backs of hairy goats shimmer in the sun as they descend en masse along a slope in the region.

> ⁶Your teeth are like the flock of ewes
> That ascend from the washing,
> Every one of them with its twin,
> There is no "miscarriage" among them.

Again, 6:6 parallels 4:2 with a single exception. In the earlier section the teeth are a "shorn flock," but here a "flock of ewes" forms the basis for the comparison. The pictures are similar, with 6:6 suggesting the whiteness of the ewes' coats, washed clean of any dirt. Whiteness, clean-ness, and uniformity contribute to the portrait of the female.

> [7]Like pieces of pomegranate are your temples,
> Behind your veil.

The final simile, in praise of the female's face (6:7), is borrowed without alteration from the second half of 4:3. The lover's temples behind her veil trace a loveliness of form that catches the eye of her admirer. At the same time, the suggestion that they are partially hidden behind the veil shows the overall effect on the male, pulling back from the intense fixation on the eyes to the admiration of the hair and finally to the observation about the temples. While admiring each aspect of the face, the male gradually relaxes his interest so that his praise can turn to the overall beauty of his beloved. Although 6:7 duplicates 4:3b, chapter 6 omits 4:3a. The first half of 4:3 describes the female's mouth as lovely and desirable. Although one could argue a scribal error at this point, in which the first half of the verse was omitted by accident,[3] the remainder of this *wasf* suggests a different direction in the male's praise. In chapter 4 he has gone on to describe in detail other features of the female's body; here, however, he avoids the greater sensuality suggested by the arms and breasts. Instead, the male wishes to praise the female in terms of her superiority to all other women. This different focus may explain an avoidance of the mouth, already noted as the most sensual of body parts described in the text.

> [8]There are sixty queens,
> Eighty concubines,
> And maidens without number.

Verse 8 turns to female members of the royal court in order to compare the beauty of the female and to establish her superiority. Pope reviews discussions of the numerical sequence "sixty . . . eighty" and concludes that this is a variant of the "three . . . four" sequence in the form of "threescore . . . four-score."[4] Hence the sequence describes a "multitude of gradations" that reflect the large number of females to be compared. The sequence appears to move from the most select group of special "wives" of the king (queens) to the larger number of concubines and finally to the young women who are either unmarried or, more likely, not yet mothers.[5] Comparisons to King Solomon's harem (1 Kings 11:3) are

---

3. Both the first half of 4:3 and the second half (the part duplicated in 6:7) begin with the same letter, *kāp*. Thus the scribe's eyes might have skipped the first half of the verse.
4. Pope, *Song*, 567–68, refers to Greenfield, Review, 257.
5. Walton, "ʿAlmāh."

not likely intended with such different and unrelated numbers.[6] Rather, as Keel (*Song*, 218–19) notes, Rehoboam's harem of eighteen wives and sixty concubines comes much closer. Only the sixty warriors guarding the palanquin of Solomon (3:7) compare in terms of numbers in the Song. In the poetry of the Song, sixty may be a number associated with royalty. In any case, the picture is one of the highest levels of royalty and the most beautiful women, whether those in the senior ranks of society or those among the most youthful of women. Although the social ranking appears to diminish as the verse proceeds, it does not provide a perfect syntactical parallel for each unit. In the case of the queens and concubines, the number occurs before the noun. In the case of the maidens, the number (actually, "without number") follows the noun and concludes the verse. The emphasis thus shifts from the status of the women to the concluding estimate of their countless number.

> [9]She is unique, my dove,
> My perfect one, she is unique.
> She is special to her mother,
> To the one who bore her.
> Daughters saw her,
> Queens and concubines blessed her,
> And they praised her.

Verse 9 begins with a nominal construction that parallels the first two phrases of v. 8. All these lines begin with a number: sixty, eighty, and here, one. For the first lines of both verses, this is followed by a pronoun ("they/she"). At this point v. 9 deviates from the preceding lines. The male then uses two successive titles of endearment, each with the pronoun suffix "my": "my dove" and "my perfect one." The male repeats that his lover is one or unique, thus emphasizing the contrast between his love for her alone and the beauty that dominates the royal court. Twice earlier the male referred to his lover as "my dove" (2:14; 5:2). The second occurrence, in 5:2, where the male knocks at the door of his lover's bedroom and calls to her, includes both terms, "my dove, my perfect one," as here. Thus the expression of the male echoes both his affection for his beloved and the desire for her that led him to her room at the beginning of chapter 5.

The role of the mother in the third and fourth lines implies a sense of the special nature of the female, already chosen from all the others by her mother. Surely it would not be surprising for a mother to choose her daughter above all others. The male may have this sense in mind.

6. Seven hundred wives and three hundred concubines.

As the mother's love for her daughter, so is the male's admiration for the same daughter. It is this powerful sense of something unique and special that the male wishes to communicate. Like the first stanza of v. 9, this two-line stanza reinforces the same point, but from a different observer. The male begins with his own perspective. Here he shifts to the mother's thoughts. Finally, he moves to the peers of the female in the remaining lines. There he begins with the daughters, who may be identical to the "maidens" of v. 8. In this line the use of the term "daughters" (*bānôt*) may carry on the family relationship initiated by the mother. However, for this to be compelling one would expect "her sisters," since the relationship is defined by the female, not her mother. It is best to see here a synonym for "maidens" in v. 8. The return to the three groups of females in v. 8 provides the male an opportunity to develop the purpose of bringing them on the scene, something not clear in the previous verse. In between the appearance of these groups of women, the sense of the unique nature of the female lover is emphasized. This leads to the great number of women, especially queens and royal courtesans, who might be expected to know beauty, affirming the surpassing loveliness of the female. Identical verbal forms, "call her blessed" (*wayĕʾaššĕrûhā*) with "and they praised her" (*wayĕhallûhā*), occur elsewhere together only in Prov. 31:28: "Her children arise and call her blessed; her husband also, and he praises her" (NIV). There the children and husband of the "woman of valor" (*ʾēšet ḥayil*, 31:10) so honor her.[7] In both cases, the verbal praise is bestowed freely and for a good reason. It is neither forced nor gratuitous.

> [10]Who is this who gazes down as the dawn,
> Beautiful as the full moon,
> Special like the sun,
> Terrible as the display <of the stars>?

Verse 10 identifies the words of praise that the queens and consorts speak. They move the word picture out of the terrestrial world and upward to the heavens. The female's beauty takes on the aspects of a goddess. Indeed, the Dawn is such a deity in the myths of Canaan.[8] Even so, the connection of vv. 8–9 with her mother provides a secure tie for the female with the world of humanity. In the whole of the Bible, the question "Who is this?" (*mî zōʾt*) with the feminine demonstrative "this" occurs only here and in 3:6 and 8:5. In the other occurrences the lover always ascends from the desert. Here she looks down from above, like the dawn shedding its rays across the landscape. Her beauty is com-

7. The second verb, where the husband is the subject, uses a singular form and so has a slightly different formation.
8. It occurs in the Birth of the Gracious Gods myth, found at Ugarit.

pared to the moon, with an unusual term for moon, emphasizing the "whiteness" of the object. Fox refers to the appearance of a giant full moon in the sky over Israel.[9] Again, the unusual and poetic word for "sun" suggests that the female is herself special and distinctive in relation to all the heavenly bodies. Müller ("Begriffe") and Long ("Lover") are correct in identifying here the vocabulary of divine imagery in the heavens. Yet the expressions are used in a climax of hyperbole where only the most exalted language (short of explicit divinization) will suffice. The last line summarizes these elements of the sky and all others as terrible in their display. It uses the same description as in v. 4, where the male begins his address. The repetition serves to envelop the entire *wasf* of praise to the female, initiated by the male and joined by the chorus of other beautiful and royal women. Therefore, this praise from the chorus (v. 10) belongs with that of the male even though there is a change in the speakers.

As noted, the theme of this address (6:4–10) is different from the first hymn of praise to the female. There the emphasis was upon the desirable features of her face and body. Here the words summarize and generalize the beauty of the female to emphasize the power of that beauty, a power that can overcome her lover's defenses with a gaze of her eyes and that can evoke praise from the finest women in the land. The central statement, that of v. 9, emphasizes how unique and therefore how special the female is. None can compare to her. Her lover learns this, not only from his own senses, but also from the praise of others. Together they observe in the female one whose beauty is a great power that can be used for good or evil. It remains for the rest of the Song to identify the female's own values that are concerned only with love and not with manipulation.

> [11]To the grove of nut trees I went down,
> To see the plants in the valley,
> To see if the vine has blossomed,
> If the pomegranates are in bloom.

6:11–12. *Female: Lingering in the groves.* Verses 11–12 could apply to either the man or the woman. The latter must be the subject of v. 12 if the final phrase is correctly understood. However, v. 11 is by no means clear. Keel notes that the metaphor of vineyard/garden is used elsewhere of the woman (1:6, 14; 2:15; 4:12–5:1; 6:2; 7:13 [7:12 Eng.]; 8:12).[10] However, the imagery here is one of a nut tree (used collectively). The

9. Fox, *Song*, 153.
10. Keel, *Song*, 222.

picture thus is distinct in terms of some of the plants that flourish in this garden or grove. That a grove of walnut trees is intended is most likely. Other than Josephus, who identifies walnut trees at the Sea of Galilee (*Jewish War* 3.10.8 §§516–17), there is no explicit evidence for them this far south in the Middle East. This therefore may describe a grove of imported plants. However, the Arabic for "walnut" (*jôs*) is preserved in the name of the Kidron Valley north of Jerusalem, the Wadi al-Jôs.[11] Although this name may be a form of "the Valley of Jehoshaphat" (Joel 4:2, 12 [3:2, 12 Eng.]), it more likely preserves an authentic memory associating this valley (wadi) with Song 6:11, walnut trees, or both. This could therefore describe the royal gardens to the east of Jerusalem, where as already seen various nonindigenous and exotic plants were kept. The need to descend reflects the demand such trees have for water and their presence along the banks of rivers and wadis. The symbol of the walnut as a picture of the male scrotum or the female vulva can thus exhibit erotic imagery that combines with the pictures found in the remainder of this verse.

The verb "to see" suggests a lingering and the evocation of fantasy regarding these symbols of sexuality and fruitfulness. The object of the lover's vision are the plants of the valley. A valley (*naḥal*, used only here in the Song) serves as a naturally protected area, likely along a wadi or stream that would flow through the valley to provide water. If this is indeed the Kidron Valley east and north of Jerusalem, then the description suggests the descent of the lover from the heights of the fortified city to the lush and verdant gardens of the king, and perhaps of nobles as well. The singular occurrence of both terms, "plants" and "valley," may suggest a new scene or speaker. However, it forms a parallelism with the next line, also introduced by the infinitive of the verb "to see."[12] There the verb "to bud" (*prḥ*) appears. It is attested once elsewhere in the Song, in 7:13 (7:12 Eng.). There as well as here, its subject is "the vine" (*haggepen*). Indeed, 7:13 (7:12 Eng.) matches the remaining phrase regarding the blooming of the pomegranates. Interestingly, in the latter passage the location of these is the vineyards (*kĕrāmîm*). The picture of vineyards provides a more particular definition for the gardens. They are primarily agricultural in nature, designed to produces grapes for wine, just as the pomegranates serve as a source for food. Nevertheless, the vine (2:13; 7:9, 13 [7:8, 12 Eng.]), like the pomegranate (4:3, 13; 6:7; 7:13 [7:12 Eng.]; 8:2), is used in this Song to evoke images of the human body (often female).

---

11. Note that the Arabic term is cognate to the Hebrew for "walnut" as used here (*ʾĕgôz*) but lacks the initial *ʾālep* of the Hebrew. Also noted by Pope, *Song*, 574–79.

12. *Lirʾôt*, describing purpose.

The budding of the pomegranate utilizes a verb (*nṣṣ*) that occurs only once elsewhere, where it describes the blossoms of the almond tree (Eccles. 12:5). The stroll around the garden is a stroll around the body of the lover. It is a description of the beauty of the lover's body as well as suggesting the pleasures of love that await the speaker. Other than in the Song, it is unusual for Hebrew poets to portray the fruit or blossom of the pomegranate in the plural. In contrast to the vine, which is singular, the plural "pomegranates" reflects a particularly strong image of fruitfulness. The fruitful yield portrayed here, as elsewhere in the Song, is concerned less with reproduction and more with the joys of love that the two may experience in the deepening of their physical relationship.

> [12]I did not realize,
> My desire set me,
> In chariotry,
> With a prince.

The picture of fruitfulness and desire prepares the speaker for the passion of love that leads to v. 12. The confession of ignorance that introduces v. 12 is not strictly temporal (as in NIV: "before I knew") but explicitly negative ("I did not know"). The sense is one of not realizing the experience rather than the suddenness of it. How it happened is not clear. In what may be a fantasy, however, this is not important. The term used to describe the female's "desire" is the Hebrew *nepeš*. This term describes the center of the desire for life. Its occurrence elsewhere in the Song often is suggestive of desire (1:7; 3:1–4; 5:6; cf. Job 23:13; Eccles. 6:3).[13]

The expression at the end of the passage (*ʿammî nādîb*) can be translated, according to the MT, as either "my uncle is generous" or "my people are noble." The LXX and Vulgate relate the term to the proper noun Amminadab, known inside and outside the Bible as a name used by both Israelites and Ammonites. Müller ("Kohelet") connects the eighth/seventh-century BC Tell Siran bottle inscription, an Ammonite poem that also mentions Amminadab. However, the presence of a *yôd* in the Hebrew text makes this an unusual spelling for the name. Further, the Tell Siran inscription is a drinking song, somewhat removed from the themes of the Song. Better is the sug-

13. Contra Deckers, "Structure," one does not need to apply an androcentric interpretation to justify this translation. To apply it as a referent for the Jewish people as a whole would be unique in a context such as this. For a gynocentric interpretation of the texts of Song, as a reflection of the strength of women within a rural peasant household setting, see Meyers, "Gender."

gestion that the initial term be taken as the preposition "with" (*ʿim*). This requires a change in the vowel pointing and the omission of a *yôd* in the consonantal text. The second element (*nādîb*) can appear as a substantive with the sense of a nobleman or prince. Thus the translation expresses the fantasy of the female lover placed beside her princely lover in a dramatic and public display of power. The term for chariot is in the plural, suggesting a squad of chariots that go to battle. The passion of desire translates into the excitement of the most adventurous and dangerous experiences known to the author. Such chariotry traditionally made up the elite of the army, those who could afford to maintain the required horses and all the trappings for the vehicle. It also represented one of the most fearful weapons appearing on the battlefield. In fact, since a chariot served as a mobile firing platform for an archer, there normally were two or three individuals on a chariot, including at least a driver and a master of the weaponry. Thus the female lover's sense of a place on board this instrument of terror is part of a fantasy of danger and excitement, which provides the climax of this experience. Away from the peaceful gardens, the chariotry of the nobles, whether in war or in procession, heightens the drama and fuels the passion of the lover.

> 7:1 (6:13 Eng.)Return! Return! O Shulammite!
> Return! Return! That we may gaze on you.
> How would you gaze on the Shulammite?
> Like the dance of Mahanayim.

7:1 (6:13 Eng.). *Chorus: Call to return.* The chorus interrupts the fantasy of the female with a call to her to return. In the context of the preceding verse, this expresses a desire to see their friend come back from the chariot ride with her prince. The women call her with four repeated imperative commands: *šûbî.* Two begin each of the first two lines and frame the only proper noun identifying the female in the entire poem: "Shulammite." The term occurs only in this verse, in the first and third lines. Its possible derivation from the root *šlm* may carry the sense of "whole, complete, perfect." In a Song that repeatedly names Solomon (1:5; 3:9, 11; 8:11, 12),[14] it is appropriate that the female counterpart should have her name derived from the same root. Actually, hers is not a personal name. The definite article indicates that it should be understood more as a title. Perhaps it carries the sense

---

14. Note that except for the first mention, the other four occurrences appear in pairs, just as the Shulammite also appears twice in this verse.

of one who is altogether beautiful. This would agree with the second and fourth lines.[15]

The desire to gaze upon the Shulammite is repeated. The use of the verb (*ḥzh*) in the third line forms a volitional statement wherein the desire of the chorus is expressed. It recurs in the following line, where it forms a question. The visual emphasis continues the motifs of the *waṣf* in the previous verses and anticipates the *waṣf* that immediately follows. The chorus thus joins in praising the visual characteristics of the female. The dance of Mahanayim forms a climactic conclusion to the verse. This alone describes the manner through which the chorus relates to the woman. The noun "dance" (*mĕḥōlâ*) comes from a root *ḥwl* (to turn/whirl).[16] It thus carries the sense of an exuberant dance, one that the Israelites performed before the golden calf (Exod. 32:19). More often, however, women are specified as the participants, and the dance has to do with battle.[17] Surprisingly, the terms occur nowhere in the poetic literature of the MT except for this single appearance in the Song. Nevertheless, usage elsewhere dictates a whirling dance of ecstatic

15. The derivation from some form of the root *šlm*, with the resultant meaning as suggested, is favored by Fox, *Song*, 157 (cf. Garrett, *Song*, 419), who summarizes some of the other proposed derivations. Albright ("Syro-Mesopotamian God") related this name to that of the Mesopotamian war goddess Shulmanitu. However, there is no reason for such a derivation in the context of a love poem, nor is the name of a foreign deity (otherwise unattested in Palestine) likely in a clearly Israelite context. Pope, *Song*, 600, relates this to Anat, the virgin goddess of love and war in the Ugaritic myths, and notes the use of *šlm* in a message given to her. That this is a nickname for the Canaanite goddess is pure speculation, however. The theory that this is a feminine counterpart to the name Solomon faces the difficulty noted above, that it is not a personal name but a title of sorts. However, the similar sounds of "Solomon" and "Shulammite" remain a possible reason for its insertion. The final theory, attested by the LXX manuscript Codex Vaticanus, that this is an alternative reading or scribal error for "the Shunemite" (someone from the Galilean village of Shunem) is quickly dismissed by Fox, who notes that she lives in Jerusalem, in a walled city (5:7–8). Shunem, however, was the home of Abishag, the most beautiful of women brought to the palace to comfort and warm David in his old age (1 Kings 1:3–4). After his death, Adonijah's request for her to be his wife led to his execution by order of Solomon (1 Kings 2:13–25). Could the Song's Shulammite be Abishag the Shunammite? (cf. Budde, "Hohelied," 36; Delitzsch, *Song*, 119–20). It is possible, but this proposal suffers from the lack of any attested involvement of Solomon with Abishag and the absence of anything else in the Song that can exclusively connect the female with Abishag (cf. Keel, *Song*, 228–29, who ultimately despairs of any certain explanation for the name). More speculative is Frolov, "No Return," who identifies the figure with Bathsheba and attempts to rearrange the text by moving 7:1 (6:13 Eng.) to a position immediately following 3:11.

16. See also Gruber, "Ten"; and for the related *māḥôl* as "dance," see Braun, *Music*, 39–40.

17. Miriam, Exod. 15:20; Jephthah's daughter, Judg. 11:34; daughters of Shiloh, Judg. 21:21 (not directly related to battle, but in a context of war); women of Israel, 1 Sam. 18:6; 21:11; 29:5.

joy such as would characterize the response of women to the warriors of their group returning from a successful battle. The women participating in such a dance were not necessarily performing an intentionally erotic display.[18] Instead, they were expressing great joy with their physical motions. The effect also entertained those who watched, for why else would the texts stress that they danced and sang before the warriors?

The final term, "the Mahanayim" (hammaḥănāyim), is meant to match the sound of the word for dance (mĕḥōlat) and to further evoke the sense of a victory dance after battle. This is because the name sounds like the word for "camp" (maḥăneh) in the dual. In fact, this may well be translated "the (two) camps." The term occurs as a place-name east of the Jordan River, first designated by Jacob after he departed from Laban (Gen. 32:3 [32:2 Eng.]). It was the region where Ish-bosheth settled after Saul's death (2 Sam. 2:8, 12, 29) and to which David fled from Absalom (2 Sam. 17:24, 27; 19:33 [19:32 Eng.]; 1 Kings 2:8). The term "camps" and the above narratives suggest a fort or place for defense in time of war. Certainly, this region is associated with threats of war. In the Song, the otherwise unattested appearance of a definite article before the word leads many scholars to recognize here not a place-name but the common noun "the two camps." While this may be true, the name could in this context designate the whole region rather than a single site. In such a case the use of the definite article would not be anomalous.[19] Further, the association of music or dance with a region is not unknown.[20] Both the term for "dance" and the region suggest a whirling dance of joy and celebration that would emerge out of a military victory. In view of the context in the Song, perhaps the chorus itself provides the music and, if only in their imagination, observes the Shulammite performing alone or in the leading role in the dance.[21] The repeated emphasis on looking accompanies the dance, which is primarily something seen rather than experienced through any other sense. The effect is to reinforce the visual emphasis on the Shulammite and to anticipate the male's description of her physical beauty in the following section.

7:2–10a (7:1–9a Eng.). *Male: Third* waṣf *for the female.* This song of praise of the female's body examines some fourteen different parts of the body, using some fifteen separate metaphors or similes. The previous

18. Even Exod. 32:19 is not necessarily primarily erotic. For a military context, see Janzen, "Character."

19. This is especially true in Transjordan, where other regions appear with a definite article, such as Gilead and Bashan (Josh. 13:11).

20. Cf. Ps. 137:1–4 and the apparent notoriety that the inhabitants of Judah and Jerusalem had gained for music.

21. As Murphy notes (*Song*, 185; cf. "Dance"), nowhere does the text indicate that the female is dancing or intends to do so.

*wasf*s of the male's body (5:10–16) and female's body (4:1–8; 6:4–10) use similar literary devices to compare the different parts of the body. This one most closely resembles the earlier *wasf* of the male's body insofar as it surveys all major parts of the body. Like all of the *wasf*s, most of the descriptions are reserved for the head. However, unlike the male *wasf* (and the others), this one begins with the feet and moves upward toward the head. The head and hair are central, being the subject of the middle verse (6 [5 Eng.]), and followed by a general exclamation of beauty (7 [6 Eng.]). However, the climax of the *wasf* comes with the repeated mention of the female's mouth (twice) and breasts (three times). These features form key points for praise. They occurred in the first *wasf* of the female body (4:1–8) but not the second (6:4–10). Hence the features of mouth and breasts frame the three *wasf*s as they do the entire Song. The Song begins by relishing the joy of the male's mouth (1:2) and concludes with the breasts of the female as the last physical attribute mentioned (8:10).[22]

More than any other *wasf* or descriptive part of the Song, this third and final hymn of praise to the female's body forms a list of comparisons. The items compared are both natural and artificial. The similes are drawn from nature at the beginning and end of the song (vv. 2–4 [1–3 Eng.]: ornaments, wine [in a bowl], wheat, fawns; vv. 8–9 [7–8 Eng.]: palm tree, date clusters, apples, wine), with the one exception of Mount Carmel in the middle (v. 6 [5 Eng.]). The artificial (of human construction or manufacture) images dominate the central descriptions (vv. 5–6 [4–5 Eng.]: ivory tower, Heshbon, Bat-Rabbim, tower of Lebanon, Damascus, royal purple). Only v. 7 (6 Eng.) contains no images whatsoever. It provides a high point as the male exclaims his love for the female.

> 2 (1 Eng.)How beautiful are your feet in sandals,
> O daughter of a prince,
> The curves of your hips are like ornaments,
> The work of an artist's hands.

The *wasf* begins in v. 2 (1 Eng.) with the male gazing upon the female's feet. The contrast of this with the previous *wasf*s has been noted. The whole poem focuses on the head, mouth, and breasts, and so this is a reasonable starting point as the description progresses toward these other features of the body. However, it also forms a logical connection with the statements of the chorus that immediately precede it. There

22. The view of Brenner, "Come Back," that this is a parody remains unproved; it seems largely based on modern interpretations of some of the metaphors described here (see note 32 below; see also Black, "Unlikely"). Even less convincing is the argument of Whedbee, "Paradox," to extend the parody to other *wasf*s.

211

the emphasis was on gazing at the female's dance. Although the whole body may be active in a dance, there is no dance without the motion of the feet. The feet and legs form a natural bridge between a vision of the female dancing and the *waṣf* that begins with this text. The expression "how beautiful" (*mah yāpû*) occurs only three times in the Bible, all of them in the Song and all used by the male to describe the love and beauty of his lover: 4:10; 7:2, 7 (7:1, 6 Eng.).[23] Only in this occurrence, however, does the expression refer to a physical feature. Elsewhere it introduces general statements from the male's perspective. The term for "feet" here is not the customary one (*regel*, as in 5:3) but a less frequent one (*pacam*; cf. 2 Kings 19:24 = Isa. 37:25; Ps. 85:14 [85:13 Eng.]; Exod. 25:12; 37:3) that refers more often to frequency (e.g., two times, three times, etc., as in Gen. 2:23; Exod. 8:28 [8:32 Eng.]; Lev. 4:6; Josh. 6:16; et al.). Indeed, it can describe a step or pace (Isa. 26:6, appearing in parallel with *regel*) and thus may be all the more appropriate following the observation of a dance.

The significance of using sandals here is not clear. There are claims that everyone commonly wore sandals and claims that the average peasant had no footwear.[24] Pope dwells on the erotic characteristics of the sandals as manifest in Judith's dressing to seduce Holofernes:

> Her sandal ravished his eye,
> Her beauty captured his soul,
> And the sword severed his neck. (Jdt. 16:9)[25]

This itself may be a reflection of the text here in the Song. However, it would not make sense in the narrative if there were not some erotic association with the sandals. Besides adorning and emphasizing the (dancing) feet, the term for "sandals" (*necālîm*) uses the root (*ncl*) related to the term for the "locked" (*nācûl*) garden in 4:12. The connection of 4:10 with the first two words of the line (already noted) may have led further to this noun (sandals). The evocation "O daughter of a prince" recalls 6:12 and the expression there, "with a prince." In both cases, the term "prince" describes an upper-class and perhaps royal environment. However, the usage here does not refer to the same "prince" as in 6:12. Rather, it describes the royal lineage of the female. Is this part

---

23. In v. 7 (6 Eng.), the Hebrew is *mah yāpît*. For the meaning of the root *yph* (beautiful) and its numerous occurrences elsewhere in the Bible, see comments on 4:10.

24. For the former, see King and Stager, *Life*, 272–73; for the latter, see Keel, *Song*, 234. Keel refers to the Assyrian reliefs of the Judean prisoners of war exiting Lachish in 701 BC. Their feet are unshod; however, this may reflect their status as prisoners rather than the common practice of Israelites.

25. Pope, *Song*, 614.

of the fantasy, hyperbolic praise for the lover, or a reality? Whatever the case, these opening words differ from the remainder of the *wasf*. Here is no simile or metaphor, but a straightforward declaration of praise. By introducing the *wasf* in this manner, the reader's/listener's attention is riveted to the picture of the female. Now it is possible to move into descriptive pictures without losing sight of the object of the praise.

The second half of the verse moves upward from the feet to the hips and thighs. The female's enticing curves are likened to the adornments of jewelry that attract attention by their beauty and thereby enhance the beauty of the one wearing them. Only the finest of artists could have produced such objects of beauty. The term for "artist" (*ʾāmmān*) occurs only here and is never used for the Creator in the biblical text; yet the principle of one who forms what is beautiful is applicable (Ps. 19). Thus there is an indirect allusion to God here. In fact, it is the allusive nature of the reference to God that serves the theological purpose of the Song. No other book in the Bible betrays such a strong sense of the metaphorical in its use of poetic language, and the Song does this from start to finish, with no prosaic interlude to explain the significance of the word pictures. The effect is one of language used as signposts for love and for its subjects and objects.

The language is about royalty and peasantry, about those who long for love and those who have found it, about the natural world and the supernatural sphere. The delights of the male in admiring his lover's curves fully embrace the carnal, but they do so in the recognition that this is good because it is more than carnal. The flesh forms not an end in itself but a praiseworthy object that both physically and metaphorically, in the language of the text, points to the source of all beauty and all true desire. It points to God himself. Yet within the rules of such poetic language it cannot do this by naming the divine. Instead, the language of the joys of creation can never reach very far behind created things because it must always remain close to the carnal, the subject of the poem. Hence the male is still concerned for his lover even when he sees her beauty as part of a larger drama. Nevertheless, he remains enchanted by her so that the praise directed to her physical appearance becomes an expression of gratitude for the One who has made it all.

> 3 (2 Eng.)Your navel,
> A round bowl,
> It does not lack spiced wine.
> Your waist,
> A heap of wheat,
> Encircled by lotuses.

Verse 3 (2 Eng.) moves the focus of attention upward toward the center of the woman's body. As has been true throughout the Song, there is no explicit mention of the pudenda. Instead, the male considers his lover's navel. Egyptian, Palestinian, and Syrian female portraits and figurines with prominent navels suggest this as a cultural focus of beauty and that a larger size was prized.[26] Thus the image of a larger mixing bowl for wine, a crater, is appropriate. The *kāp* comparative prepositions of the previous verse do not appear here. The metaphor has no introduction. Indeed, the second word in the verse, "bowl," suggests that the word pictures have a special importance in the structure of this verse. "Your navel" and "your waist" are each a single Hebrew word. These two terms alone identify the physical features, while the remaining nine words provide vivid pictures of bowls full of spiced wine and piles of wheat surrounded by lotuses. The emphasis moves from the physical attributes themselves to the descriptive images of plenty that they evoke. The mixing bowls of wine anticipate a feast and the joy and contentment that it brings.[27] Piles of wheat would be a common enough picture of plenty. However, the lotuses surrounding them are unusual.[28] It may mirror the practice of guarding the wheat, such as in Ruth 3:7.[29] However, guards or something more secure than lotuses would be expected.[30] Alternatively, since the decoration of various foods with lotuses was an Egyptian custom, plates and bowls would have decorations of such flowers surrounding the food that might be stored or served. Keel suggests that they symbolized the freshness and life that such nourishment might provide.[31] It may be similar here with reference to the female. Rather than lighter flesh tones (contrast 1:5; even less likely is the view of corpulence as an ideal), the wheat in this context symbolized the potential fruitfulness of the woman.[32] Along

---

26. Keel, *Song*, 234. Longman, *Song*, 194–95, represents those who understand the navel to be a direct reference to the female's vulva, which (unlike the navel) becomes moist when sexually excited. Even so, as noted above, it is the bowl that contains the wine, not the body part. Longman's other argument, that the navel "reminds the male of the vulva," is asserted rather than proved.

27. Pope, "Response," finds here evidence for the *marzēaḥ* festival that he sees underlying the Song, but surely the drinking of wine does not require such a festival.

28. The claim that harvested wheat was surrounded by thorns (Snaith, *Song*, 102; Fox, *Song*, 159; Bergant, *Song*, 84) seems to lack relevance here.

29. For various allusions to Ruth and, particularly, chapter 3, see Loader, "Exegetical."

30. In such a case, the use of thorns would be understandable.

31. Keel, *Song*, 235. Murphy, *Song*, 182, suggests a female garment or decoration. Cf. Pope, *Song*, 624.

32. Brenner, "Come Back," 254–55, argues that the picture is a comic one of a fat woman dancing in the nude. The wheat represents her stomach and the lily flowers picture her pubic hair. The comparison of her breasts with fawns in v. 4 (3 Eng.) furthers

with the wine, it suggests that this proximity to her body will bring her lover the joy of a feast.

> 4 (3 Eng.)Your two breasts,
> Like two fawns,
> Twins of a gazelle.

With v. 4 (3 Eng.) the male moves upward to the breasts. This text returns to the use of the *kāp* comparative preposition and so establishes a simile rather than a strict metaphor. This is a word-for-word repetition of 4:5, with omission of the final two words that describe how the fawns browse among the lotuses. Of course, that may have been assumed by the proximity of this verse to the preceding one. The picture of twin fawns is thus repeated as a description for the breasts. They become a focal point for the picture of physical beauty and for the desire that the male has for his lover.

> 5 (4 Eng.)Your neck,
> Like an ivory tower;
> Your eyes,
> Pools in Heshbon,
> By the gate of Bat-Rabbim;
> Your nose,
> Like the tower of Lebanon,
> Espying Damascus.

Verse 5 (4 Eng.) moves further upward to the neck and the features of the head. The three descriptions of the neck and nose are similes, using the *kāp* preposition; the eyes remain similar to v. 3 (2 Eng.) as a strict metaphor, with no comparative preposition. The single line following the identification of the neck contains a single comparison. This is unlike the eyes and the nose, as well as all the preceding comparisons. They all possess two lines of description after the identification of the physical feature. However, in the following verses this single line of comparison will become the more common means of association. Therefore, it is not likely that a line is missing here.[33] The female's neck has been men-

---

the "ludicrous" nature of the description. This all depends on Brenner's identification of this *waṣf* as a parody. Although she is correct in some of the distinctives of the description here in comparison with the previous word pictures, nothing in the text identifies it as a parody or requires such an understanding. Humor is difficult to identify in any alien culture and all the more so in one removed by millennia. I prefer to see here a description of one who is praised for her beauty—which appears to be the most obvious interpretation of the text.

33. Fox, *Song*, 159–60.

tioned twice previously. In 1:10 it was bedecked with jewelry; in 4:4 it was likened to the tower of David, this time decorated with shields. The sense of an ivory tower is similar here. It is not that the tower is made of ivory any more than that the furniture of Samaria was made entirely of the valuable commodity (Amos 3:15; 6:4; 1 Kings 22:39). Instead, as with the Samaria ivories, it formed a decoration. Just as with the jewelry and the shields in the two previous occurrences, this decoration beautifies the tower and makes it appear all the more strong and secure. The tower forms a natural part of the fortification and defense of a city and kingdom. The neck is vulnerable in battle as a place where a mortal wound can be effected. Therefore, it is defended and guarded. The tower serves a similar purpose, to defend and guard the strategic[34] and vital elements of a city.[35] Only here are the pools of Heshbon compared with the eyes. At the Iron Age site of Tel Heshbon, cisterns for water were discovered.[36] Perhaps as the main source of such water, the glistening pools would have not only had a natural beauty but also reflected the sole significant source to sustain life in the city. The gate of Bat-Rabbim, while in all likelihood a historical reality as the gate through which access to the pools was most easily achieved, also means "daughter of many." This may reflect the hordes attracted to the pools and passing through it (Keel, *Song*, 236). In a similar manner many would be attracted to the eyes of the female. The eyes provide a powerful magnet, perhaps to break the hearts of numerous suitors. Like the pools, their reflection and beauty promise an abundant life. However, this is not to be enjoyed by all. Hence the pools themselves, like the eyes of the female, need to be guarded by the strongest towers possible. The ivory tower has been mentioned. As the towers might be strategically placed on either side of the life-giving pools,[37] so the two towers mentioned in this verse are positioned before and after the description of the pools. This disturbs the bottom-to-top survey of the female's attributes. However, it also centers on the eyes as the focus of beauty in this description of the neck and head. The "tower of Lebanon" that espies Damascus might refer to the Lebanon or Anti-Lebanon mountains. This may well be a poetic

34. Compare the "Tower of David" on the northwestern corner of the ancient city of Jerusalem, beside the modern Jaffa Gate. As a regional high point and on the city's outer perimeter for much of its history, this site required special defense such as a tower might provide. See also the recently discovered Iron Age towers guarding the precious water sources for Jerusalem (Reich and Shukron, "Light").

35. Eichner and Scherer, "Teiche," relate this image to the following one by suggesting a reservoir in Heshbon as the "ivory *migdāl*."

36. This, not Rabbah (the site of modern Amman), should be regarded as the site to which the text makes reference; contra Brenner, "Note."

37. As with the water source in Jerusalem during the monarchy. See Reich and Shukron, "Light."

allusion to Mount Hermon, the tallest of mountains from Israel's perspective, and the one that forms the most natural observation point for any threat moving toward the nation from Damascus.[38] The picture thus is not that of a large nose but, like the neck, of the features of the face that reflect nobility, personal security, and well-being for the woman. Although alluring and desirable, the lover's description of his beloved values characteristics that suggest a personality at peace with itself and an internal strength of character.

> [6 (5 Eng.)]Your head above you,
> Like Carmel;
> The loose hair of your head,
> Like purple,
> A king is bound with locks.

Like a camera that has examined the details of the nose and eyes, the lens now pulls back to a general impression of the head as a whole (v. 6 [5 Eng.]). The emphasis on the head as being "over/above you" ("crowns you," NIV) suggests that with this verse the journey from feet to head is at an end. The poet will return to marvel at distinctive features, but the sweep of the whole body has now been completed. The comparison to Mount Carmel may suggest the similar sounding *karmîl*, the purple crimson color (2 Chron. 2:6, 13 [2:7, 14 Eng.]; 3:14) that anticipates the purple of the hair.[39] More likely, however, it completes the geographical sweep of the region's prominent cities and mountains. Beginning with Jerusalem and moving in a counterclockwise fashion, the poet stops at Heshbon, Hermon, Damascus, and now Carmel. This last mountain is crowned with green forests. The second half of Song 7:6 (7:5 Eng.) demonstrates that the emphasis here is with the hair of the head. The growth on Carmel does not represent the color of the hair; the purple addresses that point. Instead, the growth on Carmel represents the living and wild nature of the hair. This point is furthered by the sense of dangling, hanging hair in the following line. Like the thrums left on a fabric from the warp (Isa. 38:12), the loose hair cascades down over the shoulders of the female and crowns her frame with the beauty of a symbol of life and growth. This is the point of the allusion to this third prominent feature. Along with the ivory tower and the tower of Lebanon, this towering mountain of Carmel represents a place of life and fertility. The purple hue of the hair uses a term that describes the royal dye drawn

38. Pope, *Song*, 626–27, referring to Robert, Tournay, and Feuillet, *Cantique*.
39. Cf. Murphy, *Song*, 182. This difference in vocalization, while retaining the same consonants, causes Paul, "Polysensuous," to suggest a double entendre, which he designates as another example of Janus parallelism.

217

from the murex shell. In classical times it was associated with Tyre, the great coastal city to the north of Carmel. To the south of the mountain, excavations at Dor have produced evidence of purple refineries there as well. Carmel thus lay in the center of the purple industry. Its comparison to the hair has led some to understand a shade of red hair here; others find the vitality symbolized by what is essentially black hair.[40] In any case the purple theme draws into the scene the appropriate "wearer" of purple, a king. The male has become this king, no longer merely clothed, but now securely bound by the running locks of his lover. The symbolic power of hair, whether holding the secret of Samson's strength or described in the Greek myths of the Gorgons' hair as serpents, here carries the additional force of feminine seduction. The use of the hair of a woman to captivate her lover has long been the subject of love poetry. An example from Egypt illustrates:

> How skilled is she—(my) sister—at casting the lasso
>   yet she'll <draw in> no cattle!
> With her hair she lassos me,
>   with her eye she pulls (me) in,
> with her thighs she binds,
>   with her seal she sets the brand.[41]

Or again:

> [Her ha]ir is the bait
>   in the trap to ensnare (me).[42]

Of all the attributes mentioned in this poem, only the hair actively pursues and entraps the male. The defensive towers and mountains are crowned with a most powerful weapon of love.

> [7 (6 Eng.)]How beautiful you are,
> How desirable,
> O love,
> O daughter of pleasures.

Thus captivated, the male responds with an exclamation of the female's beauty (7:7 [7:6 Eng.]). In so doing he nearly repeats the expression that began his adoration in v. 2 (1 Eng.). There he cried *mah yāpû*. Here

40. For red hair, cf. Pope, *Song,* 630, who refers to the red paint on the head of an Ishtar statue at Mari. For black, cf. Keel, *Song,* 238.
41. Fox, *Song,* 73 #43.
42. Ibid., 9 #3b.

his statement, *mah yāpît*, is virtually identical, with the second-person feminine singular verb form ("you are beautiful"). This forms an inclusio that envelops the actual *wasf* and thus signals its end. The male revels in the beauty of his lover by using the term "beauty, beautiful" that occurs so frequently in the Song. Of its sixteen appearances, this is the final and climactic one.[43] Only here is it used in this particular verbal form, as though to emphasize at last that the female herself is beautiful. In the second line this term for beauty is paralleled with an expression of beauty or desirability whose root occurs only here in the Song: *nāʿamt*. It appears elsewhere in the Bible some fourteen times, often used of activities or matters that are pleasing to God or others.[44] It is used once of Yahweh's beauty (Ps. 27:4) and once of David's feelings for the fallen Jonathan (2 Sam. 1:26). In Ugaritic the cognates are used to describe the beauty of both men and women, mortal and divine.[45] Like the unique verbal form in the first line, the single use of this synonym in the Song expresses the special beauty that the male sees in his lover, something not found elsewhere. The seventh occurrence of the noun for love (*ʾahăbâ*) also appears in this verse.[46] Its isolated position, following two exclamatory phrases and preceding the final word, invites the consideration that it is used as a vocative to address the favored one. She is his love. The final term may be translated "with delights," as it appears in the MT (*battaʿănûgîm*). Of its four other occurrences, three are in some sort of construct relationship (Mic. 1:16; 2:9; Eccles. 2:8). Thus it is not at all inappropriate to propose here the same thing, *bat taʿănûgîm* (daughter of pleasures). As with the term "love," this could be a vocative form, addressed to the female.[47] Thus the first half of the verse describes her beauty, and the second half describes the relationship between the two lovers and its benefits. Each line of the verse is a direct address to the female, whether with second-person verbs or with vocative nouns. It is a climactic moment in the *wasf*. Only here will the male address his lover in her entirety, without holding back anything.

8 (7 Eng.) Your stature resembles a palm tree,
Your breasts <resemble> clusters of fruit.

---

43. Cf. 1:8, 15 (2x), 16; 2:10, 13; 4:1 (2x), 7, 10; 5:9; 6:1, 4, 10; 7:2, 7 (7:1, 6 Eng.).

44. Gen. 49:15; Ezek. 32:19; Zech. 11:7, 10; Pss. 90:17; 141:6; Prov. 2:10; 3:17; 9:17; 15:26; 16:24; 24:25.

45. Pope, *Song*, 631–32.

46. Previously in 2:4, 5, 7; 3:5, 10; 5:8. It will occur in 8:4, 6, 7 (2x).

47. Noting how "son of" or "daughter of" describes various relationships between people and things, Keel (*Song*, 242) suggests that "daughter of pleasures" implies "a woman who provides all the delights and pleasures of love."

Verse 8 (7 Eng.) returns to attributes of the female. Her "stature" (*qômâ*) is described here for the first time. The previous verses have already hinted at one of noble bearing with a strong and firm neck. However, here the female is likened to a palm tree. There is an association of this date palm (*tāmār*) with biblical women named Tamar, their attractiveness, and their involvement in sexually explicit stories: Gen. 38; 2 Sam. 13; 14:27. The verb "to be like/resemble" (*dmh*) appears elsewhere, where the male likens his lover to a mare (Song 1:9) and the female compares her lover to a gazelle or young stag (2:9, 17; 8:14). Here a plant rather than an animal is chosen as the term of comparison. Perhaps the purpose is to express the regal nobility and the statuesque nature of the female. However, in context with this and the following verse, it appears rather to set a scene that will allow the male to focus on the female's breasts. The tall and slender tree dramatically contrasts and emphasizes the abundant clusters of fruit displayed prominently. Keel (*Song*, 240–48) traces three millennia of ancient Near Eastern iconography that associate voluptuous females (divine and human) with date palms.

Prior to this *wasf* the female's breasts were mentioned once by her, as a place where her lover may rest (1:13); and once by the male in 4:5, the parallel passage to 7:4 (7:3 Eng.). The fact that they receive a threefold mention in this *wasf* and appear again three times in chapter 8 implies that there is an emphasis in this final *wasf* and the last chapter of the Song, an emphasis that did not appear earlier. The association of the breasts with clusters of fruit is made by an elliptical use of the verb "to resemble" in the first line. The similar construction, with a preposition (*lāmed*) prefixed to "palm tree" and again to "clusters of fruit," implies that the verb does double duty for both lines even though it occurs only in the first line. The term "clusters" (*ʾaškōlôt*) has occurred once before in the Song, in 1:14, where it described a single cluster, or "bouquet," of henna. Elsewhere the term most often refers to clusters of grapes (*ʿănābîm*; Gen. 40:10; Num. 13:23–24; Deut. 32:32; Isa. 65:8; Mic. 7:1). Grapes that grow on a vine do not satisfy the requirements here, however. The sense must imply clusters of a fruit such as dates. Their sweetness would form an appropriate image for a metaphor in which they symbolize the breasts of the female. The date palm thus becomes a picture of the fecund female (the "daughter of pleasures") whose fruit provides the ultimate goal of the male's joy.[48]

> **9 (8 Eng.)** I said,
> "I shall climb the palm tree,
> I shall seize its branches."

---

48. Pope, *Song*, 634, notes the similarity between the breasts of the image of Artemis of Ephesus and date clusters. However, he pushes too far to argue for an image of "polymasty" in the Song.

> May your breasts become as clusters of the vine,
> May the fragrance of your breath become like apples.

Verse 9 (8 Eng.) evokes an erotic scene of lovemaking symbolized by the male fantasizing his ascent on the date palm and his taking hold of the clusters of fruit. Not only does the preceding verse make the connection between the fruit and the female's breasts; the third line of this verse is also explicit in its description of this theme. The male longs to lay hold of the breasts of his lover, and that wish is nowhere more explicit than in the central two lines of this verse. The introductory single-word statement, that the male "said" what follows, is most unusual in the Song and worthy of note. The verb "to say" (ʾmr) is one of the most frequent words in the Bible, and yet it occurs only twice in the Song, here and in 2:10. Although a primary theme of the Song is communication between the two lovers, statements of direct discourse do not define the speeches. Every chapter uses verbal pictures and pledges of devotion, but the fact that the speakers speak is rarely noted. The only other occurrence of this verb (2:10) describes what the female remembers the male saying to her. In 7:9 (7:8 Eng.) the male again speaks. In chapter 2 he sought to entice the female to go with him. Here he expresses his own desire for the carnal delights of his lover in the physical closeness of lovemaking. Song 2:10 anticipated the female's response in seeking and finding her lover to fulfill her desires (3:1–4). Although she did not actually depart with him, she did join him. For the attentive reader, the use of this verb of saying again in 7:9 (7:8 Eng.) raises the question, Will the male's desires once more be fulfilled by the acquiescence of the female? As in the previous experience, will there be a twist on how they are fulfilled—not quite according to the male's fantasies but in a manner that will bring pleasure and happiness to both?

The term "seize" refers in the first instance to the clusters of fruit and thus evokes a picture of the male taking hold of the female's breasts. Significantly, this verb is used once elsewhere in the Song in the first person ("I/my"). In 3:4 the female speaks of seizing her lover and not letting him go before she brings him to her mother's bedroom. Here the male uses the term in reference to taking hold of the female with erotic goals in mind. The reference to the branches or panicles of the fruit uses a term not found elsewhere in the Bible (sansinnâ). Yet, when he refers to the "clusters" of fruit again, using the same term as in the preceding verse, what are described are not date clusters but clusters of the vine (ʾeškĕlôt haggepen). In midverse the metaphor changes from the date palm, which has been the image of choice to describe the female, to the vineyard and the clusters of grapes, expressing desire for the female's breasts. For this reason the actual discourse of the male introduced at the beginning of the verse is thought to have ended halfway through the verse. This better explains the rather abrupt shift of the image that forms the goal of the male's desires, from dates to grapes. The shift is necessary in order to anticipate the reference to wine in the following verse. Nevertheless, this single verse, with its four lines of imagery, encompasses a range of senses that bring about full pleasure to the male. There is the female as a palm tree, the touching of her breasts as seizing the branches, the taste of her breasts as grapes from the vineyard (amplified in the following verse), and the aroma of the lover's breath as fresh and sweet as apples. Add to this the auditory message introduced by the first word, "I said," and the twelve words of the verse provide a feast of sensuality.

The final line, with its sense of smell, evokes the use of a scent or fragrance. It uses the Hebrew word *rêaḥ*, a term that appeared five times in the first four chapters (1:3, 12; 2:13; 4:10, 11) but has not been used since. Its reemergence here emphasizes the sensual nature of the male's description as he prepares for a further description in the final verse of this chapter. The word for "breath" is identical to the one used of the nose in v. 5 (4 Eng.) (*ʾap*). Although it may provide some cohesion for the *waṣf*, the usages are distinct. The final word of the verse describes the source of the pleasant breath, the "apples" (*tappûḥîm*).[49] The image of an apple tree occurred in 2:3, where the female used it to distinguish her lover from other men. It will reappear in 8:5 as the place where the female's mother conceived her and where her lover arouses her own passions. The sole other usage of "apples" in the Song is 2:5, where as here in chapter 7 the apples themselves are mentioned (rather than the tree). In 2:5 they provide refreshment for the female overcome by her passion of love. Together these uses suggest, when applied to the female, that the apple is an image associated with the passion and desire shared between the two (cf. comments on 2:3), while simultaneously providing refreshment to continue their amorous pursuits.

10a (9a Eng.)Your palate,
Like the best wine . . .

Verse 10a (9a Eng.) begins with three words that come from the mouth of the male. The first refers to the female's palate or inner mouth. As in its previous occurrences in 2:3 and 5:16, it describes the place of intimacy where the most erotic of kisses are shared. The picture of the best wine recalls the use of this term for wine from the beginning of the Song and

---

49. There is an interesting, perhaps intentional, wordplay here. The word for "apples" (*tappûḥîm*) resembles the use of the verb "to breathe," with *ʾap* in Gen. 2:7, where God "breathed" ([*way*]*yippaḥ*) into the nostrils of the man to create a living soul.

its constant association with the love shared between the lovers (1:4; 2:4; 4:10; 5:1; 8:2). Wine as the symbol of that love and represented by kisses is found at the beginning of the Song (1:2). Only here, however, is it likened to the best wine, an image of consummate sensuality.[50]

At this point, however, the female interrupts the musings of the male because she can no longer contain her desire. She picks up the poetry and imagery of her lover to coincide her own senses of love and desire with his.

> [10b (9b Eng.)] . . . flowing smoothly to my lover,
> Gliding over sleepers' lips.

7:10b–8:4 (7:9b–8:4 Eng.). *Female: Springtime and love.* The interruption of the female nevertheless continues the thought of the male. The wine imagery that describes their kisses becomes a picture of an intimacy that they share as it flows back and forth between them. The image of that which "glides" (*dôbēb*) uses a second participle in this verse. In the whole of chapter 7 are only three participles, two of which occur in this verse.[51] The use of these verb forms, describing continuous or ongoing action, forms a pledge of love with which the female responds to her lover. It also brings to a close the reflections of the chapter on physical attributes. With this word picture the female promises that the erotic desires of the male, which are also her own, will be met and more than met in their embrace. The final line may suggest the collapse into sleep that comes after the frenzy of lovemaking.[52] However, since the term "sleepers" forms the final word in the verse, it may suggest the sleepy way in which the wine glides over the lips—just as "the best" of the wine and "the smoothness" of its flow all form adverbs at the end of each line of the Hebrew. Most probable, however, is the sense that the erotic "wine" enlivens even those who sleep so that the touch upon the lips and the effect on the inside of the mouth is to rouse and awaken to the delights of passion.

> [11 (10 Eng.)] I am my lover's,
> And his desire is for me.

---

50. Keel, *Song*, 247, comments: "Like wine, which sends both gods and mortals into a frenzy of good cheer (Judg. 9:13), thus removing the inhibitions of everyday life, so also the woman's mouth, soft and moist as wine, sends her lover into a state of intoxication when it opens to his pressure."

51. The third, "espying" (*sôpeh*), occurs in 7:5 (7:4 Eng.).

52. Keel, *Song*, 247.

Verse 11 (10 Eng.) begins with a sentiment first expressed by the female in 6:3. As there, so here it describes the union and exclusive commitment that the female vows for her lover. The second line of this verse has been the source of much discussion. This is because the term for "desire" (*tĕšûqâ*) occurs only two other times in the Bible, in Gen. 3:16 and 4:7. Fox observes that in 3:16 the man possessed the woman because her "desire" was for him.[53] Keel goes so far as to state that the effects of 3:16 are now declared reversed as the lovers share the mutual possession of one another.[54] Pope introduces problems with this conclusion.[55] First, the versions read something different. Second, both Gen. 3:16 and 4:7 use the preposition *ʾel* (for) rather than *ʿal* (upon), which appears here. To this may be added that the main concern of Gen. 3:16 should be interpreted by 4:7 rather than by a text in a completely different context and located at the other end of the Bible. In Gen. 4:7, the sense is the desire to dominate rather than sexual desire. Could the same be the case in 3:16? I believe it is and have argued elsewhere that the point of this text is to stress the conflict of the wills between male and female (Hess, "Equality"). The usage of "desire" (*tĕšûqâ*) in Song 7:11 (7:10 Eng.) is unique. Within its context it should be understood first as erotic desire. Nevertheless, more is suggested here, as well. As in Genesis, this also concerns the control of the partner's body. However, here it is no longer a negative feature. Keel is correct that the verse conveys a reciprocity of possession. The lovers give themselves to one another and possess each other's bodies. Thus the Genesis judgment of each person seeking domination is reversed, with each person now seeking mutuality and willingly giving possession of their body to their partner. In the NT this becomes the test of love between a husband and wife, that they give their bodies to one another and love each other as they love their own bodies (1 Cor. 7:2–4; Eph. 5:22–33).

> 12 (11 Eng.)Come, my lover,
> Let's go out to the countryside.
> Let's spend the night in the villages.

Verses 12–13a (11–12a Eng.) form the first direct address by the female to her lover in this section. The initial imperative is followed by three (or four) verbs in the first position in each line that all function as cohortatives and thus continue the volitional force of the initial

53. Fox, *Song*, 164.
54. Keel, *Song*, 251–52.
55. Pope, *Song*, 643.

224

verb. Each of the first four verbs is followed by a single word that in the first case describes the object of address, or for the others points to the destinations of verbs of motion. The verbs describe an adventure set in chronological sequence. The female envisions a journey out to the fields, with the couple then staying overnight in one of the villages so that they can rise early the next morning and witness the blossoms bursting forth among the vineyards. The whole plan, and what follows, is summarized in her first word, the urgent imperative "Come!" The *hê* ending on the imperative does not serve to make it more emphatic but focuses the command toward her lover, who is then addressed with the next word. Of the seven appearances of the verb "come" (*hlk*), the first four previously in the Song form a cluster whose main concern is the same as here: encouraging the lover's partner to join in an adventure of exploring the outdoors and springtime's new life found there. The four occurrences of the verb in 2:10–13 form a kind of leitmotif through the whole of the discourse. There, however, it is the male who speaks and commands the female. Here in chapter 7 the scene is reversed as the female gives her orders to the male. Rather than finding here a reversal of power roles, it is much more in keeping with the mutual love, suggested by the context, to suppose that this word balances the statements of the male in chapter 2. By saying this, the female follows her lover in expressing desire for the same thing. With the command "Come, my lover," she summarizes the whole of her message and her heart, that the two be united in this journey and all journeys of life.

A similar picture of word usage for "go out" (*ys*ʾ) emerges as it did for "Come!" Of the three other occurrences of this root, the first one, 1:8, is also a command by the male to the female to go out and find where he pastures his flock. Here the female commands the male, but this time they will go together. Their destination is to be the open fields (*śādeh*), far from the walled cities with their towers and near where the gazelles and does live (2:7; 3:5). This is not the wilderness or desert where little grows, nor is it the wild forest with its dangers. Instead, it is the open lands, best seen in Israel in the hill country, where the nation first settled. These areas, with their cultivated terraces and broad pasturelands, provide contact with the people, animals, and crops that comprise the Israelites and their country. The journey is of such length, and their start perhaps so late in the day, that they will need to spend the night in one of the villages. In its various usages the term for "village" (*kāpār*) describes a population center that is unfortified, with about one or two dozen houses (Josh. 18:24; 1 Sam. 6:18; Neh. 6:2; 1 Chron. 27:25). It refers to villages in the hill country of Palestine where the Israelites settled. These villages were generally unwalled and represented the settlements for many Israelites for much of their history before the exile. Spending a night in the villages provided safety from wild animals and thieves. It would also give warmth.

> [13 (12 Eng.)]Let's go early to the vineyards,
> So we can see if the vine has blossomed,
> If their blossoms have opened,
> If the pomegranates are in bloom,
> There I will make love to you.

Upon rising, the female hopes to go early to see the new life of the spring. Having spoken of an adventure through the countryside and in the villages, the female now takes her mind's eye off to the vineyards. Are these the same vineyards mentioned in 1:6? If so, then they are the ones that belong to the female's family, and she has some responsibility for tending them. Now she wishes her lover to join her. Vineyards attached to the families in a village might be closer than some of the more distant pasturelands and fields. This verse gives the sense of vineyards in proximity to where they stay, allowing the female and her lover to approach them early in the morning, as the sun's rays come upon the blossoms beginning to open. The picture of seeing the blossoming vines and the pomegranates repeats the same verbs and subjects as occur in 6:11. There as well the female speaks. The picture is also a metaphor of her body and its fecundity for love.[56] In this verse the drama and journey again lead to the same destination, the place of lovemaking. This is a place full of luxuriant vines and greenery, a place of fruitfulness in which the life-giving powers of physical love are represented by the giddy intoxication that the vineyard promises and the great symbol of abundant fruitfulness in Israel, the pomegranate, rich in seeds and luscious fruit. These images are the same as in 6:11. Such repetition frames the whole erotic picture of the female in chapter 7. What the male has praised concerning his lover's body, she now confirms twice in a text that frames this image of fruit and the passionate desires that it brings to the couple. Yet the repetition in "see if the vine has blossomed, . . . if the pomegranates are in bloom" itself frames the two words that occur together for the first time, *pittaḥ hassĕmādar* ([if their] blossoms have opened). This line elaborates the first, using a term for vine blossoms found only in 2:13 and 2:15 in the Song. Rhetorically, it serves to build the image and its emotional exuberance. Piling line upon line gives the impression of the entire vista of vineyards and pomegranate fields blossoming and bringing fruitfulness to the whole land. In the

---

56. Thus Madl, "Dimensionen," studies the whole remainder of the text of the Song and uncovers symbolism illustrating the fruitfulness of love. His identification of the desert imagery with death, however, is not as clear.

sense of the verse, this context becomes an erotic "chamber" in which the female climaxes the picture of new life and fruitfulness by yielding her body and its potential for fruit bearing to the embrace of her lover (7:13b [7:12b Eng.]). The garden becomes a bed in which the lovers exult in their lovemaking.

> 14 (13 Eng.)The love fruits give off their fragrance,
> At our doors are all the best fruits,
> Both new and old,
> That I have stored up for you, my lover.

In v. 14 (13 Eng.) the female changes the structure of the poetry from a focus on verbs of movement and fruitfulness to beginning each line with nouns: "love fruits," "our doors," and "my lover." The "love fruits" are mandrakes. In Gen. 30:14–16 they are associated with Leah's persuasion of Jacob to sleep with her.[57] Their association with love is no doubt related to the first three letters of the word, *dālet-wāw-dālet*, letters that spell the word for "lover" (*dôd*), used so frequently in the Song. By their pleasing and potent fragrance these emblems of desire powerfully evoke the senses for a sexual encounter. These aromatics waft their scent of love to the senses of the lovers. At the "doors" of their senses they indulge in the best of fruits. This term (*mĕgādîm*) has already appeared in 4:13 and 4:16, where it was used by both lovers as a reference to the female's body and its sexual delights. The image continues here, and the sense of "new and old" may refer to the fruits mentioned. Although many fruits have the best flavor as soon as they are plucked, the best wine may come from what has been aged. For this reason, a common designation for a type of wine in administrative records found at Samaria and Arad from the time of the monarchy is *yšn*, "old" or "aged" wine. In addition, the expression "new and old" as used of fruit may function as a metaphor for the experiences of carnal love that the two have shared. The female promises new delicacies as well as those already favored by her lover. These she has kept well so that she is able to provide them for the benefit of her lover.[58]

---

57. For the use of the love apple or fruit of the mandrake in Egypt, see Keel, *Song*, 257–59. He identifies it as an import from Palestine and Syria. He also suggests that the Egyptians, like their northeastern counterparts, regarded it as an aphrodisiac. Among the many scenes that depict this, one from fourteenth-century Amarna is a beautiful miniature of a young princess giving her prince a taste of the love apple, while her gown remains open and thus associates her physical beauty with the apples. Murphy, *Song*, 184, compares the Ugaritic Anat Epic (*CTU* 3.3.12).

58. In this sense "new and old" may form a merism that accommodates everything, an all-inclusive term. Cf. Longman, *Song*, 202.

> **8:1**If only you were like my brother,
> Nursed at the breasts of my mother,
> I would find you in public,
> I would kiss you,
> And no one would despise me.

Chapter 8 begins with a continuation of the female's desire for her lover. A theme introduced in the first verse remains constant through the first nine verses of this final chapter of the Song. It is the subject of the female's family. In successive order are mentioned her brother (v. 1), mother (vv. 1, 2), and sister (vv. 8–10). Although the brother is a fantasy, for the female only dreams of her lover as a brother, the others are real persons who function within her family. Although everyone may be expected to have a mother, the existence of a younger sister and her concerns cannot be assumed as though these are stock figures. The portrayal here is intended to reflect the love of a specific couple within the domestic world of the female's family (cf. Gen. 2:24). The first verse of Song 8 consists of two parts. In the first two lines the female creates an imaginary world in her fantasy. She dreams that her lover is her physical brother. She pictures him as a full brother, with the same mother (and presumably father) as herself. The previous mention of the female's brothers and mother occurred only in 1:6, where she declared that her brothers were angry with her and sent her out into the sun, which darkened her skin. Now, however, her attitude has changed. In place of anger, her relationship with a brother is now portrayed as one of love. In public, affectionate kissing between adults of different sexes and outside the family was apparently considered inappropriate. Thus the female fantasizes for a means that would allow her to kiss her lover in public. If they are married, this suggests that even kisses between a husband and wife are not proper in public.[59] It is not clear, however, that the scene envisioned is concerned with marriage. There is only the desire of the lovers for one another. Contrast this to the chase scenes of 3:1–4 and 5:4–7, where the female can roam the city streets at night in search of her lover. Here as well there is risk: in 5:7 the night guards catch her, beat her, and strip off her shawl; in 8:1 she worries that others might

59. Such public affection between sexes is either that of cousins (Gen. 29:11) or of prostitutes or adulteresses (Prov. 7:13). See Keel, *Song*, 261. Cf. also the Egyptian love poem in Fox, *Song*, 55 #37D: "If only mother knew my heart—she would go inside for a while. O Golden One, put that in her heart! Then I could hurry to (my) brother and kiss him before his company, and not be ashamed because of anyone. I would be happy to have them see that you know me, and I'd hold festival to my goddess." Thus it is not clear that Longman, *Song*, 204, is correct when he finds here a proof that they were not married in this verse but were maintaining a secret love.

despise her; and in 8:10 she defends herself. Nevertheless, the picture of 3:1–4 suggests pursuit in a public context. Further, the goal of the female toward her lover is set there as well in the context of her mother. Song 3:4 describes how she brought him to her mother's house after she found him. In 8:1 the emphasis upon those "nursed at the breasts of my mother" does more than evoke an image of full brother and sister. It also continues the theme of the preceding verses in this exchange in which both male and female discuss her breasts. In addition, the sucking infant evokes the senses of taste and touch, something already suggested and reiterated in the image of kissing that is central to the second half of this verse.

The second half of 8:1 begins a series of five verbs that all appear in the same form,[60] a form limited in the Song to nine verses having a total of fifteen verbs.[61] That five of those appear here suggests something significant. Previously, two appeared in 7:9 (7:8 Eng.), where the male uses the erotic image of the date palm and attests, "I shall climb the palm tree, I shall seize its branches." This refers to the female and the male's picture of sex with her. In 7:13 (7:12 Eng.) the same form appears again as the female declares, "I will make love to you." This desire for physical love reaches a new level in this series of verbs. The female moves through her fantasies, using these verbal forms that rise to a level of passionate intensity: "I would find you; I would kiss you; I would lead you; I would bring you; I would give you . . . to drink."[62] These verb forms are a regular means of conveying the personal desire and intention of the speaker. Their concentration in vv. 1 and 2 suggests an emotionally charged plan to bring about greater and greater intimacy. The significance of the descriptions should be considered in such a context. Further, there are some distinctive phrases and use of terminology in these verses. For example, the verb "to kiss" (nšq) might be thought of as a common term throughout the Song. However, as a verb it appears elsewhere only in 1:2, where the female begins with the passionate and sensual expression of her desire for kisses from her lover.

---

²I would lead you,
I would bring you to my mother's house,
You would teach me;

---

60. These are first-person common singular imperfects with second-person masculine singular suffixes on each one.

61. The fifteen occurrences of first-person common singular imperfects, with or without suffixes, are Song 1:7; 3:2 (2x), 4; 4:6; 5:3 (2x); 7:9 (7:8 Eng.) (2x), 13 (12 Eng.); 8:1 (2x), 2 (3x).

62. With the second-person masculine singular suffix attached to all five of these verbs, the cohortative form would not be marked in a manner different from the imperfect verb.

> I would give you spiced wine to drink,
> From the crushed juice of my pomegranate.

In 8:2, the verbs "to lead" (*nhg*) and "to give to drink" (*šqh*) both appear only here in the Song. The "mother's house" of the female has been mentioned in 3:4 as the destination of the couple after they found one another. Here the implications of this search suggest a reason for this destination, because her mother taught her (8:2). What did she teach her? There is no explicit answer. The context suggests the recipes for the wine and nectar that the remainder of the verse describes. Yet the metaphors of wine and pomegranates as intended to represent sexual purposes suggest something more. In addition, the concatenation of verbs, as already noted, implies an intensity of passion. Finally, the previous usage (3:4) of "my mother's house" associated it with the room where the female lover was conceived. Hence the instruction envisaged here is best understood as that of lovemaking and the joys of sexual pleasure, and the correct rendering of this verb should be "you would teach me," with reference to the male lover doing the teaching.[63] This anticipates the final verb, "I would give you."[64] The destination of the couple has been reached. Now it remains for the female to bestow the wine and nectar. The type of wine, "spiced" (*reqah*), suggests that a prepared mixture of spices has been added. The spices flavor the wine in a desirable manner. The crushed juice of the female's pomegranate also evokes an erotic picture, one already noted with various parts of the female's body so compared (4:3; 6:7) and most recently described as part of the outing that the couple envisions at the end of chapter 7 (v. 12 [11 Eng.]). In both cases there is strong evidence for erotic imagery, suggesting that the female here offers her body to her lover.[65]

> [3]His left \<arm is\> under my head,
> His right \<arm\> embraces me.
> [4]I want you to promise,
> O young women of Jerusalem,
> Do not disturb,
> Do not excite love,
> Until it desires.

The last lines that the female utters here are ones in which the physical relationship involves her sense of the touch of her lover and his

---

63. On this verb, see the first translation note at 8:2 above.
64. A first-person common singular imperfect.
65. Munro, *Spikenard*, 73, identifies the pomegranate with the female's breasts.

warm embrace. This is followed at once by another adjuration to the chorus of young women not to stir up love until it chooses the time. These lines are largely a repeat of 2:6–7, with the omission of the reference to the gazelles and does that appears there.[66] While serving to tie together the whole Song in a literary sense of inclusio, this statement here also brings the female out of the fantasy of her lover as brother to the reality of her lover beside her. It is thus a continuation of the opening verses of chapter 8.[67]

Theological Implications

The section begins the male's second *wasf* for the female (6:4–10). The first was intended to encourage the female in her beauty; this one reflects the power of that beauty and its effect upon the male. Those who gaze upon the form of such beauty are overcome and transformed by it. Whether that gaze results in good or ill depends on the purposes of the subject and object. In the context of this love, as with the beatific vision of God, the gaze becomes a source of life and well-being.

Desire draws the female to embark on a dangerous and exciting adventure (6:11–12). The chorus invokes her name, Shulammite, to call her to dance and to become the object of further admiration (7:1 [6:13 Eng.]). This introduces the most intensely erotic *wasf* in the Song, one in which the female's lover repeatedly pours forth with fruitful and luscious images of nature (7:2–10a [7:1–9a Eng.]).[68] The focus surrounds aspects of the female's body that are most arousing for the male and climaxes in his assertion that he will fulfill his desire for love with her. The first verse of this poem of desire indeed drives the source of all the beauty and desire back to an "Artist." The love that the lovers share is ultimately tied to the Creator, the Artist of the natural world. Without this good creation, the joys celebrated here would not exist.

The response of the female emphasizes the mutuality of the couple's love (7:10b–8:4 [7:9b–8:4 Eng.]). She not only finishes her lover's thought but also goes on to stress how he possesses her with his desire. She eagerly reciprocates such longing by calling him to a journey into the countryside, where she will give her body to him. She calls into service images of fruit and family to describe her readiness to yield her body. A section that begins with the male gazing upon his lover (6:4) con-

---

66. See further comments there.

67. Contra Keel, *Song*, 264, who maintains that there must be a separation of the fantasy of vv. 1–2 and the "reality" of v. 3. However, this is the same female, and the theme of sensuality remains.

68. This itself reflects an increasing intensity of expression as the Song progresses.

cludes with the two locked in passionate embrace (8:3). Once more the section moves from the lovers separated to their enjoyment of union. Once more the refrain of the female's address to the daughters of Jerusalem recurs (8:4). The poem has clearly seen the love of the couple aroused. However, they have explored it for reasons other than purely as a satisfaction of desire. Instead, their bodies with their desires, like the beauty of nature and the blessing of family, are traced back to an Artist who brings all these things into being. This unexpressed key provides for the integration of beauty, desire, and commitment. It thus allows the lovers to give themselves fully to one another without fear (1 John 4:18) and without oppression (Eph. 5, especially v. 21).

VII.
Epilogue:
The Power of Love
(8:5–14)

Translation

Chorus
5aWho is this ascending from the desert,
Leaning[a] upon her beloved?

Female
5bBeneath the apple tree I awoke you,[b]
There your mother conceived you;
There she conceived and gave birth to you.
6Set me like the seal on your heart,
Like the seal on your arm;
For as strong as death is love.[c]
As difficult as Sheol is jealousy.
Its flames are flames of fire,
A flame of the LORD.
7Many waters cannot quench love,
Rivers will not overflow it.
If one were to give all the possessions of his house for love,
They would utterly scorn it.[d]

a. *Mitrappeqet,* a hapax legomenon, occurs in Semitic cognates with the basic sense of supporting someone. Cf. Joüon, *Cantique,* 308; Murphy, *Song,* 191.

b. The female's voice is indicated by the use of the second-person masculine singular object suffix. This can apply only to the male, as she addresses him.

c. This line begins with *kî,* which here functions in an asseverative sense. Cf. Murphy, *Song,* 191.

d. The final third-person masculine singular pronominal suffix that is attached to the *lāmed* preposition (*lô*) could refer either to the man who is scorned or to his wealth.

Brothers

[8]"We have a young sister,
Who has no breasts,
What we will do for our sister
On the day when she is spoken for?
[9]If she is a wall,
We will build a silver battlement[a] on her.
If she is a door,
We will surround her with a cedar panel."

Female

[10]I am a wall,
My breasts are like towers.
So I have become in his eyes,
As one who brings[b] peace.
[11]Solomon had a vineyard in Baal Hamon,
He gave the vineyard to caretakers,
Each would bring a thousand silver <shekels> for its fruit.
[12]My vineyard is my own,
The thousand are yours, Solomon,
But two hundred are for those who take care of its fruit.

Male

[13]You who live in the gardens,
With friends attending,[c]
Let me hear your voice.

Female

[14]Flee[d] my lover,

However, the man is not the subject of discussion here. It is love and its value that forms the context. Therefore, people (in general) scorn the wealth that attempts to buy love. See Fox, *Song*, 171.

a. *Ṭîrâ*, here in construct, occurs elsewhere with the sense of "settlement" or "camp" (Gen. 25:16; Num. 31:10; Ezek. 25:4; Ps. 69:26 [69:25 Eng.]; 1 Chron. 6:39 [6:54 Eng.]). In Ezek. 46:23, the NIV translates the term as "ledge," as something that goes around (*ṭwr*) the inside of each of four courts. This sense of following alongside a ledge or wall suggests something that is built over or on top of something else.

b. Analyzing *môṣĕʾēt* as feminine singular Hiphil participle from *yṣʾ*, rather than as a Qal participle from *mṣʾ*. Murphy, *Song*, 193, translates this as a Qal ("find") that describes how the woman has found peace through her lover's acceptance of her. Elliott, *Literary*, 203, suggests an intentional use of a word that can be understood in both ways.

c. The MT accentuation and the LXX associate this verb with the following "your voice." The Vulgate and the translation proposed relate it to the "friends." See comments.

d. The root *brḥ* normally carries the meaning "to depart." However, at least in Exod. 36:33 ("they made the center crossbar so that it extended from end to end at the middle

Become like a gazelle,
Or a young stag upon spice mountains.

Interpretation

8:5a   Chorus: Search for the couple
8:5b–7   Female: The power of love
8:8–9   Brothers (quoted by the female?): Their younger sister
8:10   Female: Her defense
8:11–12   Female: Solomon's vineyard
8:13   Male: Listening
8:14   Female: Departure

> [5a]Who is this ascending from the desert,
> Leaning upon her beloved?

8:5a. *Chorus: Search for the couple.* This short section begins with
a line that occurred previously in 3:6.[1] There, as here, it introduced a
new section where someone other than the female speaks. In both cases
it is best interpreted as a question that follows an exhortation to the
daughters of Jerusalem and describes the appearance of the female. In
both cases it introduces a kind of theatrical scene in which the lover
appears. As in 3:6, so here the "desert" (*hammidbār*) sets the perspective
for an approach from a distance. Yet in this part of the verse, the male
appears to be a participant in the drama. He will be the lover and the
one who joins the female under the apple tree. As the female leans upon
her lover, the themes of their physical closeness as a symbol of the love
that they share continues the picture of v. 3, where they are seen in an
embrace. It anticipates the intimate relationship concerning which the
female will speak in the following verses.

8:5b–7. *Female: The power of love.* Verses 5–7 are the longest verses
in chapter 8. Together they form a climax to the entire book and provide an interpretive key for understanding the whole of the Song. This
key begins in v. 5b with its own structure. Each line moves forward
to develop a theme that connects the passion and love of the couple
with that of the male's line and channels the power of that passion

---

of the frames," NIV) it carries the sense of passing through or piercing. This leads Pope,
Song, 697–98, to argue for an explicitly sexual intention in the verb; Fox, *Song,* 177, settles
for a double entendre.
1. Cf. also 6:10 for the first two words.

into the hope for continuation of that line. Verses 6 and 7 develop the theme of the couple's love and project it onto the horizon of love in general, so that it becomes an object that is stronger than all and is priceless.[2]

As the female begins to speak, she continues the geographical association. The apple and its tree are mentioned three other times in the Song and only twice elsewhere in the Hebrew Bible (Joel 1:12; Prov. 25:11). In addition to the sweetness of the apple's aroma (7:9 [7:8 Eng.]) and its value as a source of strength (2:5), the female has previously compared her lover to the apple tree for his unique qualities in comparison with other young men and for the sweetness of his fruit (2:3). The comments on those verses discussed the erotic aspects of the apple tree. Here they appear in all their power as an aphrodisiac to awaken and arouse the young man for the love pleasures that the female has desired. That both senses, awakening from sleep and arousing sexually, may be present is indicated by the use of this root (*ʿwr*) earlier in the Song. The root occurs six times in the three verses where the female charges the young women of Jerusalem not to awake or stir love, most recently in the verse immediately preceding this one (2:7; 3:5; 8:4). In all these contexts it refers to romantic and sexual desire. Alternatively, in 4:16 and 5:2 the north wind is commanded to awake and the heart of the female remains awake while she sleeps.

> [5b]Beneath the apple tree I awoke you,
> There your mother conceived you;
> There she conceived and gave birth to you.

Here in 8:5b the idea is to awake from sleep. Fox thus is not incorrect when he argues that the sense of being awake can be understood here.[3] However, Pope is nearer the mark when he notes the consistent usage of this form of the verb with the sense of arousing desire in the Song.[4] As he notes, the Ugaritic myths of the West Semitic world (of which Israel was a part) portray female deities as seeking to arouse the passions of males. Recent commentators follow the MT in understanding the woman as speaking here.[5] However, as much as any other passage,

---

2. Only here in the Song is the meaning of love examined. Everywhere else it is assumed. See Longman, *Song,* 209; Sadgrove, "Song," 245; Tromp, "Wisdom."

3. Fox, *Song,* 168.

4. Pope, *Song,* 663. The verb uses the Polel stem.

5. This is based on the masculine object suffixes that she uses. Murphy, *Song,* 191, objects with the observations that (1) previously in the Song the woman has never aroused the man and (2) the mother has always been the mother of the woman. However, as noted, (1) females do arouse males in Semitic myths, and there is no reason it could not be so here; and (2) Murphy himself notes 3:11, where the mother of Solomon is mentioned.

such an understanding destroys a consistent allegorical interpretation. How can Israel or the church, the female, awaken Yahweh or Christ, the male? Probably for this reason the Syriac switched the gender of the suffixes so that the male speaks and awakes. The allegorical commentators followed this practice.

The form for "conceived" is unique to this verse in the Song, though here the root (*ḥbl*) occurs twice. Elsewhere this root, with the sense "be/become pregnant," appears only in Ps. 7:15 (7:14 Eng.): "He who is pregnant with evil and conceives trouble gives birth to disillusionment" (NIV). There it appears in parallel with the more common verb "to conceive" (*hārāh*). There is no doubt that the repetition in Song 8:5b is designed to emphasize the generational aspect, so that the erotic sense of lovemaking is set in the context of the family. It is not merely the nuclear family but especially the extended one, in which generation after generation is envisioned as safeguarding the family and perpetuating it. In the same place and manner as the current male begins a family with his lover, so his father and mother began their family. Hence the erotic tenor of the whole Song here moves beyond the inevitably selfish tendencies of pleasure seeking to describe the broader vista of fulfillment of the goal that God wishes for his people, to be fruitful and to fill the earth (Gen. 1:26–28).[6] That this should be accomplished within the bounds of committed heterosexual marriage is the only possible understanding of the remainder of the biblical text. There was little respect and no inheritance for those born outside this marriage relationship (cf. Judg. 11:1–2). This is not mentioned here because it is not the concern of the book. Nevertheless, to assume that the lovers were unmarried and celebrating a sexual relationship, as many commentators do, runs against the assumptions of this verse in the context of Israelite society. The reference to the previous generation and the expectation of one to come assume that the erotic love of the couple does not lie outside the bounds of marriage but is integral to it.

> [6]Set me like the seal on your heart,
> Like the seal on your arm;
> For as strong as death is love.
> As difficult as Sheol is jealousy.
> Its flames are flames of fire,
> A flame of the LORD.

The fulfillment of eros with the allusion to conception and childbearing leads to the climax of the entire Song, the emphasis on a commitment

6. Keel, *Song*, 268–69.

in love that is stronger than anything known. Verses 6–7 form a single unit composed of five groups of two lines each. The first line of each group in v. 6 begins with an introductory word or phrase ("set me," "for," "its flames") that is then carried along in both lines. These are identical in grammatical form. Verse 7 begins with two lines that have a close grammatical parallelism. The final two lines resemble a staircase form in which the lines follow sequentially one after the other, not unlike v. 5b. Verse 6 begins with the picture of a seal (*ḥôtām*). The seal on the heart would be one worn with a string around the neck so that it hung in front and perhaps beneath the clothes. It would be a small cylinder of stone or metal that could be impressed on clay and would contain words, pictures, and designs that identified the individual.[7] The stamp seal, made of similar materials, could also be hung around the neck (Gen. 38:18, 25) or worn as a ring on the finger (Jer. 22:24). The second line of the verse may intend this latter image, for the arm can easily include the hand and fingers. The seal secured the identity of its owner and provided a means of ensuring possession. For the female to imagine herself a seal by the heart or arm of her lover suggests that she will share his identity and become one with him, both physically (as close as possible) and legally (as taking on his name and legal identity).[8] The image of the seal was a romantic one, as found in an Egyptian love poem spoken by the male:

> If only I were her little seal-ring,
>   the keeper of her finger!
> I would see her love
>   each and every day.
> . . . .
>   [while it would be I] who stole her heart.[9]

The focus of the Song may be found in the following two lines. The strength of love is likened to death, and the difficulty of overcoming death is likened to the hold of the grave (8:6). No mere mortal can escape these, and thus they testify to the most powerful forces known.[10]

---

7. On its connection with the identity of the individual, see Hallo, "As the Seal"; idem, "For Love"; J. Sasson, "Unlocking," 14.

8. Bergant, *Song*, 97: "She wants the union that they share to be so intimate that she might represent to others the very identity of her beloved."

9. Fox, *Song*, 38 #21C.

10. Cf. Longman, *Song*, 210, who aptly cites Eccles. 9:11–12 and refers to Watson ("Love and Death," 385–86) translating a line from the ancient Mesopotamian Gilgamesh Epic (10.7.11–12): "The fine young man, the beautiful girl/when making love, together they confront death." This is particularly appropriate because a major theme of the epic is the search of the hero Gilgamesh for immortality. However, it seems unlikely that the

Their power cannot be overcome, and their hold is eternal. This is the picture of love: not only the love of the couple but here at last the sense in which the love they share partakes of a greater love that is higher and more magnificent in its awesome power than anything on earth. This love nowhere denies the erotic emphasis of the couple's love. However, it builds on that physical passion with an eternal commitment that will not let go.

"Death" here parallels "Sheol" in the next line. In the West Semitic mythology of thirteenth-century BC Ugarit, Death was personified as a deity, was described as strong, and was able to defeat Baal.[11] No such deity can be demonstrated in this brief text. However, Sheol or Death is personified and represents the abode of the dead, whose grip is so strong that no one returns after going there. Thus the love described here also forms an irrevocable commitment.[12] Longman observes that the Bible approves of jealousy in only two relationships: the worship of one God alone, and the marriage covenant:

> Humans can have only one God. If they worship another, it triggers God's jealousy. God's jealousy is an energy that tries to rescue the relationship. Similarly, a man and a woman can have only one spouse. If there is a threat to that relationship, then jealousy is a proper emotion. All this is because so much hangs on the integrity of the relationship. It is so basic, so deep, that it stirs up strong emotions and passions.[13]

The image of the flames of love as flames of fire describes a heat burning so intensely that nothing can stand in its way. The term for flames (rešep) is used of a deity in the Ugaritic myths. This Canaanite deity is well known in Egypt, where he is depicted as brandishing a battle-ax.[14] He is associated with pestilence. The name may occur as a personification of pestilence in Hab. 3:5 (cf. Deut. 32:24). However, the occurrence in Song 8:6 (in plural construct) is likely a reference not to the deity but to flames, as also occurs in the cognate languages. The emphasis of the final lines

---

point of the Song passage is that making love defies death. It may be a challenge to death, but it seems that the Song makes a comparison rather than a challenge between love and death. For this reason (and the lack of an explicit statement in the text affirming it), it also is difficult to accept the interpretation that applies the power described here to the woman (Frettloch, "O Amor").

11. Pope, *Song*, 668–69; Murphy, *Song*, 191; LaCocque, *Romance*, 170.

12. Murphy, "Dance," observes that love is portrayed not as overcoming death but as similar to it in strength.

13. Longman, *Song*, 211–12, observes that Webb ("Love Poem," 98n18) notes that Deut. 32:21–22 and Song 8:6 share similar vocabulary.

14. Pope, *Song*, 670. A love-goddess background is also affirmed by Munro, *Spikenard*, 39.

thus is on the power of fire and, no doubt, its heat as that which cannot be stopped and which inflames the passions of those it affects.

The last word (*šalhebetyāh*) is the most controversial in the entire verse (8:6). It occurs only here, and its meaning is not clear. The construction of the word invites its division into possibly a prefixed relative pronoun followed by a word for "flame(s)" (*lhb*) and then the shortened form of Yahweh, the divine name. It could thereby be rendered as "flames of Yahweh." This might reflect a superlative, the mightiest of flames (so Brin, "Superlative"), or it could imply that God is the ultimate author of this arousal of love and the heat of passion. The LXX renders it as "its flames," whereas the Vulgate interprets it as "and of the flames."[15] Nevertheless, the characteristically shortened form of Yahweh, as found frequently in the major book of biblical poetry, the Psalms,[16] suggests that here is mention of Yahweh.[17] If so, in the entire book this is the only direct reference to God, by any name. It may well be that here at the climactic point of the whole Song, the poet chooses to mention the name of God, a name otherwise hidden and reflective of his operation behind the scenes. God is not in the conscious concerns of the couple as they celebrate their sexual love, just as he is not himself ever portrayed in a sexual sense. This would prevent the erotic poetry from somehow being applied to God as though he were sexual. Still, a tendency—reflected both in the historical interpretation of the text and in the many monarchical references in extrabiblical Hebrew inscriptions to Yahweh in possession of a consort (Asherah)[18]—was to apply it in some way to Israel's deity. Nevertheless, the absence of any direct reference to God, except at this point, suggests that here the erotic love of the Song reaches a level of the love that transcends all and through which God is known. Thus God is love (1 John 4:8, 16), and those who would know and worship him must know that love. The greatest physical pointer to such love is the committed sexual intimacy between a husband and wife.

> [7]Many waters cannot quench love,
> Rivers will not overflow it.

15. The LXX: *phloges autēs*; the Vulgate: *atque flammarum*.

16. And elsewhere: e.g., Exod. 15:2; 17:16; Isa. 12:2; 26:4; 38:11; Pss. 68:5, 19 (68:4, 18 Eng.); 77:12 (77:11 Eng.); 89:9 (89:8 Eng.); 94:7, 12; 102:19 (102:18 Eng.); 104:45; 106:1, 48; 111:1; 112:1; 113:1, 9. The best-known example of this shortened form of the divine name occurs as the last syllable of the term of praise: Hallelujah.

17. Murphy, *Song*, 192, suggests that in parallel to the preceding line, a second similar term may have fallen out, so that the original would be "flames of Yah are its flames." Cf. Rudolph, *Hohe Lied*, 179–80; Robert, Tournay, and Feuillet, *Cantique*, 453.

18. Cf. those from Kuntillet ʿAjrud, Khirbet el-Qom, and Philistine Tel Miqne.

> If one were to give all the possessions of his house for love,
> They would utterly scorn it.

Verse 7 carries forward the emphasis on the value of love. Whereas the previous verse had described how strong, hard, and enduring love is, this verse continues the theme of its endurance in the face of obstacles and also adds an emphasis on its great value. With the twenty-eight occurrences of "many waters" or "mighty waters" (*mayim rabbîm*) in the Bible, there are many associations with themes of God's control over the watery powers of chaos.[19] Regarding the thematic significance, Murphy writes: "The appropriateness of the water metaphor is twofold: it contrasts with fire, and it represents the powers of chaos which only the Lord can dominate. Love refuses to be conquered even by such strength as the *mayim rabbîm* represent."[20]

The female was earlier depicted as a well of living water, and the male's eyes as doves by streams of water; these images prepare for this image of unquenchable love. The verb "to quench" occurs only here in the Song (8:7).[21] The negative connotation explains why. The Song is about love, love that by its nature cannot be subdued or destroyed. Neither the separation of the couple (chapters 3 and 5) nor the beatings of the night guards (5:7) could extinguish the desire each had for the other. This is a picture of true love. The second line of 8:7 also uses words not found elsewhere in the Song: "rivers" (*něhārôt*) and "overflow" (*štp*). The terms of this line reinforce and emphasize the inability of the powerful forces of rivers and their torrent to flood and wash love away. Neither fire nor water, the two natural forces most feared in the ancient world, is able to threaten true love in the slightest. Pope follows Robert in noting the striking identity of some five terms in these two verses with those found in Isa. 43:2: "When you pass through the waters, I will be with you; and when you pass through the rivers, they will not sweep over you. When you walk through the fire, you will not be burned; the flames will not set you ablaze" (NIV).[22] The verse assures the believers (in exile) that whatever trials may come, they will not prevail against the mission God has given his people. The vocabulary connection with the Song suggests that the poet wishes to affirm the power of love over all obstacles. Insofar as these two passages are linked (not intentionally, but in a common identification as to what is invincible), then love here

---

19. Cf. Gen. 1:2; Isa. 51:9–10; Ps. 77:17–20 (77:16–19 Eng.); May, "Some," who documents the thirteenth-century Ugaritic Baal cycle myth where Baal's opponent is "Sea" (*ym*, Yam). See also Montgomery, "Ras Shamra," 271.

20. Murphy, "Dance," 119; idem, *Song*, 192.

21. It occurs as the Piel of *kbh*.

22. Pope, *Song*, 674; Robert, Tournay, and Feuillet, *Cantique*.

must be compared with the presence of God in overcoming all barriers to its achievement.

In this couplet, as in the second couplet of this verse, the term "love" (ʾahăbâ) occurs in the middle. It appears at the end of the first line, which is the longer of the two lines. This gives it the central position that it also occupies in 8:6, where it appeared once, at the end of the first half verse. Thus "love" stands out with its three appearances in these two verses. Among the eleven occurrences of the noun "love" in the Song, only here are three clustered together in two sequential verses. The only other cluster is found in 2:4–5 (the first two occurrences of the word), where it appears once in each verse. This is another example of a framing technique in which key words appear in the first two chapters and again in the last chapter of the Song.

The final couplet, in the second half of 8:7, describes the inestimable value of love. The sense is that not even every possession of a householder could suffice to buy love. It is a commodity that cannot be bartered or bought.[23] It is free but not cheap. There is no trade for it. Instead, its value is higher than all earthly possessions. Therefore, when it is found or acquired, it must be valued and preserved beyond anything else. That such an attempt to buy love would be despised is expressed emphatically by repeating the root with an infinitive absolute (bôz). It thus attests to what forms popular opinion: love has a greater value than anything else.

8:8–9. *Brothers (quoted by the female?): Their younger sister.* Verses 8–9 are best understood as spoken by the brothers, although it is possible that their words are here quoted by the female.[24] As I see the structure of these lines, v. 8 is composed of four lines, each having three words. In v. 9 there is an alternation of 3-4-3-4 in the number of words on each line, whereas v. 10 shows a greater unevenness (2-2-3-2), though there may be more order than is apparent at first. Nevertheless, this suggests a division between vv. 9 and 10. In v. 8, the first two lines have "sister" and "breast" as their first words. The initial position of these nouns suggests that the emphasis here for the first time reaches outward, beyond the couple's focus on each other. The commentators are in general agree-

---

23. LaCocque, *Romance*, 47, finds here a criticism of the tradition of arranged marriages. While it can be taken in that way, the expression has more to do with the value of love than with a negative evaluation of marriage customs.

24. Murphy, *Song*, 192. Bergant, *Song*, 100, summarizes some of the most important arguments: (1) use of the first-person plural forms; (2) the reference to the female as "young" or "little," and thus insignificant; (3) the description of the female's breasts contradicts the male's previous praise of them. For the view that the woman speaks of her younger sister in this passage, see Exum, "Literary," 75–76; Landy, "Beauty," 70. Cf. also Delitzsch, *Song*, 149–52.

ment that the speakers of vv. 8 and 9 are best understood as the siblings of the sister, in particular, her brothers. This forms an inclusio for the whole book since the brothers are also mentioned in 1:6.[25]

> [8]"We have a young sister,
> Who has no breasts,
> What we will do for our sister
> On the day when she is spoken for?

As in every culture and especially in the history of Israel (cf. Gen. 34; 2 Sam. 13:22–33), the brothers wish to protect the honor and chastity of their sister. They are concerned about their sister's youthfulness, that she is not yet ready for love. This concern is expressed by protests of her physical immaturity. Although the concern for her breasts may seem odd, the reference to the mother's nursing breasts in 8:1 may suggest that this line describes a concern for her physical maturity and for the continuation of the family. The final line, where a passive form of the common verb "to speak" (*yĕdubbar*) appears, uses a verbal form found elsewhere only in Ps. 87:3: "Glorious things are said of you, O city of God" (NIV).[26] In the context of Song 8:8, the verb may suggest a kind of debut or announcement of marriage for the younger sister. Hence the concern of this verse is to prepare the female for her experience of love, and the brothers by tradition claim a share in the patriarchal right to make the arrangements.[27]

> [9]If she is a wall,
> We will build a silver battlement on her.
> If she is a door,
> We will surround her with a cedar panel."

Verse 9 continues the concern of the brothers with pictures of defense and adornment. The metaphor of a wall describes an image of a city wall that protects the inhabitants. Here its contrast with the door in the second half of the verse may suggest that this describes two different situations, the first where the female resists (like a wall) and the second where she acquiesces (like a door).[28] In the first case, the brothers will

---

25. Cf. Elliott, *Literary*, 201.

26. The verb mentioned appears in the Pual stem. However, its form is characteristic of that used with a masculine subject, not a feminine one, as here. Is this another example of gender incongruity?

27. Cf. Gen. 24:29–60; 34:6–17; Judg. 21:22; Bergant, *Song*, 100–101.

28. Murphy, *Song*, 193, suggests that either both images imply resistance or, as argued here, the first involves resistance while the second implies willingness. This second option may be preferred because the image of a door regularly suggests access.

build a silver battlement along and on top of the wall. In addition to the added security that they wish to provide their sister, and so protect the honor of their family, there is also the beauty or adornment that this brings. Its translation from the metaphor to the reality of their sister's condition means that the brothers remain watchful to guarantee that her honor is not compromised and that her beauty is adorned in the best way possible. The same is true of the picture in the second part of the verse, but here the female is more inclined to yield to her lover's advances.[29] The cedar panels (*lûaḥ*) of the door would provide both protection and strength, giving the door increased security. It would add beauty to the entrance so that all who pass through would be impressed by the home. The same is true of the brothers' concern for their sister. They wish to protect her and to add to her beauty as well as to the nobility of their home.[30]

These concerns pale before the reader of the whole Song, who has received the Bible's most powerful and sustained description of physical desire between the two lovers. This, along with the lovers' absolute commitment to one another, renders the brothers' concern to marry off their sister as "a wry satire of patriarchal marriage customs."[31] And this it must be, because the freely acquired desire and commitment preempts and renders foolish all artificial contrivances to guarantee the honor of the family and particularly that of the brothers.

> [10]I am a wall,
> My breasts are like towers.
> So I have become in his eyes,
> As one who brings peace.

8:10. *Female: Her defense.* With the first two words of the Hebrew (*ʾănî ḥômāh*), the female agrees with her brothers' first proposition in v. 9. She is a wall. None is able to overcome her defenses, and her virtue is secure. The reference to her breasts, in the third word of the verse, also follows on the subject addressed by her brothers in v. 8. However, the metaphor of towers (*migdālôt*) introduces a new term here, seen earlier in the Song only two times. In 4:4 and 7:5 (7:4 Eng.), the female's neck is likened

29. For ancient Near Eastern evidence for the door as a symbol of a sexually available female, see Hicks, "Door."
30. Keel, *Song,* 278–79, understands the interpretation differently: "Thus, the siblings lend their support to their younger sister, who is not ready to go too quickly into a union planned by the parents or assumed by some admirer." On the opposite extreme, Murphy, *Song,* 199, understands this statement to refer to a sequestering of the daughter by the brothers.
31. Walsh, *Exquisite,* 124.

to a tower. Here the term is distinct from that used by the brothers in
8:9 to describe the "battlement" (singular) that they would build on her
wall. These towers may stand apart from the wall. However, whether
they are connected or not, they form independent defenses. The earlier
comparison of the female's neck with a tower was intended as praise for
its beauty. Now the towers evoke an image of strength that will not be
overcome. On the one hand this disputes the claim of the brothers that
their sister remains physically immature. On the other hand the breasts
come to symbolize defenses that the woman possesses. However, the
entire theme of breasts as used throughout the Song undermines this
picture. Far from a barrier between her and her lover, the breasts represent
their intimacy. The male lies between her breasts (1:13). He likens them
to fawns that appear delightful to watch (4:5; 7:4 [7:3 Eng.]). Finally, as
the focus of the third *wasf*, he imagines them as clusters of date fruits
that he wishes to take hold of (7:8–9 [7:7–8 Eng.]). These images suggest an erotic symbol for the breasts, one that serves to portray them as
something other than defenses. The discrepancy between the female's
statements to her brothers and the past implications of the images she
evokes provides the reason that the second half of the verse has been so
much disputed.[32] Only once before have the eyes of the male received
mention. In 5:12 the female described them as doves by streams of water.
This emphasized their beauty. Here in 8:10 his eyes provide a means to
describe the viewpoint or perspective of the male, anticipating the following line. The perception of the male, as understood by the female, is
not that she is a wall of defenses without compromise. Rather, he sees her
as one who brings peace. Does this mean that she is defenseless before
him?[33] That does not appear to be the meaning of this phrase, here or
elsewhere. Rather, it suggests the absence of conflict and the readiness
to pursue good relations. The female appears to suggest that she will not
avoid the pursuit of her lover; instead, she will be open to his advances.
Rather than using her powers to resist him, she intends to pursue their
mutual well-being and delight.

> [11]Solomon had a vineyard in Baal Hamon,
> He gave the vineyard to caretakers,
> Each would bring a thousand silver <shekels> for its fruit.
> [12]My vineyard is my own,
> The thousand are yours, Solomon,
> But two hundred are for those who take care of its fruit.

---

32. See Pope, *Song*, 684–86, for a review of some approaches to understanding the
final phrase.
33. Keel, *Song*, 279.

8:11–12. *Female: Solomon's vineyard.* The passage begins with the term "vineyard" (*kerem*), which appears three times in these two verses. Verse 11 begins with a narrative that provides the background for the speaker to assert the distinctive value of the speaker's own possession in v. 12. The picture of the vineyard has been repeatedly used as the epitome of both fruitfulness (1:14; 7:13 [7:12 Eng.]) and the female's body (2:15). Here the vineyard belongs to Solomon, a figure whose name is also repeated in these two verses. This figure, whose name is associated with the Song itself (1:1), also represents the wealthiest of persons in possession of tents (1:5), carriage (3:7, 9), and crown (3:11). Thus Solomon's possession of his vineyard means that he owns the finest and most fruitful of vines. Its location at Baal Hamon may refer to a site, Balamon (*Balamōn*), mentioned in Jdt. 8:3 as near Dothan.[34] The Beelamon (*Beelamōn*) of the LXX in Song 8:11 might refer to the same place, although its significance is unclear. Alternatively, the Hebrew term means lord or owner of "multitudes" (*hāmôn* has this meaning in Gen. 17:4–5; 2 Sam. 6:19; 2 Kings 7:13; Isa. 5:13) or of "wealth" (*hāmôn* has this meaning in Ezek. 29:19; 30:4; Eccles. 5:9 [5:10 Eng.]; 1 Chron. 29:16). That Solomon possessed great wealth is without doubt. The "multitude" might refer to his wives and concubines. It is ironic that the term for the "caretakers" to whom Solomon gives out the vineyard uses a root (*nṭr*) occurring elsewhere in the Song only in 1:6. There it describes how the female was sent out by her angry brothers to care for (*nṭr*) the vineyard while she did not take care of (*nṭr*) her own vineyard. As the comments on the text observe, this clearly refers to the woman herself, who has just expressed her own concern about her appearance. The "vineyard" refers both to the literal fruit-bearing vines and also to the female body and sexuality. Solomon's vineyard is also his harem. His seven hundred wives and three hundred concubines (1 Kings 11:3–10) are symbolized by a vineyard valued at one thousand shekels, a figure calculated by Delitzsch on the basis of Isa. 7:23.[35] The question of how the caretakers relate to this story is not so clear. Theories that Solomon rented out his harem or used the women for purposes of cultic prostitution extend beyond the picture portrayed here, nor are such theories in agreement with the tenor of the poem.[36] More likely, this reference anticipates v. 12 and the "two hundred" paid to the caretakers. Such a fifth or sixth of the produce (200 out of 1,000 or out of 1,200) is less than that given to a tenant farmer, according to the Talmud (between

---

34. Snaith, *Song*, 126–27; Longman, *Song*, 219. G. Carr, *Song*, 174, identifies it with the site of Belemoth (Khirbet Balama, modern Ibleam) in the Dothan Valley.

35. Delitzsch, *Song*, 157.

36. Cf. Pope, *Song*, 691, for this view.

a half and a fourth).[37] However, that is not the primary concern. Verse 11 prepares the reader for v. 12, in which the speaker claims sole possession of a vineyard, in contrast to Solomon, who with all his wealth must share the produce of his vineyard with his caretakers. The point thus is not who the caretakers are or how they relate to the metaphor of the harem. Instead, the vineyard is a picture of true love in which the couple shares one another's bodies in an exclusive commitment.

The remaining question of this passage concerns the identity of the speaker. Is it the male or the female? A one-to-one correspondence with Solomon leads some commentators to assume that the male is speaking. Nor is it pure chauvinism to assume this, because the fact that the lovers freely give and possess one another's bodies is not unique. It is a theme of marital love in the NT (1 Cor. 7). Nevertheless, this is not the best explanation. The association of the vineyard with the female is a constant theme throughout the use of the term in the Song. Therefore, the vineyard belongs to the female, the most natural and most frequent speaker throughout this Song. When the female claims the vineyard for herself (8:12), she claims that she alone takes care of it (contra 1:6) and that she alone opens her locked garden to the one whom she loves (cf. 4:12, 16).[38] The true and committed love of this couple thus contrasts dramatically with the harem of Solomon. He can have the great wealth and the appearance of great pleasure that is demonstrated by, and (supposedly) comes with, his harem. However, the female regards her body and her love as her own and of greater worth than all of Solomon's wealth. This theme, placed in the concluding verses of this great poem, is so important. The pleasures of sex, as great and praiseworthy as they are, do not become ends in themselves. All the joy, all the sensuality, is subsumed beneath the respect for the woman and her right to use her body in a committed relationship of love.

Longman argues that these verses, with their rejection of Solomon's polygamy, support monogamy.[39] Clearly, the power of the love that the couple shares transcends all monetary and other values of this world. The committed relationship here attains a joy and human delight that multiple sexual encounters (whether polygamous or promiscuous) can never achieve. As a note that follows upon the evaluation of love as a binding commitment (vv. 6–7), the female expresses the strength of that relationship by her refusal to substitute any earthly offer, however desirable it may seem at the time.

37. Gordis, *Song,* citing *b. B. Bat.* 110a; Pope, *Song,* 688.
38. Cf. Alden, "Song," who thinks the female here addresses her brothers, refusing their continued protection.
39. Longman, *Song,* 220.

> ¹³You who live in the gardens,
> With friends attending,
> Let me hear your voice.

8:13. *Male: Listening.* The initial feminine participle and the feminine suffix "your" on "your voice" attest to the addressee being the female. The male speaks these six words, with two words to each of the three lines, according to my division of the Hebrew poetry. The whole verse hinges on the final word, the only finite verb in the verse: *hašmî'înî* ("cause me to hear!" or "let me hear"). Since this is addressed to the female, it is assumed that the remainder of the verse is also addressed to her. Nor is this a surprising assumption, because the most common person used for most of the Song has been the second person ("you/your"). The male addresses his lover for the final time. Now he describes her as one who resides (*hayyôšebet*) in the gardens. The female used this term in 2:3 to describe how she delighted to sit (*yāšabtî*) in the shade of her lover as beside an apple tree. The male had earlier described his lover as a garden (*gan*; 4:12; 5:1) and as a fountain in the garden. The female had invited him to come and taste the fruits of the garden, a metaphor for the sexual delights of her body (4:15–16; 6:2). So for the male to describe her as residing in a garden suggests that the delights of her garden are now made permanent for him. In 1:7 the female had referred to the flocks of her lover's "friends," using the same term as here (*ḥăbērîm*), where it now describes the female's friends in attendance. The masculine plural may suggest all males, perhaps reflecting that the shepherd's companions of 1:7 have now become acquaintances of the female. However, it more likely includes both men and women. The female has true friends, more real than all Solomon's wealth could buy. She also has friends beyond her own household, so that her love for the speaker is not one of desperation or dependency, but a self-giving expression that arises out of a well-balanced emotional life. The description of the friends "attending" implies more than associates. The term describes those who listen attentively.[40] These friends are listeners! Interestingly, it occurs only here in the Song. Perhaps this is because the lovers, in their passion and desire for one another, would naturally listen to each other. Here, however, the friends of the female are described as true friends, those who listen and know her heart. Among them would certainly be the daughters of Jerusalem and perhaps also the young men with whom she worked while tending the garden where her brothers sent her (1:6). Perhaps the scene is a noisy one, with many speakers. The male longs to hear the voice of his lover. This recalls the sound of the doves cooing in 2:12, where it is a

40. Here the Hiphil participle *maqšîbîm* is used.

delight to listen to them. More closely, however, is the identical form of the verb and its object ("your voice") that the male uses in 2:14, where he likens her to the dove of just two verses earlier. There as here he begs to hear his lover's sweet voice. The image evoked by these final words of the male may be that of fear of being shut out of the female's circle of friends. More likely, however, he wishes to hear her voice rather than the voices of her friends around her. He hints that he longs for them to be alone so that their passion may be consummated.

> 14Flee my lover,
> Become like a gazelle,
> Or a young stag upon spice mountains.

8:14. *Female: Departure.* As the female responds, her first word demonstrates agreement with her partner. She counsels him: "Flee" (*bĕraḥ*). As the context of the Song and of this verse in particular suggests, she does not wish him to depart from her. She wishes to be with him forever. Why then does she use a verb that generally carries the sense of running away? Perhaps because she too has listened so carefully to his words in the preceding verse. As though to show this, she takes the term for "companion" (*ḥbr*) and interchanges the root consonants to obtain the verb "flee" (*brḥ*). She thereby demonstrates careful acknowledgment of his words and her agreement to his suggestion. The Song then closes with a refrain whose words are almost the duplicate of those in 2:17 (cf. also 2:8–9). Here, however, the hills are no longer those of Bether, a place known to exist not far from Jerusalem. Instead, they are the hills of spice, a term that returns us to the erotic passions of the couple and their complementary descriptions. The female's perfume (4:10) and especially her "garden" (4:12–16; 5:1; 6:2) are of spice. The male's cheeks are likened to beds of spice (5:13). Thus the female counsels the male to depart, but not for a distant land.[41] Instead, he is to depart from the noise and commotion of the surrounding society and to taste her own mountains of spice. As he "flees," so she "flees." But it is only so that they may join one another in the privacy of their own love.

Theological Implications

The brief poetic declaration of 8:6–7 on the value of love culminates the entire book and provides a direct correlation with the NT emphasis

41. See Poulssen, "Vluchtwegen," for a review of possible interpretations of where to flee.

on love. There is a one-for-one correlation throughout the Song between the eleven appearances of the word for "love" (ʾahăbâ) in the Hebrew text and the Greek rendering of it in the LXX as *agapē*. This term forms the basis for the NT understanding of the amazing love that God has given to believers. This is most emphatically and consistently argued in the works ascribed to the apostle John: John 13:35; 15:9, 10, 13; 17:26; 1 John 2:5, 15; 3:1, 16, 17; 4:7, 8, 9, 10, 12, 16 (2x), 17, 18 (2x); 5:3; 2 John 3, 6; 3 John 6; and perhaps Rev. 2:4 and 19. In Rom. 8:35–39 Paul proclaims the excellence of God's love in terms of its inability to be overcome by any earthly force. The surpassing value of this love, which abides forever, is nowhere more eloquently stated than in 1 Cor. 13. Those who would follow Jesus as his disciples require this love alone.[42] Hence the worth of the couple's love, based on erotic experience and commitment, establishes the foundation for the Song's understanding of a love whose basis, experience, and commitment is the all-surpassing love of God (cf. Hosea 11:8–9). This provides the resource for the understanding of love that the NT apostolic writers use.

The final verses of the Song culminate in a confession of the power of love. It is stronger than any force in the universe, and it alone can vie with death and perhaps extend beyond it (1 Cor. 13). The twin emphases of commitment and desire continue to the end of the Song, and the whole remains open-ended. Love with commitment allows a freedom for the couple to play, to explore their desires with each other's bodies and persons. They do so without fear of the loss of their partner. Love burns with the passion of desire. This desire is not satisfied but continues to grow stronger and stronger. It is the secret of love and the secret of life, whether human or divine. As the couple's desire grows with their love, so the believer's desire for God enflames the divine love that knows no consummation in this world, but becomes only better and better (Deut. 6:4–9; Matt. 22:37–40; Mark 12:30–33; Luke 10:27).

The Song thus concludes, not with an erotic ecstasy of consummated love, but with an awareness of separation and a longed-for reunion. As Bergant notes so eloquently, this characterizes the nature of human love: "Human love knows no definitive consummation, no absolute fulfillment. Loving relationships are never complete; they are always ongoing, always reaching for more."[43]

It is the finitude of human love that points toward something greater and more complete. From a canonical perspective, this love points to-

---

42. Cf. Luke 14:33: "In the same way, any of you who does not give up everything he has cannot be my disciple" (NIV).

43. Bergant, *Song*, 105; cf. Munro, *Spikenard*, 89.

ward the consummation of all yearnings for a more complete love, a fulfillment that is reached in the marriage of Christ and his Bride:

> "Let us rejoice and be glad and give him glory! For the wedding of the Lamb has come, and his bride has made herself ready. Fine linen, bright and clean, was given her to wear." (Fine linen stands for the righteous acts of the saints.) Then the angel said to me, "Write: 'Blessed are those who are invited to the wedding supper of the Lamb!'" And he added, "These are the true words of God." (Rev. 19:7–9 NIV)

This scene is nothing less than a witness to the irrevocable power of love between Christ and his people, something stronger than death or any other power known:[44] "For I am convinced that neither death nor life, neither angels nor demons, neither the present nor the future, nor any powers, neither height nor depth, nor anything else in all creation, will be able to separate us from the love of God that is in Christ Jesus our Lord" (Rom. 8:38–39 NIV).

44. Cf. Provan, *Song*, 378.

Bibliography

Aartun, Kjell. "Textüberlieferung und vermeintliche Belege der Konjunktion *pV* im Alten Testament." *Ugarit-Forschungen* 10 (1978): 1–13.

Abécassis, Armand. "Espaces de lecture du Cantique des Cantiques en contexte juif." Pages 185–96 in *Les nouvelles voies de l'exégèse: En lisant le Cantique des cantiques*. Edited by J. Nieuviarts and P. Debergé. Paris: Cerf, 2002.

Albrektson, Bertil. "Singing or Pruning?" *Bible Translator* 47 (1996): 109–14.

———. "Sjunga eller beskära? Om översättningsproblem i Höga visan." *Svensk Exegetisk Årsbok* 63 (1998): 61–69.

Albright, William Foxwell. "Archaic Survivals in the Text of Canticles." Pages 1–7 in *Hebrew and Semitic Studies in the Text of Canticles*. Edited by D. Winton Thomas and W. D. McHardy. Oxford: Clarendon, 1963.

———. "The Syro-Mesopotamian God Šulmân-Eshmûn and Related Figures." *Archiv für Orientforschungen* 7 (1931–32): 164–69.

Alden, Robert L. "Song of Songs 8:12a: Who Said It?" *Journal of Evangelical Theological Society* 31 (1988): 271–78.

Alter, Robert. *The Art of Biblical Poetry*. New York: Basic Books, 1985.

Andiñach, Pablo R. "Critica de Salomón en el Cantar de los Cantares." *Revista biblica* 53 (1991): 129–56.

Apponius. *Commentaire sur le Cantique des cantiques*. Translated by Bernard de Vregille and Louis Neyrand. 3 vols. La Scuola Cattolica 420, 421, 430. Paris: Cerf, 1997–98.

Araújo, Hermínio. "O corpo humano en questao: Algumas reflexoes biblio-teológicas y éticas." *Itinerarium* 43 (1997): 441–93.

Audet, J. P. "Le sens du Cantique des Cantiques." *Revue biblique* 62 (1955): 197–221.

Auwers, Jean-Marie. "Lectures patristiques du Cantique des cantiques." Pages 129–57 in *Les nouvelles voies de l'exégèse: En lisant le Cantique des cantiques*. Edited by J. Nieuviarts and P. Debergé. Paris: Cerf, 2002.

Baildam, John D. *Paradisal Love: Johann Gottfried Herder and the Song of Songs*. Journal for the Study of the Old Testament: Supplement Series 298. Sheffield: Sheffield Academic Press, 1999.

Balthasar, Hans Urs von. *Seeing the Form*. Vol. 1 of *The Glory of the Lord: A Theological Aesthetics*. Translated by J. Riches. Edited by J. Fessio and J. Riches. San Francisco: Ignatius; New York: Crossroad, 1983.

Barbiero, Gianni. "Die Liebe der Töchter Jerusalems: Hld 3,10b MT im Kontext von 3,6–11." *Biblische Zeitschrift* 39 (1995): 96–104.

———. "Die 'Wagen meines edlen Volkes' (Hld 6,12): Eine strukturelle Analyse." *Biblica* 78 (1997): 174–89.

Bardski, Krzysztof. "Świątynia Salomona w Targumie do Pieśni nad pieśniami 3,7–5,1." *Collectanea theologica* 70/2 (2000): 79–92.

Barth, Karl. *Church Dogmatics*. Vols. 3/1 and 3/2. Edinburgh: Clark, 1958–59.

Bekkenkamp, Jonneke, and Fokkelien van Dijk. "The Canon of the Old Testament and Women's Cultural Traditions." Pages 91–108 in *Historiography of Women's Cultural Traditions*. Edited by M. Meijer and J. Schaap. Dordrecht: Foris, 1987. Reprinted as pages 67–85 in *A Feminist Companion to the Song of Songs*. Edited by A. Brenner. Feminist Companion to the Bible 1. Sheffield: Sheffield Academic Press, 1993.

Bergant, Diane. "My Beloved Is Mine and I Am His (Song 2:16): The Song of Songs and Honor and Shame." *Semeia* 68 (1994): 23–40.

———. *The Song of Songs*. Berit Olam. Collegeville, MN: Liturgical Press, 2001.

———. "The Song of Songs: An Introduction." *Bible Today* 36 (1998): 140–46.

Bernard of Clairvaux. *On the Song of Songs I*. Translated by K. Walsh. Works of Bernard of Clairvaux 2. Spencer, MA: Cistercian Publications, 1971.

———. *On the Song of Songs II*. Translated by K. Walsh. Works of Bernard of Clairvaux 3. Kalamazoo, MI: Cistercian Publications; London: Mowbray, 1976.

Biggs, Robert D. *Šà.zi.ga, Ancient Mesopotamian Potency Incantations*. Texts from Cuneiform Sources 2. Locust Valley, NY: Augustin, 1967.

Black, Fiona C. "Beauty or the Beast? The Grotesque Body in the Song of Songs." *Biblical Interpretation* 8 (2000): 302–23.

———. "Unlikely Bedfellows: Allegorical and Feminist Readings of Song of Songs 7:1–8." Pages 104–29 in *The Song of Songs*. Edited by A. Brenner and C. R. Fontaine. A Feminist Companion to the Bible, 2nd series, 6. Sheffield: Sheffield Academic Press, 2000.

Bloom, Harold, ed. *The Song of Songs*. Modern Critical Interpretations. New York: Chelsea, 1988.

Blumenthal, D. R. "Where God Is Not: The Book of Esther and the Song of Songs." *Judaism* 173 (1995): 80–90.

Blutting, Klara. "Go Your Way: Women Rewrite the Scriptures (Song of Songs 2:8–14)." Pages 142–51 in *The Song of Songs*. Edited by A. Brenner and C. R. Fontaine. A Feminist Companion to the Bible, 2nd series, 6. Sheffield: Sheffield Academic Press, 2000.

Boer, R. "The Second Coming: Repetition and Insatiable Desire in the Song of Songs." *Biblical Interpretation* 8 (2000): 276–301.

Bosshard-Nepustil, E. "Zu Struktur und Sachprofil des Hohelieds." *Biblische Notizen* 81 (1996): 45–71.

Bossina, Luciano. "I gemelli di Gazzella (Ct 4,5)." *Revista degli studi orientali* 73 (1999): 1–8.

Boyarin, D. "The Song of Songs: Lock or Key? Intertextuality, Allegory, and Midrash." Pages 214–30 in *The Book and the Text: The Bible and Literary Theory.* Edited by R. Schwartz. Oxford: Blackwell, 1990.

Braun, Joachim. *Music in Ancient Israel/Palestine: Archaeological, Written, and Comparative Sources.* Translated by D. W. Stott. Grand Rapids: Eerdmans, 2002.

Brenner, Athalya. "Aromatics and Perfumes in the Song of Songs." *Journal for the Study of the Old Testament* 25 (1983): 75–81.

———. "'Come Back, Come Back the Shulammite' (Song of Songs 7.1–10): A Parody of the *Waṣf* Genre." Pages 251–76 in *On Humour and the Comic in the Hebrew Bible.* Edited by A. Brenner and Y. T. Radday. Sheffield: Almond, 1990. Reprinted as pages 234–57 in *A Feminist Companion to the Song of Songs.* Edited by A. Brenner. Feminist Companion to the Bible 1. Sheffield: Sheffield Academic Press, 1993.

———. "*Dôdî ṣaḥ wᵉᵓdôm* (Cant 5:10–11)." *Beth Mikra* 27 (1981–82): 168–73. [In Hebrew.]

———. *The Israelite Woman: Social Role and Literary Type in Biblical Narrative.* Biblical Seminar 2. Sheffield: JSOT Press, 1985.

———. "A Note on Bat-Rabbîm (Song of Songs vii 5)." *Vetus Testamentum* 42 (1992): 113–15.

———. *The Song of Songs.* Old Testament Guides. Sheffield: Sheffield Academic Press, 1989.

———. "To See Is to Assume: Whose Love Is Celebrated in the Song of Songs?" *Biblical Interpretation* 1 (1993): 265–84.

———, ed. *A Feminist Companion to the Song of Songs.* Feminist Companion to the Bible 1. Sheffield: Sheffield Academic Press, 1993.

Brin, Gershon. "The Superlative in the Hebrew Bible: Additional Cases." *Vetus Testamentum* 42 (1992): 115–18.

Broyde, M. J. "Defilement of the Hands, Canonization of the Bible, and the Special Status of Esther, Ecclesiastes, and Song of Songs." *Judaism* 173 (1995): 65–79.

Budde, Karl. "Das Hohelied erklärt." Pages ix–48 in *Die fünf Megillot (Das Hohelied, Das Buch Ruth, Die Klagelieder, Der Prediger, Das Buch Esther).* Edited by K. Budde, A. Bertholet, and D. G. Wildeboer. Kurzer Hand-Kommentar zum Alten Testament 6. Freiburg: Mohr, 1898.

Burns, Camilla. "Human Love: The Silent Voice of God." *Bible Today* 36 (1998): 159–63.

Burrows, M. S. "Foundations for an Erotic Christology: Bernard of Clairvaux on Jesus as 'Tender Lover.'" *Anglican Theological Review* 80 (1998): 477–91.

Buzy, D. "La composition littéraire du Cantique des cantiques." *Revue biblique* 49 (1940): 169–84.

Cainion, I. J. "An Analogy of the Song of Songs and Genesis Chapters Two and Three." *Scandinavian Journal of the Old Testament* 14 (2000): 219–59.

255

Calloud, J. "Esquisse: Propositions une interpretation raisonnée du Cantique des cantiques." *Sémiotique et Bible* 65 (1992): 43–60.

Callow, John. "Units and Flow in the Song of Songs 1:2–2:6." Pages 462–88 in *Biblical Hebrew and Discourse Linguistics.* Edited by R. D. Bergen. Winona Lake, IN: Eisenbrauns; Dallas: Summer Institute of Linguistics, 1994.

Cantwell, L. "The Allegory of the Canticle of Canticles." *Scripture* 16 (1964): 76–93.

Carr, David McLain. "Ancient Sexuality and Divine Eros: Rereading the Bible through the Lens of the Song of Songs." *Union Seminary Quarterly Review* 53 (2000): 1–18.

———. *The Erotic Word: Sexuality, Spirituality, and the Bible.* Oxford: Oxford University Press, 2003.

———. "Falling in Love with God." *Bible Today* 36 (1998): 153–58.

———. "Gender and the Shaping of Desire in the Song of Songs and Its Interpretations." *Journal of Biblical Literature* 119 (2000): 233–48.

———. "The Song of Songs as a Microcosm of the Canonization and Decanonization Process." Pages 173–89 in *Canonization and Decanonization.* Edited by A. van der Kooij and K. van der Toorn. Leiden: Brill, 1998.

Carr, G. Lloyd. "The Old Testament Love Songs and Their Use in the New Testament." *Journal of the Evangelical Theological Society* 24 (1981): 97–105.

———. *The Song of Solomon: An Introduction and Commentary.* Tyndale Old Testament Commentaries. Leicester, UK: Inter-Varsity; Downers Grove, IL: InterVarsity, 1984.

Charbel, A. "Come tradurre '*ʾeškōl hak-kōfer*' (Cant. 1,14)?" *Bibbia e oriente* 20 (1978): 61–64.

Childs, Brevard S. *Introduction to the Old Testament as Scripture.* Philadelphia: Fortress, 1979.

Clines, David J. A. "Why Is There a Song of Songs and What Does It Do to You If You Read It?" *Jin Dao* 1 (1994): 1–27.

Cogan, Mordecai. "'. . . From the Peak of Amanah.'" *Israel Exploration Journal* 34 (1984): 255–59.

Cooper, Jerald S. "New Cuneiform Parallels to the Song of Songs." *Journal of Biblical Literature* 90 (1971): 157–62.

Cottini, Valentino. "Linguaggio erotico nel Cantico dei Cantici e in Proverbi." *Liber annuus Studii biblici franciscani* 40 (1990): 25–45.

Dahood, Mitchell. "Canticle 7,9 and UT 52, 61: A Question of Method." *Biblica* 57 (1976): 109–10.

———. "Hebrew *tamrûrîm* and *tîmᵃrôt.*" *Orientalia* 46 (1977): 385.

———. "Philological Observations on Five Biblical Texts." *Biblica* 63 (1982): 390–94.

Danby, Herbert, trans. *The Mishnah.* London: Oxford University Press, 1933.

Davidson, Robert. *Ecclesiastes and the Song of Solomon.* Daily Study Bible Series. Louisville: Westminster John Knox, 1986.

Deckers, M. "The Structure of the Song of Songs and the Centrality of *Nepeš* (6.12)." Pages 172–96 in *A Feminist Companion to the Song of Songs.* Edited by A. Brenner. Feminist Companion to the Bible 1. Sheffield: JSOT Press, 1993.

Delitzsch, Franz. *Proverbs, Ecclesiastes, Song of Solomon*. Translated by M. G. Easton. Vol. 6 of *Commentary on the Old Testament in Ten Volumes*. Reprint, Grand Rapids: Eerdmans, 1975.

Dempsey, Carol J. "Metaphorical Language and the Expression of Love." *Bible Today* 36 (1998): 164–69.

Dietrich, Manfried, and Ingo Kottspier, eds. *"Und Mose schrieb dieses Lied auf."* Alter Orient und Altes Testament 250. Münster: Ugarit-Verlag, 1998.

Dirksen, P. B. "Song of Songs iii 6–7." *Vetus Testamentum* 39 (1989): 219–25.

Di Vito, Robert A. "Old Testament Anthropology and the Construction of Personal Identity." *Catholic Biblical Quarterly* 61 (1999): 217–38.

Dobbs-Allsopp, F. W. "Ingressive *qwm* in Biblical Hebrew." *Zeitschrift für Althebräistik* 8 (1995): 31–54.

Dorsey, David A. "Literary Structuring in the Song of Songs." *Journal for the Study of the Old Testament* 46 (1990): 81–96.

Driver, G. R. "Lice in the Bible." *Palestine Exploration Quarterly* (1974): 159–60.

———. "Supposed Arabisms in the Old Testament." *Journal of Biblical Literature* 55 (1936): 101–20.

Driver, S. R. *Introduction to the Literature of the Old Testament*. Cambridge: Cambridge University Press, 1913.

Dünzl, Franz. *Braut und Bräutigam: Die Auslegung des Canticum durch Gregor von Nyssa*. Beiträge zur Geschichte der biblischen Exegese 32. Tübingen: Mohr (Siebeck), 1993.

Edmée, Sister. "The Song of Songs and the Cutting of Roots." *Anglican Theological Review* 80 (1998): 547–61.

Ehrlich, A. B. *Randglossen zur hebräischen Bibel: Textkritisches, sprachliches und sachliches*. 7 vols. Leipzig: Hinrichs, 1908–14.

Eichner, Jens, and Andreas Scherer. "'Die Teiche von Hesbon': Eine exegetisch-archäologische Glosse zu Cant 7.5ba." *Biblische Notizen* 109 (2001): 10–14.

Elliott, M. Timothea. "Ethics and Aesthetics in the Song of Songs." *Tyndale Bulletin* 45 (1994): 137–52.

———. *The Literary Unity of the Canticle*. Europäische Hochschulschriften, series 23, Theology 371. Frankfurt am Main: Peter Lang, 1989.

Emerton, John A. "Lice or a Veil in the Song of Songs 1.7?" Pages 127–40 in *Understanding Poets and Prophets: Essays in Honour of George Wishart Anderson*. Edited by A. Graeme Auld. Journal for the Study of the Old Testament: Supplement Series 152. Sheffield: JSOT Press, 1993.

Emmerson, Grace I. "The Song of Songs: Mystification, Ambiguity and Humour." Pages 97–111 in *Crossing Boundaries: Essays in Biblical Interpretation in Honour of Michael D. Goulder*. Edited by S. E. Porter, P. Joyce, and D. E. Orton. Leiden: Brill, 1994.

Exum, J. Cheryl. "Assertive ʾal in Canticles 1,6?" *Biblica* 62 (1981): 416–19.

———. "Developing Strategies of Feminist Criticism/Developing Strategies for Commentating the Song of Songs." Pages 206–49 in *Auguries: The Jubilee Volume of the Sheffield Department of Biblical Studies*. Edited by D. J. A. Clines and S. D. Moore. Journal for the Study of the Old Testament: Supplement Series 269. Sheffield: Sheffield Academic Press, 1998.

———. "In the Eye of the Beholder: Wishing, Dreaming, and *Double Entendre* in the Song of Songs." Pages 71–86 in *The Labour of Reading: Desire, Alienation, and Biblical Interpretation.* Edited by F. C. Black, R. Boer, and E. Runions. Semeia Studies 36. Atlanta: Society of Biblical Literature, 1999.

———. "A Literary and Structural Analysis of the Song of Songs." *Zeitschrift für die alttestamentliche Wissenschaft* 85 (1973): 47–79.

———. "Ten Things Every Feminist Should Know about the Song of Songs." Pages 24–35 in *The Song of Songs.* Edited by A. Brenner and C. R. Fontaine. A Feminist Companion to the Bible, 2nd series, 6. Sheffield: Sheffield Academic Press, 2000.

Falk, Marcia. *Love Lyrics from the Bible. A Translation and Literary Study of the Song of Songs.* Bible and Literature Series 4. Sheffield: Almond, 1982.

Feuillet, André, *Le Cantique des cantiques.* Paris: Cerf, 1953.

———. "La double insertion du Cantique des cantiques dans la vie de la communauté chrétienne et dans la tradition religieuse de l'Ancien Testament." *Divinitas* 35 (1991): 5–18.

———. "Le drama d'amour du Cantique des cantiques remis en son contexte prophétique." *Nova et vetera* 49 (1987): 81–127.

———. "La formule d'appartenance mutuelle (ii,16) et les interprétations divergentes du Cantique des cantiques." *Revue biblique* 68 (1961): 5–38.

———. "Perspectives nouvelles à propos de l'intérpretation du Cantique des cantiques." *Civitas Vaticana* 34 (1990): 203–19.

———. "'S'asseoir a l'ombre' de l'époux (Os., xiv,8a et Cant., ii,3)." *Revue biblique* 78 (1971): 391–405.

Fleming, Daniel. "Mari's Large Public Tent and the Priestly Tent Sanctuary." *Vetus Testamentum* 50 (2000): 484–98.

Fokkelman, J. P. *Reading Biblical Poetry: An Introductory Guide.* Louisville: Westminster John Knox, 2001.

Foster, John L., trans. *Hymns, Prayers, and Songs: An Anthology of Ancient Egyptian Lyric Poetry.* SBL Writings from the Ancient World Series 8. Atlanta: Scholars Press, 1995.

Fox, Michael V. "Scholia to Canticles (*i 4b, ii 4, 14bα, iv 3, v 8, vi 12*)." *Vetus Testamentum* 33 (1983): 199–206.

———. *The Song of Songs and the Ancient Egyptian Love Songs.* Madison: University of Wisconsin Press, 1985.

Fox, Michael V., and Bezalel Porten. "Unsought Discoveries: Qohelet 7:23–8:1a." *Hebrew Studies* 19 (1978): 26–38.

Frettloch, Magadelene Luise. "O Amor é forte como a morte: Uma leitura de Cânticos dos Cânticos com ohlos de mulher." *Fragmenta de cultura* 12 (2002): 633–42.

Frolov, Serge. "No Return for Shulammite: Reflections on Cant 7,1." *Zeitschrift für die alttestamentliche Wissenschaft* 110 (1998): 256–58.

Gall, A. von. "Jeremias 43,12 und das Zeitwort ʿṭh." *Zeitschrift für die alttestamentliche Wissenschaft* 24 (1904): 105–21.

Garbini, Giovanni. *Cantico dei cantici: Testo, traduzione, note e commento.* Biblica: Testi e studi 2. Brescia: Paideia, 1992.

―――. "Note linguistico-filologiche (*Cantico* vi,9; *Salmo* xx,6; *1 Re* vii,6)." *Henoch* 4 (1982): 163–73.

―――. "Il significato del 'Cantico dei Cantici.'" Pages 9–23 in *Realtà et allegoria nell'interpretazione del Cantico dei Cantici.* Genoa: Facoltà di lettere, 1989.

Garrett, Duane A. *Proverbs, Ecclesiastes, Song of Songs.* New American Commentary 14. Nashville: Broadman, 1993.

Gaster, T. H. "Canticles i.4." *Expository Times* 72 (1960–61): 195.

―――. "What 'The Song of Songs' Means." *Commentary* 13 (1952): 316–22.

Gerleman, Gillis. *Ruth. Das Hohelied.* Biblischer Kommentar, Altes Testament 18. Neukirchen-Vluyn: Neukirchener Verlag, 1965.

Ginsburg, C. D. *The Song of Songs and Coheleth (Commonly Called the Book of Ecclesiastes). Translated from the Original Hebrew with a Commentary, Historical and Critical.* 2 vols. London, 1857–61. Reprinted with a new prolegomenon by S. H. Blank. 2 vols. in 1. New York: Ktav, 1970.

Gledhill, Tom. *The Message of the Song of Songs: The Lyrics of Love.* Bible Speaks Today. Leicester, UK: Inter-Varsity; Downers Grove, IL: InterVarsity, 1994.

Glickman, S. C. *A Song for Lovers: Lessons for Lovers in the Song of Solomon.* Leicester, UK: Inter-Varsity, 1976.

Godet, F. "The Interpretation of the Song of Songs." Pages 151–82 in *Classical Evangelical Essays in Old Testament Interpretation.* Edited by W. C. Kaiser Jr. Grand Rapids: Baker, 1972.

Goitein, S. D. "*Ayumma Kannidgalot* (Song of Songs vi.10): 'Splendid like the Brilliant Stars.'" *Journal of Semitic Studies* 10 (1965): 220–21.

―――. "The Song of Songs: A Female Composition." Pages 58–66 in *A Feminist Companion to the Song of Songs.* Edited by A. Brenner. Feminist Companion to the Bible 1. Sheffield: Sheffield Academic Press, 1993. Reprinted from pages 301–7, 316–17 in *ʿIyunim ba-Mikra* [Studies in the Bible]. By S. D. Goitein. Tel Aviv: Yavneh, 1957. Translated from Hebrew by A. Brenner.

Goldin, J. *The Song at the Sea.* New Haven: Yale University Press, 1971.

Gordis, Robert. "The Root דגל in the Song of Songs." *Journal of Biblical Literature* 88 (1969): 203–4.

―――. *The Song of Songs and Lamentations: A Study, Modern Translation, and Commentary.* 2nd edition. New York: Ktav, 1974.

Gordon, Cyrus. "Asymmetric Janus Parallelism." *Eretz-Israel* 16 (1982): 26*–33*.

Görg, M. "'Kanäle' oder 'Zweige' in Hld 4,13?" *Biblische Notizen* 72 (1993): 20–23.

―――. "Lexikalisches zu HL 5,11." *Biblische Notizen* 21 (1983): 26–27.

―――. "Eine Salbenbezeichnung in HL 1,3." *Biblische Notizen* 38/39 (1987): 36–38.

―――. "Die 'Sänfte Salomos' nach HL 3,9f." *Biblische Notizen* 18 (1982): 15–25.

―――. "'Travestie' im Hohen Lied: Eine kritische Betrachtung am Beispiel von HL 1,5f." *Biblische Notizen* 21 (1983): 101–15.

Goulder, Michael D. *The Song of Fourteen Songs.* Journal for the Study of the Old Testament: Supplement Series 36. Sheffield: JSOT Press, 1986.

Graetz, Heinrich. *Shir has-shirim = Schir ha-schirim, oder, Das salomonische Hohenlied: Übersetzt und kritisch Erläutert.* Vienna: Braumüller, 1871.

Grave, Cecilia. "Northwest Semitic Ṣapānu in a Break-up of an Egyptian Stereotype Phrase in EA 147." *Orientalia* 51 (1982): 161–82.

Greenfield, Jonas C. Review of D. W. Thomas and W. D. McHardy, eds., *Hebrew and Semitic Studies Presented to Godfrey Rolles Driver. Journal of the American Oriental Society* 85 (1965): 256–58.

Grossberg, D. "Canticles 3:10 in the Light of a Homeric Analogue and Biblical Poetics." *Biblical Theology Bulletin* 11 (1981): 74–76.

———. *Centripetal and Centrifugal Structures in Hebrew Poetry.* Atlanta: Scholars Press, 1989.

———. "Sexual Desire: Abstract and Concrete." *Hebrew Studies* 22 (1981): 59–60.

———. "Two Kinds of Sexual Relationships in the Hebrew Bible." *Hebrew Studies* 35 (1994): 7–25.

Gruber, Mayer I. "Ten Dance-Derived Expressions in the Hebrew Bible." *Biblica* 62 (1981): 341–45.

Hallo, William W. "'As the Seal upon Thy Heart': Glyptic Roles in the Biblical World." *Bible Review* 1 (1985): 20–27.

———. "For Love Is Strong as Death." *Journal of the Ancient Near Eastern Society of Columbia University* 22 (1993): 45–50.

Harper, Andrew. *The Song of Solomon with Introduction and Notes.* Cambridge Bible for Schools and Colleges. Cambridge: Cambridge University Press, 1907.

Haupt, Paul. *Biblische Liebeslieder: Das sogenannte Hohelied Salomos.* Leipzig: Hinrichs, 1907.

Heim, Knut M. *Like Grapes of Gold Set in Silver: An Interpretation of Proverbial Clusters in Proverbs 10:1–22:16.* Beihefte zur Zeitschrift für die alttestamentliche Wissenschaft 273. Berlin: de Gruyter, 2001.

Hermann, Alfred. *Altägyptische Liebesdichtung.* Wiesbaden: Harrasowitz, 1959.

Hess, Richard S. *Amarna Personal Names.* Winona Lake, IN: Eisenbrauns, 1993.

———. "Eden—a Well-Watered Place." *Bible Review* 7/6 (December 1991): 28–33.

———. "Equality with and without Innocence: Genesis 1–3." Pages 79–95 in *Discovering Biblical Equality: Complementarity without Hierarchy.* Edited by Ronald W. Pierce, Rebecca M. Groothuis, and Gordon D. Fee. Downers Grove, IL: InterVarsity, 2004.

———. "*Rēaʿ.*" Pages 1144–49 in vol. 3 of *The New International Dictonary of Old Testament Theology and Exegesis.* Edited by W. VanGemeren et al. Grand Rapids: Zondervan, 1997.

Hicks, R. Lansing. "The Door of Love." Pages 153–58 in *Love and Death in the Ancient Near East: Essays in Honor of Marvin H. Pope.* Edited by J. H. Marks and R. M. Good. Guilford, CT: Four Quarters, 1987.

Holman, Jan. "A Fresh Attempt at Understanding the Imagery of Canticles 3:6–11." Pages 303–9 in *"Lasset uns Brücken bauen . . .": Collected Commu-*

nications to the XVth Congress of the Organization for the Study of the Old Testament. Edited by Klaus-Dietrich Schunck and Matthias Augustin. Beiträge zur Erforschung des Alten Testaments und des antiken Judentums 42. Frankfurt am Main: Lang, 1998.

―――. "Pleidooi voor een onderaards Hooglied: Resultaten van een cultureel-antropologische lezing." Tijdschrift voor theologie 37 (1997): 113–31.

Honeyman, A. M. "Two Contributions to Canaanite Toponymy." Journal of Theological Studies 50 (1949): 50–52.

Horine, Steven C. Interpretive Images in the Song of Songs: From Wedding Chariots to Bridal Chambers. Studies in the Humanities 55. New York: Lang, 2001.

Horst, Friedrich. "Die Formen des althebräischen Liebesliedes." Pages 43–54 in Orientalische Studien: Enno Littmann zu seinem 60. Geburtstag am 16. September 1933. Edited by R. Paret. Leiden: Brill, 1935. Reprinted as pages 176–87 in Gottes Recht: Gesammelte Studien zum Recht im Alten Testament [von] Friedrich Horst, Aus Anlass der Vollendung seines 65. Lebensjahres. Edited by H. W. Wolff. Munich: Kaiser, 1961.

Hostetter, Edwin. "Mistranslation in Cant 1:5." Andrews University Seminary Studies 34 (1996): 35–36.

Hunt, Patrick N. "Subtle Paronomasia in the Canticum Canticorum: Hidden Treasures of the Superlative Poet." Pages 147–54 in Goldene Äpfel in silbernen Schalen: Collected Communications to the XIIIth Congress of the International Organization for the Study of the Old Testament. Edited by Klaus-Dietrich Schunck and Matthias Augustin. Beiträge zur Erforschung des Alten Testaments und des antiken Judentums 20. Frankfurt am Main: Lang, 1992.

Hunter, Jannie H. "The Song of Protest: Reassessing the Song of Songs." Journal for the Study of the Old Testament 90 (2000): 109–24.

Hurvitz, Avi. "Toward a Precise Definition of the Term אמון in Prov. 8:30." Pages 647–50 in The Bible in the Light of Its Interpreters. Edited by S. Japhet. Jerusalem: Magnes, 1994. [In Hebrew.]

Hyman, Ronald T. "The Multiple Function of 'How' in the Tanakh." Dor le Dor 18 (1989–90): 84–91.

Jakobson, Roman. "Grammatical Parallelism and Its Russian Facet." Language 42 (1966): 399–529.

Janzen, J. Gerald. "The Character of the Calf and Its Cult in Exodus 32." Catholic Biblical Quarterly 52 (1990): 597–607.

Joüon, Paul. Le Cantique des cantiques: Commentaire philologique et exégétique. 2nd edition. Paris: Beauchesne, 1909.

Kampen, Natalie Boymel, ed. Sexuality in Ancient Art: Near East, Egypt, Greece, and Italy. Cambridge: Cambridge University Press, 1996.

Kautzsch, Emil. Die heilige Schrift des Alten Testaments. Vol. 2. Edited by Alfred Bertholet. 4th ed. Tübingen: Mohr, 1923.

Keel, Othmar. The Song of Songs. Translated by F. J. Geiser. Continental Commentaries. Minneapolis: Fortress, 1994.

King, Philip J., and Lawrence E. Stager. Life in Biblical Israel. Library of Ancient Israel. Louisville: Westminster John Knox, 2001.

Kinlaw, Dennis F. "Song of Songs." Pages 1201–43 in vol. 5 of The Expositor's Bible Commentary. Edited by F. E. Gaebelein. Grand Rapids: Zondervan, 1991.

Kitchen, Kenneth A. "Lotuses and Lotuses, or . . . Poor Susan's Older than We Thought." *Varia Aegyptiaca* 3 (1987): 29–31.

Knight, George A. F., and Friedemann W. Golka. *Revelation of God: A Commentary on the Song of Songs and Jonah.* International Theological Commentary. Grand Rapids: Eerdmans, 1988.

Kramer, Samuel Noah. *The Sacred Marriage Rite: Aspects of Faith, Myth, and Ritual in Ancient Sumer.* Bloomington: Indiana University Press, 1969.

Krinetzki, Leo. *Das Hohe Lied: Kommentar zu Gestalt und Kerygma eines alttestamentlichen Liebesliedes.* Kommentare und Beiträge zum Alten und Neuen Testament. Düsseldorf: Patmos, 1964.

LaCocque, André. *Romance, She Wrote: A Hermeneutical Essay on Song of Songs.* Harrisburg, PA: Trinity, 1998.

Landy, Francis. "Beauty and the Enigma: An Inquiry into Some Interrelated Episodes of the Song of Songs." Pages 35–95 in *Beauty and the Enigma: And Other Essays on the Hebrew Bible.* By F. Landy. Journal for the Study of the Old Testament: Supplement Series 312. Sheffield: Sheffield Academic Press, 2001. Reprinted and updated from *Journal for the Study of the Old Testament* 17 (1980): 55–106.

——. "In Defense of Jakobson." *Journal of Biblical Literature* 111 (1992): 105–13.

——. *Paradoxes of Paradise: Identity and Difference in the Song of Songs.* Bible and Literature Series 7. Sheffield: Almond, 1983.

——. "The Song of Songs and the Garden of Eden." *Journal of Biblical Literature* 98 (1971): 513–28.

——. "Two Versions of Paradise." Pages 129–42 in *A Feminist Companion to the Song of Songs.* Edited by A. Brenner. Feminist Companion to the Bible 1. Sheffield: Sheffield Academic Press, 1993. Reprinted from pages 183–89, 269–70 in *Paradoxes of Paradise.* By F. Landy. Bible and Literature Series 7. Sheffield: Almond, 1983.

Lapsley, Jacqueline E. "Feeling Our Way: Love for God in Deuteronomy." *Catholic Biblical Quarterly* 65 (2003): 350–69.

Lemaire, André. "Zāmmīr dans la tablette de Gezer et le Cantique des cantiques." *Vetus Testamentum* 25 (1975): 15–26.

Linafelt, Tod. "Biblical Love Poetry (. . . and God)." *Journal of the American Academy of Religion* 70 (2002): 323–45.

Livingstone, Alasdair. *Court Poetry and Literary Miscellanea.* State Archives of Assyria 3. Helsinki: Helsinki University Press, 1989.

Loader, J. A. "Exegetical Erotica to Canticles 7:2–6." *Journal for Semitics* 10 (1998–2001): 98–111.

Lobrichon, Guy. "Espaces de lecture du Cantique des cantiques dans l'occident médiéval (IXe–XVe siècle)." Pages 197–216 in *Les nouvelles voies de l'exégèse: En lisant le Cantique des cantiques.* Edited by J. Nieuviarts and P. Debergé. Paris: Cerf, 2002.

Long, Gary Alan. "A Lover, Cities, and Heavenly Bodies: Co-Text and the Translation of Two Similes in Canticles (6:4c; 6:10d)." *Journal of Biblical Literature* 115 (1996): 703–9.

Longman, Tremper, III. *The Song of Songs*. New International Commentary on the Old Testament. Grand Rapids: Eerdmans, 2001.

Loretz, Oswald. *Das althebräische Liebeslied: Untersuchungen zur Sitchometrie und Redaktionsgeschichte des Hohenliedes und des 45. Psalms.* Vol. 1 of *Studien zur althebräischen Poesie.* Alter Orient und Altes Testament 14/1. Kevelaer: Butzon & Bercker; Neukirchen-Vluyn: Neukirchener Verlag, 1971.

———. "Cant 4,8 auf dem Hintergrund ugaritischer und assyrischer Beschreibungen des Libanons und Antilibanons." Pages 131–41 in *Ernten was man sät: Festschrift für Klaus Koch zu seinem 65. Geburtstag.* Edited by D. R. Daniels. Neukirchen-Vluyn: Neukirchener Verlag, 1991.

Lundbom, Jack R. "Song of Songs 3:1–4." *Interpretation* 49 (1995): 172–75.

Lys, Daniel. *Le plus beau chant de la création: Commentaire du Cantique des cantiques.* Lectio Divina 51. Paris: Cerf, 1968.

Madl, Helmut. "Dimensionen des Menschen in Israels Lyrik: Von der Stärke der Liebe—wider ihre Verächter (Hoheslied 7,12–8,14)." Pages 227–42 in *Theologie im Dialog: Gesellschaftsrelevanz und Wissenschaftlichkeit der Theologie: Festschrift zum 400-Jahr-Jubiläum der Katholisch-Theologischen Fakultät der Karl-Franzens-Universität in Graz.* Graz: Verlag Styria, 1985.

Maier, Gerhard. *Das Hohelied.* Wuppertaler Studienbibel: Altes Testament. Wuppertal: Brockhaus, 1991.

Malul, Meir. "Janus Parallelism in Biblical Hebrew: Two More Cases." *Biblische Zeitschrift* 41 (1997): 246–49.

May, Herbert G. "Some Cosmic Connotations of *Mayim Rabbîm*, 'Many Waters.'" *Journal of Biblical Literature* 74 (1955): 9–21.

McLaughlin, John L. *The Marzēaḥ in the Prophetic Literature: References and Allusions in Light of the Extra-biblical Evidence.* Vetus Testamentum Supplement 86. Leiden: Brill, 2001.

Meek, Theophilus J. "Babylonian Parallels to the Song of Songs." *Journal of Biblical Literature* 43 (1924): 245–52.

———. "Canticles and the Tammuz Cult." *American Journal of Semitic Languages and Literatures* 34 (1922–23): 1–14.

———. "The Song of Songs." Pages 91–148 in vol. 5 of *The Interpreter's Bible.* Edited by G. A. Buttrick. Nashville: Abingdon, 1956.

———. "Song of Songs and the Fertility Cult." Pages 48–79 in *The Song of Songs: A Symposium.* Edited by W. H. Schoff. Philadelphia: Commercial Museum, 1924.

Meyers, Carol. "Gender Imagery in the Song of Songs." Pages 197–212 in *A Feminist Companion to the Song of Songs.* Edited by A. Brenner. Feminist Companion to the Bible 1. Sheffield: Sheffield Academic Press, 1993. Reprinted from *Hebrew Annual Review* 10 (1986): 209–23.

Miller, Cynthia L. "A Linguistic Approach to Ellipsis in Biblical Poetry (Or, What to Do When Exegesis of What Is There Depends on What Isn't)." *Bulletin for Biblical Research* 13 (2003): 251–70.

Montgomery, James E. "Ras Shamra Notes IV: The Conflict of Baal and the Waters." *Journal of the American Oriental Society* 55 (1935): 268–77.

Morfino, Mauro Maria. "Il *Cantico dei Cantici* e il patto elettivo: Possibili connessioni." *Theologica et historica* 5 (1996): 7–42.

Mulder, M. J. "Does Canticles 6,12 Make Sense?" Pages 104–13 in *The Scriptures and the Scrolls: Studies in Honour of A. S. van der Woude on the Occasion of His 65th Birthday.* Edited by F. G. Martinez et al. Leiden: Brill, 1992.

Müller, Hans-Peter. "Begriffe menschlicher Theomorphie: zu einigen cruces interpretum in Hld 6,10." *Zeitschrift für Althebräistik* 1 (1988): 112–21.

——. "Hld 4,12–5,1: Ein althebräisches Paradigma poetischer Sprache." *Zeitschrift für Althebräistik* 1 (1988): 191–201.

——. "Das Hohelied." In *Das Hohelied, Klagelieder, das Buch Ester.* By H.-P. Müller, O. Kaiser, and J. A. Loader. 4th edition. Alte Testament Deutsch 16/2. Göttingen: Vandenhoeck & Ruprecht, 1992.

——. "Kohelet und Amminadab." Pages 149–65 in *"Jedes Ding hat seine Zeit . . .": Studien zur israelitischen und altorientalischen Weisheit: Diethelm Michel zum 65. Geburtstag.* Edited by A. A. Diesel et al. Beihefte zur Zeitschrift für die alttestamentliche Wissenschaft 241. Berlin: de Gruyter, 1996.

——. "Menschen, Landschaften und religiöse Erinnerungsreste: Anschlußerörterungen zum Hohenlied." *Zeitschrift für Theologie und Kirche* 91 (1994): 375–95.

——. "Der Mond und die Plejaden: Griechisch-Orientalische Parallelen." *Vetus Testamentum* 51 (2001): 206–19.

——. "Travestien und geistige Landschaften: Zum Hintergrund einiger Motive bei Kohelet und im Hohenlied." *Zeitschrift für die alttestamentliche Wissenschaft* 109 (1997): 557–74.

Munro, J. M. *Spikenard and Saffron: A Study in the Poetic Language of the Song of Songs.* Sheffield: JSOT Press, 1995.

Murphy, Roland E. "Cant 2:8–17—A Unified Poem?" Pages 305–10 in *Mélanges bibliques et orientaux en l'honneur de M. Mathias Delcor.* Edited by A. Caquot et al. Alter Orient und Altes Testament 215. Neukirchen: Neukirchener Verlag, 1985.

——. "Dance and Death in the Song of Songs." Pages 117–19 in *Love and Death in the Ancient Near East: Essays in Honor of Marvin H. Pope.* Edited by J. H. Marks and R. M. Good. Guilford: Four Quarters, 1987.

——. "Form-Critical Studies in the Song of Songs." *Interpretation* 27 (1973): 413–22.

——. "History of Exegesis as a Hermeneutical Tool: The Song of Songs." *Biblical Theology Bulletin* 16 (1986): 87–91.

——. *Proverbs, Ecclesiastes, Song of Songs.* Peabody, MA: Hendrickson, 1999.

——. *The Song of Songs.* Hermeneia. Minneapolis: Fortress, 1989.

——. "Towards a Commentary on the Song of Songs." *Catholic Biblical Quarterly* 39 (1977): 482–96.

——. *Wisdom Literature: Job, Proverbs, Ruth, Canticles, Ecclesiastes and Esther.* Forms of Old Testament Literature 13. Grand Rapids: Eerdmans, 1981.

Ndoga, S. S., and H. Viviers. "Is the Woman in the Song of Songs Really That Free?" *Hervormde teologiese studies* 56 (2000): 1286–1307.

Nil d'Ancyre (Nilus of Ancyra). *Commentaire sur le Cantique des cantiques: Édition princeps, Tome I.* Edited and translated by Marie-Gabrielle Guérard. Sources chrétiennes 403. Paris: Cerf, 1994.

264

Noegel, Scott B. *Janus Parallelism in the Book of Job*. Journal for the Study of the Old Testament: Supplement Series 223. Sheffield: Sheffield Academic Press, 1996.

Ogden, Graham. "Some Translational Issues in the Song of Songs." *Bible Translator* 41 (1990): 222–27.

Orel, Vladimir. "Textological Notes 3–4: On Golden Mice of Philistines and King David in the Song of Songs." *Henoch* 16 (1994): 147–52.

Ostriker, Alicia. "A Holy of Holies: The Song of Songs as Countertext." Pages 36–54 in *The Song of Songs*. Edited by A. Brenner and C. R. Fontaine. A Feminist Companion to the Bible, 2nd series, 6. Sheffield: Sheffield Academic Press, 2000.

Paul, Shalom. "A Lover's Garden of Verse: Literal and Metaphysical Imagery in Ancient Near Eastern Love Poetry." Pages 99–110 in *Tehillah le-Moshe: Biblical and Judaic Studies in Honor of Moshe Greenberg*. Edited by M. Cogan et al. Winona Lake, IN: Eisenbrauns, 1997.

———. "The 'Plural of Ecstasy' in Mesopotamian and Biblical Love Poetry." Pages 585–97 in *Solving Riddles and Untying Knots: Biblical, Epigraphic, and Semitic Studies in Honor of Jonas C. Greenfield*. Edited by Z. Zevit, S. Gitin, and M. Sokoloff. Winona Lake, IN: Eisenbrauns, 1995.

———. "Polysensuous Polyvalency in Poetic Parallelism." Pages 147–63 in *"Shaʿarei Talmon": Studies in the Bible, Qumran and the Ancient Near East Presented to Shemaryahu Talmon*. Edited by M. Fishbane and E. Tov. Winona Lake, IN: Eisenbrauns, 1992.

Paula Pedro, Enilda de, and Shigeyuki Nakanose. "'Debajo del manzano te desnudé . . .'—Una lectura de Cantar de los Cantares 8,5–7." *Revista de interpretación biblica latino-americano* 37/3 (2000): 57–73.

Pelletier, Anne-Marie. "Le Cantique des cantiques: Un texte et ses lectures." Pages 75–101 in *Les nouvelles voies de l'exégèse: En lisant le Cantique des cantiques*. Edited by J. Nieuviarts and P. Debergé. Paris: Cerf, 2002.

Phipps, William E. "The Plight of the Song of Songs." *Journal of the American Academy of Religion* 42 (1974): 82–100. Reprinted as pages 5–23 in *The Song of Songs*. Edited by H. Bloom. New York: Chelsea, 1988.

Pilch, John J. "A Window into the Biblical World: Biblical Language and Biblical English." *Bible Today* 37 (1999): 382–86.

Polaski, D. C. "What Will Ye See in the Shulammite? Women, Power, and Panopticism in the Song of Songs." *Biblical Interpretation* 5 (1997): 64–81.

Pope, Marvin H. "A Mare in Pharaoh's Chariotry." *Bulletin of the American Schools of Oriental Research* 200 (1970): 56–61.

———. "Response to Sasson on the Sublime Song." *Maarav* 2 (1980): 207–14.

———. *The Song of Songs*. Anchor Bible 7C. Garden City, NY: Doubleday, 1977.

———. "The Song of Songs and Women's Liberation: An 'Outsider's' Critique." Pages 121–28 in *A Feminist Companion to the Song of Songs*. Edited by A. Brenner. Feminist Companion to the Bible 1. Sheffield: Sheffield Academic Press, 1993.

Poulssen, N. "Vluchtwegen in Hooglied 8,14: Over de meerzinnigheid van een slotvers." *Bijdragen: Tijdschrift voor Filosofie en Theologie* 50 (1989): 72–82.

Provan, Iain W. *Ecclesiastes/Song of Songs*. NIV Application Commentary. Grand Rapids: Zondervan, 2001.

———. "The Terrors of the Night: Love, Sex, and Power in Song of Songs 3." Pages 150–67 in *The Way of Wisdom: Essays in Honor of Bruce K. Waltke*. Edited by J. I. Packer and S. K. Soderlund. Grand Rapids: Zondervan, 2000.

Rabbe, Paul R. "Deliberate Ambiguity in the Psalter." *Journal of Biblical Literature* 110 (1991): 213–27.

Ratzhabi, Yehudah. "Biblical Euphemisms for Human Genitals." *Beth Mikra* 34 (1989–90): 192–96. [In Hebrew.]

Reich, Ronny, and Eli Shukron. "Light at the End of the Tunnel: Warren's Shaft Theory of David's Conquest Shattered." *Biblical Archaeology Review* 25/1 (January/February 1999): 22–33, 72.

Renan, Ernest *Le Cantique des cantiques: Traduit de l'hébreu avec une étude sur le plan, l'age et le caractère du poème*. Paris: Lévy, 1884.

Robert, André, Raymond Tournay, and André Feuillet. *Le Cantique des cantiques: Traduction et commentaire*. Études bibliques. Paris: Lecoffre, 1963.

Rochettes, Jacqueline des, Nicole Fresquet, Annie Laverdure, and Paule-Elisabeth Oddero. "Les mots du *Cantique:* Une polysémie symphonique." *Bulletin de littérature ecclésiastique* 102 (2001): 167–80.

Rudolph, Wilhelm. *Das Buch Ruth, Das Hohe Lied, Die Klagelieder*. Kommentar zum Alten Testament 17/1–3. Gütersloh: Gütersloher Verlagshaus [Gerd Mohn], 1962.

Rundgren, F. "*ʾprywn*: Tragsessel, Sänfte." *Zeitschrift für die alttestamentliche Wissenschaft* 74 (1962): 70–72.

Sabar, Y. *An Old Neo-Aramaic Version of the Targum on Song of Songs*. Wiesbaden: Harrassowitz, 1991.

Sadgrove, M. "The Song of Songs as Wisdom Literature." Pages 245–48 in *Papers on Old Testament and Related Themes*. Vol. 1 of *Studia Biblica 1978: Sixth International Congress on Biblical Studies, Oxford 3–7 April 1978*. Edited by E. A. Livingstone. Journal for the Study of the Old Testament: Supplement Series 11. Sheffield: Dept. of Biblical Studies, University of Sheffield, 1979–80.

Sasson, Jack M. "On M. H. Pope's *Song of Songs* [AB 7C]." *Maarav* 1 (1979): 177–96.

———. "Unlocking the Poetry of Love in the Song of Songs." *Bible Review* 1 (1985): 11–19.

Sasson, Victor. "King Solomon and the Dark Lady in the Song of Songs." *Vetus Testamentum* 39 (1989): 407–14.

Schoville, Keith. "The Impact of the Ras Shamra Texts on the Song of Songs." Ph.D. diss., University of Wisconsin, 1969.

Schroeder, C. "'A Love Song': Psalm 45 in the Light of Ancient Near Eastern Marriage Texts." *Catholic Biblical Quarterly* 58 (1996): 417–32.

Schweizer, Harald. "Erkennen und Lieben: Zur Semantik und Pragmatik der Modalitäten am Beispiel von Hld 4." Pages 423–44 in *Text, Methode und Grammatik: Wolfgang Richter zum 65. Geburtstag*. Edited by W. Gross et al. St. Ottilien: EOS, 1991.

Sefati, Yitschak. *Love Songs in Sumerian Literature.* Bar-Ilan Studies in Near Eastern Languages and Cultures: Publications of the Samuel N. Kramer Institute of Assyriology. Ramat Gan: Bar-Ilan University, 1998.

Selms, Adrianus van. "Hosea and Canticles." *Die Oud-Testamentiese Werkgemeenskap in Suid-Afrika* (Potchefstroom) 7–8 (1966): 85–89.

Shea, William H. "The Song of Seedtime and Harvest from Gezer." Pages 243–50 in *Verse in Ancient Near Eastern Prose.* Edited by J. C. de Moor and W. G. E. Watson. Neukirchen-Vluyn: Neukirchener Verlag, 1993.

Sivan, Daniel, and S. Yona. "Pivot Words or Expressions in Biblical Hebrew and Ugaritic Poetry." *Vetus Testamentum* 48 (1998): 399–407.

Snaith, John G. *Song of Songs.* New Century Bible Commentary. Grand Rapids: Eerdmans, 1993.

Soden, Wolfram von. "Die Nominalform *taqtûl* im Hebräischen und Aramäischen." *Zeitschrift für Althebräistik* 2 (1989): 77–85.

Sonnet, Jean-Pierre. "Le Cantique: La fabrique poétique." Pages 159–84 in *Les nouvelles voies de l'exégèse: En lisant le Cantique des cantiques.* Edited by J. Nieuviarts and P. Debergé. Paris: Cerf, 2002.

Soulen, Richard. "The *Waṣfs* of the Song of Songs and Hermeneutic." Pages 214–24 in *A Feminist Companion to the Song of Songs.* Edited by A. Brenner. Feminist Companion to the Bible 1. Sheffield: Sheffield Academic Press, 1993. Reprinted from *Journal of Biblical Literature* 86 (1967): 183–90.

Stadelmann, L. *Love and Politics: A New Commentary on the Song of Songs.* New York and Mahweh, NJ: Paulist Press, 1990.

Talmon, Shemaryahu. "Prophetic Rhetoric and Agricultural Metaphora." Pages 269–80 in *Storia e tradizioni di Israele: Scritti in onore de J. Alberto Soggin.* Edited by D. Garrone and F. Israel. Brescia: Paideia, 1991.

Toorn, Karel van der. "The Significance of the Veil in the Ancient Near East." Pages 327–39 in *Pomegranates and Golden Bells: Studies in Biblical, Jewish, and Near Eastern Ritual, Law, and Literature in Honor of Jacob Milgrom.* Edited by D. P. Wright, D. N. Freedman, and A. Hurvitz. Winona Lake, IN: Eisenbrauns, 1995.

Tournay, Raymond Jacques. "Abraham et le Cantique des cantiques." *Vetus Testamentum* 25 (1971): 544–50.

———. "Les chariots d'Aminadab (Cant. vi 12): Israël, peuple théophore." *Vetus Testamentum* 9 (1959): 288–309.

———. "The Song of Songs and Its Concluding Section." *Immanuel* 10 (1980): 5–14.

———. *Word of God, Song of Love: A Commentary on the Song of Songs.* Translated by J. E. Crowley. New York and Mahweh, NJ: Paulist Press, 1988.

Trible, Phyllis. "Love's Lyrics Redeemed." Pages 100–120 in *A Feminist Companion to the Song of Songs.* Edited by A. Brenner. Feminist Companion to the Bible 1. Sheffield: Sheffield Academic Press, 1993.

———. *God and the Rhetoric of Sexuality.* Philadelphia: Fortress, 1978.

Tromp, N. J. "Wisdom and the Canticle: Ct., 8,6c–7b: Text, Character, Message, and Import." Pages 88–95 in *La sagesse de l'ancien testament.* Edited by M. Gilbert. 2nd edition. Leuven: Leuven University Press, 1990.

267

Tuell, Steven S. "A Riddle Resolved by an Enigma: Hebrew גלש and Ugaritic *GLT*." *Journal of Biblical Literature* 112 (1993): 99–104.

Urbach, E. "The Homiletical Interpretations of the Sages and the Expositions of Origen on Canticles, and the Jewish-Christian Disputation." Pages 247–75 in *Studies in Aggadah and Folk-Literature*. Edited by J. Heinemann and D. Noy. Jerusalem: Magnes, 1971.

Vaccari, Alberto. "Note critiche ed esegetiche." *Biblica* 28 (1947): 399–401.

Villiers, D. W. de, and J. J. Burden. "Function and Translation: A Twosome in the Song of Songs." *Old Testament Essays* 2 (1989): 1–11.

Viviers, H. "Die besweringsrefrein in Hooglied 2:7, 3:5 en 8:4—'Moenie die Liefde rypdruk nie' of 'Steur ons nie in ons liefde nie.'" *Skrif en Kerk* 10 (1989): 80–89.

———. "The Rhetoricity of the 'Body' in the Song of Songs." Pages 237–54 in *Rhetorical Criticism and the Bible*. Edited by S. E. Porter and D. L. Stamps. Journal for the Study of the New Testament: Supplement Series 195. London and New York: Sheffield Academic Press, 2002.

Waldman, N. M. "A Note on Canticles 4.9." *Journal of Biblical Literature* 89 (1970): 215–17.

Walsh, Carey Ellen. *Exquisite Desire: Religion, the Erotic, and the Song of Songs*. Minneapolis: Fortress, 2000.

———. "A Startling Voice: Woman's Desire in the Song of Songs." *Biblical Theology Bulletin* 28 (1998): 129–34.

Walton, John. "*Almāh*." Pages 415–19 in vol. 3 of *The New International Dictionary of Old Testament Theology and Exegesis*. Edited by W. VanGemeren et al. Grand Rapids: Zondervan, 1997.

Watson, Wilfred G. E. *Classical Hebrew Poetry: A Guide to Its Techniques*. Journal for the Study of the Old Testament: Supplement Series 26. Sheffield: JSOT Press, 1986.

———. "Love and Death Once More (Song of Songs viii 6)." *Vetus Testamentum* 47 (1997): 385–86.

———. "A Note on Staircase Parallelism." *Vetus Testamentum* 33 (1983): 510–12.

———. "Some Ancient Near Eastern Parallels to the Song of Songs." Pages 253–71 in *Words Remembered, Texts Renewed: Essays in Honour of John F. A. Sawyer*. Edited by J. Davies, G. Harvey, and W. G. E. Watson. Sheffield: Sheffield Academic Press, 1995.

Webb, Barry G. "The Song of Songs: Garment of Love." Pages 17–35 in *Five Festal Garments: Christian Reflections on the Song of Songs, Ruth, Lamentations, Ecclesiastes and Esther*. Edited by B. G. Webb. New Studies in Biblical Theology. Downers Grove, IL: InterVarsity, 2000.

———. "The Song of Songs: A Love Poem as Holy Scripture." *Reformed Theological Review* 49 (1990): 91–99.

Weems, Renita J. "Song of Songs." Pages 156–60 in *The Women's Bible Commentary*. Edited by C. A. Newsom and S. H. Ringe. Louisville: Westminster/John Knox, 1992.

Wetzstein, J. G. "Die syrische Dreschtafel." *Zeitschrift für Ethnologie* 5 (1873): 270–302.

268

Whedbee, J. W. "Paradox and Parody in the Song of Solomon: Towards a Comic Reading of the Most Sublime Song." Pages 266–78 in *A Feminist Companion to the Song of Songs*. Edited by A. Brenner. Feminist Companion to the Bible 1. Sheffield: Sheffield Academic Press, 1990.

White, John B. *A Study of the Language of Love in the Song of Songs and Ancient Egyptian Poetry*. SBL Dissertation Series 38. Missoula: Scholars Press, 1978.

Wolff, Hans Walter. *Anthropology of the Old Testament*. Translated by M. Kohl. Philadelphia: Fortress, 1981.

Würthwein, Ernst. "Das Hohelied." Pages 25–71 in *Die fünf Megilloth*. By E. Würthwein, K. Galling, and O. Plöger. Handbuch zum Alten Testament, 1st series, 18. Tübingen: Mohr (Siebeck), 1969.

Young, Ian. *Diversity in Pre-exilic Hebrew*. Tübingen: Mohr (Siebeck), 1993.

Zevit, Ziony. "Roman Jakobson, Psycholinguistics, and Biblical Poetry." *Journal of Biblical Literature* 109 (1990): 385–401.

Zolli, Eugenio. "In margine al Cantico dei Cantici." *Biblica* 21 (1940): 273–82.

Subject Index

271

Author Index

Index of Scripture and Other Ancient Writings